# People, power and place

Perspectives on Anglo-American politics

Keith Hoggart

London and New York

First published 1991
by Routledge
11 New Fetter Lane, London EC4P 4EE

Simultaneously published in the USA and Canada
by Routledge
a division of Routledge, Chapman and Hall, Inc.
29 West 35th Street, New York, NY 10001

© 1991 Keith Hoggart
Typeset by Columns
Printed and bound in Great Britain by
Biddles Ltd, Guildford and King's Lynn

*British Library Cataloguing in Publication Data*
Hoggart, Keith
  People power and place : perspectives on Anglo-American politics.
  1. Local government. Political aspects
  I Title
  352

ISBN 0–415–02462–5


*Library of Congress Cataloging in Publication Data*
  People, power, and place : perspectives on Anglo-American politics
  / Keith Hoggart.
    p.  cm.
  Includes bibliographical references (p.  ) and index.
  ISBN 0–415–02462–5
  1. Local government—Great Britain.  2. Local government—United
States.  3. Political culture—Great Britain.  4. Political culture—
United States.  I. Title.
JS3111.H65  1991
320.8′0941—dc20                                                    90–9093
                                                                       CIP

# Contents

# Figures

# Tables

# Preface

Research and teaching on local politics has emerged in recent years as a vibrant field of inquiry. In truth, much of this dynamism has not come from disciplines and sub-disciplines with the most obvious interest in 'political' affairs. In geography, for example, texts on key issues in city politics have more likely emerged through the auspices of urban geography (e.g. Kirby *et al*. 1984) or have been associated with social geographers (e.g. Duncan and Goodwin 1988). Political geographers have not been inactive (e.g. Johnston 1979; Short 1982; Taylor 1985), but the locality has not occupied a prominent place in their work. Geography is not alone in this regard. In sociology, for one, some of the most notable contributions to our understanding of city politics have come from those with a primary interest in urban rather than political affairs (e.g. M.P. Smith 1988). At the same time, sociologists have been chided for ignoring the causal nexus of locality-specific forces; for neglecting the richness of the local realm by treating it as its national counterpart writ small (Urry 1987). Within political science itself, local politics occupies a junior position (albeit aspiring to adolescence in the USA) and carries a hangover from its dull, legalistic tones of earlier decades. That the local political realm now sits high on research agendas owes much to new theoretical developments. It also owes a great deal to actual political events.

Over the last decade, the accessions to premierships of Margaret Thatcher in 1979 and Ronald Reagan in 1981 did much to enliven interest. Their reductions in public expenditure and cut-backs on social programmes exposed larger, poorer cities to traumatic operational adjustments (most evident in fiscal affairs). The political left responded with a stream of polemic on government in general and on local affairs in particular (e.g., for Britain, see Pluto Press offerings such as those by Hall 1983, Manwaring and Sigler 1985, or

Wheen 1985). From the academic world polemic has also been offered (e.g. Piven and Cloward 1982; Duncan and Goodwin 1988), as have detailed analyses which dissect the rationale, evaluate the impact and assess the political significance of higher tier government policies. Some of these works are a delight to read and merit the highest praise for their precision, incisiveness and depth (e.g. Mollenkopf 1983; Midwinter 1984; Newton and Karran 1985). Supporting such analytical efforts, the stock of general texts on sub-national government has swelled (e.g. Hampton 1987; Stoker 1988). Yet there is something of a 'peculiar' air to this general literature. Empirical works which are alive with *political* discourse, such as those of Midwinter or Newton and Karran, have only touched the surface of general texts. There is a dryness to these works; as though the primary goal were to provide factual information rather than to provoke and stimulate. This last comment should be read in a comradely way, since the quality of general texts has much improved in recent years and volumes such as those by Hampton (1987) and Stoker (1988) are well worth reading. Yet, even for these contributions, the departing feeling carries a tinge of disappointment; materials are handled more as a matter of fact than as the expression of a central political theme. Certainly, these texts have organising themes. Yet, to me, both empirically and theoretically, these themes fall short by playing down the 'political' dimension. Of course, there are various ways of writing a text and it is partly because good 'fact books' exist that there is a market for placing such information within a more explicit 'story'. For this volume, the story is about politics; that is, who gets what, when, where and why (Lasswell 1958). With the exception of a few general books, such as those by John Dearlove (Dearlove 1979; Dearlove and Saunders 1984), texts by political scientists commonly seem engrossed with how governments are organised and make decisions, to the detriment of evaluating with what effects. Throughout this text a central feature is consideration of the distributional consequences of the State.[1]

A second aspect of the book is its comparative perspective. Commonly, textbooks on local politics restrict their attention to one nation. Yet similar trends are evident in many nations, even though pressures that cross national boundaries often work themselves out in dissimilar ways. Understanding how the interaction of national and local forces produce divergent outcomes is necessary to deepen our theoretical knowledge. Comparative work helps here by pinpointing the strength and dissimilar manifestations of causal forces in different settings, and by offering more realistic evaluations of nation-specific political events. Thus, when Dearlove and Saunders (1984) assert that restrictions imposed by higher tier government on British local expenditure is 'the end of local democracy', this prompts us to ask why similar legislation did not yield this evaluation in the United States? Of course, comparative investigations come in a variety of forms. This text is not a review of local politics around the world. Primarily, it has been written for undergraduates in British higher education. On familiarity grounds, it is therefore logical for the British scene to be put at its core.[2] Implanting a comparative framework around a British centre could be achieved in two ways. The first would be to pick and choose from a variety of nations to provide context. This approach has not been favoured, primarily because it raises problems of misrepresentation, given the relatively shallow knowledge that a writer has (or can impart to a reader) about numerous nations. Put simply, whereas I believe that valuable comparative texts can be produced on specific aspects of government (e.g. Newton 1980), for more general coverage superficiality or misrepresentation can too easily result. The comparative framework which constitutes the core of this text contrasts Britain with the United States. By choosing these two nations, the framework adopted is biased because these countries share many principles of local government. The specifics are not the same, but the political traditions of Britain and the United States have more in common than either does with, say, West Germany or Japan. Furthermore, as Katznelson (1985) pointed out, to the end of the nineteenth century the urban–spatial histories of these two nations were the most alike of any of the industrialised economies. At a time when fundamental values of local government were being entrenched, both the physical and the ideological environments of these nations had much in common. The principles and practices identified in this book cannot be transposed at will to other settings. Other nations have quite different traditions (Lash and Urry 1987). Yet, following a lead ably offered by Douglas Ashford's (1982) comparison of Britain and France, the desired impact of this comparative investigation is to deepen understanding of local politics in both nations.

With a disciplinary background which emphasises location, place and spatial variation, it might seem that a geographer is well placed to undertake comparative analyses of local politics. After all, as Lineberry and Masotti (1976: 6) noted: 'The politics of urban services . . . is a part of the politics of spatial advantage and deprivation.' Yet the geographical fraternity has been slow to make an effective contribution to local political studies. Partly this is because of the backwardness of political geography. As recently as 1974 it was pertinent to stress that 'there is an astonishing lack of effective connection between theory in human geography and theory in political science' (Hall 1974: 48). Today a mood of optimism is more evident. Yet advancement within the sub-discipline still has a long way to go before other political analysts will be convinced of its vitality. Illustrative of those who question its contribution is Allison (1982):

> Contemporary geography seems to many outside observers to be a tradition (and a body of people) in search of both a subject matter and a method of study to call their own. Their idea of the spatial dimension seems to offer neither.
>
> (Allison 1982: 112)

In reviewing a compilation of geographical research, Dommel (1984) likewise questioned the geographer's role:

> This rather unkind review is likely to be seen by some as the pique of a non-marxist political scientist. But if this is the best state-of-the-art analysis geographers have to offer as 'geographical imagination', then do not fault those who still think of political geography as the musty art of painting half the countries of the world map pink to show they are part of the British Empire.
>
> (Dommel 1984: 112)

Perhaps political geography aspires to academic gentrification, but it has not attained it as yet.

Within geography itself, political geography does not occupy a prestigious place. Indeed, the most articulate and coherent prescriptions for improvement in its standing have had a notably non-geographical flavour. This is exemplified in Johnston's (1980: 445) point that 'a major failing of modern political geography is its avoidance of politics'. This observation encapsulates Taylor's (1977) earlier insistence that teaching in political geography should open up political issues, not close them down. So far, Pinch's *Cities and Services* (1985) and Bennett's *The Geography of Public Finance* (1980) are the only geographical texts with a significant interest in local government. They adopt more of a 'fact book' approach to textbook writing which plays down the centrality of politics in governmental form and action. This is particularly apparent when these books are compared with texts of the same era which primarily focus on international and national aspects of political geography (e.g. Short 1982; Taylor 1985). However, the introduction of a stronger political element has consequences for the geographer's traditional concern with place and spatial variation. Political geographers have been remiss in not enthusing their work with a stronger sense of politics, but political scientists have been equally remiss in neglecting the importance of place in their research. Indeed, some political scientists have been inclined to denigrate geographical effects:

> Since all social processes have some spatial component, the inter-relationships among processes may take place via spatial locations and access structures built into them. But this cannot in itself constitute the basis of a separate field of social science inquiry, for an adequate account of spatial effects may necessitate analysing all the social processes involved. Only if a partially independent process of spatial differentiation can be identified is it possible to delimit a valid, distinct field of study.
>
> (Dunleavy 1980a: 38)

Although presented in a subtle form, this argument states the truism that things must happen somewhere, and so concludes that the geographical dimension is unimportant. But having 'removed' geography, history must be next, since things must happen at some time. Neither space nor time exists on its own. Each is constituted from social relationships. It is in studying the integration of relationships in space and time that disciplines make their contribution. Overly legalistic writings in political science, the prevalence of technically sophisticated but immensely abstract papers in economics, and a spatial fixation within some geographical contributions, are all manifestations of an a priori assumption of disciplinary primacy.

Theoretical advancement will be retarded by a 'my discipline first' attitude. This does not mean that insights from investigations of specific human activities are not valuable. Society is too complex for the depth of understanding which specialisation brings to be ignored. However, specialisation should better equip more general evaluations, rather than asserting the primacy of one explanatory perspective. Where this places the geographical contribution is not in promoting the centrality of geography, but in highlighting how social forces interact to produce dissimilar locational effects. In this regard, Savage *et al.* (1987) offer a valuable heuristic framework for distinguishing the geographical basis of social differences (this is also described in Duncan and Goodwin 1988). In this scheme, *contingent* local effects are those which arise as time–space variations on national and international trends. Thus, proximity to an airport is associated with economic activities which owe little to location other than airport accessibility. By contrast, *causal* local processes emerge from the combining of social relationships within localities to produce 'unique' outcomes which cannot be reduced to their constituent parts. In the USA, even today, industrial relations and political practices in the former confederate states cannot be understood outside the peculiar social practices that emerged as a consequence of slavery, and as a reaction to its abolition. Yet the distinctiveness that is present in the South would not qualify as a *locality* effect. This involves a further level of distinctiveness, wherein a specifically local culture is present. Anthropologists now recognise that even within advanced economies there is enormous subtlety and variety in local cultural forms (Cohen 1982). Yet the common threads that run through these subtle variations mean that an 'independent' local culture is rare (Duncan and Goodwin 1988). Hence, the more common point of distinction is whether social processes are contingent or are locally causal. To date, studies in both political geography and political science (if considering place at all) have done little to draw out these dissimilar types of relationship. Although there are numerous studies of politics in single cities, few have probed for the influence of locality-specific causal forces. That such processes are influential cannot be doubted. Investigations such as Bulpitt's (1967) of six Lancashire towns reveal that distinctive political practices arise even in nearby, seemingly similar, locations. Recent work on the character of local political cultures has tried to identify the basis of such locality-specific forces (Cooke 1985; Rees 1986; Savage 1987; Rose 1988), while some studies have sought to link these traits to dissimilarities in electoral behaviour and governmental performance (e.g. Dickens *et al.* 1985; Mark-Lawson *et al.* 1985; Agnew 1987). These morsels do not go far toward filling the vacuum of knowledge on local causal effects, but they whet the appetite for further investigation and for theoretical advancement.

It follows that this book is not so much a list of answers as an array of questions. The first question is 'where is geography?', since the material covered in this volume does not focus on issues common to many political geography texts (boundaries, externality effects and so on), neither is spatial variation nor location the centrepiece of the text. What this volume primarily seeks is an understanding of causal forces. In doing so, it draws attention to the manner in which differences in local politics have a place-specific foundation. As a personal evaluation, I would say that the balance of the book favours understanding causal forces more than drawing attention to this place-specific focus; in effect, it 'generalises' rather more than it should. Quite apart from the limited development of locality based studies, this bias must be put down to the author's own weaknesses, alongside the orientations of personal interest. Perhaps most notable in this regard is the sense that work on localities still has a long way to go in understanding how social structure intersects with human agency. Despite protestations to the contrary, much work on local politics has an overly deterministic, an overly structuralist and an overly reductionist tone to it. Both Whitt (1984) and Swanstrom (1988) hit the nail on the head in arguing that theorising remains excessively abstract and contentless. Accompanying this, there is a strong tendency to sentimentalise. Writers of the left are particularly guilty of this when discussing the working class and (particularly) trade unions. Those on the right reveal the same myopia when commenting on the middle classes and business. In both cases there appears to be an unwillingness to inquire about how human agents really behave; preferring instead to rely on a screen of assumptions consistent with ideological disposition. Politics is much 'dirtier' than most academics seem inclined to acknowledge. As the former leader of the Greater London Council expounded:

> I have often thought that Mario Puzo's *The Godfather* is a much more honest account of how politicians operate than any of the self-justifying rubbish spewed out in political biographies and repeated in academic texts.
>
> (Livingstone 1987: 115)

Put simply, much of what happens in political affairs is not 'convenient' for the neat bundle of concepts and linkages that make up academic theories. Theorising needs to become much 'dirtier' (or more complex, if you like; Mann 1986). Just as the insights of structuralists reveal the weaknesses of accounts which purely concentrate on human agency, so the lulling simplicity of structuralist formulations must be guarded against. Combining agency and structure in convincing theoretical models is still some way off.

Inevitably, then, this book has many rough edges and awkward passages. That there are not more of these owes much to other writers in the field from whom I have learnt a great deal. In particular, the contributions of William Domhoff, Pat Dunleavy, Thomas Dye, Ira Katznelson, Ken Newton and Ken Young have always proved illuminating. Another aid in producing this book arose from the calming effect that living with Linda Newson has on my otherwise turbulent character. In particular I have to thank her for gaining an invitation to teach at the University of California, Berkeley, around which I was able to conjure the sabbatical leave which gave me time to write much of this volume. Somewhat with tongue in cheek, I acknowledge the role of my employer, even if reluctantly, in granting this leave. More seriously, some of the information in this text was derived from projects funded by the British Academy, the Nuffield Foundation and the University of London Central Research Fund, all of whom have my thanks. Carolyn Adams made very valuable suggestions on Chapter Two and both Roma Beaumont and Gordon Reynell merit praise for putting up with my meagre cartographic knowledge and for using their skills to produce the Figures for this volume. Finally, I should like to thank Peter Sowden of Routledge for prompting me to tackle this project.

While I cannot make claims about the quality of the product there is a challenge in writing textbooks. Students of King's College and the London School of Economics who have taken my Urban Politics course will find substantial differences between this text and those lectures. I see the writing of a text not as an exercise in placing lecture notes into fuller form but rather as an exercise in teasing out themes and ideas from courses and extending them conceptually, empirically and theoretically. It involves delving into realms not previously considered, challenging assumptions and seeking deeper insight on interrelationships. This leads to new reading, and a variety of new challenges, heartaches, disappointments and excitements, plus the usual nervous tensions and uncertainties of academic writing. If history repeats itself, by the time that the book is published, I shall have been asked to relinquish existing teaching commitments in order to plug a hole in departmental provision. Perhaps when this volume takes its place on library shelves it will hardly be noticed by its author; after all of the struggling during the production process, the result will cause barely a stir. Someone had better tell Jimmy Greaves that it is not only football that is a funny old game.

Keith Hoggart
September 1989

# 1 Local politics in comparative perspective

In the United States, the upsurge in academic interest in local politics came earlier than in Britain. Most would see the catalyst for US research as Floyd Hunter's (1953) *Community Power Structure*, which challenged core ideas in political science by questioning whether local government was democratic. Thomas Dye (1966) further boosted the research imagination when his statistical analysis concluded that political differences had an insignificant effect on public policy compared with economic circumstances. In 1975 the vitality of research was recharged when New York City was bankrupted and the potency of local fiscal stress became evident. At this time, British research was about to 'take off'. By the late 1970s, there were only a few impressive British studies (e.g. Dearlove 1973; Newton 1976a), some done by American visitors (e.g. Danziger 1978; Glassberg 1981). Paradoxically, in a country which in 1966 formally started a process of major local government reorganisation, there was little quality research on these institutions. The last decade has seen most progress (e.g. Saunders 1979; Dunleavy 1981; Midwinter 1984; Newton and Karran 1985; Parkinson 1985). If a chasm now separates British and US work, it is not in the quality of research. More likely, it is in dissimilarities in theoretical emphasis.

Of course, it is dangerous to refer to British studies and US studies as though they are cohesive entities. They are not. For one thing, divergent ideological interpretations exist on the same phenomena. In addition, reminiscent of what many have seen as the previously dull, dark, boring days of local government studies, some reports are still somewhat legalistic or present descriptions in an atheoretical manner. However, amongst those publications which have sought either theoretical explanation or *political* interpretation, broad distinctions exist across the two nations. In part these can be tied to the historical period in which research on local politics developed. The earlier emergence of US interest placed the formulation of questions and methods of investigation in an era dominated by positivism, wherein the general tone was one of identifying activity styles, rather than questioning reasons for the form and operations of State institutions. As Greenberg (1974) explained, assumptions about the State were implicit:

> Generally working under the unexamined, axiomatic assumption that, with minor exceptions, the American [sic] system is democratic, efficient and just, it [contemporary political science] devotes its time to methodologically sophisticated examinations of the ways in which the wondrous mechanism operates.
>
> (Greenberg 1974: 238)

Fortunately, over time, shifts in emphasis have been evident, as in the emergent 1970s concern with the distributional impacts of government policies (Clark 1975). However, these shifts did not reorient either the conceptual or the theoretical agenda. They owed more to disenchantment with the increasingly sterile debate between those who believed localities were dominated by small, cohesive élites and those who saw a pluralist democracy (Elkin 1987). What forged the break with this seeming impasse was the emergence of a new theoretical perspective originating in Europe. Manuel Castells (1977) and Cynthia Cockburn (1977) were the innovators here. Their contributions came less from any new empirical evidence than from the application of structuralist ideas to the urban realm. These two books came at an opportune moment for British researchers. Most notably in sociology and geography, this was a time when the role of the State and the limitations of consumer choice explanations were becoming widely recognised. Researchers now saw a multitude of constraints on people, as expressed in the growing attention to 'urban managers' who had 'control' positions in key institutions (such as building societies or local authority housing departments; Pahl 1975). Yet this initiative was also running out of steam as the limits on managers' freedom of action became apparent. Increasingly, as the 1970s progressed, attention switched to how managers, and by implication State institutions in general, were constrained by the logic of the capitalist mode of production. As the surge in European work on local politics occurred, theoretical attention was less on human agency (as in the USA) than on the social organisation of society and its links to the State.[1] Such focuses are now integral to many US investigations (e.g. Gottdiener 1987; M.P. Smith 1988).

However, on both sides of the Atlantic, new ideas have not led to the eradication of old ones. Instead, greater variety has resulted. Despite this, in much governmental research, the interpretation of the State that informs an investigation is often implicit (Taylor 1983). Yet it is inevitable that even unstated assumptions permeate all aspects of research and writing, from the questions posed, to the categories employed in analysis, through to result interpretation.

## THEORIES OF STATES

Publications on the State have become something of a growth industry. This is not a criticism. If negative comments deserve to be made, these should be directed at the time that it took to recognise the centrality of the State. A multitude of recent books merely confirms the shallowness of writings in the past (e.g. Jessop 1982; Carnoy 1984; Block 1987; Dunleavy and O'Leary 1987). Yet these presentations give so wide a variety of theoretical schemes that they make one ponder how many ways a circle can be divided. A bewildering array of classificatory divisions exists, each of which seems to offend the theoretical divisions pervading other schemes. Even realms which reasonably can be expected to offer consistency are marked by a maze of themes, suppositions and contradictions (e.g., on divergent views in the neo-marxist literature, see Jessop 1982, Carnoy 1984 or Isaac 1987). Inevitably, then, within the space devoted to this topic here, only a broad outline can be offered. Readers are strongly encouraged to follow up on materials in the text.

In a sense, the above comments exaggerate dissimilarities amongst theories of the State because division lines are evident between two main camps. This does not mean that two core schools of thought exist, since such an assertion would endow these blocs with greater coherence than they possess. However, there are sharp differences between theories which explain the (capitalist) State in terms of its structural position within the capitalist mode of production (or more generally in capitalist society) and those which view the State from the perspective of human agency. That these two camps are not self-contained should be stressed, since agency and structure are now evident in most theoretical positions. Further, running across the agency–structure separation is a division between radical and status quo ideas of the State. Instrumental neo-marxist accounts readily illustrate this, because they emphasise human agency (e.g. see Dunleavy and O'Leary 1987), when more recent radical formulations stress structure. What is more, new right State theories have more allegiance with prescriptive accounts of what should be than with descriptions of what is (Barry 1987). Thus, a variety of strands runs through the agency–structure divide which makes it a far from 'clean' break. Nevertheless, this is a valuable division for explanatory accounts.

## Social structure and the state

Most commonly associated with neo-marxist writings on the State, structuralist accounts have usually been classed as radical because an overtly discriminatory message lies at their heart. Principally, this is seen in the assertion that the State is not neutral in its effects on society at large but has built-in biases carried in the structure of capitalist economies. This is most evident in the dependence of the State upon capitalists, given that wealth is created primarily in the private sector. Of course, the State could generate wealth itself (prior to Thatcher government privatisation Britain did precisely this for telecommunications, electricity and gas production, oil production and sales, air travel and aircraft production, to name a few). However, the further a nation goes toward a government-run economy, the less likely capitalists will find it an attractive investment site (partly because there will be less investment opportunities, partly because the prevailing ethos is less likely to favour purely private gain). In addition, with the United States as the parent of massive corporate investments overseas, reductions in the role of the private sector incur the wrath of the world's dominant power. On both an economic and a political front, the most likely result is the destabilisation of a nation's economy.[2] Where electoral politics is integral to the national scene, such disruptions are likely to induce governmental defeat, with a new administration reversing past policies to regain business confidence. Hence, States in capitalist societies ultimately depend on private sector profitability (Offe 1984). It does not matter whether revenues come from taxes, service charges or in other guises, so long as a substantial proportion of the national wealth is generated in the non-governmental realm, public institutions will be structurally dependent on profit-making. By the nature of capitalism itself, an unavoidable outcome of this relationship is the perpetuation of the advantages of the bourgeoisie over the proletariat.

From a neo-marxist perspective, in order to maintain private sector profitability, the State must at times organise capitalists, as well as thwarting popular aspirations. These two processes operate on a broad front. Governmental trade delegations to increase exports are an obvious example of the former, as is the provision of efficient transportation systems. As regards the thwarting of popular aspirations, an obvious example is the combined cut-backs in public services and welfare payments which have featured in Britain and the United States in the 1980s. These contradictory trends must be set alongside State-awarded benefits for the general public. These are granted partly for electoral reasons, partly because politicians have personal commitments to particular programmes[3] and, most commonly dwelt upon in radical accounts, partly because a disgruntled population would threaten the stability of the social order; short-term profitability might be enhanced by 'keeping the population down', but the surety of long-term profits is reduced by this ploy (cf. the Republic of South Africa). The acquiescence of the general population is preferable to their subjugation on the grounds of cost, morality and political ambition. Hence, government leaders promote the legitimacy of social arrangements, even though these maintain inequalities in opportunity and outcome. Put caustically, O'Connor (1981: 45) charged that the process of 'legitimation can be defined as the reasons which the State gives to the public to cover up the real purposes of State programs and policies'. This passage is characteristic of much neo-marxist writing, in that it plays down the effects of ethical, ideological, moral and personal values. This is because the State is conceived as having little autonomy (i.e. capacity to contradict dominant societal forces). As Coates (1980) warned those on the political left:

> The labour movement has got to grasp that the strength of capitalism lies not simply in its *institutions* but also in its *processes*; and that the 'capture' of key institutions (by public ownership, planning agreements, worker directors or whatever) cannot of itself change the imperatives to which the new Labour [Party] men [*sic*] of power would be subject.
>
> (Coates 1980: 264)

Put simply, the dictates of profitability work against awarding too generous a proportion of societal benefits to non-capitalists.

The difference between abstract theory and the real world comes in the form of confusions of purpose and uncertainties of effect. In fact, State leaders have autonomy of action because of the contradictory pressures that capitalists place on them. These contradictions are apparent from O'Connor's (1973: 6) categories for State expenditure. On the side of promoting capitalist profitability are *social capital* commitments. These come in two forms. *Social investments* are projects and services which directly increase the productivity of labour and increase profits (expenditure on research and development, improved transport systems and industrial parks are examples). Alongside these, *social consumption* commitments lower the reproduction costs of labour and so increase profits (e.g. educating the workforce and health services). Seen more as a cost to be set against profits are *social expenses*. These are projects and services which maintain social harmony and the continued legitimacy of the social order. Welfare is one example, as is defence spending, if only in terms of images of national sovereignty. The key here is the word 'images'. How is defence spending evaluated by capitalists and the general public? For defence contractors, it is regarded as a bounty no doubt, but for those not involved in defence work its returns are intangible, even though its costs are high. Defence is not alone in this regard. The costs of public education are similarly difficult to evaluate. How much school spending is required to promote economic growth and what kinds of provision are most suited to the task? Conversely, at what point does education spending produce diminishing returns for growth promotion and under what circumstances can education provoke challenges to the status quo? From a structuralist viewpoint, competition amongst politicians (and their parties) is primarily concerned with dissimilar images of where the most appropriate balance lies. It cannot afford to be other than this, since a government that 'unduly' restricts profits builds up trouble for the future, just as much as the heavy-handed thwarting of public desires provokes social unrest.

At the margins, compromise positions are affected by the values of political leaders and electoral prospects. Depending upon their character, force and longevity, these effects can alter structural restraints on the State. Because they are an 'active' (human agency) phenomena, these forces have the potential to change behaviour norms by adjusting definitions of 'acceptable' State action. Structural anthropologists, intent on explaining how cultures persevere yet change over time, account for this by the inevitability of reproduction processes producing a transformation: 'one may question whether the continuity of a system ever occurs without its alteration, or alteration without continuity' (Sahlins 1981: 67). To grasp this point, 'structures' should be seen as repeated behaviour patterns which carry within them the norms of 'acceptable' action.

The links between agency and structure are not fixed since there are 'grey areas' of uncertainty over the 'appropriateness' of particular acts. For example, if a government of the left were elected, capitalists might make few new investments for fear that legislation will reduce their returns. Conceptually, this response is little different from electors signifying through opinion polls that they have lost faith in a ruling party. To stay in office, the ruling party must appease powerful interest lobbies which are reluctant to support it; in effect, the behaviour options of the ruling party are constrained because the structure of society gives a 'lobby' power to terminate its governance. That these structural limits do not determine behaviour should be clear. The ruling party could decide to press on with its programmes although its demise seems assured. Alternatively, if its actions do not rile powerful lobbies, it might barely feel the weight of these structural constraints (hence structure is not always self-evident in behaviour). Then again, even if interest lobby preferences are contradicted, so long as such lobbies can be persuaded of the contrary, State functionaries need not be constrained in their actions. Hence, 'contending [political] groups attempt to generate support for their positions by drawing on one or another strand of ideology, and they challenge opposing groups by showing that their proposals are inconsistent with accepted ideological premises' (Block 1987: 18). It follows that an amalgam of forces originating within the State apparatus itself, amongst the populace at large, and amongst capitalists, combines to determine the character of the State. For social stability, compromises are reached between these competing forces. Yet the circumstances under which compromise holds differ across nations. What is more, present-day compromises give orientation to future compromises. Hence, even if they had started from a common base, over time the State would take differing forms across nations. The central values of the capitalist mode of production give communality to all manifestations of the capitalist State, but built around this communality are nation-specific packages of compromises which establish 'unique' ground rules for 'acceptable' behaviour by State agents, capitalists and the populace.

Of course, these three social groups are not equally influential in moulding attitudes and expectations. Power relationships have a key role to play in this. Given the dependency of the State on capitalist profitability, the structuralist argument holds that the bourgeoisie has the leading edge in setting structural limits on the State (though this is not from coordinated action, but from similarity of response when profits are stimulated upwards or downwards).[4] However, adjustments to structural limits vary over time. For neo-marxists this primarily comes from class struggle: as the power of the proletariat increases, the State leans in their favour, but when capitalist strength is in the ascendancy, State actions emphasise capital accumulation.

To the extent that class struggle alone provides the core of neo-marxist explanations, it reveals an overly deterministic and economically reductionist account of the State. Crucially, such conceptualisations portray State processes simply as a reflection of social structure. Caveats on the existence of State autonomy cannot disguise the essential point that the State is seen as a reflection of class forces. This neglects the independence of State agents. It also offers a parochial image of the State. Explicitly, this is because nations are treated as isolated entities. This is unacceptable. Each nation operates in the context of dissimilar pressures, limits and opportunities depending upon its standing within the world political economy. As Mann (1988) argued, modern states are dual entities in which internal affairs and geopolitics operate with some measure of independence, but wherein one informs and structures possibilities of action for the other.[5] As the next chapter will show, and as others such as Katznelson (1986) make clear, it is inconceivable that national class structures and States can be validly understood outside their international setting. With dissimilar incentives and restraints, State agents can manipulate both capitalists and the populace, but in differing measure across nations and over time.

Within the vast literature on structural determinacy there is variety in emphasis. For some, the primary distinguishing feature of the State is its role in maintaining the legitimacy of the capitalist social order. For others, the State is principally an arena of class struggle, with more recent French and Italian writings conceptualising the State as the scene of working class victories (Carnoy 1984). Others portray the State as fundamentally a supporter of capital accumulation, with the more 'political' views of those such as Offe (1984) and Block (1987) emphasising the autonomy of the State set in the context of continued attention to long-term capitalist interests. Compared with even five years ago, there is little doubt that most researchers are pulling back from explanations in which social structure is taken as the central determinant of precise behaviour. This is symbolic of a growing maturity in this theoretical tradition, since as Dickens *et al.* (1985) pointed out:

To identify structural mechanisms of capitalism is not the same as explaining what happens in particular capitalist societies. It is the characteristics of these societies, the multifarious ways of institutionalising practice, that determine how, in many ways, or if at all, such structural mechanisms work. Furthermore many of these features do not have their origin in capitalist social structures.

(Dickens *et al.* 1985: 1)

It follows that structuralist explanations are incomplete without theories of human agency.

## Theories of human agency

Most usually, reviews of the State break down human agency theories into three groups: instrumentalist, managerialist and pluralist. Stated in simple terms, these titles translate into models which stress, respectively, business dominance, control by public bureaucracies and responsiveness to the public. In reality, these three are separated by two distinct ideas. For pluralism, this is that the State is democratic; it is not subject to direction by a minority, vested interest but arbitrates between competing groups. For instrumentalism and managerialism, the State is held to operate at the behest of an élite, with little input from the general public. Crossing this divide are public choice theories. These not only assert that (elected) governments are responsive to the electorate (e.g. Downs 1957) but also contend that public institutions are controlled by their bureaucracies (e.g. Niskanen 1971). What puts such dissimilar postures in the same theoretical camp is their core assumption that State agents act principally from self-interest (plus the belief that their behaviour can be explained by neo-classical micro-economic theory). When public institutions are responsive to the public, this is because politicians find it in their best interests to be so. When they are not, this is because public sector bureaucrats are advancing their own careers. In terms of its own internal logic, the public choice perspective is riddled with self-contradiction (e.g. Dunleavy and Ward 1981; Dunleavy 1985) and offers little to State theory. Its notion of what drives State action is self-contained, in that revenue requirements (the power of capital) and system legitimacy (the power of the electorate) are subsidiary to the self-interest of State functionaries. Most obviously for public bureaucracies, this does not go far in explaining how popular and revenue supports are maintained. Yet the State cannot justify itself (except when external factors give legitimacy, as for wars). It must be legitimate in the eyes of the electorate and maintain the confidence of investors. Unless it is assumed that there is a smokescreen surrounding government self-interest, which others have failed to see through over the centuries, theories of human agency require a grounding in ideas about popular support (pluralism) or revenue support (instrumental élitism).

Two features distinguish élite theories from their structuralist counterparts. Firstly, élitist conceptions place more emphasis on the directing role of human agents in policy-making. Whereas in neo-marxist accounts the structure of capitalist society produces outcomes favourable to capitalists, in élite theories élites themselves are central participants in policy determination. Secondly, unlike structuralist explanations, which generally fall within radical perspectives of the State, élite theories range along a spectrum from radical (neo-marxist instrumentalism) to reactionary (public choice bureaucratic). This is because élite theories largely outline the style of power relationship rather than its ideological content. Perhaps most explicitly, this is outlined in Vilfredo Pareto's (1901: 36) assertion that 'the history of man [sic] is the history of the continuous replacement of certain élites: as one ascends, another descends'. Intrinsic to this view is the belief that élites are principally motivated by self-interest. In this framework, it is a misconception to expect government leaders to treat people equitably, since: 'People agitate for equality to get equality in general, and then go on to make countless numbers of distinctions to deny it in the particular. Equality is to belong to all – but it is granted only to the few' (Pareto 1935: para. 1222). As Wildavsky (1971) argued, recent challenges to existing societal arrangements offer comfort for this view:

> the revolutionaries of contemporary America [sic] do not seek to redistribute privilege from those who have it to those who do not. These radicals wish to arrange a transfer of power from the élites who now exercise it to another élite, namely themselves, who do not.
>
> (Wildavsky 1971: 29)

More generally, Arblaster (1987: 30) noted that the meaning of 'democracy' has changed over time in order to preserve élite domination. Thus, while 'some notion of popular sovereignty provided the only plausible basis on which to challenge the theory and practice of absolutism . . . the language of popular sovereignty is by its very nature universalist'. This raised problems, most especially after the 1789 French Revolution, because 'the old [élitist] fear of the mob was intensified by the now much greater possibility of the people obtaining real political power and political rights' (Arblaster 1987: 33). The solution to the 'threat' of popular control was to manipulate the meaning of 'democracy' to justify continuing élite rule.

These last comments might read like political history, but they are far from this. It is a truism that in large nations everyone cannot have equal influence on the State. In some measure an élite must exist. The critical issues are whether this is a self-perpetuating group and how responsive it is to the general populace. The pluralist argument is that the élite is not self-perpetuating, but is responsive. Encapsulating the main tenets of this last argument, former British Prime Minister Harold Wilson described 'the State machine' as neutral:

> It is like a car waiting to be driven. Whichever way it is steered, the machine will go. What matters therefore is the driver. If the man [sic] behind the machine is a Labour man, the machine will move towards Labour. Not only Parliament, but the vast machinery of the State which it controls – the police force, the army, the judiciary, the educational institutions, the BBC, etc. are politically neutral, loyal to their political masters.
>
> (from Coates 1975: 142–3)

For pluralists, those who dominate the State are elected and responsive to the general public because they want to stay in office and, in some formulations, wish generally to serve the public good. In 'purest' form, the pluralist ideal recognises that competing interests exist but finds unbiased responses to them. The State arbitrates between competing claims owing to the self-interest of politicians and to a desire to serve the common good. In the long term, the State is neutral in its stance. Elitists cast aside this idea of neutrality. They argue that those who really decide State policies are not elected and have no worries about electoral consequences. It is politicians who 'front' for the élite who are concerned about elections; hence their attempts to project the myth of their indispensability to the masses.

To grasp what divides élitist and pluralist conceptions of the State, two points should be kept in mind. The first is that pluralists do not hold that the State will never be biased. It is accepted that decisions will be made that favour some groups above others (with potential electoral consequences). Further, as in Michels' (1959) 'iron rule of oligarchy', there are those who believe that political leaders inevitably become more isolated from their constituents the longer they are in office and thereby fail to appreciaté biases in their actions (see Iannaccone and Lutz 1970). Neither of these is inconsistent with pluralist ideas so long as the advantages bestowed on groups are not cumulative and, were they to be so, the general populace could show its disfavour by removing leaders from office.

The second point is that pluralist theory does not rely on interest groups exerting equal influence (Dunleavy and O'Leary 1987: 35). What it expects is that criteria which distinguish group influence are legitimate in a democracy (e.g. group size, mobilisation success, intensity of members' preferences). This is a critical point, since it brings normative ideas from pluralism into close proximity with élitist expectations. This arises because many pluralists not only acknowledge interest group inequities but also praise them. These commentators are not offering a modern-day equivalent to nineteenth century denouncements of 'the mob', but they do caution against the exercise of power by 'the masses'. From this perspective: 'Mass politics in democratic society is . . . anti-democratic' (Kornhauser 1960: 277; see also Lipset 1960: 32), because 'the classical picture of democratic man [sic] is hopelessly unrealistic . . . [since] an increase in political participation by present non-participants could upset the stability of the democratic system' (Pateman 1970: 3). In a nutshell, demands made by present-day non-participants are likely to be 'alien' to democracy. The explanation for this is that such demands would come from today's 'outsiders', largely those of lower socio-economic status, who favour short-term, self-satisfying goals rather than the general, long-term needs of society as a whole. Also infused within this notion is the idea that democratic governments inevitably respond to public pressures, thereby increasing govern-mental involvement in everyday life (here the argument takes a decidedly new right tone; Barry 1987). For society as a whole, this is said to be detrimental in two major ways. First, if there is an extension in welfare provisions, there will be an erosion of 'traditional values' – such as the work ethic and family life – which enabled the State to extend its activities in the first place. Unless corrected, the success of capitalist democracy generates its own downfall. Second, in response to such pressures, the State will 'transgress' into spheres where it is ineffective, such as productive (i.e. profitable) areas of economic activity (similarities with new right ideology are again evident). This leads to 'ungovernability' (Dunleavy and O'Leary 1987). Thus, the stability of a democracy is maintained by restricting policy-making influence, rather than widening its population base. As Dye and Zeigler (1978) expressed it, the irony of democracy is that its survival rests on the shoulders of an élite.

In this pluralist formulation, democracy is safe in the élite's hands both for personal and for institutional reasons. Elites are assumed to internalise democratic values more strongly than others (partly on account of their success within the existing system), with the attainment of high office further heightening the sense of societal responsibility (Dye and Zeigler 1978: 17). Even if this is not the case, so long as there are genuine competitive elections, the ideals of pluralist democracy should be advanced. As Schumpeter (1943: 269) reasoned: 'the democratic method is that institutional arrangement for arriving at political decisions in which individuals acquire the power to decide by means of a competitive struggle for the people's vote.' The nub of the argument is not that the State is not élitist, but that it is responsive to the general populace. Elitism might well lead to dissonance in the goals of leaders and followers, but this is not problematical, if, in the long term, the State is not cumulatively discriminatory and the population decides on its leaders. Today, even stalwarts of the pluralist camp cast doubt on these assumptions in favour of neo-pluralism (e.g. Lindblom 1977; Dahl 1982). Arblaster (1987) explained the stimulus for this:

> It is one of the paradoxes of contemporary political thinking that at the same time as much conventional theory has tried to restrict the idea of democracy to that of choosing a government from competing élites, it is also widely admitted that the theoretical sovereignty of those democratic governments is not in fact matched by their actual powers over society . . . If so much power lies outside the domain or the control of elected governments, it is surely odd to hold that the requirements of democracy are met when government alone is popularly elected.
>
> (Arblaster 1987: 64)

Ironically, aspects of the neo-pluralist argument are difficult to distinguish from the neo-marxist:

> Because public functions in the market system rests in the hands of businessmen [*sic*], it follows that jobs, prices, production growth, the standard of living, and the economic security of

everyone all rest in their hands. Consequently government officials cannot be indifferent to how well business performs its functions. Depression, inflation, or other economic disasters can bring down a government. A major function of government, therefore, is to see to it that businessmen perform their tasks.

(Lindblom 1977: 122–3)

Critically, where these ideas differ from business élite formulations is in insisting that entrepreneurs are not key participants in policy-making. The policy-making process is held to nurture business interests in general, but not in the particular. By contrast, in instrumental élitist models, State processes are dominated by business vested interests.

Critics have charged that a major failing in élite theories is their lack of attention to élite 'defeats'. For example, if business leaders do dominate government, how can we explain the successes of labour unions and environmental groups in winning better work conditions and less pollution? The élitist response is that the élite is not a cohesive, all powerful body. Competition occurs amongst élites, and between élites and non-élites. Over time, the personnel of the élite changes. History is 'a graveyard of aristocracies' (Pareto 1935: para. 2053), as well as a scene of struggle between groups seeking ascendancy. Both to attain and to maintain élite standing, élites require support from non-élites. To obtain this, concessions are offered. Hence, élites 'will share the product of their labors to the extent required to insure the survival and continued productivity of those others whose actions are necessary or beneficial to themselves' (Lenski 1966: 44). However, what élite theory warns is that these alliances are for convenience rather than joint-interest:

After the victory the new aristocracy will perhaps allow some concessions of form and language to the new proletarians; that is, to the weak, the improvident, or the incapable, but actually these latter will probably have to bear an even heavier yoke than the one they are bearing now. The new masters will not, at least for a little while, have the senile weakness of our bourgeoisie.

(Pareto 1901: 87; also Michels 1959)

Elites in decline make more concessions to non-élites than those in the ascendancy, but both 'buy' support from non-élites. Since maintaining support can be costly, élites seek to legitimise their standing in the eyes of non-élites. For many élite theorists, it is this search for legitimation that has led to 'democratic' procedures and to the sharing of portions of society's benefits. In the United

Kingdom, for instance, Miliband (1982: 3) described how 'it is no exaggeration to say that it is the wish to contain pressure from below which provides the key to the nature and spirit of the British political system: all else depends upon it'. Indeed, for Europe in general: 'To be historically accurate a political account of the development of the welfare state should probably begin with 1848 when those grasping the remains of aristocratic power realised that major institutional adjustments were needed' (Ashford 1986: 9). Elite theorising acknowledges that contradictory forces are at play within society. It does not accept a static, unchanging world and would not sit unhappily alongside Dahrendorf's (1959: 163) stipulation that: 'We cannot conceive of society unless we realise the dialectics of stability and change, integration and conflict, function and motive forces, consensus and coercion.'

This point ties into a second uncertainty over élite theory which concerns disagreement over precisely what constitutes the élite. First and foremost, an élite is identified by the *relative* permanence of the power it exerts. With regard to the State, the groups most commonly ascribed as élites are business entrepreneurs and public bureaucracies. Theories linked to these have often been labelled *instrumental–marxist* (or just instrumentalist) and *managerialist*. However, to be consistent with central tenets of élite theory, it is more appropriate to term them *individualist* and *organisational* élitism. This distinction is preferable because it pulls away from the implied association between instrumentalism and the private sector, and managerialism and the public sector. More significantly, an individualist–organisational divide focuses on fundamental changes in advanced capitalist societies over the twentieth century. In particular, it leaves scope for acknowledging that family capitalism has been replaced by the capitalism of large organisations (Scott 1985) and that the increased bureaucratisation of social life is as much a feature of the private sector as of the public sector (Breton and Wintrobe 1982). Hence, élite theory does not have to be divided into two competing models for, on the one hand, capitalists and, on the other, public sector bureaucrats. Instead, élite domination can be conceived as a struggle between a once dominant but fading élitism, in which personal self-interest is expressed through individual benefits, and a newer, now dominant élitism, within which personal self-interest is satisfied through organisational advancement.

Readers might hold that there is inconsistency between the above argument and the previous contention that theories of bureaucratic power cannot provide a valid account of the State. In fact, the previous paragraph does not contradict this stipulation. What it suggests is a step towards more coherent theory. For this it must be emphasised that élites are defined by their power. This conceptual-isation of what an élite is differs somewhat from that found in much of the sociological literature, wherein élites are seen to be functional groups, mainly distinguished by occupation, which have high status in society (Bottomore 1964). For the State such stipulations are unnecessary, since those who exert most power need not be of high status. The leaders of working class political machines in US cities in the late nineteenth and early twentieth centuries are good (local) examples. To maintain the legitimacy of the State, influential voter groups and major revenue providers are given privileged access to channels of policy-making. So too are public bureaucracies, because their compliance with elected leaders' goals is central to projecting an image of competence in government. The issue is thus not one of discounting particular influences but of theorising causal importance. For this we need to be clear about the comparative standing of causal processes linking to human agency and social structure.

## AGENCY, STRUCTURE AND POWER

The literature on agency and structure is now a large one, yet the theoretical issues raised in it remain unresolved. Expressed in simple terms, the root of the controversy concerns how far the actions of human agents (individuals, groups and organisations) are decided by rules and resource distributions over which they have little control (i.e. by the structure of the social system). In short, should principal emphasis in theories of political action be placed on freedom of choice or on the dissimilar constraints and opportunities offered by the structure of society? For Wilson (1987) the real problem is one of causal balance:

> Today, social theorists seem to agree that no theory that treats either structure or agency as residual is satisfactory, but the agreement seems to stop there. As specific theories are worked out, theories of power, social transformation, deviance and the like, . . . biases and leanings to one side or the other quickly reveal themselves, leading the other side to cry foul and issue forth with a theory to rectify the fault.
>
> (Wilson 1987: ix)

For State theories, élitist and pluralist formulations stand in the agency-first camp, whereas neo-marxist accounts stress structural determination. On both sides, however, ideas have gone some way towards compromise. This is not to say that theoretical accord is in the offing. On the contrary, there is little prospect of pluralists changing their minds over the centrality of democratic practices, even if they accept that their high ideals are tarnished (Lindblom 1977; Dahl 1982). Likewise, there seems little prospect that neo-marxists will downplay the key effects of class conflict, even if they admit that democratic processes are not completely an ideological smokescreen. Too great a chasm has to be crossed for accord to be reached. Seemingly, there is potential for a closer integration of neo-marxist and business élite theories, although one prominent élite theorist has now cast aside his 'long-held delusion' that he can constructively engage in debate with neo-marxists (Domhoff 1986: 56). Besides which, there are dangers in combining theoretical insights from traditions with different philosophies (Pickvance 1980; Taylor 1983; Alford and Friedland 1985).

This does not mean that theory has to stay entrenched in either the structuralist or the human agency moulds. On the contrary, this would be a formula for shallow explanation. This particularly applies when events are 'distorted' to fit theoretical categories in such a way that they lose their realism. Precisely this is at the heart of much disenchantment with structuralism. Dunleavy (1986) captured this dissatisfaction:

> Many writers of the left endlessly rework discussions of the strategies of right-wing parties, especially in constructing hypo-thetical linkages between their actions and the 'needs' of capital. In these accounts there is usually a very 'loose fit' between the policies of parties or political leaders and capital interests.
>
> (Dunleavy 1986: 131)

For non-marxists, structuralist theorising is seen to be excessively abstract and contentless (Whitt 1984; Swanstrom 1988), with explanations largely reducing government actions to the requirements of capitalist profitability (Domhoff 1986). Neo-marxists would not accept this assessment, because, in addition to the varied approaches within this tradition (Jessop 1982; Carnoy 1984; Dunleavy and O'Leary 1987), there is recognition that the State has (some) autonomy from capital. However, as Saunders (1982b) makes clear, there are problems with this relative autonomy idea; if State support leads to labour victories over capital, this can be explained by relative autonomy, but if the bourgeoisie wins, this seems to confirm the domination of capital. 'There is, one suspects, little that the state might do which could be used as a check on the validity of such a theory' (Saunders 1982b: 10). This problem hits a target, since there has been a loss of confidence in neo-marxist accounts. Wickham's (1988) commentary on historical research has wider applicability in this regard:

> this has been a decade when the intellectual self-confidence of Marxist historians has been severely shaken. The moment is naturally itself not unconnected with the political advance of the right; but it is also in large part (in Western Europe at least) the result of the inconclusive way in which structuralist Marxism, the most novel 'western Marxism' of the 1970s, has been absorbed into traditional Marxist history. Structuralist theory had a positive effect on many people . . . but its impact on history as a whole was largely negative; for its brief reign principally showed historians how difficult their subject was, and how many levels of analysis (discourse) it was necessary to operate on at once to get a properly articulated synthesis together. Furthermore, the complexities of structural articulation . . . had a clearly functionalist element to them; although this in many respects added power to the models, it proved as a result excessively difficult to show how significant historical change could take place at all. When structuralism abruptly began to dissolve as a project around 1980, it had only shown most historians how *not* to do their subject, not how to do it.
>
> (Wickham 1988: 78)

Not surprisingly, some recent neo-marxist studies reveal a lack of connection between theoretical posture and empirical analysis (cf. Duncan and Goodwin 1988). Again, Wickham (1988: 78) highlights a broader trend in noting how 'remarkably few Marxist historians . . . are currently doing much beyond nuanced (and committed) empirical description'.

Is there a way out of this unsatisfactory position? If there is, it is one that as yet is not widely accepted. This is inevitable, since:

> each theoretical perspective on the state has a home domain of description and explanation. That is, the meaning of 'state' depends on whether the vantage point for analysis is individuals, organizations or societies and also upon the fundamental assumption made about the relationships among those levels of analysis.
>
> (Alford and Friedland 1985: 3)

Yet an argument can be made that progress has been made. In this regard, the work of Offe (1984) should be looked at seriously. On his theoretical conception, Pickvance (1980) made the significant point that while Offe's ideas are placed by many in a neo-marxist framework, they actually represent an original alternative to neo-marxism; one that precludes its being added to the neo-marxist stockpile. Moreover, in analysing the main propositions that Offe makes, it becomes clear that he not only offers a framework in which agency and structure are integrated, but does so in a consistent way. Even so, Offe's ideas require extension, elaboration and empirical verification. He provides no panacea, just a useful starting place for an account of the State which integrates agency and structure.

The critical point of Offe's contribution is the combination of a structuralist perspective with a recognition of the key role of 'strategic groups'. In effect, a model is presented which brings together ideas from neo-marxist and élitist theorising. For Offe (1976), advanced capitalist nations are characterised as follows: (a) the State is largely excluded from capital accumulation; (b) consequently, government institutions are largely dependent on capital accumulation for their revenues, so programmes which maintain the popularity of elected officials and the legitimacy of the system depend on private sector profitability; (c) the State has a central role in maintaining and enhancing capital accumulation; and (d) to maintain the image of a 'democracy', all of (a), (b) and (c) must be concealed from the general populace. How these structural dimensions are tied into an understanding of human agency is through the mechanisms which perpetuate (a), (b) and (c). Put simply, State institutions forge alliances with 'strategic groups' whose acquiescence and support are crucial for the persistence of the social order. At the national level, strategic groups include oligopoly capital, organised labour and public sector bureaucracies. In the compromises reached with factions of each, those with the least political power lose out. They bear the brunt of disbenefits produced by 'buying-off' strategic groups. In essence, then, the élitism of the State is that of coalition bias (Stone 1986).

This does not mean that coalitions are the primary force behind State actions, since societal structure makes it essential that the broad outline of policy is conditioned by a long-term drive for capital accumulation. Further, even with coalition bias, less powerful and minority groups can be locally influential owing to the geographical concentration of social groups. To gather more geographically dispersed benefits, strong organisation is needed. Sustaining organisations for large population groups is not easy (especially if resources are scarce). Consequently, the population at large tends to exert influence primarily through elections and over specific, short-term issues. 'While such external pressures are fully capable of determining the outcome of any single issue, they appear to be ill suited to controlling a policy direction' (Stone 1976: 201). However, voter group influence is variable – functionally, geographically and temporally. The same applies for social group participation in coalition bias, because the 'value' of élites to State agents is not universal. In so far as their general support is essential, they can never be treated with disdain. However, over specific issues, State functionaries can play off one interest against another (and in many cases specific interests can be ignored because for them the issue at stake is marginal). The requirements of maintaining system legitimacy, the necessity of organising society for coordinated action (especially for economic growth), the strength of the ideological claim that some must lose for the 'common good', and genuine uncertainties over the 'best' course of action, all give State agents scope in decision-making. Put simply, the State is not a mere reflection of powerful interests in society, since it forges room for independent action. Groups can be judiciously played off against one another. Hence, while the power of élites results from their strategic value, that strategic role must be acknowledged by State functionaries; élites hold their status because State agents depend upon them, not because of some objectively defined position. The range of options goes from élites contriving their own special place to having it bestowed on them by State personnel. There is fluidity in the processes that are involved, such that misperception, tactical manipulation and force are all elements which transform the 'objective' standings of groups into their operational positions. The State cannot be read from 'objective' reality because there is a dynamic interaction between State agents, capitalists and civil society. Hence, the division between élites and non-élites is fluid both across policy arenas and over decision issues. Further, as Giddens (1984), Pred (1984) and Urry (1987) make clear, this fluidity has a temporal and a geographical specificity (i.e. groups that are strategic in one locality might not be elsewhere, with temporal changes in 'the issues of the moment' leading to dissimilarities in group centrality). Presently, our knowledge of what produces stability, change and variability in the time–space matrix of political action is too meagre to move us far forward in theoretical modelling. Why Offe's lead merits investigation is because he links structural advantage to the strategic role of human agents. Within this formulation, what ties structure and agency in a causally significant way is political power (Giddens 1984; Pred 1984).

## Political power

In social science there is rarely agreement over the precise meaning of key concepts. Integral to any definition is an ideological or theoretical predisposition. This is clear for definitions of political power. Consider, for example, the following passage from Poulantzas (1973):

> The concept of power cannot be applied to 'inter-individual' relations or to the relations whose constitution in given circumstances is presented as independent of their place in the process of production, i.e. in societies divided into classes, as independent of the class struggle.
>
> (Poulantzas 1973: 106)

Viewed in this manner, power must be 'the capacity of a social class to realise its specific objective interests' (Poulantzas 1973: 104). A completely different view is put forward by Debnam (1984: 21), for whom: 'The only way in which we are justified in going beyond the individual in identifying power actors is where we can establish that the image of a collectivity acts as a motive in the minds of individuals.' Applying this criterion inevitably leads to rejecting the notion that social classes have power, since classes are rarely conscious collectivities. In effect, Debnam and Poulantzas offer stalemate: Debnam denies the legitimacy of Poulantzas's conception of power, and the sentiment is reciprocated. What lies at the heart of this impasse is theoretical incompatibility. Poulantzas adopts a structuralist stand in portraying political action as derivative from class conflict. Debnam, by contrast, puts human agency first, with abstractions such as social classes deemed irrelevant unless voluntarily entered into. The chance of compromise between these positions is slim. In their insistence on the sanctity of their own definitions, these researchers signify that political power is a contested concept (Cox *et al.* 1985).

This is seen in the varied definitions offered for this concept, and indeed in their links to theories of the State. Following Lukes (1974), many theorists acknowledge that there are three main interpretations of power. These Lukes called the dimensions of power. The first is *decision power*. Here 'A' is understood to have power over 'B' to the extent that 'A' gets 'B' to do things that 'B' otherwise would not do (Dahl 1961). Power is exerted even if 'B' does not do exactly what 'A' wants, so long as 'B' has responded to pressure from 'A' and a behaviour change has resulted. Analytically, this conception raises significant methodological problems. In particular, how do we assess the extent of change in the actions of 'B' and how do we justify concluding that these were brought about by 'A'? When studying institutions, addressing these issues involves conducting time consuming and labour intensive interviews which identify the roles of participants in decision processes. This heavy load is inevitable, since: 'Groups with the most established and routinized channels of political influence are the least likely to acknowledge that they are in fact exercising such influence' (Verba 1987: 264). Case histories must therefore be constructed so that the motives, information, beliefs and actions of participants are identified (see Dahl 1961). Conceptually, what is distinctive about this approach is its focus on actual behaviour.

This contrasts with the *nondecision* concept of power. The key notion here is that 'B' does not act, owing to beliefs that 'B' holds about the likely reaction of 'A'. Theoretically, the critical distinction between decision and nondecision power dimensions is that the former has been adopted by pluralists, whereas élitists have been willing to accept the latter. This match is not perfect, since élitists also hold that their ideas are confirmed in decision power. However, élitism is strongly linked to the notion of agenda rigging which is an integral part of nondecision-making. Thus, Bachrach and Baratz (1970) defined this power dimension as:

> a decision that results in suppression or thwarting of a latent or manifest challenge to the values or interests of the decision-maker. To be more nearly explicit, nondecision-making is a means by which demands for change in the existing allocation of benefits and privileges in the community can be suffocated before they are even voiced; or kept covert; or killed before they gain access to the relevant decision-making arena; or, failing all these things, maimed or destroyed in the decision implementing stage of the policy process.
>
> (Bachrach and Baratz 1970: 44)

Methodologically, this definition also raises major problems. When a policy option is voiced, then its 'suffocation' can be analysed in the same way as decision power is investigated. However, what if a proposal never reaches the decision-making agenda? Given that an infinite number of issues could be raised within a locality, how can we distinguish between non-issues (those not thought of) and suppressed issues? Zelditch *et al.* (1983: 14) offered one solution when suggesting that: 'An issue not on a polity's agenda is a nondecision if and only if, in the absence of some identifiable factor X, the issue is on the agenda of otherwise similar polities.' Using this criterion, nondecision-making seems to be a critical dimension of local politics. For illustration, US cities with economies dependent on polluting industries have been notably reluctant even to discuss restrictive air pollution legislation (Crenson 1971; Phelan and Pozen 1973; Friedman 1977). Hence, at the heart of nondecision power is a fundamental political issue. As Crenson (1971: 184) put it, nondecisions 'are not all politically random oversights but instances of politically enforced neglect'. Hence, to examine only issues which reach the public agenda 'is merely to study what happens to the political crumbs strewn carelessly about by an élite with its hands clasped firmly around the cake' (Saunders 1979: 30–1).

In the *structural* dimension of power this idea is taken further. As Lukes (1974) expressed it:

> is it not the supreme and most insidious exercise of power to prevent people, to whatever degree, from having grievances by shaping their perceptions, cognitions and preferences in such a way that they accept their role in the existing order of things, either because they see it as natural or unchangeable or because they value it as divinely ordained or beneficial? To assume that the absence of grievance equals genuine consensus is simply to rule out the possibility of false or manipulated consensus by definitional fiat.
>
> (Lukes 1974: 24)

Hence, for Lukes (1974: 34), structural power is where 'A' has power over 'B' in so far as 'A' affects 'B' in a manner contrary to the interests of 'B'. This raises the immediate question of what those interests are. Since these must of necessity be defined by the researcher ('B' not being able to identify them owing to 'false consciousness'), they are overtly value laden. On this basis many reject Lukes's scheme (e.g. Martin 1977). Yet for Lukes (1974: 26) this is not problematical, since 'power is one of those concepts which is ineradicably value-dependent'. It is difficult to disagree with him. Indeed, Gaventa (1980) has shown how the workers in one single-industry Appalachian community were manipulated by their employer so that they did not challenge practices which were detrimental to them.

Each of these dimensions of power has something to offer in furthering our understanding of the State. Inevitably, any interpretation of power will be value laden. Entertaining the possibility that any of these dimensions might be crucial in the determination of social practices should not therefore be shied away from on the grounds of subjectivity. What these three dimensions really identify is the exercise of power through different channels of agency and structure. For decision power, agency is to the fore, just as structure is for structural power. As for nondecision-making, this straddles the two. This is not intentional. At the time that Bachrach and Baratz wrote, their nondecision-making idea challenged the overtly behavioural focus of prevailing views on power. But in presenting their ideas they bundled together quite different aspects of power. This is seen in the passage quoted above (Bachrach and Baratz 1970: 44). Here they argue, on the one hand, that nondecision-making is 'a means by which demands for change in the existing allocation of benefits and privileges in the community can be suffocated before they are even voiced', but go on to hold that this concept also applies when pressure for change is 'maimed or destroyed in the decision implementing stage of the policy process'. These are very different. The former refers to the organisation of the policy-making process, the latter to what happens within that process. In effect, in the second of these two interpretations, Bachrach and Baratz offer nothing beyond decision power. All they point to is the manner in which demands for action can be defeated; this is decision-making, not nondecision-making. Yet the first element of their specification is quite different. Here they do not focus on the power that a group has over another when action is contemplated, but highlight the differential power to act (Isaac 1987). This formulation is not fundamentally different from that of Lukes (1974). In general terms, this aspect of nondecision-making is part of the *mobilisation of bias*. This comes from Schattschneider, who offered the following explanation: 'All forms of political organization have a bias in favor of some kinds of conflict and the suppression of others because *organization is the mobilization of bias*. Some issues are organized into politics and others are organized out' (Schattschneider 1960: 71). In effect, 'the rules of the game' are structured so that the action scope of some agents is constrained while for others it is enabled.

What is thus meant by power is the capacity to act, whether or not that capacity is used. Power is conditioned by the structure of society, but at the same time is part of that structure. As Pred (1984: 281) explained: 'the structural properties of any social system express themselves through the operation of everyday practices at the same time that everyday practices generate and reproduce the micro- and macro-level structural properties of that social system.' In other words, human actions are influenced by the norms (or set of 'rules') that govern behaviour, but in acting in a manner which is consistent with those rules people reproduce underlying structures (Sahlins 1981). Structure informs action but in acting that way behaviour norms are reinforced. Freedom of action is present, both because norms allow some interpretive choice and because people can act contrary to the rules of the game. Thus, while college lecturers expect students to listen in lectures, a student could instead decide to sing loudly. The chances are that such an act would not be in the long-term interest of the student, so that the capacity to act on a short-term 'whim' could affect the ability to attain longer-term goals (such as a degree). However, if all the students in a lecture proceeded to sing raucously, this might have a different meaning. Here, the 'norm' has been broken but the lecturer might view this positively or negatively (celebrating a birthday or drawing attention to an appalling standard of lecturing). Let us focus on the second, as this introduces a further element of choice; namely, how will 'the authorities' react? The options here are that the students' lot might be improved (by removing the lecturer or encouraging more effort in lecturing) or might deteriorate (the students could all be suspended – the authorities not accepting such challenges). This reveals a further aspect of power, since the authorities must have resources which enable them to enforce such steps. These could be based on authority (e.g. the legal right to fire the lecturer), but they might depend on incentives (financial inducement for the lecturer to leave). There are a vast number of resources that can be called upon, ranging from violence to moral pressure, from withdrawal of labour to withholding investment, and from dictatorial fiat to persuasive cringing. In its own right, of course, pleading is not a resource, but the ability to do it well is. Put simply, everyone has resources, as these do not have to be physical artefacts, but not everyone uses them with equal 'efficiency' (given £10,000 each, people chasing the same goal are unlikely to be equally successful). Hence, the structure of society is comprised of both rules of behaviour and resources (Giddens 1984), but rules can be changed and resources can be used inefficiently. To be complete, theories of power must explain both the social relationships which establish and maintain societal rules, and the differential ability of agents to attain their goals. As Giddens (1984) and Isaac (1987) rightly emphasise, the starting place must be structure, since this establishes the framework in which human agents find their capacity to act differentially constrained and enabled. It follows that the first step in understanding local politics is appreciating structural power relations which provide the context in which local agents act. This involves understanding the character of national political arrangements, and, leading on from this, an appreciation of how local political scenes are integrated with, while also standing apart from, their national counterparts.

## THE LOCAL STATE

Each element of confusion and contradiction that surrounds theories of the State holds in magnified form for the local State. For some, the local State is a manifestation of the State at a sub-national level. In effect, the term draws attention to the unity of the State, no matter what its precise organisational forms (e.g. Cockburn 1977). For others, the term is used more in an institutional manner. By referring to the local State, rather than local government, attention is directed at the manifold ways in which public institutions are organised at the sub-national level. (For example, why are local functions in the hands of locally elected councils in some nations but reside in the hands of national government appointees in others?) In other formulations, dissimilarities in the balance of class forces across localities (e.g. Duncan and Goodwin 1988) and differences in the character of power relationships (e.g. Cawson and Saunders 1983) are held to distinguish the local and national contexts of the State.

As at the national level, a division should be drawn between 'local State institutions' and 'the local State'. Concern for the institutional dimensions of the State at the local level is welcome, since this highlights the significance of non-elected organisations and warns that a focus on local 'government' alone offers too narrow a field of vision when analysing the State (and democracy) within localities. However, the designation 'local State institution' lacks theoretical content, as it is merely a statement of subject interest. For theoretical expositions, the phrase 'the local State' is more appropriate. At present, however, there is ambiguity over what the term 'local State' means. Paris (1983: 97), possibly a little harshly, charged that this concept is: 'apparently a theoretical category based on Marxist theory, but on closer inspection turns out to be a convenient slogan with little or no analytical rigour'. Fincher (1987) is also critical and recommends that the concept be abandoned because a locality basis for the social relationships of the State does not exist and because no general marxist theory of the State is possible. In effect, both authors identify confusion about this concept and acknowledge its marxian heritage. On both counts this is a sound assessment of its history. Whether it is a pointer to the future is more debatable.

The fact that researchers have adopted the phrase 'the local State' without qualifiers reveals much. In fact, even if this phrase is understood as the social practices and class conflicts that are metered through State institutions at the local level, it is still questionable whether 'the local State' exists. What do exist are theories of the local State. Theoretical postures on social practices and conflicts within localities are not singular. They come in a variety of guises. Perhaps it is tempting to believe that neo-marxist accounts differ from pluralist and élitist formulations because their field of vision is broader. In truth, it is not. As Duncan and Goodwin (1982) concluded with regret, without changing their arguments, the word 'State' could be replaced by 'government' in most neo-marxist writings on the local State. Too often, the phrase 'local State' has done little other than signify support for a neo-marxist view (Paris 1983). More than this is needed. Theories should be concerned with local State institutions, and not simply with local government. This does not mean that they should concentrate merely on the organisational principles of (or the distribution of functions amongst) public institutions. Their scope should be broader. Specifically, theories of the local State should explain the locality basis of the State; in other words, why can we not account for socio-political practices at the local level by directly transposing theories of the State down to the locality?

On both the left and the right, a modicum of agreement exists on this score. From Duncan and Goodwin (1988: 41), the argument of the left states that: 'social relations are unevenly developed, hence on the one hand [there is] a need for different policies in different places and, on the other hand, a need for local state institutions to formulate and implement these variable policies'. In effect, 'without the uneven development of societies there would be little need for local – that is subnational – institutions in the first place' (Duncan and Goodwin 1988: 45). This view sits rather comfortably alongside Paul Peterson's (1981) public choice perspective. Here the first line of argument is that 'by comparison with national politics local politics is most limited', which leads to the expectation that uneven economic development has a major impact on local public policies:

> Because cities have limits, one explains urban public policy by looking at the place of the city in the larger socio-economic and political context. The place of the city within the larger political economy of the nation fundamentally affects the policy choices that cities make. In making these decisions, cities select policies which are in the interests of the city, taken as a whole.
>
> (Peterson 1981: 3–4)

Where these two views diverge is over what a city's 'interests' are. Immediately following the above statement, Peterson (1981: 4) asserted that: 'It is these city interests, not the internal struggle for power within cities, that limit policies and condition what governments do.' Yet for Duncan and Goodwin, it is the local specificity of class struggle that produces the distinctiveness which demands a local State theory. In other words, there is no such thing as a city's interest, just the outcome of class struggle. Even if the interests of cities could be defined unequivocally (which Duncan and Goodwin would reject), these should vary across localities, since class forces are unequally distributed. In effect, Peterson's schema holds that there is a unitary interest for cities; that the force which drives the local State machinery is nationwide in its application. Of course, in one respect this point also fits Duncan and Goodwin's (1988) case, since they hold that class conflict alone holds centre stage in theorising the local State. What in neo-marxist accounts occupies the forefront is thereby simply transcribed to the local scene.

This will not do. Localities, as with nations, are comprised of two major relationships; those aligned with the accumulation of wealth and those concerned with community formation (Mollenkopf 1981). The class conflict perspective highlights just one of these and so offers a lopsided account. As Katznelson (1981) energetically pointed out:

> American [*sic*] urban politics has been governed by boundaries and rules that stress ethnicity, race and territoriality, rather than class, and that emphasize the distribution of goods and services,

while excluding questions of production or workplace relations. *The centrepiece of these rules has been the radical separation in people's consciousness, speech, and activity of the politics of work from the politics of community.* This subjective division has been such a powerful feature of American urban life that it has been operative even in situations where blue collar workers live in immediate proximity to their factories.

(Katznelson 1981: original emphasis)

The point is that as well as class forces being spatially uneven, so leading to dissimilar policy pressures on local public institutions, so too is the incidence of other social divisions within localities. Conflicts around community values are not equivalent to those between capitalists and labour (Mollenkopf 1981; Domhoff 1986). 'State, culture and economy are all important structuring networks; but they almost never coincide' (Mann 1986: 2). Of course, few researchers discount the role of (non-work) community divisions (to do so would raise the charge of economic reductionism) but some afford them scant attention:

The issues that reach public agendas (and are therefore available for pluralists' investigations) do so precisely because they are matters on which élites have, in effect, agreed to disagree. Only under rather extraordinary circumstances is this consensus endangered.

(Logan and Molotch 1987: 51; also Peterson 1981)

The problem with such reasoning is that it denies community a role in policy determination when in fact 'nothing guarantees that either the laws of the market place or the power of economic élites will successfully dominate society . . . Politics . . . counts heavily and can be ignored only with peril by those who are presently winning the game' (Mollenkopf 1981: 321). Market forces are critical in policy determination, but their roles are conditioned by their interaction with community values. There is an iterative process between the two, wherein messages exchanged between proponents of different values are informed by the responses of others, which then alter the character of future messages (and hence future responses). This is not an assertion of the vitality of pluralism, since the primacy of structural economic forces is central to the argument. However: 'What is needed is a theory of *political* economy, not an economic theory of politics' (Swanstrom 1988: 88).

Where does this leave us in terms of understanding the local

State? Firstly in a position which lacks coherent support. As with theories of local democracy (Sharpe 1970), much writing on the local State is more a public display of personal prejudice than an explanatory account of the State at a local level. There is still a long way to go for theoretical accounts to be convincing. Much more is needed than class conflict and capital accumulation. These are important, but so are non-work, community based processes. What is more, just as an understanding of the State demands analysis of internal and external relationships, so does an appreciation of the local State. This applies not simply with regard to the compromises and conflicts of local and national forces concerning the decision-making autonomy, functions and organisation of local institutions. It is also manifest in inter-institutional interactions at a local level. To understand the local State requires that its processes be placed in the context of the broader political economy. With regard to the standing of localities in Britain and the United States, elucidating these national settings is the task of the next chapter.

# 2　The national context of local politics

In its simplest form local government refers to governmental institutions with policy-making authority organised on a locality basis. Dissecting each word of this definition reveals that we cannot easily come by a precise definition of local government. For instance, what is meant by 'local'? In the United States, New York City, with a 1980 population of 7,071,639, is classed as a local government, whereas Alaska, Wyoming and Vermont are states whose 1980 populations were 401,851, 469,557 and 511,456 respectively. New York City is 'subservient' to a state government in Albany which has the same constitutional authority as Alaska, Wyoming and Vermont, yet these latter states have lower tier (local) governments within them. Some conceptions of 'locality' would get around this 'problem' by categorising both local and state institutions as 'local'. However, this is a simplification. Certainly, there can be tiers within 'local' government. The English system of districts and counties, as with US municipalities and counties, attests to this, since both local levels are on an equal footing with regard to higher tier authorities. Yet, in federal structures, states and provinces stand in a different position because they have legally encoded autonomy from their national counterparts. To illustrate the difference, the *ultra vires* stipulation under which British local authorities operate holds that they cannot legally undertake an action unless authority can be traced to an Act of Parliament. By contrast, the Tenth Amendment to the US Constitution holds that authority which is not delegated to the federal government in the Constitution belongs to the states. Here *ultra vires* operates 'in reverse', restricting the scope of national action rather than that of sub-national agencies. Further, since US local government is constitutionally a state responsibility, federal influence on the lowest tier must principally be indirect (viz. through the courts and by encouraging compliance through financial incentive). It would be easy to throw even more complexity into the pot, as in noting that in some countries local governments can take any action not explicitly forbidden in national legislation (e.g. Norway) and that 'home rule' provisions can insulate lower tiers from higher tier interference. But such complication is unnecessary. Already it should be evident that there are no hard and fast rules about the size or operational procedures of local government within nations, let alone between them. Local arrangements are not decided by universal laws. Rather they emerge and are sustained by forces of domination, compromise, inertia and expediency, the dynamics of which cannot be divorced from social practices at both sub-national and national levels.

This also applies to the circumstances of local government within the spectrum of local State institutions. There are a variety of governmental units at the local level which most commentators do not accept to be governments. In England, District Health Authorities, area offices of the Department of Social Security, and Job Centres are of this kind. As with district and county councils, these can be created, be dissolved, change functions, lose or gain funding sources, or have their administrative areas altered, at the behest of Parliament. Yet these institutions are really part of the administrative machinery of the national government rather than local governments. The distinction here is grounded in the ideals of local democracy. Organisations without local elections are deemed to lack responsiveness to local electorates. They might be part of a democratic governmental system, but this funnels into a national arena. Hence, 'local' policy-making is presumed to be absent. The accuracy of this viewpoint is questionable. In reality, it is not valid to distinguish administrative agencies from governments because their officials are appointed. On this count many special districts in the United States would be discounted, even though their officials are appointed by (or come directly from) locally elected councils. Likewise, control by bureaucrats does not mean that policy-making does not occur (Page 1985; Laffin 1986). Even when there are local elections, bureaucrats make significant policy contributions (e.g. Table 2.1), and in local arms of national organisations the overview of politicians is likely to be less intense. Providing one example of this, Lojkine (1981) has reported that area officials of French national agencies such as *Agence d'Urbanisme* have closer ties with local politicians than with members of their own national organisa-tion. (LeGates [1972] recorded a similar pattern for Housing and Urban Development officials in San Francisco.) Moreover, just

*Table 2.1* North Carolina city managers' views on policy-making 1987

| Statement | % Agreeing |
|---|---|
| Managers should advocate major policy changes | 81.4 |
| Managers should assume leadership in shaping policies | 79.9 |
| Managers should advocate new services to promote equity for low-income groups and minorities | 88.2 |
| Managers should maintain neutrality on issues where the community is divided | 46.6 |
| Managers should advocate policies to which important parts of the community may be hostile | 58.6 |
| A manager should act as an administrator and leave policy matters to the council | 51.6 |

*Source*: Svara (1988: 31)

because appointments are made nationally does not mean that said appointees are not responsive to local issues, norms and moods. After all, if only for convenience, such administrators commonly have roots in the locality.

A further problem with assuming that elections lead to a locally grounded government comes from the interdependencies of local and higher tier institutions. In Sweden, for example, an estimated 80 per cent of local government expenditure is devoted to programmes directly prescribed by Stockholm (Heidenheimer *et al.* 1983). Similarly, Lovell and Tobin (1980), in their analysis of five US states, found that cities and counties had to adhere to 1,260 federal and 3,414 state mandates. That such mandates can be expensive to comply with is now recognised, with some states (admittedly half-heartedly) requiring compensation for the costs of meeting them (Walzer 1978). Perhaps, therefore, in expenditure terms at least, it is more accurate to conceptualise local government as administering on behalf of higher tier authorities rather than as independent entities. This view is consistent with commentaries on how local autonomy declines with dependence on higher tier grants (made evident when the latter are cut; Levine and Posner 1981). Elected or not, this does not mean that local institutions are mechanistic automatons that translate commands from superiors into action. They have a vitality of their own. They plant a unique stamp on nationwide policies within their localities. Moreover, what autonomous space exists in policy processes is not fixed, but is fought for and, for preservation, fought over. The very autonomy of local agencies is symbolised by the differential use to which policy-making arenas are put; some agencies use this space to the full, others rarely feel the discomfort of approaching its boundaries. What is more, even where the long arm of higher tier authorities keeps a tight grip on local actions, there is variety in response. Some authorities shield, enhance and manipulate wherever possible to ensure local values receive the maximum possible expression. Others find compliance easier to stomach. The strategy pursued is not rigid. It varies in time and space. However, set amidst this dynamism and differentiation are distinctions that should be recognised.

First and foremost are national political circumstances. These define the rules and the distribution of resources that comprise the structural power context of local politics. To exemplify the importance of structural power, this chapter proceeds by adopting a funnel approach which takes us from the more abstract to the more immediate issues of local–central government relations. The key point is that local institutions cannot be understood to be independent of their national counterparts. At the most general level, this national setting establishes prevailing political cultures. These place broad limits on the norms of political behaviour and legitimise resource distributions. It is primarily at the national level that the ideology of governmental responsibility and action is laid down. Thus, in the second section of this chapter the aim is to highlight how dissimilar expectations are attached to governments within Britain and the United States. This is followed by a section on the actual practices which demarcate local political behaviour. Whereas the first section is concerned with the national arena first, this section examines linkages between local and national spheres. Its intention is to specify the dimensions of local autonomy. Finally, the chapter closes with a consideration of local–central relationships over the last decade. Given the ideological premises of the Thatcher and Reagan administrations, plus bewailing from the left over the 'damage' inflicted on local institutions, it is pertinent to ask whether the 1980s has seen the breaking of long established moulds.

## NATIONAL POLITICAL CULTURES

A problem that seems endemic within social science is the extension of explanatory positions beyond the time–space dimensions for which they are best suited. This danger is very real for theories of the State. Increasingly this is acknowledged in theoretical formulations, although there is still a tendency to think in global terms. This is unfortunate for political practices are built upon social structures and behaviour norms of preceding social arrangements. Sen (1982) exemplifies this in his neo-marxist evaluation of the State in India. In this account he is critical of the imposition of abstract marxist categories on to the Indian political economy. Primarily this is because the State in India does not comply with mainstream marxist assumptions of structural dependence on capital. On the contrary, the State has substantial autonomy. Pursuing a line of argument reminiscent of Offe (1984), Sen charged that for capitalist domination to arise, State functionaries must believe it is in their interests to favour the capitalist class. In India such identification has been weak, partly because colonial rule produced an overseas orientation in government, and partly because the pre-colonial social order made legal rights of ownership as well as surpluses from production subject to imperial regulation. Even well into the twentieth century, State officials have failed to identify with the incipient capitalist class. As elsewhere, capital–State relationships are deeply embedded in the peculiarities of national social structure.

Stated with a broader geographical and temporal stroke, Moore (1966) sketched a similar picture in his *Social Origins of Dictatorship and Democracy*. Encapsulating the main line of thought here is the argument that previous social evolution has a major effect on the present-day State. Nations which have experienced bourgeois revolutions, such as England, France and the United States, are inclined to develop governmental forms favouring democratic methods. Where a capitalist path was followed without a strong revolutionary urge, or where the revolution was a conservative one, the State is inclined to be reactionary and possibly fascist (as in pre-1945 Germany). Further, pursuing a line contrary to Marx, Moore held that communist governments are more likely to emerge where feudal relations persist (because the absence of an independent class of town dwellers, and the convergence of interests amongst upper strata town and country dwellers, favours resistance to change, a thwarting of worker–peasant aspirations, and the build-up of radicalism). Stated so boldly, Moore's (1966) account seems deterministic. In fact, it is not, since he emphasises that 'starting points' do not decide future developments. Societal structures are composed of recurring behaviour patterns, and, while actions both draw on and reinforce structures (Giddens 1984; Pred 1984), there is no one-to-one correspondence between the two. Provoking a major change in norms is not easy to achieve, but society is ever evolving. If it were possible for two social systems to start from exactly the same position, over time they would most likely develop different social forms merely by dint of the cumulative accretion of incremental changes. It might well be that primary casual forces were the same – in effect, that abstract theories capture the driving forces in both contexts – but outcomes are contingent. They are determined by the peculiar interplay of underlying structures, directions of social change, specific short-term opportunities and even chance events. With the same causal foundations, quite different outcomes can result. Once built into societal norms, these differences provide a platform from which further distinctions can, though they need not, emerge.

The relevance of these comments to a comparative analysis of Britain and the United States arises first and foremost in warning against expecting uniformity in political practices. Institutional forms, the scope of governmental involvement in everyday life and power relations within State processes, differ. This will be expressed in the political culture of a nation, that is in 'the values, beliefs, and emotions that give meaning to political behaviour . . . [and] disposes its members to regard certain forms of political behaviour and institutions as "normal" and others as "abnormal"' (Kavanagh 1985: 9). Political culture provides the framework within which present-day conflicts and practices are situated (thus, challenges to cultural norms are easy to denigrate owing to their 'illegitimacy'; Dearlove 1974). Critical to understanding political culture is acknowledging that it is embedded in the power nexus. Political culture does not arise in a vacuum, but reflects outcomes of past political struggles as winners turn valued goals into behaviour norms (hence, had the South won the US Civil War, slavery would undoubtedly have been granted a different place in history books than it has today). Rulers who transgress the political norms of a society thereby sit on top of an unstable regime. Norms can be changed, but rarely overnight; new impositions must be accepted either through general agreement or because challenges to them seem futile. Time is a crucial component, since practices which are detrimental to major population groups can expect to be challenged in the long term, thereby requiring vigilance and reinforcement for survival (a good example is the adaptations used by white élites to maintain black subjugation in the US South; e.g. Greenberg 1981; Trelease 1981). For new rulers seeking to 'change society', time is not usually on their side. Hence, to contradict dominant national values in a major way is a recipe for rule by repression rather than government by acceptance. This is exceptionally 'wasteful', because whatever surpluses are produced within society will be disproportionately eaten up by the cost of maintaining social order. It follows that ruling parties seek the compliance of the populace. Elites must 'buy' support from non-élites to maintain the sanctity of the system (Offe 1984). Yet those critical of system maintenance at some point do not inevitably retain this position. Furthermore, as a result of inter-élite competition, a ruling coalition might require support from 'unexpected' quarters (a renowned example is the 1938 non-aggression pact between Germany and Russia). No matter whether the source of élite support is surprising or *passé*, the compromise reached, in so far as it is integral to political culture, produces an 'impure' expression of élite values. Such impurities exist in all polities, though the trace elements which disfigure virgin forms vary.

Implicit in the above comments is recognition that political cultures are not unitary. They have a number of dimensions, trends or traces within them, so nations cannot be conceptualised as fitting neatly into one character type. On this account, the core dimensions of the concept 'political culture', and so its explanatory utility, are open to disagreement. As Grant (1987: 5–6) warned: 'Used improperly, culture can easily become a garbage can variable to which everything that cannot be explained in other ways is too easily assigned.' This situation should not arise when this concept is used as a heuristic devise to draw attention to central dissimilarities in the *modus vivendi* of polities. Explanations for the emergence of these differences are still immature but, by tracing the historical evolution of social formations and power struggles, we can identify multifaceted value dispositions that specify the acceptability of different forms of action. Political culture cannot be read from social structure (Rees 1986), but emerges from the juxtaposition of forces in fields of class relations, community sensibility, political practice and 'external' relations (e.g. Rose 1988).

From the ideas of Wildavsky (1989; and, in partial form, Douglas and Wildavsky 1982), a significant dimension to political culture is found in the attitudinal and behavioural relationships between non-élites and élites. The foremost manifestations of these loosely fall into five 'life ways'. Where *egalitarian* styles exist there is an assumption of equal prospects for citizens, with a communal care that outcomes are not too unequal. By contrast, in *individualist* political cultures the sanctity of individual freedoms and opportunities for personal self-advancement are stressed, even if these produce marked inequalities. Here personal talent is assumed to bring advancement in economic and political spheres (hence inequalities are acceptable). Government should therefore be restricted largely to guaranteeing and fostering personal freedoms. Where *hierarchical* value dispositions are dominant, such freedoms are less important, since a key value in this political culture is acceptance of rule by higher (status) authorities. Those at the top are assumed to know best and are seen to occupy their positions by 'right'. Non-élites rarely challenge élites because their legitimacy is a fundamental cultural value. A different situation emerges under *fatalist* styles, in which the dominant feature is a conviction that nothing can be done to change the social order. It does not matter who comprises the élite or what rulers claim are their goals, the result is believed to work inevitably to the detriment of non-élites. It follows that challenges to the established order are rare (or require severe provocation). The same applies under an *autonomous* philosophy, where people rely on others to motivate and drive the political machinery. They want to 'do their own thing', but the extremely individualistic character of this value system leaves little scope for input into government. Such people are 'freeloaders' who allow others to grasp the ruling reins and direct them at will, provided they are 'left alone'. Readers can probably identify aspects of these 'cultural' positions amongst persons known to them. However, at a national level, dominant values are not comprised of a simple aggregation of personal stances. Far from it, since as Elazar (1966) points out, the positions of the present inevitably build on values which have evolved from the past, so a layering of interacting and intersecting cultural forms exist. Furthermore, the value stance that attains supremacy owes much to the differential power of those holding to alternative positions.

How the variety of categories listed above is translated into national character codes is as the outcome of complex historical processes which are nation-specific. Referring to the end point of these processes, Elazar (1966) characterised the general features of a United States political culture as an amalgam of three subcultures: the individualistic, the moralistic (viz. egalitarian) and the tradition-alistic (viz. hierarchical). When comparison is sought with Britain, it at first seems that the same three should be emphasised. However, the weighting of each of these differs. One illustration of how hierarchy is more strongly entrenched in Britain is seen in the discomfort in the British electorate over electing an 'untried' Liberal or Democrat party into government. By contrast, both Jimmy Carter and Ronald Reagan were 'outsiders' to Washington when taking office but this did not harm their electoral prospects.[1] This is consistent with the differential balance of individualist and hierarchical forces that Almond and Verba (1963) identified in a comparative study of electors. They concluded that the 'civic culture' of the United States laid stress on participation (emanating from a stronger sense of individualism), whereas its British counterpart was more deferential (i.e. hierarchical). In no sense does this imply that both traces are not evident in each nation. To give one example, at the end of his second term as President, Ronald Reagan received the accolade of 66 per cent of opinion poll respondents over the way he handled his job. Yet amongst the same respondents, 53 per cent rated his judgement negatively, more than 50 per cent (and commonly over 60 per cent) thought he had done a poor job on civil rights, education, housing, welfare and ethics in government, and 80 per cent evaluated his handling of the budget deficit unfavourably.[2] Since defence, US–Soviet relations and general economic policies were more positively viewed, the contradictions inherent in these figures suggest that 'respect' for position was influential (although this 'respect' had to be maintained, as seen in the misfortunes of Lyndon Johnson and Jimmy Carter). As for egalitarianism, again differences can be noted. In fact, it is probably fair to state that many people, on both sides of the Atlantic, do not appreciate the egalitarian impetus on the other side. The overtly hierarchical status system of Britain and an associated preoccupation with 'class' bemuse many Americans (including academics), though aspects of that hierarchy – most especially the Royal Family – seem to derive as much respect on the western shore of the Atlantic as on the eastern.[3] Conversely, British commentators are mystified (perhaps horrified is more accurate) by the lack of social 'conscience' in the United States. This is seen in the opposition of US leaders to the State adopting a redistributive role (Verba 1987) and in a visible landscape of appalling housing conditions, shabby health care provisions and overt discriminations against low-income and minority populations. Visitors from one country to the other perhaps emphasise different dimensions of their host nation's egalitarian failures, but both countries have them, dressed up in one guise or another. That they are recognised as 'failures' by those from the other nation arises because both countries have strong elements of egalitarianism in their political cultures. Within both nations there are traces of individualism, hierarchy and egalitarianism. But they unfold in different ways and their dissimilar manifestations and intensities feed into the rules and practices of national and local politics. This can be readily appreciated by examining the political culture of each nation in turn.

## Political culture in Britain

At a personal, local or national level, it is not valid to tie single political cultures to specific subjects. Cultures are always imbued with traces of different value dispositions. At times one is so dominant that subjects can be placed unequivocally under its label. But over large geographical expanses this is inappropriate. Cultural traits conflict, intersect, reinforce and unfold in different ways across localities and nations. They provide a kaleidoscope of historical paths and present-day manifestations, distinguishable by directions of change, dominant attributes and complexity. In Britain and the United States complexity and subtlety are especially apparent.

Perhaps the key to understanding Britain's position lies in the word 'first'. More accurately perhaps this should be 'one of the first', but the essential point is captured in the single word. In essence, although it grossly simplifies historical trends, the character of the nation can be traced to the early incidence of critical events which later changed other nations. Thus, in examining the 'peculiarities' of the English, Edward Thompson (1965) pointed out that the English bourgeois revolution of 1642 occurred before industrialisation and the development of working class political movements. A consequence was the failure of England (and later Britain) to develop a manufacturing-based, class conscious bourgeoisie. In a country that many US observers find 'infatuated' with class issues, this might seem a strange observation. Yet Britain does lack the kind of class consciousness that is present over much of continental Europe. Its upper classes were slow to organise collectively (Lash and Urry 1987) and, despite the politically motivated rantings of the tabloid press, British trade unionists are notably lacking in radical commitment (Pelling 1968; Katznelson 1986). Again, the word 'first' captures this phenomenon, because the onset of the Industrial Revolution came at a time when the British working class lacked the theoretical inspiration that Karl Marx gave to those industrialising later. The early onset of capitalism in Britain, both in its mercantilist and later industrial forms, also made a deep impression on the British economic and political élite. As Ingham (1984) persuasively argued, capitalism required a 'regulator' to provide world trade with a trustworthy currency (to facilitate product exchange), an efficient means of settling international accounts, insurance and possibly credit for commodity trade, and arrangements to facilitate the shipment of goods. In the early nineteenth century Britain was ideally placed to take on this mantle. For one thing, the importance of existing mercantilist activities meant that the home institutions, as well as the commercial and military infrastructure to support and protect shipping interests, were already entrenched. Then, as the first nation to undergo industrial transformation, there was more demand for these services than in other countries. What is more, there were entrepreneurs eager to supply the required services.

A development which grew from these patterns was the separation of industrial and finance capital. With its interests firmly set on the international scene, 'the City' had few links with industrial endeavours throughout the nineteenth century. Funding for industrial expansion tended to be from internal sources, from friends and patrons, and from provincial banks and stock exchanges. In effect, the main centres of finance and industrial capital operated side-by-side rather than in cooperation. Of the two, finance capital was the strongest. Personal wealth gives one indication of this, with the bulk of nineteenth century millionaires coming from finance rather than industry (Brown 1988). Social status provides another indication, as the more 'aristocratic' lifestyles of landed and financial élites enticed industrialists away from the endless quest for higher profits, provoking them to invest in land rather than manufacturing expansion, even when this gave substantially lower returns (Wiener 1981; Tylecote 1982). This attachment to social status is seen in the anti-industrial, old Tory culture which still has a persuasive grasp on the public mentality (Gamble 1974). As O'Leary (1987b: 379) expressed it: 'The old Tory idea of England remains essentially rooted in rural arcadias and green suburbs in the Home Counties inhabited by former tea planters.' In effect, those who 'made it' in industry frequently adopted the attitudes and social niceties of aristocrats (Wiener 1981; Tylecote 1982). For those at the top, 'the lines between wealthy nobility, gentry, and the upper reaches of business and the professions were blurred and wavering' (Moore 1966: 36).

In a governmental context, this aristocratic–mercantilist vision has been evident in a willingness to accept policies which harm industry so long as they benefit the international financial community. The roll call of such actions is legend, but includes such monuments to national economic decline as the return to the gold standard in 1926 and, until the 1970s destabilisation of the international monetary system, the obsession of post-1945 governments with defending the value of sterling. Accepting the mentality of the City in governmental circles brought mutual advantages. On the one hand, British governments needed City financiers to support policy initiatives (the Napoleonic wars brought early demands for underwriting the national debt, with ventures into colonialism and military engagements extending this need into the twentieth century). At the same time, to support its strong position in world financial markets, the City required the home government to subjugate the national interest in favour of the international capitalist economy. Holding a position of economic pre-eminence for so long, British governments readily accepted this role, and a false sense of grandeur led to this stance continuing long after the nation could 'afford' it (evident after 1945 in the slow withdrawal of military commitments overseas). It would misrepresent what actually occurred to blame the separation of finance and industry for starving manufacturing of funds, but where British industry did miss out was in the impetus given by German and US financiers to the rationalisation of industrial production (Lash and Urry 1987). Only in the 1930s, when the gloss of the City was tarnished by the Depression, did the City actively promote industrial mergers and rationalisation; and then often under the threat of government intervention (Hannah 1983). Even today, research on interlocking directorships shows that British manufacturing firms are poorly integrated with one another and with finance capital, when compared with other nations (Scott and Griff 1985). Possibly this comes from a continuing business emphasis on status attainment rather than out-and-out profit maximisation. It also owes much to a tradition of individualism which led to a reluctance to merge companies or lose control of them by floating shares on the stock market. (For example in the 1930s, William Morris refused merger offers from both Austin and Vauxhall because his personal wealth was insufficient for him to dominate the resulting car producers.) In combination, these conditions produced a manufacturing sector that was economically weak compared with its competitors and politically weak compared with the City. It was largely in latching on to the City's spirit of internationalism that industrialists found political favour. In 'no other metropolitan country is international capital so overwhelmingly *politically* powerful. In no other country, perhaps, is non-internationalised industrial capital so backward and undynamic' (Massey 1986: 47). With the re-emergence of the City, thanks to the existence of US trade deficits since 1958 and the resulting burgeoning Eurodollar market, the economic and political scene was well laid for a Thatcher government strategy of 'abandoning' industry in favour of a 'Big Bang' to enhance the City's world role (Brown 1988). The seeming abnormality of British capitalism has in fact been an international necessity.

Where all this intersects with the emergence of a national political culture is in the City's providing opportunities for aristocratic domination long after this was feasible in other nations. Industrial expansion helped to promote an individualistic trait amongst industrial capitalists, but this aristocratic flavour induced an ongoing adherence to deferential social forms. The closer ties of the City to government was influential here, since England, and through consolidation Britain, went through an early centralisation of political power, with an accompanying early articulation of national identity. All of this long preceded pressures for democratisation. And when the impetus for democracy did build up, British leaders were able to draw on and reinforce the genuine sense of national identity which existed, as well as cultivating a sense of *national* mission (viz. the emergence of 'Great' Britain). Today this nationalist orientation is still entrenched, with trade unions for one acting more as 'class national' than as 'class' actors (Vogler 1985). The consequences have been significant for everyday political life, since the Establishment has a long attested, 'legitimate' grip on government. Additionally, the international role of the 'nation' made challenges to élite domination difficult to mount and sustain, as they were easily labelled illegitimate. Furthermore, on account of their long gestation, political practices carry within them hangovers from feudal times. This was a system that 'worked', for those at the power apex at least, so it should be preserved. Yet, with no constitution, the maintenance of the system depended on informal codes and conventions that could be abused by those unfamiliar with the governing terrain. Hence, with democratisation, with the formal opening of government to the lower classes, the Establishment saw prospects of destabilisation in the existing political order. To counter this, the general public was not to be given freedoms that could challenge the State machinery:

> The British have traditionally emphasised a negative view of political and civil liberties, one which left the citizen free to do as he [*sic*] wished, unless the activity was formally proscribed. There are still few positive legislative guarantees of personal liberties and no formal bill of rights.
>
> (Kavanagh 1985: 50)

'In effect there are no barriers to official prying into any activity "the authorities" please to call subversive' (Leys 1984: 66). This has not meant government by a repressive State apparatus. On the contrary, compared with its continental neighbours, England has been marked by the tameness of State impositions on the populace. (As Katznelson [1985] pointed out, this tradition was established before the Industrial Revolution, being aided by the country having a small army – being beholden to the Channel and the navy for its defence – and by a reliance on unpaid, independent, justices of the peace to maintain social order, rather than paid royal officials.) Repression was not necessary because the Establishment was not seriously challenged, and the State machinery ran in a flexible, non-militaristic style.[4] All this owes much to a tradition of seeking national consensus. That this was attained owed much to the nation's international role, but it also had roots in 'aristocratic' values such as a 'sense of fair play' (cf. instruction in school sports). It also infused a touch of egalitarianism into political life (as in one-nation ideals within the Conservative Party which stretch back as far as the Factory Acts of the 1830s and 1840s, span Disraeli's welfare legislation of the 1870s, and, perhaps, have only been challenged in rhetoric during the Thatcher era). The underlying rationale is that the weak shall not 'fall' too far.

This does not mean that societal benefits are scattered around carelessly. Elites need non-élites and reward them for services rendered (Lenski 1966). Yet uncertainty inevitably arises over when and what concessions should be granted. Elites seek concessions on their own terms and in a manner benefiting themselves (e.g. promoting system legitimation). When élites lose face in granting concessions, usually this can be traced to miscalculation over the necessity of granting them in the first place. In terms of understanding the evolving character of British government, this is critical, since in Britain concessions have been handed out with astute political aplomb. For one thing, as Leys (1984: 64) indicated: 'popular control was introduced in institutions that could be relied on to respect and protect property rights so long as they were monopolised by the middle class'. The cultivation of the middle classes has been crucial to preserving hierarchy within the British political culture, because it played on traces in the British character – most especially those of social status (Roberts 1971) – by emphasising social rank; put simply, it entrenched hierarchy such that social divisions could be emphasised in a non-conflictual way, while indicating that those who 'behaved' could move up the ladder:

The view is very much one of the population from the top down rather than the bottom up; the public is all those people whom the state and its Establishment wish to address or acknowledge as their own . . . In a sense 'the public' is clearly coterminous with something like 'polite society'. Whether or not one is one of the elect to the polite, responsible or respectable is, of course, a matter of judgement by one's betters.

(Johnson 1985: 233)

In effect, access to governmental authority has been manipulated to protect agencies from the general populace:

as the state expanded, the principle of patronage – i.e. appointment by secret process of private citizens to public office – was extended to almost every branch of the state apparatus for which the illusion of 'representativeness' was judged desirable, but where it was desired *not* to represent, let alone give power to, ordinary people, e.g. the Health Authorities, the governing bodies of the BBC, the ITA, the public corporations, the Arts Council, the Science Research Council, etc.

(Leys 1984: 63)

As former Prime Minister Anthony Eden stated in a 1928 speech in the House of Commons:

We have not got democratic government today. We have never had it and I venture to suggest to Honourable Members opposite that we shall never have it. What we have done in all progress of reform and evolution is broaden the basis of oligarchy.

(from Guttsman 1968: 368)

Set alongside such élite rule is a constant reiteration, by members of all major parties, of the democratic character of British politics. This message is reinforced by regular statements in the British media, the ownership of which is closely tied to the Establishment (Curran and Seaton 1988). As beneficiaries of the élite character of the governmental system, it is no surprise that politicians also take keen interest in the messages projected by the media. From Margaret Thatcher this is evinced in her active part in ensuring that *The Times* fell into the hands of the right-wing, interventionist newspaper magnate, Rupert Murdoch (Evans 1983), and in her attempts to tone down criticism of her government from the BBC by warning that it was to the left of Gorbachev (W.L. Miller 1988).

With corporate domination of the private television channels as well, the media stacks are heavily biased in favour of presenting the élitist, hierarchical character of British government as 'democratic'. Even when a government avowedly rejects the prevailing consensus over egalitarian ('fair play') concerns, as the Thatcher governments have done, hierarchy continues to dominate, with opposition parties at a loss over how to react. In effect, they are constrained because the hierarchical character of political practice has favoured 'strong' government, wherein a first-past-the-post electoral system,[5] and tight party discipline in Parliament, grant to one party a monopoly over government. This is no United States of America, where executives often face legislatures ruled by opposition parties, hostile judiciaries, and colleagues prone to put person before party. The British Cabinet sits at the apex of a governmental system whose practices, by international standards, are rigid and insensitive to divergent views from party leaders. Not surprisingly, in the long term, the British public has 'learnt to internalise its own subordination' (Johnson 1985: viii). All in all, the scope for governmental action is substantial, as Harold Laski recognised over 50 years ago:

> What seems to emerge from our historic experience is the lesson that a government can impose its will upon the citizens of a constitutional democracy so long, but only so long, as the citizens are in fundamental agreement about the actual purposes of the state.
>
> (Laski 1935: 92)

In part, of course, precisely this accounts for the relative absence of repressive tendencies within the British State.[6]

Added to this hierarchical overtone is the dominant position of the Treasury within the State apparatus. Critical to its position has been Britain's role in the international capitalist economy. As the world centre for international finance, close cooperation developed between the City, the Bank of England and the Treasury. In effect, they supported each other. So long as national attention was oriented to this international role, all benefited, since policies for internationalism gave each institution enhanced power (Ingham 1984). Even when the influence of the City waned (e.g. from the 1930s until the 1960s), the Treasury retained its dominance. Built on its past eminence and its central economic role, links with other national ministries perpetuated its hegemony. 'Treasury influence rests not on hard nosed interpretation of formal powers but in personal networks, sensitive bargaining, and up-to-date information that operate to create habits of mind leading to anticipation of Treasury reaction' (Heclo and Wildavsky 1974: 380). This has put the Treasury in good stead. Although it has singularly failed to manage the post-1945 economy effectively, it has persuaded politicians – ably supported by City interests – that the fault lies in its not having enough control over the public sector (Sharpe 1982). The consequences of this are apparent in the reduced institutional effectiveness of local government. As early as the late nineteenth century this was seen in Treasury designations of the (national) Local Government Board as a second level ministry (departments dealing with international affairs took the premier ranks), so it was denied the backing to be innovative. Being overworked, underpaid and understaffed, the Local Government Board was forced to divert legislation away from itself to other departments (especially in social fields; MacLeod 1968). The result was a fragmented system of national overview of local government. The absence of Treasury trust, vision and understanding which was evident at this time is equally apparent in today's meddlings in local finance (Meadows and Jackson 1986).

## The United States in contrast

It is unimaginable to conceive of a State institution holding the sway of the British Treasury within the political economy of the United States. The US Constitution itself limits the authority and informal power of any institution; checks and balances are a keynote in the Constitution. However, while there is a democratic tone to these legal arrangements, their initiation and continued operation are imbued with élitism.

The essential dissimilarities between Britain and United States start from the self-evident fact that the USA is a new country. As a partial outcome of attempts at nation building, an inward looking political culture emerged. Until recently, what has dominated national politics has not been international affairs but the infusing of a national spirit and the integration and development of national bounds. Only since 1945 has the United States become much concerned about territories not adjacent to its frontiers. Hence, political practices have a distinctly 'localist' tone. Aiding this process have been waves of immigration which brought a variety of ethnic and racial groups to North American shores and provided a litany of divisions within the population. Kavanagh (1985) pinpoints the comparative difference:

Britain is overwhelmingly white, urban, Anglican, and English. The claims about social homogeneity and the emphasis on social class in Britain derive from the relative weakness of these other cleavages. It is very different from the ethnic melting pot in the United States.

(Kavanagh 1985: 5)

Even so, those who now hold the reins of power are overwhelmingly male, white, Anglo-Saxon Protestants (male WASPs).[7] This is little different from the time of the American Revolution. Yet the revolutionary struggle is usually painted in democratic rather than élitist colours. As Moore (1966: 112–3) points out, this view 'may be good propaganda . . . [but] it is bad history and bad sociology'. In reality, independence was spurred by English government demands that colonists pay the cost of defending them against attacks from the French and their allies. Now the British authorities might well have acted unwisely at this time, since payment was demanded for services already rendered (the French had been beaten off). But the idea that war was declared on the issue of 'no taxation without representation' stretches reality beyond the bounds of credulity. Representation of a sort there had been, because the English government responded to requests to protect colonists. However, in nationalist ideology, recourse to higher principles is essential to disguise self-interest. Those who had most to lose from higher taxes were the wealthy, yet, without the support of ordinary working people (who would have paid little of the taxes), the possibility of breaking away from the parent nation was slight. However, as many colonialists were born in Britain and others had firm attachments to it, an ideologically acceptable prop was critical. This was provided by the democratic tone of the revolutionary cause.

The catch in this revolutionary clarion call was that the promise of democratic government had to be made good (civil unrest was rife in US cities during the revolutionary era owing to price rises and food shortages; Warner 1968). Had this commitment been broken, the propertied élite[8] would likely have faced the wrath of a more numerous, heavily armed public. Hence, the constitutional arrangements of the new nation were not easy to devise. 'The merchants, bankers and landowners who gathered at Philadelphia to write a constitution had become nation-builders precisely because they wanted national policies to protect and enhance property' (Piven and Cloward 1982: 78). It was essential to provide the framework within which property rights could be enshrined, profits could be enhanced, and yet what Madison saw as the 'impudence of democracy' could be guarded against. The checks and balances which were introduced owed much to a desire to restrict the power of government, but this was as much against democratic tendencies as against autocratic ones:

> in 1787 self-consciousness of property, and a desire to limit the electoral role of people was uppermost in the minds of those who framed the Constitution, and was reflected in the erection of such institutions as a non-popular Senate, selected by the states; an appointive judiciary holding office for life; and a president elected through the indirect and cumbersome means of an electoral college.

> (Bell 1962: 105)

What was to be encouraged was a commercial society that placed individualism and property in high accord (Elkin 1987). Yet because this was a new nation, it also sought a communal identity. Hence, alongside the individualism favoured by those of property (Warner 1968), was a desire for communalism, for a sense of commonwealth. Today both sentiments are important in cultural traits in the USA (Elazar 1966). How they led to the emergence of distinctive political practices can be illustrated by the experiences of working class political organisations.

It should be noted that by the late nineteenth century there were many similarities in the mood of working people in Britain and the United States. In both nations skilled artisans tended to be the more radical, with political apathy common amongst the less skilled (Katznelson 1986). Even in the early decades of this century, populist and socialist urges amongst workers in the USA were not so different from those in Europe. 'It was by no means clear in the first few years of the twentieth century that mass socialist or labor parties had a more promising future in some European countries than they appeared to have in the United States' (Katznelson 1981: 8). As Ashford (1986: 42) put it: 'By 1914 the United States was as aware of poverty and social inequality as most European countries but lacked the institutional capacity to weave the diverse strands of social concern, including fears over the assimilation of immigrants, into legislation.' A number of conditions led to this institutional failure (apart from the constitutional provisions which worked against 'strong government'). First and foremost, as a consequence of the independence struggle, the vote was available to the labouring classes (or their male contingent at least). Hence, unlike

Europe, the labour movement could not garner kudos or support from struggles for the franchise (indeed, many trade unions discouraged party political involvements for fear of offending members). Following from this, US labour–capital conflicts were less intense than in Europe. Certainly, trade union organising was thwarted by armed private militia and by the police siding with employers, by federal troops keeping workers in check and by singular judicial interpretations of the law. But such incidents lacked coordination. Through the ballot box workers did control some municipal governments (and hence their police forces), working people did sit on juries and many judges had to be elected. Both in its formulation and implementation, anti-union legislation was milder in the USA than in Britain (Katznelson 1985, 1986). Additionally, the working classes posed less threat to property in the USA than in Europe. The size of the nation played a part here, since slow transportation made coordination more difficult for both capital and labour. Additionally, biases in the Constitution led political party conflict to channel disagreement away from threats to property, thereby allowing for policy flux in search of votes:

> Perhaps the decisive fact about American political structure is the two-party system. Each party is like some huge bazaar with hundreds of hucksters clamoring for attention. Life within the bazaars flows freely and licenses are easy to obtain; but all trading has to be conducted within the tents; the ones who bank their wares outside are doomed to few sales. This fact gains meaning in considering one of the striking features about American life. America [*sic*] has spawned countless social movements, but comparatively few long-lived political parties for, in contradiction to European political life, few of the social movements have been able to transfer themselves into permanent political parties. Here is one of the sources of flux yet stability in American life.
>
> (Bell 1962: 103)

Whereas in Britain the non-ideological disputes of nineteenth century Conservative and Liberal parties were interrupted by the Labour Party, in the USA no working class organisation consistently challenged existing arrangements. Yet when workers were provoked they did resist:

> The labor campaigns of 1886–1887 had demonstrated once again that workers would rise up in anger against the Democrats and Republicans when public officials elected by the major parties

blatantly used their authority to help capital in its conflicts with labor, but this outburst, like earlier ones, subsided after the major parties made some concessions; workers then returned to their former political homes. The labor campaigns of 1886–1887 and the Populist campaign of the early 1890s also demonstrated that a majority of middle-class voters could be whipped into hysteria, and their loyalties to the major parties reinforced, by the charge that these efforts represented nothing less than an attempt to ferment class warfare in the United States and involved an assault on the institution of private property.

(Shefter 1986: 262)

In seeking to thwart such 'disturbances,' propertied élites called on the fundamental values of communalism and individualism.

The first of these was particularly apparent in violent responses to socialist advances in the second and third decades of this century. Most especially after the 1917 Russian Revolution, the charge of foreign (communist) subversion provided a justification for jailing socialists. For Weinstein (1967: 327), when socialist advance was occurring: 'To make the world safe for democracy, the Wilson Administration sponsored a reign of terror far worse than any conducted in Europe, either among the [First World War] Allied Powers or within the German Empire.' Such tactics were not the only ones adopted. Recognising the broad appeal of socialist policies – albeit socialists controlled only a few cities (e.g. Bennett and Earle 1983) – the main parties adopted a number of socialist reform proposals (e.g. the 1913 introduction of income taxes and the direct election of senators). Many immigrant groups, already subjected to decades of abuse for threatening US communalism by introducing 'alien' ways, saw anti-socialist crusades as an opportunity to 'prove' what good Americans they were (Bell 1962). In Britain the propertied classes attacked socialism for its supposed restraints on personal freedom and its economic inefficiencies (making labourers 'work shy' and restricting the free hand of capital), but in the USA it was more openly denigrated for being un-American.[9]

The immigrant base of the US population was important for another reason. In the era of industrial expansion between 1865 and 1900, when working class communalism was spreading its organisational tentacles across Europe, new immigrants added a net figure of 14 million on to the nation's 1861 population of 40 million. This inflow came in response to unfavourable conditions elsewhere and to the enticing prospects of the New World. Whichever the case, the expectation was that the USA would bring personal betterment. For many this meant little more than gaining wealth before returning home (between 1901 and 1914, for instance, 39 per cent of all immigrants returned, this figure rising to 53 per cent for 1914–22; Kolko 1976). Hence, social mobility was consciously aligned with geographical mobility as elements of 'the American dream'. In Britain improved work and living conditions appeared easier to achieve through 'voice' than 'exit' (Hirschman 1970), but for many US immigrants: 'The easiest mode of protest and salvation was to implement the standing intent of returning home' (Kolko 1976: 70). The imagery of 'the frontier' further strengthened the idea that if success were not forthcoming in one location others might be fruitful (e.g. Vance 1972), so the 'actual effect of the westward trek . . . was to strengthen the forces of early competitive and individualistic capitalism by spreading the interests of property' (Moore 1966: 131).[10] The basic ethos of the nation encouraged ceaseless movement in home[11] and workplace. This instability reinforced the impetus toward materialism, since uncertainty placed a premium on resources which could be drawn on in times of need.

Emerging from this ideological stance, though not wholly explained by it, are two further cultural traits that distinguish Britain from the United States. The first is centred on corruption. Compared with Doig's (1984) conclusion that the British political scene is largely free from corrupt practices (also Pelling 1968), the review of Berg *et al.* (1976) suggests that it is central to the US political system (see also Amick 1976 and Etzioni 1984). Even when Britain was more open to 'shady' practices, it was looked on by US commentators as a model of virtue. Thus, at the turn of the century, 'whereas to Britons the United States represented a warning of what to avoid, to many American "reformers" the United Kingdom offered a model to be copied' (Searle 1987: 416–7). Explanations of these dissimilar patterns have pointed to the effects on the USA of the formal separation of government authority and of the need to assimilate parvenu groups. Thus, the constitutional system of checks and balances made 'the exchange of favours' a pragmatic means of concerting action and overcoming institutional rigidities, while informal exchanges are said to have helped new immigrants, unfamiliar with democratic practices, to be integrated into US society. In both cases, there is merit in these points, but if they are key causes their influence should have waned, given more than 200 years of nationhood, over 60 years since immigration made a major impression on population growth, and a century of 'progressive' pressures for more 'scientific' administrative procedures. Yet the spoils system is still a virulent one, suggesting that societal norms are significant. Indeed, as Bell (1962) reported, while moralism is so characteristic of the American temper, it has had

> a peculiar schizoid character: it would be imposed with vehemence in areas of culture and conduct – in the censorship of books, the attacks on 'immoral acts', etc., and in the realm of private habits; yet it rarely was heard regarding the depredation of business or the corruption of politics. On this the churches were largely silent.
>
> (Bell 1962: 114)

By contrast, amongst those holding public office in Britain there has been a high sense of public duty, with a long expressed sentiment that the best defence against corruption lies in the character of public appointments (Searle 1987). Behind such sentiments lies a social class bias, but this ideal persisted as the social base of elected positions broadened with the rise of the Labour Party. Perhaps Britain's position as 'referee' of international capitalism in the nineteenth century inspired a sense of 'fair play' that carried into national political affairs.

This sentiment is less evident in the USA, where public office has more commonly been seen as a basis for furthering sectional interests and securing personal gain.[12] This sentiment was established early in the nation's history:

> The early settlers and founding fathers, as well as those who 'won the West' and built up cattle, mining, and other fortunes, often did so by shady speculations and a not inconsiderable amount of violence. They ignored, circumvented, or stretched the law when it stood in the way of America's destiny [*sic*] and their own – or were themselves the law when it served their purposes. This has not prevented them and their descendants from feeling proper moral outrage when, under the changing circumstances of the crowded urban environments, latecomers pursued equally ruthless tactics.
>
> (Bell 1962: 148)

Learning from the practices of the propertied classes, it is no surprise that the less fortunate adopted tactics which would be shunned in 'polite society'. Thus, crime

> simply meant acquiring the material goals a society idealized by the only means left available to the dispossessed and scorned.

Less invidious was to gain a political office or become a policeman, but for the ethnic it was in reality all a part of the same sordid game.

(Kolko 1976: 89)

The US brand of individualism more than justified the use of State office for personal aggrandisement. Greer's (1979) report that until recently it was normal for the mayor of Gary (Indiana) to retire as a millionaire after four years in office is symbolic. As Carl Stokes, the 1967–71 mayor of Cleveland, recounted in 1982:

The only interests I could see being served by councilmen [*sic*] were petty and pecuniary. They counted their success by whether the office brought them money – so much for allowing a new gas station, so much for a zoning change, so much for allowing a cheat spot to operate. Being elected to the council wasn't a mandate to legislative responsibility, it was a ticket to a bartering system.

(from Clavel 1986: 60)

This ticket was sought after with some gusto by members of all social classes. This pursuit of self-benefit was most organised on a locality basis. With slow transport links over vast territories, a cohesive national élite was slow in emerging. Only for the present century is it realistic to think of such a group. Prior to this, the broadest geographical basis for élite groupings occurred on a regional level, wherein common interests arising from shared geographical circumstances produced sectionalism in the national arena which persists to this day (as in Sunbelt–Frostbelt conflict; Elazar 1966).[13] This feature of the US political tradition is extremely important, since it not only led to a more fractured political culture but also left space for local working class dominance. Most evidently, this is seen in ethnic political organisations.

The emergence of these organisations was aided by the inhospitability of the US experience for new ethnic groups. For one thing, despite its nineteenth century imagery as a land of milk and honey, within the USA there was much hardship. Even though labour shortages pushed up wage rates, poverty was rampant (around 40 per cent of the population were said to live in that circumstance in the 1880s; Husbands 1976; Shefter 1986). Furthermore, as the century progressed, new immigrants became isolated from mainstream society. Comprising just 10 per cent of entrants in 1875, immigrants from eastern and southern Europe were in the majority by 1896. Resented by the upper classes for their 'alien' ways (Baltzell 1964), despised for living frugally (often on account of a desire to return home; Kolko 1976; Parmet 1981), and scorned by trade unions for being strike breakers (Shefter 1986), these immigrants were 'outsiders' for whom the US experience was threatening. As Griffith (1974b: 67) explained, what immigrants sought 'was a morality in which ethnic loyalty, human sympathy, constant helpfulness, gregariousness, keeping promises, all figured largely'. This sentiment, along with the isolation of language and the hostility of others, led to group solidarity. These groups had emigrated to 'make it' and organisations sprang up to help them to do so (or at least to raise them off the bottom rung). These organisations were aided by the weakness of the labour movement, since an effective channel for representing the working classes was absent.[14] The atmosphere was fertile for the emergence of political machines dominated by single ethnic groups. In exchange for material support, machine leaders asked merely for each immigrant's vote. Since many entrants were as yet untouched by democratic practices, this was a small price to pay. Mutual support was a much more valued commodity than the competing claims of honesty and economy. Immigrants were sufficiently grateful not to be perturbed if the machine was accused of shady practices. Northern cities became renowned for their extravagance and corruption, with machine leaders regularly using the advantages of public office for personal aggrandisement (Shefter 1976).[15] The same holds for trade union leaders, who were associated more with corruption and organised crime than with representing members' interests.[16] As Edelstein and Warner (1975) summarised:

> American business unionism involves an ideology of fighting for more money rather than for social reorganisation, usually through the application of 'business-like' techniques which place a low priority on rank-and-file involvement in the running of the union. By the turn of the century it was becoming associated, in many unions, with an ethic which justified the self-enrichment of union officials through high salaries and even corrupt practices.
>
> (Edelstein and Warner 1975: 16)

The absence of an aristocratic tradition within the nation meant not only that US workers lacked a strong sense of class consciousness, but also that an aristocratic sense of *noblesse oblige* (the devotion of time to 'good works') was undeveloped. Union officials saw their jobs as careers, whereas European unionists more often saw them as 'callings'. On a broader front, hostility to new immigrants, and the preference for self-interest over communal betterment, have been manifest in the emergence and continuance of crime syndicates such as the Mafia.

All these organisational forms and practices did not emerge in a vacuum. On the contrary, they were supported and nurtured by elements of the propertied classes. This was not through grand strategy, but as piecemeal responses to issues of the moment. Two particular advantages accrued to propertied élites from these organisations. The first was enormous profits for some business segments (e.g. fat contracts for thin municipal projects and buying off trade union leaders in return for 'restraint' on worker demands). The second was more nebulous and long term, with only a limited number of localities experiencing an 'immediate' impact. This was the benefit from 'legitimising' personal over class interests. In Hildebrand's (1979) words, for trade unions:

> the journeymen who founded American unionism are probably viewed most accurately as akin to independent businessmen who contracted to supply their skilled services to master workmen under uniform competitive conditions, in the same spirit of acquisitiveness and property mindedness as the master workmen and merchants of the time.
>
> (Hildebrand 1979: 7)

These organisations lessened the chances of class based challenges to property. Societal élites did not produce this effect, but aided its emergence by structuring and using opportunities to nurture and legitimise their own values.

However, while many propertied interests benefited from these social practices, there were segments that did not (e.g. in so far as municipal taxes were inflated, those not directly gaining incurred significant costs). Within the governmental sphere, there arose amongst such 'losers' strong pressures for a more professional approach to public sector management. This Progressive Movement learnt from procedures in the corporate economy. In the 1880s, a decline in investment opportunities in railways led US banks to seek new openings for accumulated funds. A wave of corporate mergers resulted that fuelled the drive for scientific management, made necessary by the size of new institutions (Lash and Urry 1987). To establish a reference point, the internationalism of the British scene was readily apparent at this time, because in responding to similar pressures, British banks sought investments overseas (Edelstein 1982). Consequently, in Britain there was no strong push for mergers and no emphasis on professional management. Whereas the United States developed a strong, though not universal, attachment to 'experts' (first in the corporate sector and then in government), the professionalism of British institutions had a 'feudal' character of guilds requiring lengthy training to learn 'proper' conduct (e.g. in the law and in accountancy). Outside such fields, the British relied on generalist 'amateurs', with 'experts' achieving slight access to channels of power.[17]

At all space–time points, at whatever geographical scale, traits of corruption and professionalism have been evident within the USA. At times, one or other is seemingly at slumber but is not difficult to arouse. In some instances, as in Burlington, Vermont in the 1980s, the offer of 'good government' inspires the public to vote for socialist administrations (Clavel 1986). Then again, as Blydenburgh (1975) makes clear for New Jersey, even with legislation to end nepotism and patronage-laden practices, politicians introduce so many caveats to 'normal' procedures that, behind the guise of professionalism, the dictates of self-interest abound.

That these arrangements have found acceptance with propertied élites is evident from the character of US political parties. Going back to the country's formation, élite compromise has played a major part in US society (the breakdown of that compromise – over the kind of society that would hold sway in western lands – was the ultimate cause of the Civil War). Compromise has been built into the practices of political parties. 'Whatever the popular political label has been – "Federalist", "Democrat", "Whig", "Republican", "Progressive", "Conservative" or "Liberal" – American leadership has remained committed to the same values and ideas that motivated the Founding Fathers' (Dye and Zeigler 1978: 58). These have not included competition over national goals and programmes, but have sought social consensus, limited political conflict and the sanctity of property as a fundamental value. Elite compromise is an important element of the US political culture which owes much to the newness of this land, not simply in terms of its nationhood (since if this alone were important, the same condition would hold in Germany and Italy), but also in the absence of 'ancestry'. As with other new lands, the United States has sought to construct an identity for itself, but owing to turbulent population origins, this has proved fragile. As Elazar (1988: 2) explained: 'Frenchmen [*sic*] and Italians can survive crises of regime and of constitution without threat to their "Frenchness" or "Italianness"; Americans cannot weather even relatively modest crises (by non-American standards) without challenging their very right to exist as a nation.' Set alongside the primacy of individualism has been a 'forced' imposition of collective identity. But where nationalist sentiment is brittle, and national policies are class discriminatory, élites are best served by directing political differences away from class issues.

Throughout the nation's history, political parties have proved efficient instruments in furthering this goal. Ideologically, their overlaps are considerable; they cover a narrow range of the political spectrum (made clear in the ease with which politicians switch parties). Central to the institutional procedures of the party system is the controlling hand of property. One manifestation of this is the manner in which, at all levels of government, attaining electoral office is first and foremost a matter of money (and the higher up the hierarchy one's aspirations lead, the greater the cost of election campaigns). To seek office requires personal wealth or the backing of the wealthy. In either event, propertied interests are likely to be satisfied. Not that some candidates have not 'bucked the system'. However, when this occurs, élite compromise reacts. 'The simple truth is, a party will dump any election whenever its control over the party will be weakened by the victory of its own party's candidate' (Karp 1973: 19). If primary elections produce challenges to a party hierarchy, party officials are inclined to support the opposition against its own candidate (e.g. Greer 1979).

All this implies that the United States has a highly coordinated national élite which is closely integrated with government. This is a wildly different image from that which political and economic élites project and which most Americans recognise. Yet an abundance of research carefully documents the existence of an élite over a long period. Even presidents have added their stamp of approval, as with Dwight Eisenhower who (notably on retirement) popularised the concept of a 'military-industrial complex' which he held was subverting the democratic rule of government. However, it is essential to caution against too literal an interpretation of the word 'élite'. There is no assertion that a small group of people decide everything or that their views are always victorious when conflicts of interest arise. For one thing, there are divisions within the élite, though the impetus to iron these out before they become public is strong. Likewise, non-élites score victories in the face of élite opposition. It is quite obvious, for example, that the civil rights, environmental and peace (or anti-Vietnam War) movements of the

1960s had marked effects on the American mind, as well as on government policy. Each took élites by surprise because of the unexpected quarter of their origin. (For example, for the environmental and peace movements, primary instigators were the middle classes, who previously adopted a compliant attitude to the established order.) Unsettled by these attacks it took a decade or so to develop effective responses to them. But even before Ronald Reagan, military-industrial interests had again grasped the governing mantle, as environmental regulations were watered down and defence procurements soared upwards (e.g. Vogel 1983). The élitism of US society is not seen in this reassertion, but in the structural restraints that non-élites faced in mounting challenges to the established order. For the peace movement, for example, the media adopted a 'three monkeys' stance towards illegal acts by the federal government. Thus, bombing raids into Cambodia and Laos were kept from the public even though the press knew what was taking place. Overt media opposition to the peace movement was paramount until the war began to turn sour. Meanwhile, local, state and federal agencies were mobilised to discredit leaders and policies of this 'opposition party' (even if this involved abusing civil rights and breaking the law). Yet the successes of the peace movement (even if significantly benefiting from military reversals) do point out that 'even the effective system of ideological controls of the United States has its limitations' (Chomsky and Herman 1979: xii).[18] The crux of élite rule is domination of rules and norms. It does not mean that élites always win.

Even so, unusually for an advanced economy, US élites adopt a hands-on approach to government. As one sign of this, Freitag (1975) reported that 76.1 per cent of presidential Cabinet members between 1897 and 1973 had interlocks with the nation's largest corporations (the actual percentage might have been higher, as the standing of 11.7 per cent was unknown). For every single Cabinet over that period at least 60 per cent fell into this category. Significantly, these representatives were primarily leaders of the capitalist class. When Mills (1956: 9) strove to highlight how 'the warlords, the corporation chieftains, the political directorate – tend to come together, to form the power élite', he was handicapped by a shortage of supportive research. Today, investigations by Domhoff (1975, 1983), Dye (1986a), Mizruchi (1982) and Useem (1984) have added meat to Mills's bare bones. For Useem:

Rather than defensively protecting only their own company's interests, those in the highest circles of corporate leadership now share a clearer understanding that what divides them is modest compared to what separates them from those who would presume to exercise power over economic decisions from bases other than those of private economic power.

(Useem 1984:6)

In effect, a 'special segment' of the capitalist class exists which represents the fusion of financial and industrial interests (Zeitlin 1982). Assisting this coordinating group is a network of interlocking directorships amongst the largest companies, which binds financial and industrial capital together (this integration was forged in the last century when banks coordinated corporate mergers; e.g. Mizruchi 1982). A complex of charitable foundations adds further impetus by pushing university research and welfare provisions in favoured directions. Then, at the federal level, this coordinating group dominates policy agencies which seek to have their policies transformed into governmental action (e.g. the Council on Foreign Relations, the Committee for Economic Development and the Trilateral Commission). Lest the effectiveness of these groups be questioned, it is worth pointing to specific signals of relevance, such as President Carter appointing twenty members of the Trilateral Commission and fifty-four from the Council of Foreign Relations to senior government posts. That this special segment of the capitalist class constitutes an 'élite' is evident from its position at the apex of economic, political and social institutions (half of the members of the Council on Foreign Relations are in the *Social Register*, for example; Domhoff 1969). That there is a concerted attempt to breathe coordination into their actions is further shown by their use of social functions, such as the two-week annual event at Bohemia Grove, a California redwood 'camp', or the riding week at Rancho Visitadores near Santa Barbara, both of which attract numerous executives from the largest corporations (Domhoff 1975). That Hunter (1959) found that the most powerful people in the USA thought it natural to know one another should not surprise us. In a society with a coherent, coordinated ruling class this is indeed 'natural'.

## LOWER TIER–HIGHER TIER INTERFACES

How dominant themes in the political character of Britain and the United States have been projected on to the field of lower tier– higher tier governmental relationships is not a straightforward question to answer. The primary reason for this comes from the multidimensional character of such interchanges. In broad terms, cross-national differences can be distinguished. Consistent with the hierarchical character of the British scene, the centre has kept for itself the key role in influencing local policy. 'Britain is perhaps the most extreme case where the national political élite remains the major source of policy guidance and their power is further protected by the various ways they are isolated from political and administrative influence at other levels of government' (Ashford 1982: 19). As Ashford (1981: 68) made clear in an earlier publication: 'What differentiates Britain from France, which also has a unitary system, is how easily national policy-makers can act without careful consultation with local government and how easily national objectives are imposed on this vast subnational structure'. Signifying the notable dissimilarities between these nations, national politicians in Britain retain almost no formal connection with local authorities, even though somewhere around one-third of Members of Parliament were once local councillors (Mellors 1978). By contrast, many senior French officials jointly hold national and city appointments. (Schain [1985] reported that 68 per cent of National Assembly deputies were either mayors or councillors and only 17 per cent had never held local office.) That the national core has exerted such direction over British practices arises because local and national leaders have shared a common purpose for much of the nation's history. Even those who like to portray themselves as 'radicals' (such as Labour ministers and, more recently, the Thatcher administrations) have not seriously threatened élite favoured norms (note Labour's failure to act on the private school, Oxbridge educated, social biases of top civil servants; Hetzner 1985). As Bulpitt (1983: 157) identified, the national political scene 'was managed by "chaps", "sound chaps" in London, who did their best to get on with equally sound, but sometimes socially suspect "chaps", in the periphery'. Those in positions of authority outside Westminster and Whitehall might not be from as 'sound' a social stock, but they knew and adhered to 'the rules of the game'. The British

> resolved the contradiction of local self-government and 'partner-ship' with the unitary system by manufacturing a common culture at both the Centre and in the periphery; a culture in which the 'chaps' involved (both bureaucrats and politicians) would behave themselves, would not overstep the mark. In short, everything depended on an elaborate system of compromise and mutual

deference between political and administrative élites at the Centre and in the periphery.

(Bulpitt 1983: 223–4)

Local–central relations have traditionally been a partnership, not a dictatorship.

The British system of government operates in a gentlemanly fashion. Central government departments may complain of the waywardness of individual authorities, just as local authorities may complain of the obtuseness and pedantry of ministries, but the relationships are generally smooth even when they are not cordial. Though there are considerable reserves of power at the centre these are diffuse and are operated with care.

(Cullingworth 1966: 63)

The centre could do as it wished, but most of the time revealed little inclination to do so.

The United States is more decentralised than Britain and yet it is more controlled. Constitutional law makes the direct regulation of local governments a function of their state counterparts, with federal authorities having an overview role (e.g. in non-discriminatory employment laws). Given that there are fifty states, there is great potential for variability in lower tier–higher tier interactions. However, broad trends across states reveal consistencies. Amongst these has been the tendency of state leaders to 'interfere' with local government. In Adrian's (1972: 89) words: 'Local governments are the children of the state. The state has been most unwilling to allow its children to grow up.' This is hardly surprising, given the strength of sectional interests. Having responsibility for local affairs meant state officials could further favoured causes. Characteristic of nineteenth century practices was the contraction of New York City's public services, as Republicans won control of the state assembly and sought to weaken the patronage base of the Democrat controlled city, only for Democrat victories in Albany to reinstate functions (Shefter 1976; more generally see Griffith 1974a). Indeed, in the second half of the last century, state legislatures became so embroiled in local affairs that it created a heavy workload (in some states, such as Kansas, this continued much later, with around a third of legislative time going on local government in the 1950s; Drury 1965). To counter this work pressure, states began to prohibit legislation for single localities (e.g. Helstrom 1977). Instead laws had to refer to all or to specified categories of local council. (Often, for the largest cities, a category might contain one place, but if population changes pushed cities over the size threshold they became subject to the same provisions.) At the same time, under specified circumstances, some states passed 'home rule' restrictions on the application of state laws to specified areas of municipal jurisdiction. Often such provisions enhanced the power of local citizens (e.g. enabling them to call a referendum to decide policy issues or allowing them to 'recall' officials to election if dissatisfied with their performance). That these measures enhanced local autonomy should not be taken as a symbol of changed attitudes. As with easing regulations governing the formation of new municipalities, these actions owed much to the perpetuation of vested interest. In northern states, the proportion of city voters who were immigrants was rising fast. WASP élites sought ways to insulate themselves from ethnic populations (e.g. Hugill 1989). Geographical separation helped but was no guarantee of élite insulation, because there was the spectre of ethnic machines wresting control of state assemblies. Hence, some isolation from state government was essential. With self-interest a powerful motive force, these arrangements also incorporated a disposition which was favourable to tax restraint, indeed to 'limited government'. A stress on business management further strengthened these strands. What is more, by state dictate, political parties were barred from numerous municipalities (today only 27.4 per cent of cities are partisan; Adrian 1988), which restricted working class access by denying necessary organisational forms. As Sharpe (1973) argued, despite the appearance of great local autonomy, municipal rule is structured to restrain effective government (for some interests more than for others). In this, the heavy hand of the individualist, sectional tone of US political values is clear.

## Evaluating local autonomy

The above brief account of links between national political culture and lower tier–higher tier relationships has been deliberately kept at the general level. Political cultures are the articulation of dominant themes in societal organisation, but commitment to mainstream values is far from complete. Set amidst a prevailing ethos, value dispositions are fragmented, inconsistent and unevenly appreciated. The same is true for structures and practices which bind the local State into the nation State. Cockburn (1977: 47) was correct in pointing out that: 'In spite of its multiplicity . . . the state

preserves a basic unity. All its parts work fundamentally as one.'
Yet this does not get us far if the intention is to understand precise
government policies, because there is slippage between institutional
practices and the political goals of those at national and local levels.
Further, even with the same goal at all tiers, there will be different
readings of how abstract vision is best transposed into practice,
differential capacities to grasp occasions for implementation,
unequal efficiencies in pursuing aims, and varying responses to the
unexpected by-products of policy initiatives. Any central trend will
be beset by distracting forces, blurred edges and faint impressions.
Yet both the central trend and the paraphernalia that surrounds it
are central to the experience and performance of government.

So, while interpretations of local politics should be informed by
an understanding of national political culture, a framework is still
required which breathes sense into the confusions of political life. In
the context of lower tier–higher tier relationships, a valuable
device for achieving this has been provided by Page and Goldsmith
(1985). They stress that links between sub-national and national
processes (or the centralisation of State authority) are not
unidimensional. Three criteria distinguish higher tier controls.

The first concerns the *functions* that local institutions perform, as
these specify the scope of local authority. There can be enormous
complexity here, since the responsibilities of local councils are
various. Thus, whereas in England local authorities of one class
share the same functions, this is not the case in many nations (e.g.
in the United States, even within states, cities can have different
responsibilities; Liebert 1976). Additionally, within service categories
there are interpenetrations of responsibilities between tiers. For
example, many nations are characterised by a division of local and
regional transport responsibilities across tiers, so that services within
a locality fall under different tiers. Yet in some nations the
intermixing of responsibilities goes well beyond any logical spatial
fix (as in France, where local council responsibility for education is
largely restricted to school buildings while teachers' pay, curriculum
and teaching supplies rest in national hands). Of course, what
distinguishes the local role is not simply the functions performed,
but also the ability to carry them out. Page and Goldsmith (1985)
put such considerations in their second dimension, but it is pertinent
to note that responsibility for a function carries little weight if local
councils are denied the resources to fund it. This is no criticism of
Page and Goldsmith, but is a reminder that structural arrangements
have an important bearing on actual operations.

The second criterion concerns the *discretion* that sub-national institutions have in policy-making. Incorporated here are questions of how far local actions are directed from above, whether decisions are subject to higher tier approval or overview, whether institutions have the financial back-up to pursue locally determined goals, and the manner in which institutional arrangements circumscribe the actions of local policy-makers. A split second is sufficient to recognise that the range of discretionary issues is so large that evaluating this component of local autonomy is complex. Clark (1985) offers some guidance by suggesting the principles of initiative and immunity for evaluation. Put simply, what is the realm over which local councils can act on their own initiative and how immune are they from having decisions changed by other institutions (including the courts)? Conceptually these ideas are a help, though the practicalities of applying them are immense. There are three points that need to be borne in mind in this context. The first is that the existence of a legislative provision does not mean that it is complied with. Thus, in Britain, local councils are *ultra vires* if they cannot trace authority for their decisions to parliamentary legislation. Yet, 'in practice the doctrine of *ultra vires* does not have the effect of holding a local authority within a legal straightjacket' (Dearlove 1973: 15). 'While the rhetoric of *ultra vires* sounds strong, the number of cases that have been brought on the grounds of unreasonable decisions could be counted on the fingers of two hands' (Henney 1984: 45). Illustrative of this is a tendency for new services to be approved retroactively by national legislation (as for the provision of insulin for diabetics; Swann 1972). Secondly, it is critical to recognise that local councils make differential use of their discretionary authority. Milch (1974) makes this point admirably in his analysis of the divergent policy stances of Montpellier and Nîmes, where the higher priority given to local control in Montpellier led to national housing grants being rejected (as their stipulations did not meet local approval). Thirdly, it is rare to find 'purity' along a continuum of complete control to no control in lower tier–higher tier interactions (almost at the 'no control' extreme is the Netherlands, where the national government determines almost all local council funds). Black and white are not appropriate colours to paint the landscape of inter-governmental relations. Various tones and shades are needed, because intensities vary within single inter-jurisdictional links (e.g. in Britain education attracts more central overview than cultural services; Page and Goldsmith 1987) and between interaction networks (hence larger cities with more professional bureaucracies can receive less detailed attention than smaller places). Furthermore, once a particular pattern is established it frequently becomes endowed with all manner of virtuous attributes. Consider, for example, the horror expressed by Dearlove and Saunders (1984) over the introduction of rate capping, a procedure which restricts the ability of British local authorities to draw on their property tax bases:

> The imminent demise of local government as a democratic and reasonably accountable system has been forecast many times before. Rate-capping makes such forecasts a reality, for it totally constrains a local council to follow the line laid down by the centre by removing its one autonomous sphere of revenue. Effectively stripped of the power to raise taxes beyond a level determined by the centre, local authorities cease in any meaningful sense to function as systems of government and are reduced to the status of local outposts of the government in Westminster. Like the wicked queen in the story of Snow White, the centre has administered a poisoned apple to its one competitor and can now be reassured that it has no challengers. Unlike Snow White, however, the local authorities are likely to find that the dose does indeed prove fatal.
>
> (Dearlove and Saunders 1984: 389)

This colourful description must strike a peculiar note for American readers, since numerous US states impose restraints on local budgeting (Table 2.2). For instance, at the heart of New Jersey's 'cap law' is a provision not dissimilar to rate capping (California's Proposition 13 is different as it was opposed by the state government and was passed as a voter initiative). The cap law is different from rate capping in that targets are not changed annually (figures are fixed generally for a five-year period), but to stress this distinction would ignore the annually changing list of 'exceptions' granted under cap legislation (each of which has discriminatory effects across localities). The widely differing reactions which rate capping and the cap law have spawned are reminiscent of Langrod's (1953) mystification over British arguments about the sanctity of local democracy; after all, the French governmental system was highly centralised, yet it was considered democratic. What we now know is that once local autonomy is viewed in its complexity, once the assumption of unidimensionality is rejected, then a multitude of give and take processes are apparent. 'While we often think of the French political system as more centralised than the British, in

*Table 2.2* State government restraints on US municipal finance 1978–85

| Restraint | Number |
|---|---|
| States with maximum rate of property tax without a referendum | 5 |
| States with limits on property tax levy (typically with regard to annual percentage increase) | 12 |
| States with general revenue limitations (all sources) | 4 |
| States with general expenditure limitations | 2 |
| States with limits on property tax assessment increases | 6 |
| States with full disclosure or truth-in-property taxation (i.e. must advertise and hold public meetings on tax increases) | 6 |

*Source*: Howard (1987: 9)

practice the policy process in France disperses more power to lower levels of government than in Britain' (Ashford 1982: 7).

This last point dovetails into Page and Goldsmith's (1985) third criteron in which they stress that the *access* of local policy-makers to national decision circles is important. France is the most renowned case of a local–central interchange which is characterised by informality, since the rigidity of the French system provokes demands to by-pass it. These are manifest in a social network, or *relational réseau*, that binds local and national politicians through informal influence peddling (Becquart-Leclerq 1977); such ties strengthen, as well as necessitate, local leaders' attainment of national office. Local governments in Britain and the United States have nothing to compare with these informal networks. Local authority associations in Britain have attempted to develop closer links with national authorities, but their effectiveness has been limited. Their support has been called on when the centre seeks compliance with its aims, but their opposition has been ignored when the centre is convinced of its actions (Rhodes 1986). More akin to the French arrangement are the professional alliances and networks associated with particular policy fields. These so-called professional communities overlap in differing degrees with the 'policy communities' which bring together leaders in policy sectors at local and central levels. Signifying the relevance of policy communities, Newton (1976a: 203) reported that in Birmingham: 'It is said that there are only three major parties on the council – the Conservative Party, the Labour Party, and the Education Committee.' Yet, across services, policy communities vary in strength, as does their overlap with professional communities. In good part, the importance of bureaucrats appears to depend on whether an occupation was placed on a 'professional' standing prior to expanding in the public sector. The professional community for highway engineers, for example, is dominant in the transport policy community, whereas housing policy initiatives are largely in the hands of politicians (Laffin 1986). What confuses the local–central relationship is the prospect of professional and policy communities strengthening national support for local initiatives, but when these are adopted as national policies they meet some fierce local opposition (an example is comprehensive schools; Fenwick 1976). Local discretion on one occasion can lead to its subjugation on another. Such patterns are also evident in the United States (especially within states, where a few cities can be dominant), but the vehicles of influence are somewhat different. In the USA, identifiable professional and policy communities are less apparent. More common is political lobbying. This occupies a major position in policy-making. Local authority associations in Britain have their counterparts in lobby organisations which represent groups and even single cities at federal and state levels. In reality, however, these pressure groups compete for attention alongside a host of other lobbies. The lack of strong links between bureaucrats at federal, state and local levels, beside the near mutual exclusion of politicians at these levels, means that local officials have few privileges of special access to higher tier authorities. In the 1980s the accession of a new right leadership has been charged with having the same effect in Britain (e.g. Dunleavy and Rhodes 1983). For some, this follows from the general belief that, on both sides of the Atlantic, the accession of the new right has broken old moulds. This claim merits careful scrutiny.

## THE 1980s: A TURN TO THE RIGHT?

The 1980s has been something of a political paradox. Commentators on the decade have been tempted to see it as the dawning of a new age, as right-wing leaders have come to the fore in numerous advanced nations. Ronald Reagan and Margaret Thatcher are the most obvious examples perhaps, but even Sweden had an interlude of rightism which broke decades of social democratic governance and West Germany elected a conservative as Chancellor. Yet in France the reverse happened. The right was thrown out and, in President Mitterrand, the left was installed. Just as the British and United States electoral systems provided rightist incumbents with repeated victories, so the French system confirmed the left's rule. In much of the literature on the 1980s, there has been a tendency to ignore the French case. National parochialism, pleasure in victory and hurt in defeat (depending on political perspective), seem to combine to blinker some commentaries. Perhaps France is exceptional, but this seems unlikely. After all, President Mitterrand found trends in the world economy too strong for his early policies and dramatically changed their central thrust within two years of taking office (Hall 1987). France was as susceptible to world trends as other nations. And it is in these trends that we find a key to understanding the 1980s. To do so we must acknowledge the turbulence of the world economy in the 1970s, since by its middle years the central features of the decade were clear:

> every section of the political élite, from trade union leaders through Cabinet Ministers to bankers and industrialists, throughout the Western World were 'running after events' in the 1970s, were trying with greater or lesser degrees of desperation to cope with an agenda of problems – inflation, unemployment, stagnation, balance of payments deficits – common to them all but which no one of them either initiated or desired.
>
> (Coates 1975: 16–17)

Economic chaos abounded. Sitting governments were hoisted on their own electoral petard, given claims that they were most fit to govern, but were also unfortunate to be the ruling party of the day. Whatever the precise reasons, those in office were blamed for all manner of ills which they often could do little about and over which their opponents equally floundered (despite the rhetoric). Yet, on their attaining office, the depressed state of the world economy was to prove significant. 'Precisely because of the economic and ideological effects of the recession the significance of right-wing parties' control over state power has grown enormously' (Dunleavy 1986: 134). Where political doctrine leads to support for a smaller public sector, tax cuts and less welfare assistance, economic depression offers a convenient backcloth for assertions such as 'we need to tighten our belts', 'enterprise must be unleashed' and 'people are work-shy'. Economic conditions have made it easier for the right to impose preferred policies. This is nothing new. In the 1960s the relative buoyancy of western economies allowed leftist governments to support expansions in the public sector (albeit in Britain economic problems led to some cuts even then). For Rose (1984), change in British government policy since 1945 (including

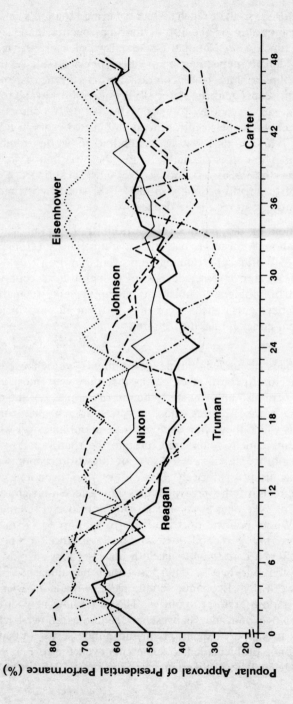

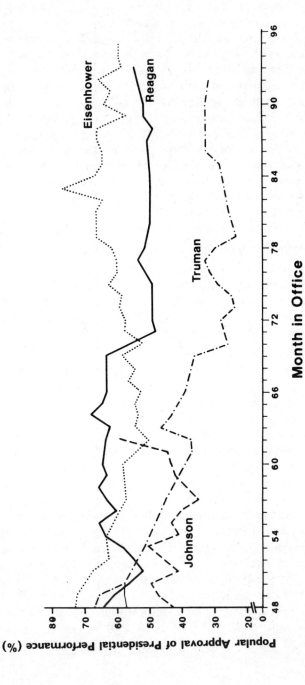

*Figure 2.1* The popularity of President Reagan 1981–9

*Source*: University of California, Berkeley, Institute of Governmental Studies, *Public Affairs Report*, 30 (2), March 1989: 8–9

the 1979–83 Thatcher administration) owes little to ideology but much to the state of the economy (as with the Mitterrand experiment).

Some commentators have fallen into the temptation of accepting rightist rhetoric and letting this colour evaluations of performance. It should be borne in mind that Ronald Reagan and Margaret Thatcher did not emerge as national leaders on account of mass support for their policies. In Ronald Reagan's case this is readily apparent in his popularity levels whilst occupying the presidency; his standing compared with other post-1945 presidents was middling to poor (Figure 2.1).[19] For Margaret Thatcher, the story that has to be told spells 'chance'. As Gamble (1988) describes, Margaret Thatcher's accession to the Conservative Party leadership drew largely on disgruntlement with the previous leader, Edward Heath. Yet in a party that places unity as a primary goal, those most favoured as the next party leader would not at first challenge him in a leadership contest:

> The curious situation had developed that those who wanted a leader other than Heath could only have a chance of getting who they wanted by voting initially for someone they did not want, namely a candidate from the Right of the Party who had no inhibitions about challenging Heath.
>
> (Gamble 1988: 82–3)

Margaret Thatcher was not a strong leadership candidate. Indeed, her 'emergence as the standard-bearer of the anti-Heath forces in the Conservative Party was unexpected, but just credible enough to make her challenge a serious one' (Gamble 1988: 82). Yet with astute management by her aides, and by playing down her own beliefs (Peele 1988), she was able to present the view that she could get enough votes to persuade Heath to resign. At that point the 'real' leadership contest was to take place. However, her campaign managers were so successful that she not only brought about the demise of Edward Heath but also sat within a few votes of becoming leader. With a head of steam behind her, and helpers again proving competent electioneers, she clinched the leadership on the second vote. 'Almost by accident the new right found that they had captured the most important position in the Conservative Party' (Gamble 1988: 83). Significantly, however, they had not captured the party itself. On forming a new government in 1979, the Cabinet was almost the same as 1970 (with the exclusion of Heath). As for policies, again little had changed. The main proposals of the Heath government were prominent, save for the monetarist emphasis on controlling the money supply (itself understandable given that monetarist policies had been adopted by the retiring Labour government and that Keynesianism was discredited after the US allowed the dollar to float in 1971). Moreover, policies which are now seen as 'radical' elements of Thatcherism – with the exception of public housing sales, this includes the privatisation of public assets – were not in the government's plans. Indeed, much to the disappointment of those supporting privatisation, the dominant theme in British policy has been revenue attainment rather than encouraging competition and entrepreneurship (Aharoni 1988). Furthermore, most especially in the early years of Thatcher rule, the government changed its policies repeatedly in the face of public and backbench opposition (e.g. Bulpitt 1983; Burch 1983), although without ever succumbing to a full U-turn (Jessop *et al.* 1988). In more recent years, returns from asset sales have provided a cushion against policy change, yet the much touted attack on anachronistic institutions and practices has been muted (e.g. Johnson 1985). Much window dressing has occurred, but new right advocates continue to be disappointed with Thatcher government achievements in critical areas such as trade union reform, private sector competition, deregulation, and reducing the size of the public sector (Gamble 1988). On the other side of the Atlantic, President Reagan's impact was also more restrained than supporters expected (Niskanen 1988). His administration's efforts were concentrated on a narrow range of issues (most obviously defence and the economy), with an avoidance of confrontation over social liberalism (Girvin 1988).

These points are not meant to suggest that the 1980s has not seen significant policy change. They are meant to warn against too simplistic a linking of governmental change to policy change. This point is emphasised by examining lower tier–higher tier relationships for three policy arenas central to the new right: macro-economic policies, the distribution of societal benefits and the structuring of power relations.

From the outset, it should be recognised that the macro-economic policy most identified with new right administrations (viz. monetarism) pre-dated both Ronald Reagan and Margaret Thatcher as national leaders. In fact, macro-economic indicators show little break with past trends on their accessions. By their stated objectives, both administrations have been failures. In Ronald Reagan's case, this is most obviously seen in a huge federal budget deficit (effectively mortgaging the country's future for short-term

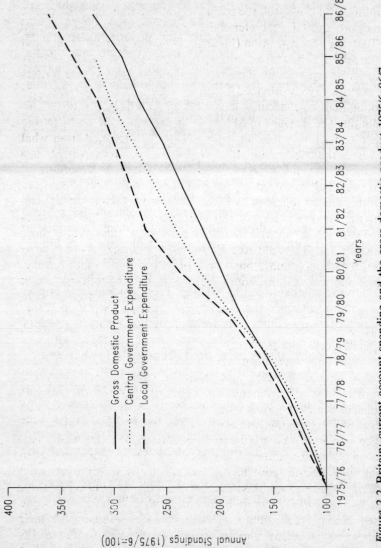

*Figure 2.2* Britain: current account spending and the gross domestic product 1975/6–86/7

*Source:* Central Statistical Office (1988) *Annual Abstract of Statistics, 1988*, HMSO, London

political gain). In Margaret Thatcher's case, it is seen in continuing increases in local and central government expenditure as a proportion of the gross domestic product (Figure 2.2) and in rates of inflation above the West European norm. Contrary to the commitment to claw back the public sector, the ratio between public expenditure and GDP accelerated upwards on the accession of the first Thatcher administration (Figure 2.2). Readers might object that this largely resulted from the rapid growth of social security payments brought on by increased unemployment. Indeed writers such as Peele (1988) provided excuses for the Thatcher performance by noting that social security payments are politically sensitive. This will not do. The message of Margaret Thatcher herself has been that she is a conviction politician, who will not be deflected from what she sees as the 'right' path. Reducing social security payments is a high priority for the new right (note the constant reshuffling of welfare regulations to reduce the number of recipients). Failure to act in this area is repeated by cutting hospital spending rather than taking the unpopular step of reducing general practitioner services (e.g. Figure 2.3). Convictionism makes good rhetoric, as does nationalism (as in Ronald Reagan's homely messages about making 'America' strong again), but much of it has been sabre-rattling. Despite their convictions, both governments have bent in the face of pressure from electorally sensitive constituencies.[20] Electoral concerns are 'realities' for any government, so perhaps it is pertinent to 'ignore' direct services to the public. Yet, as suggested by the size of the public sector labour force, whatever changes have occurred since 1979 have not been very effective (Table 2.3). Indeed, although intense pressure has been brought to bear on local authorities, the government has been unsuccessful in winning compliance with its wishes (e.g. Rhodes 1984; Smith and Stewart 1985).[21] Analysing this pattern, Adams (1989) argued that the Reagan administration has been more successful in achieving cut-backs in local expenditure than the Thatcher government, even though the federal government has no jurisdiction over local spending. In good part, this results from different political cultures in the two nations. The more hierarchical ethos of the British scene creates an expectation that national authorities will care for their junior wards, whereas the more individualistic overtone in US philosophies more easily allows cut-backs in grants (since state and municipal administrations are expected to stand on their own feet). Nationally, in Britain more than the USA, there is an impetus towards inertia in higher tier–lower tier relationships which

*Table 2.3* British central and local government employment 1975–85

| Year | Column* | | | | | | | |
| | 1 | 2 | 3 | 4 | 5 | 6 | 7 | 8 |
| --- | --- | --- | --- | --- | --- | --- | --- | --- |
| 1975 | 5544 | 4327 | 1878 | 1410 | 1027 | 460 | 20578 | 5241 |
| 1976 | 5627 | 4377 | 1947 | 1428 | 1074 | 450 | 20885 | 5685 |
| 1977 | 5652 | 4343 | 1973 | 1392 | 1094 | 431 | 20729 | 5711 |
| 1978 | 5641 | 4270 | 2021 | 1371 | 1079 | 405 | 20696 | 5673 |
| 1979 | 5744 | 4313 | 2059 | 1354 | 1105 | 427 | 20983 | 5658 |
| 1980 | 5728 | 4237 | 2079 | 1317 | 1140 | 427 | 20877 | 5475 |
| 1981 | 5621 | 3984 | 2107 | 1256 | 1179 | 436 | 20487 | 5399 |
| 1982 | 5532 | 3898 | 2117 | 1180 | 1198 | 429 | 20143 | 5280 |
| 1983 | 5495 | 3872 | 2150 | 1173 | 1210 | 429 | 20136 | 5185 |
| 1984 | 5449 | 3811 | 2206 | 1127 | 1209 | 432 | 20149 | 5043 |
| 1985 | 5417 | 3845 | 2245 | 1124 | 1208 | 436 | 20137 | 4980 |

*Column 1: education (lecturers and teachers)
 Column 2: education: (others)
 Column 3: social services
 Column 4: construction
 Column 5: police (all ranks)
 Column 6: police (others)
 Column 7: total local government employment, England and Wales
 Column 8: total central government non-industrial employment

*Notes*
(a) These figures are for full-time equivalents expressed in hundreds; data on those employed in job creation schemes (these accounted for 4,000-5,000 jobs a year only) are omitted.
(b) Only services with at least 100,000 workers have been listed.
(c) Since 1979 central government employment figures have been 'massaged' in a manner that gives a greater sense of workforce reduction than has applied. (Hence 1100 employees at the Victoria and Albert Museum came off the list in 1984, as the Museum received 'trustee' status, and in 1986 a further 1100 in the Directorate of Historic Monuments and Ancient Buildings were transferred to a commission which is not in the employment count.)

*Source*: Central Statistical Office, *Monthly Digest of Statistics*, various, HMSO, London

restrains the freedom of action even of purportedly radical leaders. On account of its federated polity, the USA has a different form of inertia built in, since state governments are quite capable of undoing federal cuts by aiding local agencies. Perhaps for this reason, total public sector employment losses in the USA bear few scars from the Reagan era (Table 2.4).

Yet the public has favoured more emphasis on social programmes than these administrations have supported (e.g. Gyford *et al.* 1989).

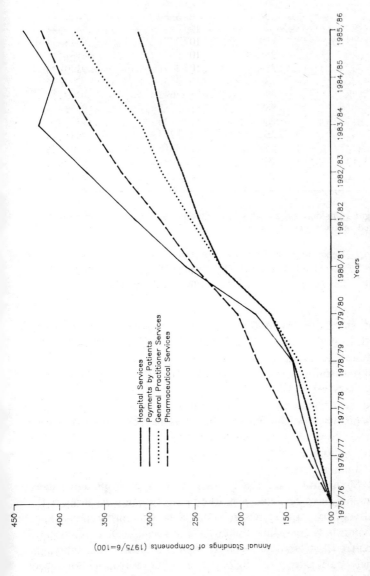

*Figure 2.3* Components of National Health Service spending 1975/6–85/6

*Source*: calculated from Central Statistical Office, *Annual Abstract of Statistics 1988*, HMSO, London

*Table 2.4* United States government employment 1975–85

| | Full-time and part-time numbers in 000s | | |
|---|---|---|---|
| Year | Federal | State | Local |
| 1975 | 2890 | 3271 | 8813 |
| 1976 | 2883 | 3343 | 8831 |
| 1977 | 2848 | 3491 | 9120 |
| 1978 | 2885 | 3539 | 9204 |
| 1979 | 2869 | 3699 | 9403 |
| 1980 | 2898 | 3753 | 9562 |
| 1981 | 2865 | 3726 | 9377 |
| 1982 | 2848 | 3744 | 9249 |
| 1983 | 2875 | 3816 | 8965 |
| 1984 | 2942 | 3898 | 9596 |
| 1985 | 3021 | 3894 | 9685 |

*Note*
These figures are only head counts, not full-time equivalents, so they should be interpreted with a degree of caution.

*Source*: US Department of Commerce Bureau of Census, *Statistical Abstract of the United States*, various, US Government Printing Office, Washington D.C.

In this regard, these leaders have acted at variance with public opinion, since the distribution of societal benefits has undoubtedly changed. In both nations, there have been significant tax cuts for the wealthy and for large corporations. Personal income distributions have shifted to favour the wealthy (e.g. Table 2.5) and tax systems are now less progressive (Figure 2.4). Thus, President Reagan is credited with having awarded the largest business tax break in the nation's history (Joe and Rogers 1985), while the cumulative impact of tax and allowance provisions in Thatcher government budgets has made only those earning over £400 a week, the retired and one-parent families better off in real terms than in 1979 (Dilnot and Stark 1986; Dilnot *et al.* 1987, 1988). Over specific policies, these governments have revealed a marked disinclination to support the politically and economically weak. Public housing programmes have been deliberately cut. Much tinkering with social security regulations has occurred, so that it is now more difficult to qualify for assistance, easier to lose eligibility, and more trouble to collect benefits. Support for collective services has likewise diminished (e.g. hospitals and public transport in Britain). Unwilling to tackle the major issue of reorganising the welfare state (or, for the USA, of restructuring social liberalism), these governments have set their sights on the weak, who will cause less political 'trouble'. When their earlier, bold steps proved to have built-in restraints for future action (as in the massive increases in unemployment consequent upon the Thatcher government's 1979–81 economic policies; Martin 1986), they turned to more modest steps which would not unduly alarm the public and which could be explained as 'good housekeeping' (as in rises in prescription costs for National Health Service medicines; Figure 2.3). This is not death by a thousand cuts. It is slimming by a hundred shavings. The impact on local government has been both direct and indirect. Directly, the higher tier has restrained lower tier aid to the poor (although perhaps only by withdrawing grant aid). Indirectly, in discarding the poor and needy, these administrations have broadened and heightened demand for local public services. To the extent that local units have responded to these demands, their policy-making has become more frantic, more uncertain and more conflictual. In Britain, intense local–central antagonism has resulted, with the go-between of state governments ameliorating local–national conflict in the USA.

Yet in fuelling this antagonism, what has been more significant than particular policies has been the attempt to redirect power relationships. Here sharp distinctions should be drawn between the two nations. Emphasising a policy made prominent by Richard Nixon, Ronald Reagan's redistributive urge has sought to give more authority to local and state authorities. Within a US context, this power nexus is a logical one for conservatives (accepting that defence and macro-economic concerns are in national hands). At the local level, conservatives are most likely to hold sway. Although Europeans tend to think of almost all US politicians as conservative, for those in the Ronald Reagan school of thought, Washington is a hotbed of liberal advocacy. By investing more responsibility at local and state levels, the sum total of governmental authority should move towards the right. Since capital mobility in the USA is high (encouraged by generous provisions for writing off investment costs against taxes, so their abandonment is cost effective after a few years), the strengthening of rightist control offers the prospect of nurturing business. With an expectation (or perhaps hope is more accurate) of capital flight from places governed by liberal coalitions, a 'disciplining' of all local leaders is anticipated.

The position in Britain is quite different. The idea of giving greater responsibility to localities would not be in keeping with political traditions within the nation; new right advocates see the

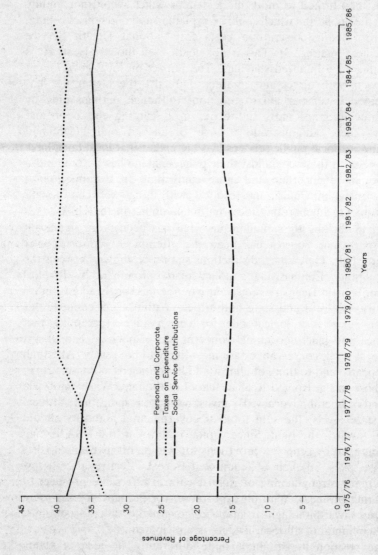

*Figure 2.4* Sources of British central government revenue 1975/6–85/6

*Source*: Central Statistical Office, *Monthly Digest of Statistics*, HMSO, London

*Table 2.5* The distribution of income in Britain 1976–85

| Year | Income bracket | | | | |
|------|--------|--------|--------|--------|---------|
| | *Lowest* | *Second* | *Middle* | *Fourth* | *Highest* |
| 1976 | 7.4 | 12.7 | 18.0 | 24.0 | 37.9 |
| 1981 | 7.1 | 12.4 | 17.9 | 24.0 | 38.6 |
| 1984 | 7.1 | 12.1 | 17.5 | 24.3 | 39.0 |
| 1985 | 6.7 | 11.8 | 17.4 | 24.0 | 40.2 |

*Notes*
(a) The numbers refer to the percentage of total income received by those in the lowest to highest (20 per cent) income bands once households are ranked by the size of their incomes.
(b) These figures are based on income levels after tax and cash payments (such as pensions) have been taken into account (i.e. they refer to 'money in the hand').

*Source*: Central Statistical Office (1988) *Social Trends 18*, HMSO, London

necessity of strengthening the State first in order to unwind the tangles of social democracy and the welfare state (Gamble 1988). In the long term, the international orientation of Britain's economy has emphasised national control. Britain is a small country in which the economic costs of geographical location are insufficiently variable to have much impact on corporate performance. Hence, inter-local differences are less important to corporate leaders than the national framework (both in terms of internal conditions and in sweetening operations overseas). To fulfil new right promises of an improved profit-making environment, it was not localities that needed strengthening but the centre. This being so, and given loud protestations of convictionism and radicalism from the new right, it is reasonable to suppose that the nettle would be grasped and individualism would be breathed into the heart of British institutions. If this is what new right advocates hoped for, they must be disappointed:

Although some Conservatives have favoured a new constitutional settlement that would end the formal sovereignty of Parliament and entrench individual rights, including property rights, traditionalists, including Mrs Thatcher, have showed no inclination whatsoever to tinker with Britain's existing political institutions. If there is any intellectual justification for this it must depend on the idea that ultimately it is 'ideas' that are the causal factors in social change. It also assumes that the masses are in a modern democracy more or less inert. Therefore on this view the strategy should be to change the ideas of élites rather than design institutions appropriate for the protection of individualism.

(Barry 1987: 129-30)

Rather than forging a new conservative vision for the nation based on enterprise and individualism, the Thatcher administrations have sought to turn the clock back to reinforce the hierarchical structure of the nation. 'At the end of the Thatcher experiment it seems certain that the pro-modern and anti-democratic encrustations in British society will have been measurably strengthened, not weakened' (Johnson 1985: x). Yet in so far as Thatcherism is a 'recrudescence of fundamental forces in British economy and society which date back at least to the eighteenth century' (MacInnes 1987: 6), it inevitably focuses on an re-emphasis on hierarchy and an antagonism to 'deviance'. The aim is ideological, in that the goal is compliance with conservative ideals (Jessop *et al.* 1988). In striving for this aim, inroads have been made into the authority of opponents of the ruling party. Money has been no object in this quest (as demonstrated by the response to the coal miners' strike of 1984–5). If the estimates of Coopers and Lybrand (1984) prove correct, the cost of the 1986 abolition of the six metropolitan county councils will save no money but could cost up to £60 million extra per year. Add on the Greater London Council and the costs are higher. Yet for the government, control of the capital by a committed left-wing council, along with its alternatives to government policies (e.g. Mackintosh and Wainwright 1987), proved too discomforting to be allowed to persist. As for rate capping, which has led to just twenty councils per year having to reduce their property taxes (Grant 1986), incremental change has been preferred to tackling core issues. The Thatcher administrations have responded to issues of the moment and 'troublesome' institutions or practices. It is questionable whether a strategy has existed (despite the implicit and explicit assumptions of some neo-marxists) or whether, as Mullard (1987) contended for public expenditure policies, there have merely been tactics to meet short-term issues. This is not a radical approach to government. It is an incremental one whose impact is significant largely because the Conservative Party has been in government for so long.[22] Yet built within this incremental path have been two clear trends. Firstly, by 'isolating' opposition groups from broader support, alternative economic, social and political practices have been diminished. Secondly, there has been a notable centralisation of power. These have produced changes in local–central relationships.

## RESUME

The aim in this chapter has been to outline a framework within which cross-national dissimilarities in the character, norms and practices of local institutions can be appreciated. The essential points are the differential emphases placed on individualism and social hierarchy within the two nations. Both are élitist, but the different weightings of individualism and hierarchy, as well as of national and international interests, leads to their dissimilar articulation. This is captured in the divergent responses of higher tier authorities to their lower tier counterparts. In many respects, it would be appropriate to conceptualise the British national government as the parent of local institutions, whereas in the USA higher tier authorities are more like school teachers (with the states in the classroom and the federal government as the principal). The former has a more encompassing and intense involvement with each 'child'. The latter is firm at times but more often provides advice and encouragement. As governments (and economic conditions) change, so do the messages these institutions receive from above. In the 1980s the messages received have not been as new as some commentators would have us believe. Their main themes were set down by administrations in the 1970s and their basic principles have much longer roots. Nevertheless there have been important shifts in circumstance, most especially in weakening national commitments to alleviating human deprivation and in redistributing authority amongst governmental units. For both countries, class conflict has been an important element in these moves. Yet these conflicts have taken different forms. In essence, they have represented a reinforcement of foundations within each nation's political culture. In Britain this has meant centralisation, in the United States decentralisation. How these forces have played themselves out in structuring local political affairs is examined in the next chapter.

# 3   Structuring local politics

In this chapter the basic concern is the institutional frameworks around which local political activities are organised. The significance of such frameworks is that institutional arrangements, by their very nature, have biases which favour some groups more than others. Hence, central to understanding politics – that is, who gets what, when, how and where – is identifying how formal structures distribute advantages differentially amongst social groups and geographically defined populations. To anticipate material in later chapters, the reader should evaluate the ideas in this chapter against the backcloth of agency–structure relationships. A structural framework does not determine behaviour, but it does predispose actions in some directions more than others. Within the same structural mould, agents can forge different behaviours. Since structure depends on the repetition of the behaviour norms which support it, a reorientation in action paths will induce an evolution of structure (provided that it is sustained long enough). However, a distinction needs to be drawn between structures which are institutionalised (and hence are more rigid) and those that are informal. *Ceteris paribus*, municipal government in a city of predominantly white, middle income, Anglo-Saxon protestants operates in a different structural context from one which services a population of poor black families. Yet both population groups have fluidity (i.e. residential mobility). Newcomers are likely to have similar characteristics to those leaving, but this is not inevitable. Through practices such as block-busting[1] or from more incremental change, the character of a population can alter, producing a dissimilar set of opportunities and constraints for municipal officials (as in the gentrification of inner city neighbourhoods). Such structural changes are informal in that they do not depend upon an explicit change in the rules of political engagement. Restructuring local government systems is a more formidable mechanism of structural change (as it re-writes operational rules). Although institutional regulations can be changed incrementally, the history of political organisation reveals that inertia is built into institutional practices. Once a governmental organisation is founded it is imbued with merits of localism, community and democracy by those who seek its preservation. Thus, the creation of the Greater London Council in 1965 was seen by some pundits as an abrogation of local democracy in that it 'distorted' governmental forms away from a 'natural' community, yet, when its abolition was planned for 1986, commentators from the same bloc (predominantly the Labour Party) held that dissolution would be undemocratic – the removal of a bastion of local democracy! Once you institutionalise, you provide a focus for corporate identity, as well as an access structure which advantages particular groups. Threaten to change that organisational form and you threaten a sense of belonging. What is more, change means uncertainty, and uncertainty raises the possibility of losing privileged access. Hence, there is a strong tendency toward inertia within formalised political organisation (made more tenuous by ghastly performances, to be sure).

The essential point is that an understanding of structural opportunities and restraints requires not simply that institutionalised practices be focused upon, but also that less formal frameworks be taken into account. The latter take a variety of forms but, in the context of local politics, are obviously expressed in the spatial arrangement of socio-economic activities. This imposes a structure on behaviour in the same way as does the formal organisation of government, yet these two surfaces do not lock tightly together. Rather they slide over one another. A government framework set up to mirror or even entrench the vested interests of particular socio-economic groups at one time can be out of phase with the same (or another) dominant interest at a later stage. However, because of the formalised nature of political arrangements, there is a time lag (and possibly a long one) between a reordering of the socio-economic landscape and the reorganisation of political institutions. Perhaps this is seen most obviously in the 'under-bounding' of city governments as suburbanisation extends a city's sphere of socio-economic domination beyond its boundaries. Such mismatches usually generate conflict or tension in governmental operations. This is a feature of all political systems, because alongside questions on the spatial extent of institutions are equally significant questions on the scope of local authority and the division of authority amongst institutions. Even if governmental jurisdictions have a tight fit with socio-economic patterns, this will not prove satisfactory if institutional authority is so circumscribed as to have little effect on major trends. Further, even if sufficient authority is available, conflict will be prevalent if coordinated or effective policies are difficult to mount. At the very least, tension is inevitable because issues of appropriate size, spatial arrangement and functional responsibility for local institutions are contentious. It follows that the form that institutions take is ineradicably inter-meshed with the power relations of intra-local and sub-national life. The impositions, compromises and victories of power groups latch governmental arrangements on to socio-economic surfaces. That these two structural frameworks provoke clashes of interest is evident in the geographical fix of local governmental units.

## GEOGRAPHICAL FIXES

For the vast majority of people there is little correspondence between what they see as their locality and the local authority in which they live. Even before the average local unit was enlarged in 1974, only 2 per cent of British rural dwellers equated their home area with their local authority, and fully 85 per cent thought of it as a parish or an even smaller area (Royal Commission on Local Government in England 1969). Evidence from urban centres revealed the same pattern, as Hampton (1970) found for Sheffield, where almost three-quarters of respondents described their home area as the few streets around their dwelling. In many countries, institutions of this size have existed in the past but reorganisation has removed them. Among nations in this class must be counted Britain, Sweden (which has seen municipal numbers fall to almost 10 per cent of their 1950 figure), Denmark (down from 1,300 to 275), the Netherlands and, though incomplete in coverage, Canada. In other nations small units have persisted, giving expression to the oft touted desirability of equating social communities with municipalities. Such an equation finds a ready home in many places in the United States (Table 3.1), with France, Italy and Spain also having small units.[2] What distinguishes nations with small institutions from those without them is no single factor, although the importance of local politics in the national political arena has a part to play (Page and Goldsmith 1985).

*Table 3.1* US local government populations 1987

| Population class | Municipalities | Townships |
|---|---|---|
| Over 100,000 population | 183 (41.3) | 33 (11.1) |
| 1,000–25,000 population | 3804 ( 4.0) | 3722 (11.4) |
| Under 1,000 population | 9369 ( 2.6) | 9143 ( 6.5) |
| All institutions | 19205 | 16691 |

*Note*
The figures standing on their own refer to the number of institutions within a population class and the figures in brackets refer to the percentage of the total population of a local government type living in institutions of that population class.

*Source*: US Department of Commerce Bureau of Census (1988) *1987 Census of Governments Volume One: Governmental Organization*, US Government Printing Office, Washington D.C.

Additionally, there are considerations of functional responsibility. Most reorganisation proposals for municipal institutions have been couched in the language of finding appropriate spatial units for the functions that local governments perform. From this perspective, smaller units are not necessarily inappropriate provided functions are few, but as they grow in number (and cost) larger units are preferable. Behind this argument lies a strong ideological stance. In deciding on the structure of new local government systems, policy-makers are confronted with two organisational principles: the efficiency of supply and the effectiveness of demand. The former is centred on economics, in that it lays stress on the cost efficiency of service provision. The latter is more political, in inquiring about responsiveness to citizen preferences. These principles are liable to clash. According to democratic theory, local government occupies a special place within a polity when its size is small enough to encourage public participation and so engage citizens in learning about democracy:

> local assemblies of citizens constitute the strength of free nations. Town meetings are to liberty what primary schools are to science; they bring it within the people's reach, they teach men [*sic*] how to use and how to enjoy it. A nation may establish a system of free government, but without the spirit of municipal institutions it cannot have the spirit of liberty.
>
> (Tocqueville 1835: 55)

To instil this spirit, citizens must be encouraged to participate. The more closely that municipalities approximate social communities, the more people are expected to do so. However, operating against this impetus towards smallness is the danger of impotency. As Vidich and Bensman (1968) highlighted so admirably, there is a problem in small places that the desire for social cohesion leads to inaction on controversial matters and a lack of new initiatives. As when social homogeneity results in few intra-local goal differences, the end product can be stultifying for the development of democratic values (Greer and Greer 1976; Newton 1978). Hence, while there are advantages in smallness, disadvantages also exist.

For many analysts, the most prominent amongst these is cost inefficiency. This does not refer solely to cost per unit of service provision. If it did, then the claims for size would be less forceful, since evidence on economies of scale in local government is not convincing and there is a suggestion that as size increases public satisfaction with services falls (Ostrom and Parks 1973). However, larger units do have two significant supply advantages. The first is that their size reduces the importance of externality effects. In other words, the (negative and positive) effects of local policies are more likely to be contained within the authority; they are less likely to spill into surrounding jurisdictions. The second is that larger units have a population sufficient to justify specialised services (e.g. schools for the specially gifted or custom built facilities for those with severe physical disabilities). The Royal Commission on Local Government in England (1969) emphasised the importance of the last of these. Yet, as public choice theorists stress, it is assumed too readily that ideal demand and supply conditions are mutually exclusive (Bish 1971). This need not be the case. Small units can purchase services from large providers (e.g. the municipality of Lakewood purchases almost all its services from Los Angeles County or from private companies; Miller 1981) and so gain the advantages of smallness alongside the benefits of scale. This is not the place to discuss the merits of the Lakewood scheme, merely to point to its potential. However, it should be noted that when local units are small, an unwillingness to place wider concerns above those of the locality raises problems for regional planning (Lineberry 1970). How important this may be is partly dependent upon the responsibilities of local units. If functions requiring region-wide solutions are not in local hands, but rest in the care of a provincial or state agency, this issue is less significant.[3] Yet what appears to be reasonable in the abstract often finds complex expression in actuality. This is illustrated by comparing English and

United States systems of local government. These have similarities in stated aims and, broadly, in functional responsibilities, yet they are notably dissimilar in emphasis.

The British approach to local government has stressed order, central control and service provision. Local choice and the encouragement of democracy have not attained the primacy found in other nations. The basic tone is well expressed in the Wheatley Commission's proposals for reforming Scottish local affairs:

> Local government . . . exists to supply public services. If it does this well it justifies its existence; if badly, its *raison d'être* is at once in doubt. Those who in the evidence have placed self-expression, self-determination and other virtues on a higher plane than effectiveness, and possibly in opposition to it, are failing in our judgement to take a realistic view of the place and purpose of local government within [British] society.

(Royal Commission on Local Government in Scotland 1969: para. 138)

More recently, the Audit Commission (1987: 11) restated the low emphasis attached to democratic values in arguing that 'there are far too many councillors in local government' (although their number has declined from 44,000 to 24,000 owing to 1970s reforms, a figure that contrasts with France's 450,000; Ashford 1981: 175). In official circles, local government has been seen less as an element of a democratic system and more as a necessary adjunct to a centralised State. It is at the centre that democracy is found, not in localities. In law this position is often, though not inevitably, evident in judicial rulings on local responsibilities which further the centralisation of authority (Johnston 1983). This view contrasts with the United States. Here, as Syed (1966) made clear, there are good reasons for acknowledging that there is a right to local self-government, even if the courts have been somewhat inconsistent in their treatment of this claim (Clark 1985). But what unites the two nations is a common thread of local government systems reflecting the preferences of the more powerful.

**Municipal maze USA**

An important difference in British and United States local government arrangements is found in the existence of unincorporated areas within the USA. In Britain every location is covered by a tier of government below that of the county (or region in Scotland), so that for one unit to increase its area another must lose ground. In the United States the system is more complex. In New England, towns (generally called townships elsewhere) preceded the establishment of counties and stayed as the primary local units, whereas elsewhere primary responsibilities rested with the county tier. However, even though New England's towns often contained fairly urbanised sections, in the main both counties and townships (the latter existing alongside counties in some states) were principally geared for dispersed settlement, where service demands were few. To enable places to render the services required for higher population densities, units could follow provisions in state law to incorporate themselves as villages, boroughs, towns or cities (the precise name varies across states and today bears little relationship to population size). Such incorporations increased the responsibilities of urban centres and gave them a distinct jurisdiction from unincorporated places (whose local government was the township or county). Today around 10 per cent of the nation's population lives in unincorporated areas. In the past it was much higher. The importance of this is that one of the primary forces deciding the present-day structure of elected local governments has been conflict over the future of unincorporated places. In this regard, the year 1873 was something of a watershed, since in that year Boston became the first city to stop its areal expansion because it had no unincorporated zones adjoining it. (It was surrounded by a ring of suburban incorporations.) The date itself is symbolic rather than separating eras in city history. 'The beginning of a real suburban trend can conveniently be dated to the founding of the Country Club, at [the Boston suburb of] Brookline, Massachusetts, in 1882' (Baltzell 1964: 123). At this time suburban growth was an upper class phenomenon, with country clubs as the focus of social exclusiveness. Private day schools followed as symbols of the upper-crust flavour of suburban areas (as in the opening of Philadelphia's Haverford School in 1884 and Chestnut Hill Academy in 1895 or in Baltimore's Gilmore School in 1897). Many northern and midwestern cities had room to expand in the early years of the twentieth century, but the creation of upper class suburbs stiffened resistance to the annexation of unincorporated zones. By contrast, in southern and western states opposition to city expansion was less marked, and even today is part of the fluidity of municipal boundaries (Table 3.2).

The geographical reference markers in the last section are critical, because an obvious distinction between municipalities in the United

*Table 3.2* US municipalities: changing boundary structures

| Type of boundary change | Annual mean average | |
|---|---|---|
| | 1980–6 | 1970–9 |
| Incorporations | 36 | 68 |
| Disincorporations | 6 | 9 |
| Mergers or consolidations | 3 | 9 |
| Annexations | 5819 | 6136 |
| Area annexed (square miles) | 770 | 877 |
| Population annexed (000s) | 228 | 317 |
| Detachment actions | 119 | 103 |
| Area detached (square miles) | 38 | 46 |
| Population detached (000s) | 6 | 9 |

*Note*
These figures are for places of over 5,000 population only.

*Source*: J.C. Miller (1988)

States is their regional dimension. This has emerged as a consequence of underlying causal forces that were evident in dissimilar suburban resistance to central city growth. At heart what stirred suburbanites to resist annexation was fear over the growing dominance of new immigrants in central city politics. As the character of new settlers entering northern and midwestern cities took on a stronger Irish or eastern and southern European accent, the dominant position of the white, Anglo-Saxon, protestant (WASP) élite was challenged. Through the auspices of political party machines, recent immigrants were quickly integrated into the political system, exchanging their votes for support in finding homes, obtaining jobs, learning a new language and settling into a new lifestyle (Griffith 1974a; Shefter 1986). With immigrants having different visions of municipal government than the propertied classes, suburbanisation offered a means of circumventing 'foreign' practices (Hugill 1989). However, if the central city could easily annex new suburban settlements, whatever respite was attained would only be short lived. Consequently, pressure was brought to bear on state governments to ease procedures for incorporating new municipalities, while also making annexation more difficult. These changes were relatively easy to achieve, since their justification drew on principles of local self-government and state officials were drawn from the same social backgrounds as those seeking the changes. In southern states, where late nineteenth century immigrants comprised a small proportion of the population, and where the primacy of the propertied classes was not challenged, restrictions on annexation were weaker.

Across the nation, though, there was acceptance of the idea that municipalities could have small population bases. In New Jersey, three households were enough to create a municipality, with California's minimum of 500 persons standing toward the upper end of the spectrum. With legislation being primarily permissive in character, the scene was set for the manipulation of municipal government for personal advantage. At times, aims were clearly stated in municipal titles. City of Industry in Los Angeles County, for instance, is effectively just that: a geographical area which is zoned for industry, so that the expensive services that householders require are kept to a minimum (so taxes stay low) and industrial requirements receive priority. Being in California, this municipality had to meet a 500 population mark (which it achieved by drawing up its boundaries to include 169 patients and 31 employees in a mental hospital; Miller 1981), but less stringent rules elsewhere have produced institutions effectively devoid of people. Thus, the seven police officers employed by Teterboro (New Jersey) do not principally safeguard its seven households but the manufacturing plants that dominate its tax base. Similarly, in order to provide its members with longer drinking hours, a New Jersey golf club was transformed into the municipality of Tavistock (populated by three households). The Cleveland municipality of North Randall was created so as to provide a home for gambling, two horse-racing tracks and 107 inhabitants (Swanstrom 1985). Lakewood, with its innovative contracting system of service provision, was largely designed to stop Long Beach from annexing a new shopping centre, so that retailers' taxes would be low (Miller 1981). Even agriculturalists have used land-use zoning authority consequent on incorporation in order to protect land holdings from urban encroachment (Fielding 1964). As Gottdiener (1987: 26) correctly assessed, municipal government 'has been open to control by the most powerful interests intent upon seizing it'. Yet because groups which grasp the reins of control have different goals, the resulting arrangement has variety (e.g. Figure 3.1). This is no municipal system but a municipal kaleidoscope.

Lest there be any doubts about the social standing of an area, land-use planning restrictions could limit access by poor families. That such restrictions are significant should not be queried. By the early 1970s, 90 per cent of remaining open land in the suburbs of

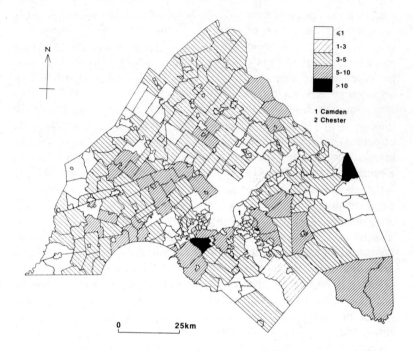

*Figure 3.1* Municipalities in the Philadelphia metropolitan area

*Notes*
(a) Property valuations per capita were calculated from (i) New Jersey Department
    of Community Affairs (1986) Forty-Seventh *Annual Report of the Division of
    Local Government Services 1984: Statements of Financial Condition of Counties
    and Municipalities*, Trenton, NJ; and (ii) Commonwealth of Pennsylvania
    Department of Community Affairs (1985) *Local Government Financial Statistics
    1982*, Harrisburg, PA.
(b) Index scores for per capita property valuation ratios had as their base the ratios
    of Camden (for New Jersey municipalities) and Chester (for Pennsylvania
    municipalities). Different base cities had to be used on account of differences in
    property assessment practices in the two states. These cities were selected as
    they were large with low property valuation ratios. In the key, 1 refers to places
    with per capita property valuations equal to the relevant base city, 5 refers to a
    ratio five times greater than the relevant base city, and so on.

New York City was zoned for single family housing, with 82 per cent in northern New Jersey zoned for minimum lot sizes of half an acre, and three-quarters of suburban Connecticut being set aside for lots of at least an acre apiece (Muller 1975). More recently, and more particularly in rapidly growing areas, similar effects have been produced by insisting that new housing meets strict environmental impact regulations. Until the 1970 National Environmental Protection Act, municipalities more or less relied on zoning to guide development. In many states all large projects now require an environmental impact statement (all federal projects do). California municipalities are particularly active in using these provisions. Residential developers are increasingly being asked to foot the bill for municipal services for their projects, as well as making provision for any identified negative externalities (Dowall 1984). Such 'impositions' have escalated housing costs, irrespective of lot sizes. Yet there is variety in municipal response. Those places which favour growth or which have deficiencies in their property tax base are much less inclined to restrain residential expansion.

There is little doubt that zoning and environmental restraints are linked to the residential segregation of income and racial groups within metropolitan areas. Yet, as Logan and Schneider (1981) show, there are significant regional differences in the evolution of municipal income disparities across the nation. In the South, where pro-growth strategies are more prevalent and restrictions on the expansion of municipal boundaries are less intense, municipal wealth inequalities in the same metropolitan area are trending towards convergence. Exactly the opposite is found in the North, where tighter zoning regulations and greater restraints on municipal expansion are linked to a growing divergence in inter-municipal wealth. The discriminatory effects of such provisions have been recognised explicitly in a variety of government statutes as well as in court rulings (see Burchell *et al.* 1983). For instance, in 1965 the Pennsylvania Supreme Court ruled that a zoning ordinance requiring a minimum lot size was unconstitutional as it worked to the detriment of a region's welfare. In New Jersey's Mount Laurel decisions, the right of municipalities to exclude low income housing was revoked and each jurisdiction has been instructed to prepare to take a fair share of its region's low income housing. Either as a court ruling or through civil statute, steps have been taken in California, Massachusetts, New York and Virginia to make it easier for lower income housing to be constructed. (With regard to the causes of such trends, the pressures identified in Note 3 [p.280] merit research attention.) How effective these steps have been remains to be seen, as some legislation is permissive rather than enforcing, and the legal challenges which struck down zoning provisions are not transferable to environmental impact provisions. Also, there is uncertainty over exactly how important municipalities are in perpetuating residential segregation.

Individual cases will always be found where municipal policies were driven by a segregationist intent. For one, the Cleveland suburb of Parma has been found guilty of intentionally excluding black families by employing tactics such as: denying building permits to privately sponsored low income housing; insisting on 2.5 parking spaces per dwelling; mandating that all subsidised housing requires voter approval; and limiting all future residential structures to a height of 35 feet (Swanstrom 1985). Further municipal barriers between income and racial groups are evident in failures to expand. Thus, in the Yazoo Delta (Mississippi), where annexation is not difficult, municipalities show reluctance to take in certain new lands (Aiken 1987). Areas with black populations are much less likely to be encroached upon than white residential zones. Amidst havens of the very rich, exclusionary practices are even more overt. The Los Angeles municipality of Rolling Hills, for one, is guarded 24 hours a day, with trespassers being liable to a fine of $500 as well as the possibility of six months in jail (Hoch 1984). Hence municipalities are active agents in the spatial structuring processes (Logan and Schneider 1981; Bollens 1986).

Nevertheless, the significance of municipal structures in generating uneven socio-economic surfaces should not be exaggerated. For example, in the case of Rolling Hills, it is unlikely that proposals for low income housing would be forthcoming under a different municipal regime, since land prices are too great a disincentive. Viewed in the context of the urban political economy as a whole, the generation of spatial wealth inequalities is integral to suburbanisation *per se*. Irrespective of precise municipal arrangements, the suburbanisation process has been more an abandonment of the (more highly organised) physical, political and labour environments of central cities than an enticement to suburban municipalities of a particular kind. As Walker (1981: 388–9) noted: 'The possibility of escaping political control, on everything from smoke-ordinance to zoning decisions, by seeking out "friendly" jurisdictions or even drawing up new ones, has been fundamental to spatial segregation and the suburbanisation process in US cities.' For employment units, green field areas in the suburbs offered weaker local governments, undeveloped worker organisations and cheaper sites for land extensive production processes. At the same time, backed by federal insurance guarantees which were denied to inner cities, by enhanced suburban accessibility from federal freeway constructions, and by federal income supports for home ownership (e.g. for veterans), incentives favoured suburban expansion. Offering higher rates of return, and a surer market for developers, the new suburban residential blocks mainly sought a middle class clientele (those of higher income could afford to move without the enticement of mass produced housing). Central cities thereby lost much of the high yield, secure investment that they derived from profitable employment agencies and better paid householders, with 'friendly' suburban locations taking the gain. The whole process was underwritten by the federal government, but it was orchestrated by large corporations in housing construction and manufacturing (Checkoway 1980; Walker 1981). For most home owners, income limitations mean that housing opportunities are tightly structured by the actions of corporate and real estate interests. The new suburban landscape was not a product of middle class consumer choice, but of corporate intent. 'The suburbs are not middle class simply because the middle class lives there: the middle class lives there because the suburbs could be made middle class' (Walker 1981: 397).

In this regard householders were not so different from municipalities. This is because there was an abundance of 'friendly' jurisdictions willing to respond to (or unable to resist) corporate overtures. An example is San José which, with a real estate and contractor dominated planning commission, paved the way for residential growth by expanding the city's area by 700 per cent between 1950 and 1970 (Cox and Nartowicz 1980). Within numerous municipalities, public leaders with small business and professional backgrounds – such as lawyers, shop owners, and realtors – had much to gain from growth (Molotch 1976). If a friendly local unit was not available, the laws in southern and western states were lenient for corporate backed incorporation proposals. Hoch (1984) brought home this point in a California study which showed how post-war incorporations have been largely instituted to satisfy business, with the public at large finding it difficult to meet the conditions for a new municipal creation. Additionally, southern states have been more generous in allowing central cities authority over annexation and the control of new constructions beyond their bounds. Here we see the effect of a more cohesive, growth promoting, economic élite, since in southern states

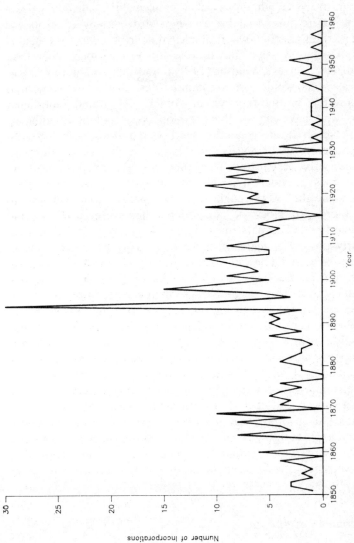

*Figure 3.2* The incorporation of municipalities in New Jersey 1850–1960

*Source:* New Jersey Department of Community Affairs, Division of Local Government Services (1977) *Municipal Incorporations of the State of New Jersey According to Counties*, Trenton

there has been less challenge to traditional leadership structures, and a stronger coincidence of interest amongst local and state leaders. In northern and midwestern states the strategy had to be different, because numerous small municipalities already existed and the desire for social exclusiveness drove many to introduce severe planning restrictions. If municipal policies led to socio-spatial segregation this is where this process should have been prevalent. Yet, for New Jersey, Windsor (1979) found that zoning ordinances were easier to avoid than is commonly assumed. This view finds corroboration in the research of Amick (1976) and Gottdiener (1977), who have shown that developers are adept at inducing zoning changes (more generally, see Logan and Molotch 1987). In addition, some rural councils did not visualise the coming threat of large scale urban expansion. Their rural character and distance from central cities provided a false sense of security, so when urban growth came they were caught without a land-use plan which gave the authority to block or ameliorate schemes (e.g. Dailey and Campbell 1980). This pattern would have been even more evident in the early post-1945 years, since very suddenly extensive plots of rural land acquired a new desirability as corporations built new style mass produced housing. Small, high income municipalities were more likely to resist invasion because their size, their already built-up character and their existing planning restrictions (introduced to maintain social exclusiveness and property values) dissuaded such proposals. However, these small places were irregularities on a landscape moulded by corporate decisions and were not central to determining evolving spatial structures. In effect, precise municipal arrangements were not fundamental to growing wealth disparities between suburb and central city. In northern states, peak periods of municipal incorporation occurred well before the post-1945 suburban explosion (e.g. Figure 3.2). In southern and western states the two were more temporally connected but, throughout the nation, business, not householders, dominated the process (Hoch 1984).

*Metropolitan government*

Although the fragmented nature of municipal systems has not been a major impediment to corporate activities, it has become an irritant. Local zoning ordinances raise construction costs and, as environmental concerns grow, restrict developers' freedom of action. It is no surprise, therefore, that there is a sentiment within the construction industry favouring regional planning (Walker and Heiman 1981). Adding to calls for reform are technocratic justifications for more ordered systems of governance. The US municipal maze is criticised because it creates a mismatch between the geographical areas over which metropolitan problems occur and the jurisdictional frameworks available to tackle them (e.g. Lineberry 1970). Adding further grist to the mill, analysts have questioned whether existing organisations are not anti-democratic in that they formalise the separation of social classes and races so that the merits of learning democratic values from reconciling goal differences are missed (Newton 1978). Indeed, as a result of the 'contrived homogeneity of many suburbs' (Haar 1974: 4), 'it is clear that all the elaborate structure of popular democracy results in government which is non-competitive, often inactive, and unaccountable to the view of the people' (Greer and Greer 1976: 203).

On the economic front, complaints have likewise been plentiful, since fragmentation is held to intensify the problems faced by central cities (Nathan and Adams 1976; Logan and Schneider 1981). This is said to occur not simply by drawing off rich investments but also, in the absence of a higher tier metropolitan authority, by means of an ongoing suburban exploitation of central cities. This central city exploitation thesis draws on the idea that suburbanites make extensive use of the services of central cities – its parks, museums, the subsidies provided to bring in jobs, the protection offered by its police force for city workers – and yet make scant donations to their cost (a metropolitan authority, it is argued, could distribute these costs more equitably). This hypothesis is difficult to evaluate (e.g. Weicher 1972; Greene *et al.* 1974; Hodge 1988). For one thing, central cities do not simply rely on property taxes for revenues. Suburbanites pay sales taxes on purchases and, where state governments allow, pay a proportion of their income to the city because they work there. Besides which, numerous suburbanites do not work downtown and some central city householders make use of suburban shopping and work facilities. Assessing the balance of these forces requires that a variety of 'guestimates' be made (since available data are only rough proxies of complex interactions). Assumptions must also be made about how things would be under other arrangements. Thus no precise answers about central city exploitation can be given (on account of varying tax, employment, retail and municipal structures, the answer is probably specific to single metropolitan areas anyway), but many believe that it occurs. What is more, suburban municipalities at times act as if they know that this is the case; an example being the deliberate exclusion of central cities from councils which coordinate and initiate regional policies (e.g. Pittsburgh and Wilkes-Barre in Pennsylvania [Helstrom 1977]).

Recognising that fragmented municipal systems restrict the potential to handle regional problems, a variety of solutions has been proposed. Most notable amongst these have been calls for the reorganisation of municipal structures. In general, such proposals have met with failure. Some reorganisations there have been – Dade County (Miami), Jacksonville, Nashville and Indianapolis are examples – but between 1947 and 1976, the peak period of interest in restructuring, only 13 proposals were approved out of 56 referenda in 40 cities (Lyons 1977). Given nationwide concern over the fragmentation problem, the meagre success of reorganisation efforts is probably less important than the sparsity of attempts. Where restructuring was attempted, specific local issues usually forced the hand of officials. In Jacksonville the breakdown of the sewer system and the threat of the school system losing its accreditation provided the spur, in Nashville deterioration of services was also critical, while intolerable traffic conditions emanating from inter-municipal parochialism and antagonism provided the impetus in Dade County. That efforts in southern centres were more successful perhaps owes much to the stronger standing of county government in that region, as this gave a familiar focus to reorganisation. However, the general stipulation of approval by public referendum limited options.

The neo-marxist argument that the State is restructured to meet the changing demands of capital finds little support here, since many referendum campaigns saw the defeat of business supported proposals (e.g. Hawkins 1966; with Dade County as an exception). What did produce voter approval? Contrary to Williams's (1971) propositions, lifestyle differences did not seem to be influential, and even expectations about tax increases had an uncertain role (e.g. Hawkins 1967; Lyons and Engstrom 1973). In fact, even with strong support for change, it was difficult to impress the general public with the merits of new schemes. When reorganisation happened it was a pale version of its British counterparts, usually characterised by weak coordinating roles for regional bodies and allowing some municipalities to retain independent status as islands in the midst of new regional structures (Hawkins 1967). Easier to institute were metropolitan administrations which were based on the cooperation of existing municipalities. The federal government did much to encourage these by tying grants for particular programmes to the existence of regional bodies. Yet such units were little more than single function special districts with little independent authority; and municipalities often had a policy veto which restricted initiative. Put simply, municipal systems established in the nineteenth century favoured the propertied classes *as home owners*, but the ideological envelope in which they operated proved less conducive to propertied interests *as entrepreneurs* in the later twentieth century (e.g. Heiman 1988). Factions within corporate capital might well want to restructure municipal government, but they have had to operate within it. That this has not proved so onerous is because precise organisational forms are not essential for the operations of market processes. In reality, there are a number of ways of skinning a rabbit.

## Explaining the maze

In identifying the causal impetus of propertied élites in determining the existing municipal kaleidoscope, the image portrayed so far is at variance with traditional theories on municipal organisation. For example, in Tiebout's (1956) public choice model, the justification for fragmentation is choice for electors. Variety is much lauded in this account, because it enables people to choose amongst localities with different packages of services and tax structures. It hardly needs to be stated that such an interpretation adds little to our understanding of how municipal arrangements arose. In effect, it merely justifies the status quo. At its heart lies an assumption that reveals its inherent bias, since it holds that consumer choice is critical, when in fact many people have little choice over where they live. In particular, the poor are unlikely to circumvent restrictions of zoning and environmental impact provisions in order to enable them to move to the wealthier areas that can afford the services they seek. Staying within a poor municipality is unlikely to help, since lack of resources restricts municipal ability to provide services for the poor. For large proportions of the population, constraint rather than choice decides action horizons; whatever choice does exist is limited and is disproportionately open to the wealthy.

This idea is central to Oliver Williams's (1971) social access explanation. Here Williams offers a lifestyle account of municipal character. Particular social groups are presumed to dominate each municipality and direct policies to preserve the sanctity of their lifestyle. Small institutions are desirable because they enhance control over lifestyle provisions. Thus, lot size regulations are seen as an attempt to limit access to those social groups which already live in the municipality. Although the competing claims of lifestyle preferences and economic self-interest (keeping out those with high service demands and low tax yields) have not been, and possibly cannot be, disentangled within analytical frameworks, there is some support for Williams's position. In the work of Thomas Dye, for example, we find evidence that annexation proposals are more likely to be approved the more similar the social standing of annexing and to-be-annexed areas (Dye 1964). Similarly, inter-municipal co-operation over service provision is more likely between those of equivalent social position (Dye *et al.* 1963). Yet two important provisos need to be made about this model. First of all, it is not necessary to have a municipal framework to produce the effects that Williams identified. For example, while municipal structures might appear to institutionalise racial segregation, such spatial distinctions also exist within US cities. Even in small towns, the spatial arrangement of social groups is such that clear social groupings are apparent (e.g. Duncan 1973). Further, while the very rich have maintained separation through house price disincentives, in places like Chicago, low income whites have used violence as their mechanism for maintaining racial segregation (Hirsch 1983). On a gentler note, the development of specialised communities for the elderly has taken place whether or not the resulting residential zone has sat in an existing municipality or comprised one of its own (Muller 1981). In cities with no zoning bye-laws, such as Houston, we still find deluxe neighbourhoods, low income areas, jumbled land-uses and a commercial downtown, much as anywhere else (Logan and Molotch 1987). Secondly, what Williams offers is less of an explanation of how the system evolved than an account of how it is used today. Amongst early suburban authorities there were traces of lifestyle concerns and economic self-interest; after all, a primary goal for high income WASPs was to escape from political machines with 'ethnic' flavours. Yet much suburbanisation since 1945 has not been in exclusive suburban incorporations. Instead, it has occurred in small towns, where incorporation was sought to provide infrastructure, and in the countryside. This is readily apparent from examining maps of municipal boundaries (e.g. Figure 3.1), since many suburban units are far larger than the ideal, were the aim merely to control social access. This should not lead us to discount Williams's proposition, as it has merit in pinpointing how municipal arrangements can further social segregation. This might be fine-tuning, but it can be important. What is more, research by Young and Kramer (1978) in England and Ostendorf (1986) in the Netherlands, shows that the USA is not alone in its municipalities being used to preserve social distinctions. However, how a system is used once established and what brought it into being can be different things.

Overall, then, neither of the above accounts offers a complete explanation for the emergence of municipal systems. Cox and Nartowicz (1980), amongst others, offer a more convincing account by tying arrangements to the dictates of the corporate economy. In truth, however, this explanation does not go far enough. Certainly it is a valid description of much that has happened in some states (e.g. Hoch 1984). However, in the northern and midwestern states, the early formulation of suburban units was related more to concerns of social exclusion than to production (as seen in many factories staying in central cities).[4] Moreover, in the resistance of suburbanites to regional government we see a continuation of social access considerations. Once a system is established, and most especially once imbued with the ideology of democracy, it can prove difficult to shake apart. Large corporations have been irritated by existing arrangements (Walker and Heiman 1981), but they have not been fundamentally damaged by them. To circumvent the nuisance of municipal policies, they are amongst the largest contributors to political party coffers (Gottdiener 1977; Logan and Molotch 1987), and when such legitimate 'bribery' (Etzioni 1984) has not worked, they have shown a ready willingness to resort to its illegal cousin (Amick 1976). Precise organisational forms are not essential for corporate dominance and so capitalist profitability has not been the sole driving force behind municipal organisation. Reversing the logic of this point, it follows that municipal organisation has not been the primary cause of uneven local wealth. Fragmentation is linked to disparities in municipal wealth (Hill 1974; Logan and Schneider 1981) but it does not cause them.

## England's ordered arrangements

There are two critical contrasts between local government in the United States and in England. On the one hand, control over the form of the English structure has been more highly centralised (being in the hands of central government). On the other hand, and not unrelated to the first point, English systems reveal a stronger sense of uniformity. Telling the story of the formation of English local authorities is consequently more straightforward than it is for the USA. Yet there are similarities across these nations, most especially with regard to the manipulation of organisational frames to advantage the powerful.

Dating back to the thirteenth century, England had the rudiments of a local government system in the form of justices of the peace. Counties, boroughs and parishes also existed from medieval times, although these in no sense constituted a local government system. Only in 1835 was the principle of elected councils, responsible to local ratepayers, introduced (and then only for urban centres). The authority of these municipal corporations was initially limited, and individual Acts of Parliament were required both to approve incorporation and to grant more responsibility. The city bias in incorporations at this time was not problematical, because it was here that improved services were desired, both for business (e.g. gas supply, water and sewer systems) and for addressing social problems (e.g. disease, crime). The organisational division of town and country also corresponded with the reality of party government, since the Liberals (Whigs) inhabited the corridors of city power, while the countryside was firmly clasped to the Conservative bosom. By the late nineteenth century the Liberals saw a future in extending their tentacles into the countryside by imposing municipal forms on the Tory heartland (Fraser 1979). Multiple objectives lay behind these pressures. Among them were genuine beliefs in popular democracy, a desire to weaken the Conservative Party, recognition that new organisations were needed to expand social programmes, and a growing dissatisfaction with the sloth and corruption of some municipal agencies (as with the London Metropolitan Works Board). As Hennock's (1973) work has brought out, moves to introduce a modern local government system were highly controversial. The City of London was fearful of having to share its enormous wealth with surrounding areas and showed its antagonism to reform by resorting to bribery, to the issuance of false reports and to violence in a campaign against an elected government for the capital (Wheen 1975). Once these acts became public knowledge, the City's cause was discredited; most especially when set alongside the strength of Quaker support for reform, as this endowed the movement with a moralistic overtone (Hennock 1973; Fraser 1979). Reinforcing these attitudes was civic pride and an antipathy amongst local economic élites to the centralisation of authority in London.

In the end, the combination of moral crusade, business interest, evidence of skullduggery, and the merits of better services, won through. In 1888, county councils were created to run affairs in rural areas, with county boroughs providing an urban governmental base. The separation of rural and urban was deliberate (in part Conservative landed élites were relieved to lose the 'radical' cities from their administrative zones). Anyway, with a Conservative majority in the House of Lords it was infeasible to suggest their integration, since this would have led to rural inhabitants paying for services in urban areas. Besides which, suburbanisation was not foreseen as the major force it later became, so functional arguments favouring rural–urban integration were weak. Generally, historic counties were taken as given and large cities were afforded the status of county boroughs. A second tier of local institutions was created in 1894 (1899 for London) with the formation of urban district councils and rural district councils. These fell within county council areas, with the services provided by the two tiers being mutually exclusive. Occupying a lesser geographical extent, county boroughs had no lower tier and remained as unitary authorities. .

The principles of the system were evident for all to see. First of all, a strong sense of history was to be preserved through the formalisation of counties into councils. Only the peculiar demands of large cities disrupted this historical pattern. Even then, county borough status was not given away lightly. Pressure from city leaders produced changes in the 1888 legislation which lowered the minimum population size from 150,000 to 50,000, but in 1926 this was raised to 75,000 and no new county boroughs were formed between then and 1958. Within counties, there was again a concern to preserve tradition, as seen in the granting of urban district status to market towns (with the result that some remarkably small units were created, such as Childwall in Lancashire with 219 inhabitants and Kirlington-cum-Upland in Yorkshire with 255; Keith-Lucas and Richards 1978). Yet, unlike the United States, all parts of a county were covered by a lower tier administration (and whether this was a rural district or an urban district, the authority of the institution was broadly similar). Furthermore, the arrangements were not designed to separate high status suburban dwellers from their associated central city. Rather, reflective of élite value dispositions, rural 'arcadia' was to be kept distinct from urban industry. As in the United States, even after some rationalisation, as of the early 1970s, the result was a patchwork (Figure 3.3).

It would be foolhardy to claim that there were not vested interests at play in setting up this system. However, there was balance

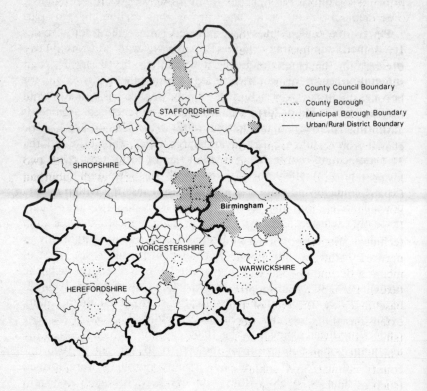

*Figure 3.3* Local authorities in the West Midlands in 1973

between the claims of the Liberals and the Conservatives. There was no labour–capital conflict at the heart of proposals, since this was a dispute between competing factions of capital.[5] That the victor in bringing about local government reform was the manufacturing lobby, the weaker of the two in the long term, should be interpreted in the context of two trends outside the immediate dispute. The first was the relative decline in Britain's economic performance, which added weight to manufacturers' claims that they needed better services. The second was fears within Lord Salisbury's Conservative government that a long-term consequence of not introducing reform could be pressure to broaden the franchise, so opening the door to the working classes (Young 1986). Once the principle of reform was accepted, compromises could be reached over details.

Up to 1965, when the local government structure of Greater London was reformed, the basic principles of local authority organisation changed little. Perhaps only the 1902 abolition of separate school boards, with their responsibilities going to county boroughs and county councils, marked a real change. (The dissolution of the Poor Law Guardians hardly counts since local authorities lost their functions within the decade.) Yet more minor changes did occur. County borough status had a definite appeal, and 21 English towns were added to the original 59 by 1926 (with two losing this status over the same period). Similarly, with suburban expansion gathering pace, the government agreed to extend county borough boundaries more than 100 times during these years (Minogue 1977). In the main, these changes were stirred by the technical application of 1888 legislation on to the evolving urban network. However, every areal extension for a county borough meant a decline in county council size (as well as a loss of property taxes). Perhaps more important, with the Labour Party's electoral base in cities, the rise of this party meant that county borough extensions threatened Conservative and Liberal electoral prospects (since some of their supporters now lived in city constituencies which these parties had less prospect of winning). In addition, as county councils and county boroughs took over more functions (such as education), losses to county boroughs were viewed more seriously by landed élites (Keith-Lucas and Richards 1978). Facing mounting opposition to urban expansions, regulations governing the creation and growth of county boroughs were tightened in 1926. (For expansions, for instance, the approval of surrounding local authorities had to be obtained after this date.) With the exception of a few county borough creations after 1958 (Luton, Solihull, Teesside and Torbay), the basic county borough–county council arrangement was stationary from 1926 until 1974. What changes did occur in spatial arrangements were restricted to a 1931–7 reduction in the number of district councils from 1,606 to 1,048. These amalgamations resulted from reviews undertaken by county councils themselves (although the central government had to approve the changes; Minogue 1977). No major power struggle was at stake, although authorities like Poplar, which had proved troublesome in opposing the national government in the 1920s (Branson 1979), found that these reviews spelt their death knell. How intentional this was is another matter, since the literature is peculiarly silent on this round of organisational change.

These mergers were the main adjustments (outside London) for nearly half a century. This was not because of a groundswell of support for existing arrangements, since the need for change was well recognised (as shown when local government boundary commissions were set up in both 1945 and 1958). What was missing was the political will to introduce reform.

## London

In London, however, the situation was getting out of hand. A number of county councils covered parts of the continuous built-up area, but the growing size of individual boroughs made requests for county borough status difficult to resist. If these had been granted it would have weakened institutions with the widest geographical vision (viz. counties). Since London had always been treated as a special case, legislation affecting the capital alone was not problematical.[6] This did not mean that it was easy to introduce. Initial proposals by the 1955 Minister for Housing and Local Government, Enoch Powell, met with fierce resistance from within local Conservative circles, because the plan to replace councils within the County of London with seven unitary authorities of at least 450,000 persons was threatening to local Conservatives. However, the Conservative Party had long chafed at the capital's being controlled by political opponents (Young 1975a); the need for reform was obvious, and Conservative Central Office appears to have been convinced (and to have convinced party leaders) that reform could place London in Conservative hands (Young and Garside 1982). The creation of a Royal Commission was no doubt intended to assuage local Conservative fears or at least deflect criticism from the government. In the end, the Herbert Commission took three years to prepare its 1960 report. The government then took a further three years to place legislation on the books.

Under Herbert Commission proposals, a two tier system would have been created, comprising of one regional authority and 52 boroughs (Minogue 1977). The higher tier was to cover 760 square miles (extending well beyond the Enoch Powell proposals), with boroughs housing populations varying from 100,000 to 250,000. The bulk of functional responsibility was for the boroughs, with the regional body having authority over roles which would be ineffective at a local level (e.g. strategic planning).

The response of the government was conditioned by party political considerations. Most notably, in order not to offend supporters in the greenbelt, the boundary of the Greater London Council was brought in so that it covered only 616 square miles. Although this was expected to reduce the number of Conservative voters in the Greater London area, the Labour Party was not pleased. As the then party leader Hugh Gaitskill explained: 'it would not be unfair to describe this as a squalid attempt on the part of the Tory Party to snatch the banner of London for itself by altering the boundaries because they cannot get the votes' (from Johnston 1979: 147). Some academic commentaries of this era reached the same conclusion, although from a different perspective. Freeman (1968: 168), for instance, made the poignant observation that 'the definition of Greater London was activated more by political forces than by a serious consideration of what was in fact London as an entity'. Yet both local councils and national opposition parties responded in a manner not dissimilar to headless chickens. Only Surrey County Council put forward a serious alternative, when it argued that the proposals were unjustified because the Greater London Council was too small for strategic planning, which was to be its main role (Ruck and Rhodes 1970). Precisely this point became a justification for another Conservative government, this time in 1986, abolishing the council.

Structuralist explanations provide little insight on the London reorganisation. The British economy was not in recession, so restructuring to enhance profitability was unnecessary, and there was no particular business pressure for change. Most agreed that reform was needed, but this had been the case for some time and could have come earlier (perhaps not between 1945–51, when the Labour government was establishing the welfare state, but certainly during the 1950s).[7] To date no convincing theoretical explanation for the timing of the changes has been put forward. But once the idea of reform had gathered steam, political party considerations became extremely important. There seems little doubt that Conservative Party leaders expected to win control of Greater London after reorganisation. Indeed, when the 1964 elections placed the Greater London Council in Labour's hands, it was not long before Conservative activists started calling for its abolition (Young 1975a). The irony is that, had the Conservatives retained the Herbert Commission's proposals, Greater London probably would have been in their hands. Labour foresaw its grip loosening, but offered no constructive criticism or a viable alternative. Needless to say, by the time local government in the rest of England was reformed, both parties had learnt from the London experience.

## Reorganisation in 1974

The backcloth to the reform of local government in England and Wales (1975 in Scotland) was the emergence of a technocratic overtone to government policy. Prime Minister Wilson was intent upon revitalising the British economy by infusing technological progress into its archaic practices. Local government reform was in keeping with this quest for improved efficiency, although it was not a component of the 1964–70 Labour government's major platform. Indeed, placing reform on the agenda seems to owe much to the personal initiative of the then Minister of Housing and Local Government, Richard Crossman. As his diaries reveal, the announcement that reform was to be considered caused uproar in his own department, because it was made without consulting senior bureaucrats (Crossman 1975). Yet arguments in favour of reform had been rehearsed already for London: larger units allow specialised service provision, socio-economic activity patterns should match governmental arrangements and larger units allow effective planning. As with London, a Royal Commission was formed which took three years to report (1966–9). Its proposals were sweeping in intent. Town and country divisions were to go under a new system of city–region authorities. These were to be single tier, with the exception of the three largest metropolitan centres. A minimum of 250,000 persons was recommended, so the existing 1,210 local authorities would be replaced by 81 (58 unitary, three metropolitan county and 20 metropolitan district). The lesson that the Labour Party appeared to learn from London, if indeed it came from that source, was that of accepting a Royal Commission's report on a controversial scheme. Labour almost wholly followed the Commission's recommendations. Those changes that were proposed, such as having five rather than three metropolitan counties and giving metropolitan counties responsibility for education rather than the districts, only tinkered at the edges. What is more, the government took little time to present its proposals, since its White Paper was before Parliament within a year of the Commission's reporting.

For those supporting the new plan, Labour did not act fast enough. Before the scheme entered the statute books, a General

Election was called, Labour was defeated, and a new Conservative government was in office. What the Conservative Party appeared to learn from the reform of London was that if you want to gain political party advantage you should do it properly. Of course, the Conservatives were not alone in hoping for advantage from local government change. The location of local boundaries had acute significance for national political parties, since parliamentary constituencies did not cross them. Institutionalising party advantage at the local level was therefore a serious matter, as Richard Crossman (1975) made clear:

> First of all I had to deal with the local government boundaries of Plymouth. I have been thinking and thinking of how I can best adjudicate to avoid bringing Conservative suburbs into Labour cities like Leicester and Nottingham and so undermining safe Labour parliamentary seats in four or five years' time . . . Harold [Wilson] was obviously concerned to make sure that I was doing my job as politician on the local boundary decisions, that no adjustment was politically disadvantageous to us. He was equally concerned to make sure that the Home Secretary was doing his job with regard to the warding of the reorganised boroughs.
>
> (Crossman 1975: 175 and 189)

That Labour accepted the Royal Commission's proposals possibly owed much to their one tier nature, since this offered large units within which a number of parliamentary constituencies would sit. Perhaps believing his own statement that Labour was the natural party of government, Harold Wilson might have felt that his continued presence at 10 Downing Street would enable Labour to control the boundary issue.[8] Certainly the Conservative victory in 1970 was a surprise for many, which perhaps added impetus to Conservative plans to reinforce structural advantage.

This came via major changes in Royal Commission recommendations.[9] As instituted in the 1972 Local Government Act, there was to be a two tier system throughout the nation. Significantly, the lower tier, which would be allocated only around 10 per cent of total local spending, was to be granted primary lifestyle functions (such as public housing and land-use planning). Middle and upper class enclaves now had the ability to sustain their social compositions. As experience with the Greater London Council had shown, if Labour controlled a higher tier authority with housing responsibility, pressure for low income housing in higher income areas could result (Young and Kramer 1978). This was not going to be allowed outside

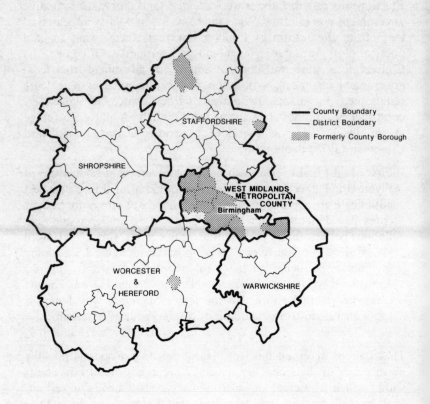

*Figure 3.4* Local authorities in the West Midlands in 1975

the capital. So, although the 1972 Act retained 250,000 as the minimum population target for a higher tier authority, it did not allow the Royal Commission's proposal of town and country integration to be taken too far. Compared with Royal Commission recommendations, county councils were drawn more tightly around major urban centres (Figure 3.4); 'in a style reminiscent of an American gerrymander . . . basing reorganisation on giving the large conurbations over to Labour (which controlled most of them anyway) and of reserving the countryside for themselves' (Jennings 1977: 24). By doing so, wealth inequities across local authorities were heightened, although not to the scale of the USA (Bristow 1972). In the precise placement of boundaries, party advantage was again important; to the extent that the division of Glamorgan was so flagrantly party political that Lady Sharp, a member of the Royal Commission and the former Permanent Secretary of the Ministry of Housing and Local Government, took the unprecedented step of accusing the government of indefensible gerrymandering (Sharpe 1978). In any structure some party advantage is inevitable (one way or another) but this system not only provided a rigid frame for wealth differences but also minimised party competition. In Dunleavy's (1980b) estimation, the new system placed three-quarters of the English and Welsh population in areas where the highest spending tier was unlikely to see a change in party control (58 per cent being under the Conservatives and 20 per cent under Labour). That this prediction has proved inaccurate owes nothing to the 1974 scheme, but comes from the weakened hegemony of the two party system (Leach and Stewart 1988).

## Metropolitan abolition 1986

That the English local government scene has been moulded primarily to reflect the Conservative Party's view of its self-interest is further shown in the 1986 abolition of the Greater London Council and the six metropolitan county councils (and in the 1990 termination of the Inner London Education Authority). Of all the changes in local government that have been instituted this was the most overtly party political. It also symbolises the frailty of 'local democracy' in England. In terming the abolition a 'farce', O'Leary (1987b) does not stretch a point at all. Remember, it was the Conservative Party that decided the form of both the Greater London Council (GLC) and the metropolitan county councils. This party was now advocating abolition because these units were too small for strategic planning (Flynn *et al.* 1985); something that was a direct consequence of a self-interested decision to tighten boundaries. Conservative criticisms of the GLC have a long history associated with that party's failure to control London (Young 1975a). Indeed, less than ten years earlier, Conservative antagonism had led to the setting up of the Marshall Inquiry to evaluate the merits of this council (Freeman 1979). This investigation was completed in under a year, so it was hardly the exercise of earlier royal commissions. Nevertheless, it favoured strengthening the GLC (e.g. giving it more responsibilities) and devoted more serious analytical thought to its proposals than the government did over abolition. Thus, despite government protestations that abolition had been considered for a long time, the leader of the GLC Conservatives was informed of it only three days before it became public knowledge (Wheen 1985: 25). Most certainly the financial implications had not been worked out, because when Coopers and Lybrand (1984) challenged the claim that millions of pounds would be saved, the government backtracked by asserting that savings were not the real aim.

Politically the government miscalculated. Public support for the GLC, in particular, was high (Flynn *et al*. 1985). In opinion polls the median percentage of Londoners opposing abolition was 66 per cent (Husbands 1985). If anything, the government revived the fortunes of local Labour parties by giving them a rallying point and providing them with ammunition in attacking an 'anti-democratic', un-professional and party political act. What is more, the step was unnecessary. 'By 1983 the GLC had been effectively crushed as an instrument of redistribution by bourgeois suburbia even before the Thatcher administration decided to put an end to it' (O'Leary 1987b: 376). By taking key functions from the GLC (such as housing and public transport), the government had stripped its scope for action. Furthermore, through rate capping, the government could restrict the spending of all metropolitan authorities (and these councils were in evidence on early rate capping lists; Grant 1986). This was not enough for Tory leaders. Greater restrictions would not remove the ideological threat. Cabinet Minister Norman Tebbitt illustrated the government's logic:

> The Labour Party is the party of division. In its present form it represents a threat to the democratic values and institutions on which our parliamentary system is based. The GLC is typical of this new, modern, divisive version of socialism. It must be defeated. So we shall abolish the GLC.
>
> (from Wheen 1985: 7)

These authorities had not accepted government dictate willingly. They had resisted and, most especially in fields of ideological importance such as the promotion of employment (Mackintosh and Wainwright 1987),[10] they offered alternatives that Conservative leaders found unpalatable. For a government that was intent on reviving traditional Tory statecraft (Bulpitt 1983), on strengthening the hierarchical character of political practices, such challenges were unacceptable. Even so, in its response the government miscalculated. It provided a stimulus to Labour support and harmed its own legislative programme by devoting a great deal of time to what had become a somewhat trivial component of governance. Even for a farce, this act had mediocre performances from the central players. The audience and bit-players met this buffoonery with a mixture of ribaldry, anguish, disgust and disquiet. Only those not watching or listening could have found room for respect.

The London experience alone highlights notable differences between the United States and England (or Britain for that matter). This emerges both in what stimulated local government form and in what its character has become. In the USA individualism is apparent, even if it is played out within the confines of strong themes which are tied to propertied interests. The hallmarks of national political cultures make obvious impressions on these differences. In the USA this is seen in the slower emergence of a united national élite, so that locally variable solutions became the norm. What is more, with an individualistic, participatory thrust in political values, small local units and the entrenchment of establishing lines of organisation find favour. That the values of both participation and property still have significant roles in municipal structure is seen in channels of support and opposition to regional government. The balance of divergent values which induces inertia over such proposals is much less apparent in England. As the 1986 abolition of metropolitan authorities showed, fashioning change in English local government requires little thought or justification, as long as the government has the will to carry it through. Hierarchy rules. Previously the desire to maintain trust between local and national élites meant that changed local arrangements were rare. When change has been enforced, its rationale has been carefully presented and implemented. This caution has most often led to change being instituted well after most commentators felt that it was necessary.

Local government organisation in England has been linked to class advantage. Yet the form of local institutions owes more to political party conflict. In 1888, for example, Lord Salisbury favoured reform because of fears over the franchise. But the main thrust of the organisational form that emerged came from conflicts between Conservatives and Liberals, from intra-class conflict, not that between classes. More notable for their inter-class tone were the 1926 regulations governing the extension and creation of county boroughs, since these were spurred by a desire to limit working class control (in the form of the Labour Party). However, by the 1974 reshuffle, these fears were less pressing. Local bastions of left-wing radicalism in the 1920s and 1930s, such as those dubbed 'little Moscows' (Macintyre 1980) or participants in 'Poplarism' (Branson 1979), had ceased to exist as separate entities or had lost their verve. By the late 1960s the ideological enthusiasm of local Labour parties was slumbering. Where the 1974 reforms were perhaps class related was in pressures for more technocratic approaches to government, since the implications of official pronouncements on this theme favoured an increase in middle class representation amongst local government officials (Dearlove 1979). In the 1980s, the hand of capital was not behind the abolition of the metropolitan counties (although Aims of Industry did make its opposition to the GLC very evident). Unlike the United States, although propertied interests have benefited from organisational outcomes, gains have been indirect rather than deliberately sought. In the end, it has been at the national level that British firms have sought advantage, not locally.

## FUNCTIONAL RESPONSIBILITIES

Three issues are central to the examination of local functional responsibilities. The first concerns the appropriate range of activities for government *per se*. The second focuses on the most appropriate government tier for task responsibility. Then there is the issue of how to organise tasks at the local level. For each there are no right and no wrong answers. Aspects of functional responsibility are open to technical examination (as over the existence of economies of scale), but solutions to questions of functional allocations are not unidimensional, so weightings must be placed on the relative importance attached to various considerations. At this point objectivity is lost (if it were ever possible), since such weightings necessarily draw on political beliefs. Understanding what is, is vastly different from expressing what should be. But as governments are vehicles for injecting values into the body politic, they are important in deciding public sector tasks.

### The scope of government

The most important idea in many discussions on the 'proper' arena for government action is that of 'public goods'. As defined by Samuelson (1954), a public good is one that can be consumed by an individual at a rate independent of its consumption by others. Clean air and national defence are primary examples. The essential features of public goods are that it is not feasible to ration their use nor is it desirable to do so. In welfare economics, public goods necessarily must be in the hands of government because they are not suited to market mechanisms. In terms of defence this is obvious, since a polity which allowed secrets to be sold to the highest bidder would not stay independent for long. However, there is a broader dimension to the problem of providing public goods. This comes in the form of free-riders. If government does not provide and pay for public goods, and instead each individual is required to pay a contribution towards these provisions, many will not do so. After all, the benefits from public goods are indivisible (everyone gains from clean air whether they have paid or not). For economists, the possibility of gain at no cost inevitably leads to personal interest taking precedence over communal interest. In order that communal welfare is not damaged by free-riders, government must take a positive role. At the other extreme, the more divisible the service (that is, the more its consumption by one person restricts access to it by another) and the more the service can be rationed, the greater the prospect that governmental involvement interferes with the efficient operation of the market, leading to a loss of communal welfare. Hence, government involvement should be kept to a minimum in areas such as manufacturing, retailing and housing.[11]

There are two main issues concerning the application of a public goods framework to identifying appropriate areas of government action. The first is that few activities are wholly divisible or wholly indivisible; the extremes rarely appear in pure form. Medicine, for example, can be purchased on a market basis (as in the USA and West Germany) or it can be mainly in the State's hands (as in Britain). Education, housing and transport are all capable of allocation via market or non-market principles. Which is preferred is not a matter of theory but of ideology (tainted with electoral reality). Secondly, even where pure public goods exist, provision is not wholly the responsibility of one sector. For example, for manufacturing, the State both directly supports profit-making (as in providing infrastructure) and dampens potential worker unrest through labour legislation (O'Connor 1973). Put simply, there is no 'free market' because profitability depends upon State intervention. It takes no marxist to recognise the strength of these arguments. Any analysis of international economic relations (e.g. Blake and Walters 1987; Gilpin 1987) makes it abundantly clear that national governments are active agents in distorting economic relationships in order to benefit their nation's producers. If we really had a free market, then the likes of Chrysler, Ford, General Motors and the Rover Group would have much smaller sales and Honda, Nissan and Peugeot would have larger ones. The way in which governments structure national markets advantages some producers more than others. In O'Connor's (1973) formulation, how important such manipulations are depends upon the economic power of companies. Enterprises with an effective monopoly over their market sector go a long way towards writing their own meal ticket. The oil industry is an example. Here, competition has been dowsed as corporations have drawn on their importance for defence and trade in order to encourage governments to cocoon them against the rigours of market competition, while, at the same time, leaving them a free hand to maximise profits (and, for 'the sake of the nation', even subsidising them in their efforts; Odell 1986). 'The [US] federal government felt a need for regulations, but this need was somehow felt to be satisfied through providing an umbrella under which the privileged companies could determine their own fate' (Davis 1974: 54). In more competitive market sectors, economic returns are likewise conditioned by government frameworks, with even short-term profits being dependent upon concessions wrested from national administrations (O'Connor 1973; Offe 1984). Those in politically influential competitive sectors are likely to receive the most concessions, as the dissimilar fortunes of British and French farmers transparently shows (Hill 1984). How groups fare will vary in the short term, since struggles between capital, labour and the State are guided by issues of the moment, changing fortunes and the ideological dispositions of key participants.

In terms of specifying the appropriate role for the State, the view in Britain's Conservative Party is that government owned industries are inappropriate because they are inefficient and unprofitable. This view sits uncomfortably alongside the circumstances in which many industries were taken into government custody, because, while the history of nationalisation in Britain is complex, two themes emerge in initial take-overs and the continuance of government ownership. These are the inability or unwillingness of private owners to organise themselves to meet emerging demand (as for airlines, electricity and gas) and the singularly unsuccessful efforts of private sector managers to run existing operations (as with coal and the railways; see Robson 1962). If an inefficient tag is tied to nationalised industries, primarily this is for arenas in which the private sector long ago failed or which are now in decline (e.g. coal, rail and steel). In promoting the ideological message that private sector management is best, what can be conveniently neglected are the economic successes of the public sector (such as the telephones, gas and airlines). But, today, the Conservative Party keenly advocates privatising profitable public enterprises: if it makes profits, sell it to the private sector, if it makes losses, it confirms that the public sector is inefficient.[12]

Behind the arguments about public or private sector provision lies the issue of political ideology. For services to the general public, the assumption that the private sector is more cost effective is far from convincing. For instance, early incursions by English local authorities into public housing construction often relied on direct labour organisations (i.e. their own employees) because costs were much less than private sector alternatives (e.g. Ryder 1984). When the cheaper, public sector option was not used, this was commonly because business dominance of councils led to a preference for private provision (e.g. Dresser 1984). As we move into the 1920s and 1930s, however, the balance of costs between construction by private and direct labour organisations often changed. As Ryder (1984) identified for County Durham, at a time of high unemployment, many councils used housing construction as a mechanism of unemployment relief; more were employed than was strictly necessary and many workers had no previous experience of this kind, so lowering the efficiency of operations. This tactic is a legitimate one, in that a local institution has jurisdiction over a variety of aspects of local life; the whole can be furthered by making sacrifices for single parts. Of course, such a logic is anathema to the new right. But the logic of their alternative – that efficiency should be assessed by focusing on parts and letting the whole take care of itself – is also ideological. It is based on a primary attachment to the private sector and a preference for low costs above other considerations. One consequence of this mentality is suggested by Mehay's (1979) comparison of police services in Los Angeles, where he found that provision by a municipality's own workers was more expensive but provided a better quality service. This pattern is mirrored in private sector responses to Thatcher government proposals to privatise public services. For one, companies have often not been interested in whole services, only in the most profitable parts of them (hence the constant fears of privatisation leading to cut-backs in rural public transport). Additionally, one reason why many local councils have not renewed service provision contracts with private companies, and why many have not taken them out at all, is the poor standard of service provision. (Even the

Conservative government's favourite local council, the London Borough of Wandsworth, has had to impose stiff fines on its private contractors for shoddy work; Manwaring and Sigler 1985; Ascher 1987.) Arguments about privatisation are ideological, not technical. Set alongside the savings that some authorities have achieved through privatising services (e.g. Southend lowering its refuse collection costs by 20 per cent; Henney 1984) are instances of savings accruing from terminating private sector contracts (e.g. Boston lowering costs by $867,000 per year on its street light maintenance; Stone *et al.* 1986). The truth is that the issues are much more complex than they have been painted. Certainly, the efficiencies of both private and public sector provision depends significantly on precise contractual arrangements (Edwards and Stevens 1978). That private sector means competition (and efficiency) and public sector means monopoly (and inefficiency) might be good rhetoric, but it reveals a feeble mind. In far too many instances private provision occurs on what is effectively a monopoly basis:

> In general, local governments have neither the time, the staff, nor the funds to devote to a comprehensive analysis and evaluation of alternative means of providing services. For these jurisdictions, a continuation of the status quo is frequently the most feasible option.
>
> (Florestano and Gordon 1984: 261)

As DeHoog (1984) made clear, there is often an absence of reliable private contractors for many public services[13] and a lack of independent information to review performances. Just as government–run services can be made more costly in order to satisfy political party aims, so can private contractors be kept on under political pressure. All in all, the outcome of opening up services for private contracting is uncertain. The issues involved are not simply tied to cost, quality and provision performance, but also to the tactics that are used to attain them. The CK Coaches saga in Cardiff shows one aspect of this (Evans 1985). In response to government legislation which opened up the city's bus network to private companies, the city council pursued tactics reminiscent of large capitalist enterprises whereby it ran services at a loss in order to force out competitors, then raised prices once its monopoly was re-established. This is one dimension of council resistance to national government dictate.[14] Another tactic is to impose tight stipulations for contract compliance, which commonly makes private firms reluctant to take on services

(Ascher 1987). Crying 'foul', pro-privatisation pressure groups have recently reported 75 councils to the British government for such 'anti-competitive' tactics.

In effect, there is no technical answer to the question of the proper scope of government. If there had never been government support for national capitalists, purely private goods might be identified. But to theorise as if this were so is like modelling transport flows assuming that time travel is possible, that the costs of movement are nil and that there are no oceans. The proper scope of government is defined by power struggles, value stances and images of immediate and long-term goals. Adopting the welfare economics approach of specifying that government intervention is justified by market failure, by distributional questions or as a means to ward against short-term profit threatening long-term survival, does not help to understand reality, because such evaluations are value charged. What is counts more than what should be, since this tells us how temporally and geographically specific forces have impinged on the State.

## Lower tier–higher tier functional splits

Welfare economics informs us that the distribution of services across governmental tiers should be based on the geographical spread of service benefits (whether local, regional or national), on externality effects and on whether inequalities are acceptable across localities (e.g. Stiglitz 1986). All of these play a part in decisions about functional splits, but the way in which they are interpreted, the emphasis placed on them and the relevance of other considerations, are all variable. The result is a complex myriad of service responsibilities.

Giving some feel for this complexity, even in the ordered arrangements of England, Bulpitt (1983) provided the valuable analogy of describing allocation across tiers as a marble cake rather than a layer cake. Liebert (1974) noted a similar US pattern in that the responsibility of state governments for roads within municipalities ranges from 66.7 per cent in South Carolina to 5.0 per cent in California. The USA most certainly provides more varied local provision than Britain, since, both within states (e.g. Table 3.3) and across them, cities have different service and decision responsibilities (Liebert 1976). In some instances these are easy to explain. The cities of New York, Philadelphia and San Francisco, for example, have merged with their coterminous counties. As a consequence,

*Table 3.3* Municipal functions in mid-Atlantic cities

| Municipal service | Percentage of cities providing a service in | | |
|---|---|---|---|
| | New Jersey | New York | Pennsylvania |
| Fire protection | 100 | 95 | 100 |
| Health services | 99 | 72 | 69 |
| Highways | 100 | 100 | 100 |
| Libraries | 100 | 100 | 75 |
| Police | 100 | 88 | 100 |
| Recreation facilities | 100 | 100 | 99 |
| Refuse services | 95 | nd | 82 |
| Welfare | 100 | 0 | 0 |

*Notes*
(a) These figures were calculated for urban centres with a 1970 population of at least 10,000 people.
(b) Following the practice of Liebert (1974) and Farnham (1986) each service was held to be provided by a municipality if it spent at least $10,000 per year on it. Places listed above as providing such services met this stipulation for each year between 1961 and 1982 (1976–84 for New York). Only a small number of centres listed above as non-providers would have been classed as a provision point for shorter blocks of time.
(c) 'nd' means no data available.

*Source*: calculated for Hoggart (1989)

they have both municipal and county responsibilities. Other fairly obvious distinctions come from dissimilar state policies. Often noted amongst these is the tendency for southern states to control welfare services, whereas in northeastern cities this is more likely to be a municipal function. Within states other differences emerge because, often distinguished by their population size, categories of municipality are entitled (or required) to offer dissimilar service packages. To understand the range of functions in local hands in the United States, the complexity of local–state relationships should be acknowledged. Drawing sustenance from Judge Dillon's classic 1868 statement, analysts most commonly view local units as wards of a state:

Municipal corporations owe their origin to, and derive their powers and rights wholly from, the legislature. It breathes into them the breath of life, without which they cannot exist. As it creates, so it may destroy. If it may destroy, it may abridge and control. Unless there is some constitutional limitation on the right, the legislature might, by a single act, if we can suppose it capable of so great a folly and so great a wrong, sweep from existence all municipal corporations in the state, and the corporation could not prevent it. We know of no limitation on the right so far as the corporations themselves are concerned. They are, so to phrase it, the mere tenants *at will* of the legislature.

(from McCandless 1970: 51)

In appearance, then, municipal responsibility rests in the hands of higher tier government. If this were true, the USA would be little different from Britain. However, the situation is more complex than this (Johnston 1983; Clark 1985). Partly this is because court rulings question the generality of Dillon's Rule, partly because court interpretations of this ruling vary, and partly because some states grant some municipalities immunity from some state directions. Because the US situation is more intricately woven than that of Britain, it is perhaps not surprising that no theory explains the hierarchy of its functional responsibilities (sharply distinguish descriptive *explanation* and *normative* proposal here). Yet the same was true for Britain prior to the presentation of Saunders's dual state model (e.g. Cawson and Saunders 1983).

From the outset it should be recognised that Saunders's model was never meant to be a rounded account of local–national political differences. It was an ideal-type from which analysts could draw inspiration and, hopefully, mould theoretical advancement (Flynn 1986). Some researchers have indeed found it valuable when interpreting both the British scene and that in other nations (e.g. Tonbee 1986). The aspect of Saunders's approach that has drawn applause is his insistence that a single theory cannot account for the organisation of the State. Theoretical dualism is said to be required to reflect the dualism of the State. The dualism is conceptualised as:

a corporate sector located at national and regional levels of government and producing investment policies designed to support capital accumulation in the monopoly sector of the economy and a competitive sector located principally at the local level of government and producing social consumption policies in response to popular pressures but within an overall context of political and economic restraint.

(Saunders 1981: 45)

For Saunders, the State is organised so that functions which are related to economic production are at the national level (e.g. trade union legislation, wage and price controls, trade policy, corporate and personal taxes). Here policy-making is more corporatist in style (i.e. arrangements are worked out between labour, capital and the State, though principally the latter two) and the influence of the general populace is weak. The remit for local institutions is to handle consumption services (those which maintain social order, such as education and social housing). At this level, politics is held to be more pluralistic, as the smaller size of governmental units makes it easier for the public to participate. This pluralism is seen to be functional for capitalism since it fosters the image of a democratic society. In his more recent work, Saunders (1985) has extended these ideas in arguing that services central to profits which require locality-specific modes of articulation are allotted to a non-elected regional government tier (e.g. the water boards, and, before privatisation, the electricity and gas boards).

There are numerous criticisms that can be levelled at this model, but at first these should be set aside in recognition of Saunders's achievement in theorising service distributions. Becoming bogged down in the fine print of his account is unnecessary, as it is an ideal-type. This is not meant to be a model about which analysts nit-pick.[15] More important is whether the dual state model furthers understanding of the British State. On this score, two main points cast doubt on its empirical veracity (as a stimulant for other researchers its role is obvious). The first is that it tends to treat its analytical categories in too monolithic a fashion. This perhaps is a general tendency in ideal-types, but here the categories are so broad as to devalue the general contribution. In the first place this is because both local and national government are treated as unitary entities, when they are comprised of a multitude of institutions and segments, each with its own goals, power complexes and inter-organisational interactions. Key policy-making relationships at the national level might well be corporatist in some arenas, but the same can hold true in localities (e.g. Simmie 1981), and at both levels this will not hold for all agencies. This is not a quibble about empirical details but a comment on styles of theoretical presentation. The same applies for the lack of historical foundation in the model. Saunders presents an account of the situation today without developing a framework for analysing how and why it has reached this point. This is inappropriate. Whatever exists at one time is merely a transient stage in an evolutionary process. It is the trends in this evolution, not what is concrete for an instant, that need theorising. Quite feasibly, the neat pattern painted at one point reveals a wholly different shading further down the line. A snapshot of time can conceal underlying themes which pull in different directions. If Saunders is correct then the central features in his explanatory account should be manifest in the history of municipal functions.

In a British context, the first theme that emerges from such a review is change. In the early years of local government, the granting of municipal functions was by Acts of Parliament specific to single cities. Prior to 1888, services were aligned largely with the interests of locally dominant factions of capital. Services which brought direct economic benefits for producers came in a number of guises. Some would be considered production related then and now (as with gas and electricity). Others, while directly benefiting production, were consumption related. Public health services are a classic case, since disease and illness were robbing manufacturers of much of their workers' time. Indirectly, care was also given to promoting values which were favoured by local élites. For this, both stick and carrot were applied. Philanthropy transmitted values of the propertied classes: 'There seem indeed to have been few institutions or activities in the Victorian industrial town which did not have the transmission of appropriate values as part of their intended or hoped-for function' (Garrard 1983: 47–8). Libraries and cultural facilities offered inducement for middle income groups, but for the poor the harshness of the workhouse was a strong stimulus for avoiding 'welfare' (Roberts 1971). Even after 1888, local influences on service provision remained strong, because a dislike of centralisation, aligned with local pride and initiative, led to a regular procession of parliamentary bills designed to extend local functions (in 1900 Parliament handled 291 local acts; Keith-Lucas and Richards 1978).

Over time, the range of services offered changed significantly. Most notable amongst the gains were school education being placed in the hands of county boroughs and county councils in 1902, low income housing provision joining the municipal ranks in the years after the First World War and land-use planning emerging as an important local task after the next world conflict. Yet losses also occurred. Prisons went in the 1870s, trunk roads in 1936, hospitals in 1946, electricity in 1947, gas in 1948,[16] and, with welfare functions starting to drain away from 1934, water and sewer services were lost in 1974. This list highlights that not all losses directly impinged on production. However, concern over local institutions controlling certain functions was nevertheless quite apparent. Thus, Parliament cast a watchful eye over attempts by socialists to use municipalities to extend public ownership (as in its refusal to sanction Swansea's 1920 attempt to establish a municipal bank; Stone 1985). Likewise, the use of municipal and poor law guardian funds to provide 'zealously' for the poor (e.g. Branson 1979) was undoubtedly a stimulus to the eradication of the poor law guardians and to the quick transfer of welfare functions to central government. The emergence of large corporations with global markets meant that the contribution of single localities to production was becoming paltry. Added to which, the rise of the Labour Party within cities threatened the local dominance of the propertied classes, which further stimulated a preference for higher tier control (Chandler and Lawless 1985). Yet these issues were not simply tied to class conflict. Behind the switch to more nationwide legislation was concern over the workload for legislation on single places. Greater financial involvement by central authorities, especially after increasing grant aid in the 1929 Local Government Act, also stimulated central intervention, as did the fiscal traumas of councils during the 1930s. Besides which, much centralisation, such as the 1946 National Health Service Act and the 1948 National Assistance Act, was instituted by the Labour Party, not to handicap councils but to raise service standards.

There is no evidence that there has ever been a master plan for the allocation of functions to councils:

> At no stage of English history has any government held a consistent logical policy on the range and limits of municipal services. Local government was not evolved to provide a coordinated system of administration for a logically defined range of services; it emerged piecemeal, in answer to a succession of needs and demands.
>
> (Keith-Lucas and Richards 1978: 35)

The allocation of functions has been too messy to be captured by so neat a formulation as the dual state model. Central authorities might well favour nationwide uniformities in some policies, but there are different reasons for this. Saunders latches on to one in focusing on the insulation of production decisions from public gaze. Another justification is to impose uniformity of standards. The right might see the national level as the most appropriate for production decisions, but the left generally sees it as where the redistribution of wealth is most effectively achieved. Furthermore, in both contexts, national control shifts benefits in favour of specific social groups. National control of mainstream health and welfare services enables

Labour to raise standards for working people, as it now allows the Conservatives to encourage private sector options by cutting back on national health hospitals and reducing social benefits. Similarly, while national control enhances the influence of capital under Conservative rule, under Labour the trade unions provide more colour to legislation. The picture overall is more subtle than that painted by Saunders. But stating more than this is not possible, given our current knowledge (unless we opt for blind faith and dogma). The British literature on the causes and political significance of functional allocations across tiers is not sufficiently developed for deeper insight.

The same is true for the United States. Here the complexity of the situation is marked (Liebert 1976) and the reasons for functional change are confused. Moreover, there is little stability in the division of responsibilities. Councils have been robbed of patronage-rich functions by state legislatures which are controlled by opposition parties (Griffith 1974a). Cities have given up services to save money (in the 1970s, Cincinnati persuaded Ohio to take over the city university and Buffalo gave its zoo to the Buffalo Zoological Society; Wolman and Davis 1980). Likewise, when functions have a strong technical component (e.g. crime laboratories) or, as with jails, when provision is unpopular, many municipalities have been happy to be relieved of the mantle of responsibility (Murphy and Rehfuss 1976). In reality, there is no seething mass of disgruntlement over a higher level assumption of services. Thus, when Ronald Reagan proposed decentralising federal authority to local and state governments, he found a lack of lower level support (Peterson 1984). This does not mean that there is strong satisfaction with existing arrangements. But at a time of fiscal uncertainty, a lack of enthusiasm for enhanced local responsibilities is understandable (significantly, local élites warmed to having more say on policy implementation in their areas). The allocation of functions between tiers can be less important than access to policy formulation and implementation.

At present the literature on US local government lacks a Saunders-type model. Any such model would be different from that of Saunders, owing to the dissimilar political cultures of Britain and the USA. However, given the hierarchical nature of British political traditions, Saunders's assertion that local government is pluralistic and participatory strikes a discordant note. This would not be so for the United States, where there is more attachment to individualism and participation (Almond and Verba 1963). At the national level, there is little reason for not transferring to the USA Saunders's idea that activities critical to the economy are insulated from public pressures. However, it is feasible to go further than this, since even at the local level much economic policy-making has been strategically placed to avoid popular control.

**Lower tier themes**

If one aspect of local government in the USA has received less attention than is merited, this must be single function special districts. This neglect is surprising, since these organisations are controversial on two counts. The first criticism arises because they provide services or make decisions that otherwise would be in municipal hands. This is said to intensify problems of service coordination, as well as confusing channels of responsibility between electors and elected (Liebert 1976). This criticism is not dissimilar to that levelled against the fragmented spatial structure of US municipal systems. On this account, these points will not be replayed here. The criticism that is distinctly directed at special districts is that they increase operational inefficiencies and weaken the democratic basis of government. These charges are far from easy to pin down (e.g. DiLorenzo 1981), since there is no theoretical agreement on the optimum size for local organisations, nor for the package of services that make local units most effective. All such evaluations are value-laden.

Many critics of special districts would not respond too adversely to this point. Nevertheless, they would press home the second charge that special districts weaken the accountability of government and, partly because of this, but more significantly to promote this, they are vehicles for pursuing vested interests. 'Special districts

*Table 3.4* Number of local government units in the USA 1962–87

|  | Local government type | | | | | |
|  | County | Municipal | Township | School district | Special district | Total |
| --- | --- | --- | --- | --- | --- | --- |
| 1962 | 3043 | 18000 | 17142 | 34678 | 18323 | 91186 |
| 1972 | 3044 | 18517 | 16991 | 15781 | 23885 | 78218 |
| 1987 | 3042 | 19205 | 16691 | 14741 | 29487 | 83166 |

*Source*: US Department of Commerce Bureau of Census (1988) *Census of Governments 1987*, US Government Printing Office, Washington D.C.

*Table 3.5* Number and type of US special districts 1977–87

| Special district type | Number | | % Change |
|---|---|---|---|
| | *1977* | *1987* | *1977-87* |
| School districts | 15174 | 14741 | -2.9 |
| Natural resources (including flood control, soil and water conservation) | 6595 | 6473 | -1.8 |
| Fire protection | 4187 | 5063 | +20.9 |
| Housing and community development | 2408 | 3460 | +43.7 |
| Water supply | 2480 | 3056 | +23.2 |
| Multiple functions | 1720 | 1917 | +11.5 |
| Cemeteries | 1615 | 1629 | +0.8 |
| Sewerage | 1610 | 1605 | -0.3 |
| Parks and recreation | 829 | 1004 | +21.1 |
| Libraries | 586 | 830 | +41.6 |
| Hospitals | 715 | 784 | +9.7 |
| Education (primary school building) | 1020 | 707 | -30.7 |
| Highways | 652 | 620 | -4.9 |
| Health | 350 | 481 | +37.4 |
| Airports | 299 | 367 | +22.7 |
| Others | 1489 | 896 | -39.8 |

*Source*: US Department of Commerce Bureau of Census (1988) *1987 Census of Governments Volume One: Governmental Organization*, US Government Printing Office, Washington D.C.

reflect the ultimate in local independent control of the provision of services, illustrating the ethos of privatism' (Johnston 1979: 33). As such, they are accused of furthering personal over communal goals. As Harrigan (1976: 209–10) explained: 'The major reason for the popularity of special districts undoubtedly lies in the fact that they can raise money for needed services at the same time that they maintain a low political and fiscal visibility.' With the exception of school boards, these local agencies have become more prevalent over time (Table 3.4). Yet the districts which are the butt of most criticism are mainly of one type (those aligned with production functions). Criticisms levelled at them are real, but the special district issue is broader than these institutions alone (Hawkins 1976).

Overwhelmingly, special districts are single purpose authorities. Looking at the services that they cover reveals a varied compilation, and few of their functions are not provided by mainstream, multi-purpose, locally elected councils (Table 3.5). Amongst these functions school districts stands apart. These authorities were authorised more than 200 years ago with the intention of keeping educational issues away from the hustle and bustle of competitive politics (Institute for Local Self Government 1970). How successful they have been in achieving that end is a matter of dispute, since school districts have been subjected to the same political vagaries as mainstream municipal institutions. In Chicago the school board was unable to escape the clutches of the political machine and became integral to its patronage politics (Nelson 1982). In Youngstown, Ohio, it was almost bankrupted when a referendum requirement for tax increases coincided with weak political leaders who failed to assuage public ignorance over the necessity of greater expenditure (Brunn *et al.* 1969). That such occurrences are not limited to smaller cities is shown by Cleveland's experience in seeking a higher rate of local income tax (Wolman 1982). Additional political failings have come from school board members becoming isolated from the public, leading to an upsurge of discontent and confrontations over leadership (Iannaccone and Lutz 1970; Hennigh 1978). That school district politics differs from mainstream municipal politics is nevertheless evident from the decline in their numbers over time (Table 3.4). In this we see the strong influence of the education professions. They have pressed for school consolidation in order to advance educational objectives (Sher and Tompkins 1977). These professional values have undoubtedly conflicted with more localist sentiments and, as the continued existence of many small districts shows (Table 3.6), professionalism has not achieved an outright victory as yet. Yet the aims of school district formation have perhaps been satisfied by the importance of the education professions, but, if so, only marginally, by degrees of shading rather

*Table 3.6* Size of school districts in the USA 1987

| Size | Number |
| --- | --- |
| One school | 3461 |
| Two schools | 3604 |
| Three to nine schools | 6118 |
| School enrolment under 100 pupils | 2079 |
| School enrolment 101–500 pupils | 4068 |
| School enrolment 501–1000 pupils | 4771 |
| All school districts | 14741 |

*Source*: US Department of Commerce Bureau of Census (1988) *1987 Census of Governments Volume One: Governmental Organization*, US Government Printing Office, Washington D.C.

than colour. In effect, school districts are part of the regular municipal scene, but have worn a different institutional garb. A more complex pattern holds for other special districts.

In many circumstances, technical considerations have played a key part in special district formation. An example is when benefits are sought from cooperation across municipal units. What should be placed alongside the contention that special districts circumvent mainstream electoral procedures is the fact that in 1987 only 24.3 per cent of special districts (excluding school districts) had boundaries coterminous with a single county or municipality. Often, districts have been set up in response to federal requests for organisations with region-wide remits. With many states imposing limits on municipal debts, federal aid also encouraged special authority formation. As Bennett and DiLorenzo (1983: 102) explained, around 30 per cent of special district funding now comes directly from the federal government: 'So anxious are federal politicians to distribute and local politicians to receive federal aid, that there are literally thousands of OBEs [off-budget enterprises] in existence which do nothing but collect federal grants'.[17] It is relevant to remake the point that by vesting responsibility for local government in state hands, the US Constitution laid the foundations for great variety. This is seen in the inability of municipalities in some states to vary their tax rates to allow for dissimilar service demands; in this context special districts provide for improved service allocations in return for special tax assessments (Stetzer 1975). Moreover, most evidently seen in fire protection agencies, some districts are effectively remnants from the past, in that they give legal and financial backing to volunteer fire departments (even in the 1980s only 35 Pennsylvania municipalities had full-time fire departments). Moreover, many districts are really separate arms of the city or county that created them and have no independent authority for taxation or for setting service standards. The funding bases of these districts would not look out of place if they came under a municipal umbrella (Table 3.7). And one survey has found that districts which are independent of municipal control are 98 per cent governed by elected boards (Hawkins 1976).

Despite this seeming normality, there are sound criticisms of the special district system. In particular, the general public is little aware of their operations. Where special districts abound, the combination of differences in geographical coverage, uncertain chains of command (which district is independent and which tied to a municipality?) and lack of clarity over responsibility (what does

*Table 3.7* Main funding mechanisms of special districts 1987

| Funding mechanisms | Number |
|---|---|
| District-wide property taxes | 12853 |
| Other taxes (e.g. sales) | 823 |
| Special assessments | 4028 |
| Service charges or sales | 7116 |
| Shared taxes, grants, rentals or other government reimbursements | 8976 |

*Source*: US Department of Commerce Bureau of Census (1988) *1987 Census of Governments Volume One: Governmental Organization*, US Government Printing Office, Washington D.C.

the Estero Municipal Improvement District do?), make for confusion. Not surprisingly, special district elections have extremely low turnouts (one California survey reported that 80 per cent of water district elections were cancelled for lack of competing candidates, with just over half of the 'elected' officials acquiring their posts by appointment rather than the ballot box; Institute for Local Self Government 1970). Excluding school districts, whose actions are very visible, the activities of special districts are poorly publicised. By itself this seems somewhat suspicious, given the charge that these units are often clandestine operations promoting private sector profits (e.g. Cox and Nartowicz 1980). However, this critique should be treated somewhat carefully since a minority of districts are of the enterprise type. What nevertheless gives force to this charge is the financial importance of these units (Hawkins [1976], for example, reported that while such authorities made up 34 per cent of special districts they spent 80 per cent of all funds). As with the New York Port Authority, some districts which control vast sums of public money are effectively free of electoral accountability. Other districts have been created solely to subsidise private profit. In the San Francisco Bay Area, for example, the Estero Municipal Improvement District came into being so that a residential developer could issue $55 million in tax exempt government bonds in order to cover the building of 35,000 homes (Harrigan 1976; see Cox and Nartowicz 1980 for a similar Houston example). More generally, Bennett and DiLorenzo (1983) provided a long list of large corporations, including Allied Chemical, Atlantic Richfield, Exxon, Ford, Goodyear, K-Mart, Mobil, Nabisco, Proctor and Gamble, and Pepsico, all of which have had special districts created for them so that they can have investments backed by tax exempt bonds. These are not isolated cases but part of a general pattern. 'In the agricultural districts, notably, policy decisions will almost universally be made by directors clearly in the position of self-interest and personal benefit' (Institute for Local Self Government 1970: 25). No matter what a person's political disposition, special district actions are discomforting. Those of the right object to the circumvention of debt and expenditure limits, plus extravagance in institutions whose actions are not properly vetted (e.g. Bennett and DiLorenzo 1983), just as those on the left are repulsed by manipulations to enhance purely private profit. Special districts make circumventing democratic processes easier either because of their low visibility or because their funding mechanisms exclude them from debt and expenditure limits.

That special districts are deliberately created in order to avoid debt, tax and expenditure requirements cannot be doubted. In New Jersey, for example, after a cap was placed on municipal expenditure increases in 1977, there was a flurry of special district creations which added 74 to the stock before the state called a halt in 1982 (Connors and Dunham 1984). The growth in redevelopment agencies in California from 1981 onwards is suggestive of the same phenomenon (Table 3.8), as this was when state aid became more constrained (as surpluses dried up) and the full impact of the tax

*Table 3.8* New community redevelopment agencies in California 1973–87

| Year | Number created |
|------|----------------|
| 1973 | 16 |
| 1974 | 14 |
| 1975 | 11 |
| 1976 | 14 |
| 1977 | 4 |
| 1978 | 5 |
| 1979 | 8 |
| 1980 | 9 |
| 1981 | 27 |
| 1982 | 26 |
| 1983 | 27 |
| 1984 | 18 |
| 1985 | 20 |
| 1986 | 14 |
| 1987 | 5 |

*Source*: California State Controller (1988) *Annual Report of Financial Transactions Concerning Community Redevelopment Agencies in California 1986/7*, Sacramento

limitations in Proposition 13 began to be felt (Citrin 1984). However, there is a general trend toward hiding local spending by placing it in special districts (Table 3.4). Most particularly this is seen for functions associated with economic development and public utilities, which not only hold the promise of large revenues but also generally receive less public supervision since their income is drawn from fees and sales. However, the number of districts created is more than needed to avoid tax and expenditure limits or to promote private profits. A more general process is at work; one that owes much to the unwillingness of the public to accept tax increases. As Bennett and DiLorenzo (1983) noted, with only around one-third of referenda on expenditure questions being approved, local councils have an incentive to remove services from public overview whenever they expect problems in raising revenue. That this circumvention of local accountability has worried state governments is apparent in the number that have limited growth in this organisational form (e.g. California, Nevada, New Jersey, New Mexico, Oregon and Washington).

Yet what lies behind the creation and sustenance of many special districts is the simple fact that local, state and federal leaders find it advantageous to implement policies in an arena about which the public knows little and understands less. This practice has a questionable democratic heritage. However, the root cause lies not simply in politicians' self-interest. Also important is the public's weak understanding of governmental affairs. In a system which draws heavily on referenda approval for spending and tax increases, as well as imposing arbitrary limits on both, this can easily result in the denial of resources to provide basic services (Brunn *et al.* 1969). In New Jersey, for example, between 1977 and 1980, a time of relatively high inflation, 57 per cent of referenda seeking to overturn the state's 5 per cent cap on annual expenditure increases were defeated (Wolman 1982). Recognising that its own limits were too low to meet real cost increases, but lacking the will to change the law openly, the state government approved a long, seemingly ever growing, list of exemptions from the cap, so enabling council spending to stay technically within legal limits. The roots of such circumventions owe much to individualist values. This drives the public toward rejecting taxes and services from which they gain little personal benefit, and encourages those who expect gain to use government channels for personal advancement. Neither tendency occurs by chance. As analyses of the media show, the public is not well informed about government, except for 'personality' stories, and is encouraged to strive for personal rather than societal benefits (Bagdikian 1983; Parenti 1986). These values are well suited to an élitist control over government which directs rewards towards the already strong.

Although individualism does not provide a complete account of special district formation, the significant part it plays provokes the expectation that this organisational form is less important in Britain than in the USA. It further suggests that under the new right government of Margaret Thatcher – so avowedly intent on changing communalist values into personalised ones – special districts will increase in importance. Both expectations are confirmed by actual practices. This is not to say that such authorities have not existed for a long time. Most obviously seen in the case of London, where urban growth has produced demand for inter-authority policy integration for over a century, such organisations have a lengthy heritage. Cousins (1988) highlights this in noting that there are at least 1,000, if not 2,000, pseudo-governmental organisations within Greater London (e.g. Lea Valley Regional Park Authority and London Transport). Some of these are vestiges of the past, others have arisen to meet new demands. Some come under the jurisdiction of the national government, others fall under the control of joint committees representing a number of councils, and yet others take in both private and public concerns. Until the last decade, what distinguished the vast bulk of these organisations – with the exception of the Metropolitan Police or London Transport – is that they controlled few resources and could be justified on 'technical' grounds.[18]

Where more recent years break with the past is in the establishment of agencies to circumvent local authority control. Most clearly, these are seen in enterprise zones. These geographical areas have been taken out of local authority hands and awarded the right to offer incentives to attract investment (Anderson 1983). The clarion call of these central government impositions is revitalising the economy by giving incentive to the private sector (in the form of less government regulation and lower taxes). In a declining economy, it is not surprising that large numbers of localities have applied for such special favours (Hoare 1985). After all, in many respects the programme merely provides central funds for what the bulk of local authorities do of their own accord (Keating 1988): compete for mobile firms in order to increase employment (Hampton [1987] reported that by 1982 over 80 per cent of district councils were providing sites and over half premises for manufacturers). As Chandler and Lawless (1985: 3) observed, 'support and development of the local economy is now a top priority for almost every local authority'. Yet local priorities are not those of their national counterparts. Attempts in London's docklands to develop an economic development plan to meet the needs of local residents was thwarted by the establishment of the London Docklands Urban Development Corporation, whose actions have mainly benefited large corporations. Such a pattern is not part of the government's publicity messages, but, as Anderson (1983) made clear, the advantages which enterprise zones like the Docklands offer are less suited to small firms. The primary tenants in these zones are major corporations, many of which merely move location from one part of a metropolitan area to another. (National surveys suggest that only 4–12 per cent of firms in enterprise zones might not have started up without them, with 90 per cent of relocations coming from within the same region; Keating 1988.) There have been obvious political party and social class dimensions to this policy. That the government has used enterprise zone designations to feather the party's electoral nest is only evident at the margins of the allocational process (Hoare 1985). That the policy was used to steal the thunder of alternative local programmes – such as those headed by the Greater London Council and the West Midlands County Council – is more apparent. Yet these two visions directly contradicted one another. Under the enterprise zone scheme firms are offered subsidised business relocation which can be used to restructure production processes, reduce workforce levels and weaken trade union power (most evidently seen in newspapers abandoning Fleet Street for London's Docklands). By contrast, many local regeneration efforts have stressed trade union involvement, small business ventures and community cooperation (Duncan and Goodwin 1985; Mackintosh and Wainwright 1987).[19] In disbanding councils for metropolitan counties, the government signified its attachment not only to autocratic governance but also to one vision of economic change.

Of course, in comparison with the United States, private-regarding impulses within a special district format are weakly developed. Counting all formally designated Urban Development Corporations and enterprise zones together, the list still runs to under 100. However, the longer the Conservative Party has stayed in national office, the more attractive this means of weakening local councils has been. In 1985, for example, legislation was passed forcing local authorities to create companies to manage their participation in airport and bus operations. The abolition of the higher tier metropolitan authorities has likewise increased the special district role in local politics. Recent legislation holds out a future of further growth, with the government encouraging individual schools to opt out of local authority hands, set up their own governing board and receive funds direct from Whitehall. In the form of Housing Action Trusts, the government has reiterated its position: to break up municipal 'empires', public housing estates will be financially and legislatively encouraged to operate outside local authority view. In promising more task forces to guide inner city revival, the government is again threatening to take a role from locally elected officials (although the government's experiment in task force operations on Merseyside was so singularly unsuccessful that, without substantial change, this proposal will carry the threat of a paper tiger; Parkinson and Duffy 1984). Overall, the accumulation of proposals affecting local government add credence to the claim that it is under siege. As Davies (1988) notes, much of this threat can be assuaged by councils being more responsive to citizens' concerns. The Thatcher government might well hope for a re-run of the wooden horse of Troy in its search to implant private-regarding values into the local government sphere. But if local authorities are sufficiently adroit, the government might face a Stalingrad. Then again, if local councils do not respond positively, the outcome could bear more resemblance to Massada.

## FISCAL DILEMMAS

The Thatcher administration's proposals for local government promote person-centred sentiments not only by weakening the authority of those institutions which have shown most concern for social provisions. In addition they intensify personal positions, even within the family, by proposing to change the local tax base from a household to a person-centred system (viz. the community charge or poll tax). The aim in moving from property taxes to a tax on all adults is to bring home to people the cost of services. Like referendum proposals in the USA, such a system has the potential of bringing self-interest to the fore as expenditure increases are seen more overtly (i.e. local taxes will no longer be hidden in rent payments and, although rebates will be allowed, few will legally escape from paying the tax). The hope is that local spending will be kept under control, as high spending should be more of a threat to electoral prospects. As an additional bonus for Conservative supporters, this new poll tax will be regressive (on account of the greater importance of extended families for some immigrant groups, it also has racial overtones). Under this proposal all adults in a local authority, bar the few who obtain rebates, will make the same tax payment, irrespective of income. With regard to understanding the restraints that this will place on local authorities, recognition must be given to the accompanying proposal that tax rates for non-residential property be set by the national government. The political significance of these steps could be profound. By adjusting non-residential rates of taxation, or by changing central grants, the national government could put single authorities in the highly charged atmosphere of having to raise its poll tax or else raise service charges to balance its budget. Either solution would have regressive consequences for local income distributions. Additionally, by placing more of the revenue burden at the lower end of the income spectrum, the government hopes to provoke traditional Labour supporters into resisting higher expenditure. If local Labour groups respond to such pressures, the government 'wins' in that its goal of lower public expenditure is attained. If they do not respond, the government also hopes to 'win' when (and if) Labour supporters vote Conservative in order to lower taxes. For Labour supporters and those of lesser income, this seems to endow property taxes with a halo of virtue. This is far from the case. All taxation schemes are biased in one form or another (Schattschneider 1960). Moving from one revenue scheme to another might change the character of the bias, but it will not eradicate it.

The implications that this has for the structuring of local politics can be visualised from two angles. The first sits against the cheek of local populations. It asks how revenue raising distributes cost benefits and disbenefits within the locality. The second sits inside the council policy-making apparatus. It considers how the operational structures of revenue collection determine institutional responses. Both are political in that they are concerned with the distribution of societal benefits. Where they differ is in their field of vision. The first focuses on the intra-local field, examining how advantages and disadvantages accrue to householders. The second pinpoints inter-local disparities, highlighting how revenue systems differentially ease and retard policy formation and implementation. Intrinsically, one is not more important than another. Also, they are not mutually exclusive; a householder who gains much intra-locally could be a heavy loser in the inter-local stakes. Being so central to politics itself, both should be investigated. Here, we start at the intra-local level. The next chapter explores the inter-local ramifications.

## Local resource bases

Within both Britain and the United States the main source of local revenue has long been the property tax. This is not the case in all nations. For example, with Norwegian communities levelling income taxes at the maximum rate of 22 per cent (Newton 1980), it is not surprising that 84.2 per cent of the nation's local revenues comes from this source (Karran 1988). In Sweden (92.9), Denmark (90.7), Finland (90.4) and Switzerland (87.0), the percentages are even higher, making the US figure of 5.8 per cent look miserly. Yet this figure misrepresents the true role of income taxes within the USA, as only nine states allow municipalities to use them (MacManus 1983). Moreover, even in states that do, not all authorities find it open to them (thus, in New York State only New York City is entitled to levy both a personal income and a corporate tax). Even so, the prospect of an income tax must look fabulous to British local officials. As Karran's (1988) international survey shows, with the exception of Ireland, and until the poll tax became operational, the United Kingdom was unique amongst the advanced nations in not allowing councils to tax citizens directly. Instead, drawing on a single tax base, all charges were levied against property. British councils are precluded from drawing on sales taxes, although these are available to councils in more than half of the states in the USA. Admittedly, the US position is not as rosy as might be imagined, since rates of income, property and sales taxes are commonly limited by state regulations. The pattern is somewhat different in West Germany, where *Länder* (provinces) fix rates for corporate, income and value added taxes which local units cannot change (Brosio 1985). Further complexity comes from the varying importance of inter-governmental (i.e. higher tier) grants. In Canada, for example, the percentage of municipal revenue from own sources ranges from under 15 in Prince Edward Island to around 67 in British Columbia (Bird and Slack 1983).

Not to be forgotten in the array of fiscal sources is the dynamism of the revenue manifest. For example, since the so-called US tax revolt of the late 1970s, there have been notable changes in the well from which local funds can be drawn. Comparing the ratio of revenue receipts to personal income in cities for 1979 with the same

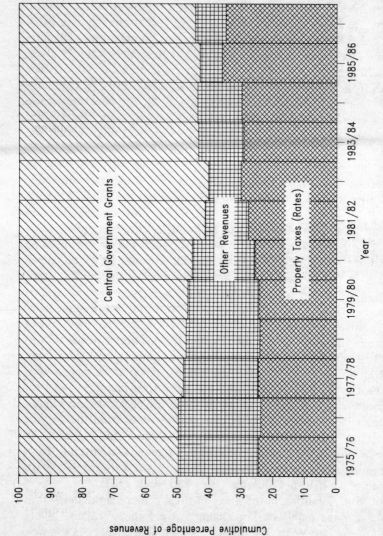

*Figure* 3.5 Rates and grants as a percentage of total local revenues: England and Wales 1975/6–86/7
*Source:* Central Statistical Office (1989) *Annual Abstract of Statistics 1989*, HMSO, London

calculation for 1984 yields a figure of 0.90 for property taxes, whereas for sales and income taxes it is 1.56 and 1.43, with charges for municipal services recording 1.68 (Howard 1987). Put simply, rates of property tax increase have not kept up with income growth, whereas other revenue sources have grown faster than income. In Britain the property tax has also had a declining part to play (Figure 3.5). Cut-backs in central grants have pushed councils toward obtaining a higher proportion of their funds from user charges and fees (such as swimming pool entrance charges and planning application fees). This process has not come about just because grants have fallen. It has been deliberately engineered by national policy-makers by means of threatening to limit access to property tax resources (e.g. rate capping) and by regulations which have pushed up fees. Most obviously, the latter has been seen in housing. Consequent upon the 1980 Housing Act, which forced councils to sell their dwellings to sitting tenants who wished to buy (Forrest and Murie 1988), the government made home purchase more attractive by sharply increasing rents for council owned dwellings. This provided no bounty of extra resources for local authorities because the means of achieving rent increases was to lower those grants which subsidised rents by the very amount by which the government wanted rents to rise. Hence, councils were left with some choice in the matter; although, with the spectre of rate capping hanging above them and more general grant reductions to contend with, their scope for action was limited. Even so, Labour councils did make their opposition to government policy felt in restrained responses to central initiatives (Hoggart 1985). In this regard Labour councils have tried to shield those of lower income from shouldering the burden of fiscal restructuring. This objective draws inspiration from regard for that party's electoral prospects, since council house tenancy is associated with Labour support (e.g. Johnston *et al*. 1988). However, it also has ties to the party's commitment to helping the poor.

## Local revenue discriminations

Every form of taxation sets a pattern of extraction which differentially benefits people, either in terms of use or income. From the perspective of the individual, those educated in private schools or outside a nation are in a sense discriminated against when they pay taxes to support public education because they have received no personal benefit, just as those who contribute higher proportions of their income to pay a universal tax are discriminated against. In general, such individualistic views are answered by noting that there are communal benefits from service provision (a better informed population, for example) and that the discriminatory impact of single taxes is not crucial so long as the total burden of taxation is not unduly biased. For this last point, a rider should obviously be added, because if the revenue mechanisms which are available to single institutions are significantly discriminatory, this can place a brake on the willingness to act. The organisation can collect money, but the more it collects the more it hurts one segment of the population. This is the position that many local councils face when they rely heavily on property taxes. More than this, in the USA at least, there are regressive tendencies in total local and state tax collections (e.g. Figure 3.6).

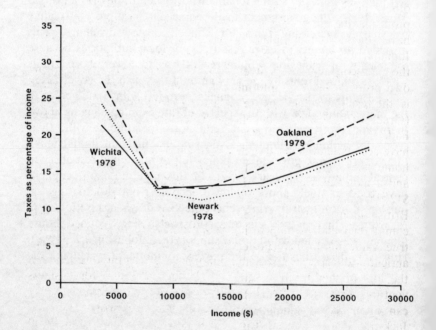

*Figure 3.6* Local and state tax burdens by income class: Newark, Oakland and Wichita

*Source*: Menchik, M.D., Pascal, A., De Tray, D., Fernandez, J. and Caggiano, M. (1982) 'Fiscal Restraint in Local Government', Rand Corporation Report R–2645–FF/RC, Santa Monica, CA, 7 and 9

A primary reason for this is the regressive features of property, sales and fee revenues. For property taxes, for example, US evidence shows that assessed property values are not equitably applied. Comparing the assessed taxation value of 13,679 Boston properties with their sales prices, Oldman and Aaron (1969) found that single family homes were assessed at 34 per cent of real value, two family residences at 41 per cent, five family residences at 52 per cent, and for properties with at least six families (tenements and apartment blocks) the ratio was 58 per cent. Not surprisingly, ratios of tax value to real value were lower in wealthier areas, where single family homes predominated. Similar findings have been reported for Chicago (Berry and Bednarz 1975), Hamilton, Ontario (Thrall 1979), and for both Derby (Wyatt 1983) and Woking in England (Ford and Brown 1978). In the Boston investigation, business properties had the highest ratio, a finding consistent with some others in North America (e.g. Bird and Slack 1983). However, profit-making enterprises have not always treated this as given and have sought to manipulate ratings to their advantage. In Gary, Indiana, for example, the dominant local employer has long been the giant corporation US Steel (now USX), which effectively sets its own property taxes by informing the council how valuable its plant is; the resulting valuations are apparently well below real investment (Greer 1979). Deriving benefits in a different manner, Thomas R. Fadell, the tax assessor for Calumet County, Indiana, is reported to have accumulated three trucking companies, a trailer park, a mobile home sales company, a law practice, extensive real estate interests and a motel in Miami, all in a few years and based on an annual $12,500 salary (Amick 1976: 97; also Hayes 1972). For a long time British industry did not need such underhand practices, because commercial and manufacturing properties were rated below their true value until 1964 (Foster *et al.* 1980); and in many nations agricultural land and associated buildings are zero rated. Even with the loss of this privilege, there are hidden subsidies for business ventures, since (as in Britain) the property taxes that companies pay can often be set against corporate income taxes (Meadows and Jackson 1986). Special cases are also visible when political advantage is at stake, as in Chicago where the lowest assessment ratios were in Mayor Daley's neighbourhood (Berry and Bednarz 1975; also Oldman and Aaron 1969).

This perhaps reads like Robin Hood in reverse, but so far only part of the story has been told. In Britain, for example, rate rebates were introduced in the 1966 Rating Act for those of low income.

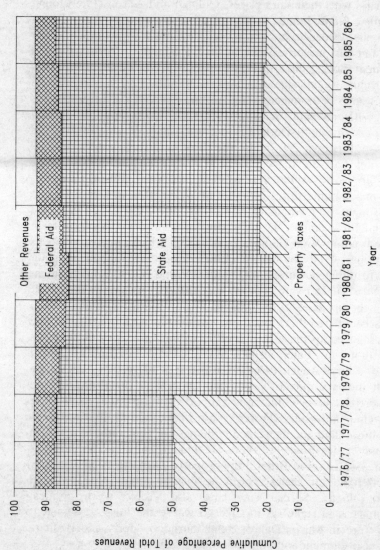

*Figure 3.7* Revenue sources for California school districts 1976/7–85/6

*Source:* State of California (1988) *California Statistical Abstract 1987,* Sacramento

These have gone a long way toward reducing the regressiveness of this tax (Committee of Inquiry into Local Government Finance 1976). Similarly, in various parts of the United States, legally binding restrictions have been placed on local reliance on property revenues. In the ruling on *Serrano* v. *Priest*, for instance, the 1971 California Supreme Court invalidated local property taxes as a mechanism for financing public education. This provision was overturned in the US Supreme Court, on the grounds that unequal school district wealth did not inevitably led to inequalities in opportunity, but its spirit has lived on a variety of rulings (as in the introduction of a state-wide income tax to fund schools in New Jersey and in the increasing share of school district funds which come from the state in California; Figure 3.7). In addition, a total of 28 states have introduced circuit-breaker provisions in their tax codes (for 19 of these for the elderly only), wherein tax payments which take an undue proportion of income are refunded by the state (Chicoine and Walzer 1985). Offering further amelioration, stipulations for property assessment have been tightened. In England this came about when the Inland Revenue took over assessment from local officials in 1948. In the United States it has been seen in the assumption of assessment control by many county governments (reducing the threat of intra-municipal bias) and by state government requirements that assessments be based on market values (upgraded every few years). In addition, a high percentage of local revenue comes from non-domestic tax payers, which, save in a few places such as Delaware (Phelan and Pozen 1973), have no vote in local elections. In effect, as those on the right keenly point out, this is taxation without representation. (In Britain over 50 per cent of property taxes comes from non-domestic sources, yet, until recently, councillors have had little incentive to weigh the concerns of these tax payers in their assessment of tax increases.) Although there are regressive tendencies within property taxation, much less is asked of householders because of the contribution of the non-domestic sector.

All this perhaps reduces concern about regressiveness in local taxation but, in practice, attempts to iron out inconsistencies and biases have had questionable effectiveness. For instance, despite a state requirement that property valuations in New Jersey be upgraded every three to four years, in 1980 the cities of Camden and Newark had not been assessed since 1959 and 1963, respectively (De Tray *et al.* 1981). Likewise no revaluation has occurred in England since 1973, which has meant that cities with declining economies, where property values have risen much slower than elsewhere, are receiving substantially less central grant than they should, since one element of grant payments is based on comparative rateable values (Parkinson 1985). The party politics behind this should not be lost on readers. When property revaluation was implemented in Scotland in 1985 it provoked a major anti-Conservative backlash, as the tax burden swung away from commerce and industry on to householders; and given rate rebates for those of lowest income, the changes particularly hit middle and higher income households (Bailey 1986). Placed in an English context, a similar implementation has the potential of tearing large chunks out of Tory votes in its heartland in South East England; the region that has benefited most from changes in the British economy in the 1980s but where the environmental and community based concerns of the Liberal Democrat and Green parties has some appeal for middle class voters. The introduction of the poll tax in Britain is not simply a means of redistributing income, nor is it merely a way of damaging the Labour Party; it gets the Conservative government out of a sizeable political hole. So, while this tax is controversial, it might prove less damaging to the Conservative vote than a revaluation of property.

As well as understanding the fabric of taxation systems, attention should be directed at the circumstances in which tax resources can be relied upon. The recent controversy over the Greater London Council's Fares Fair policy highlights the importance of such circumstances. The Fares Fair policy reduced ticket prices on London's underground railway and buses by 32 per cent. It produced a 10 per cent increase in public transport usage in three months and a 6 per cent reduction in the number entering central London by car (Wheen 1985). To pay for these reductions, increased revenue from ticket sales was supported by the council's general funds (raising the GLC subsidy from 29 to 56 per cent of London Transport's total costs, a figure well below those for New York at 72 per cent, Milan at 71, and Brussels at 70, and only just equalling that for Paris; Wheen 1985 and Livingstone 1987). The London Borough of Bromley, a suburban municipality with few public transport services, no underground railway and high rates of car ownership, took the GLC to court over this usage of ratepayers' money. When the House of Lords ruled in favour of Bromley, Lord Wilberforce explained that the GLC:

> owes a duty of fiduciary character to its ratepayers who have to provide the money . . . in deciding to proceed to make a grant to

support the fare reduction, once it became apparent that the ratepayers' burden would be approximately doubled it acted in breach of its fiduciary duty as defined above. It failed to hold the balance between transport users and the ratepayers as it should have done.

(from Henney 1984: 39)

Lord Diplock backed this judgement while making a more general point about local authority responsibility:

it is well established by the authorities . . . that a local authority owes a general fiduciary duty to the ratepayers from whom it obtains monies needed to carry out its statutory functions, and that this includes a duty not to expend those moneys thriftlessly.

(from Henney 1984: 39)

British local authorities, it seems, must take care when spending local funds in order to maintain a balance between the beneficiaries of spending policies and the payers of taxes. Put simply, any policy which provides direct benefits for lower income residents could be deemed illegitimate unless councils are responding to national government dictate. This follows because the balance of payees and recipients is lopsided. The justification that a council has an electoral mandate for its policy – Fares Fair was in the GLC Labour Party's 1981 election manifesto – holds little water in British courts; national governments are allowed the justification of a mandate, local councils cannot be so certain.[20] Unless counteracted by other legal stipulations, the requirement that a council has a fiduciary duty to ratepayers presumably would permit an expenditure bias favouring the wealthy, since those paying most would receive most. In fact, though, this fiduciary duty stipulation has not been a major restraint on council decisions, other than as a warning against inefficient management.[21] Its importance arises from signifying how complex municipal budgeting can be. Most especially in nations with so long a history as England, there are innumerable 'sleeping' regulations that the courts can interpret as relevant to council decisions.

The regulations and processes that surround taxation schemes can either increase or weaken regressive tendencies. For example, one outcome of placing limits on property taxation in the United States has been that local taxation has become more progressive, since greater reliance has been placed on income taxes and fees (Wolman 1982; Pascal *et al.* 1985). The reference to fee income might strike readers as a strange one in this context. After all, fees and user charges have a regressive image given that the poor pay as much as the rich. However, the situation is not so sharply defined. When the 1979 Conservative government raised British value added taxes (i.e. sales taxes) from 7.5 per cent to 15 per cent for 'luxury' items and from 2.5 per cent to 15 per cent for 'non-luxuries', the outcome was regressive. However, had luxuries been increased (say) to 25 per cent and non-luxuries kept as they were or reduced, a more progressive tax structure could have resulted. Similarly, after Proposition 13, California municipalities relied more on user fees (Figure 3.8), but the charges which increased most had progressive elements in them (e.g. tourist and business travellers paying the transient lodging tax). Taxation changes do not have predictable distributional consequences. Their impact is dependent upon their precise implementation. At times, their main effects might even be outside the taxation system. Thus, following massive reductions in property taxes after Proposition 13, those renting homes in California expected to write smaller rent cheques. When this did not materialise, indeed as rents continued to climb, a few municipalities, such as Berkeley and Santa Monica, imposed rent freezes on all landlords (Clavel 1986). Even if higher tier authorities have a specific objective, local agencies do not automatically follow their spirit or intent. Thus, the Conservative government's recent stipulation that British councils give business a special place in budget deliberations – by formally consulting them on tax and expenditure decisions – has not produced the hoped-for infusion of stronger business influence. Councils have controlled whom they take advice from, and also whether they take it (Martlew 1986).

A number of agents are involved in filtering demands into policy enactments. In a wide variety of contexts, as fiscal stress has imparted itself on local government, powerful interests have manipulated responses toward goals which they favour. Often, fiscal stress has enabled local leaders to change tax and spending policies in a manner which they favour but were previously reluctant to implement for fear of upsetting electoral balances built around the status quo (e.g. Levine *et al.* 1981; Citrin and Levy 1981). Change incorporates varying objectives. This variety warns against too literal an acceptance of O'Connor's (1973: 203) argument that: 'Every important change in the balance of class and political forces is registered in the tax structure. Put another way, tax systems are simply particular forms of class system.' The weakness in this contention comes from the slippage which occurs between its first and second sections: class and political forces in the first are reduced

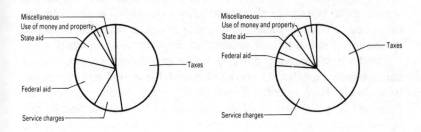

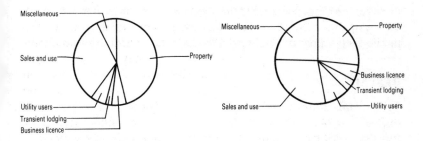

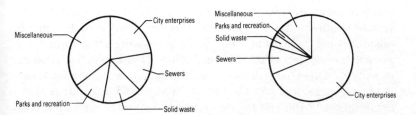

*Figure 3.8* Revenue sources for California cities 1977/8 and 1986/7

*Source*: California State Controller (1988) *Annual Report of Financial Transactions Concerning Cities of California*, Sacramento

to class alone in the second. It could be argued that since politics is concerned with the distribution of societal benefits, class systems are central to it. This is indeed the case, but the two are not equivalent. There are significant dimensions to distributional issues other than class (e.g. gender, race, age). What is more, government is not simply about ruling but also about getting elected. The introduction of a poll tax in Britain shows that electoral considerations are important. Similarly, the restraints on property taxation which some US states have introduced are so feeble that their justification must surely have simply been to make electors believe that something was being done (Peretz 1982; Gold 1984). Additionally, the internal dynamics of government institutions must be brought to bear on our understanding of taxation processes. In Britain, for example, the fact that local authorities have only one taxation source cannot be understood outside an appreciation of strong Treasury pressure not to allow a more flexible revenue base. Although government appointed committees have recommended more flexible (and progressive) taxation systems (e.g. Committee of Inquiry into Local Government Finance 1976), the Treasury has fought hard to block their implementation, seeing them as a threat to its control over public sector finance (Ashford 1980; Meadows and Jackson 1986).

**RESUME**

The organisation of State institutions at a local level follows quite different paths across nations. There is little uniformity in the functions of local units, in which responsibilities are at a national or local level, over their spatial fixes, in their funding systems, and in the manner in which they are integrated into or kept apart from mainstream electoral politics (e.g. Karran 1988). That having been stated, it can be seen that the primary values in a political culture, which in themselves are a reflection of dominant power relations in society, both in the past and to this day, are reflected in the organisational forms that emerge. Each organisational form has a particular consequence for the distribution of benefits and advantages in society. Often such forms have contradictory emphases, albeit in the aggregate it is possible to identify strong trends. But between organisational form and the gains (and losses) of persons and social groups there is slippage. Structures set up orientations in patterns of advantage but they do not sustain them; for this, agents within those structures must act in a manner which is consistent with the logic of its formation. In reality, there is no uniformity in response to structural arrangements. For one thing, even amongst the most powerful elements in (local or national) polities, there are divergences in values. These might be minor, being more matters of interpretation or of tactics than of goals, but they still lead to openings for divergent views to find succour within structures. Then there are differences in local reactions to the same structure. These can vary across geographical areas, perhaps aligned with differences in local political culture, or they can arise from changes in local leadership. That there are biases in favour of societal élites in the arrangements of both the English and the US systems of local government is clear (even though they have not had everything their own way). What now needs to be assessed is whether the processes that operate within these structures reinforce those biases, or if political practices sing a different distributional tune.

# 4 Local political cultures, local political practices

No generally agreed typology exists for local political cultures or even for the dimensions that distinguish prevailing political orientations within localities. This perhaps is not unexpected, since value dispositions are complex. Young (1975b) explained the predicament:

> Value analysis is without doubt a theoretical and methodological minefield. It is clear that different dimensions of belief and evaluation bear upon different policy areas; that levels of analysis problems arise in the identification of whose values are potent for policy; that decision outcomes often arise from the *negotiation* of conflicting value positions within the decision system; and that many aspects of service delivery are determined at the interface between organisation and client – a point at which the 'policy process' hardly claims to bear. Ultimately, however, the tangled skein of values must be unravelled if we are to understand better what government does.
>
> (Young 1975b: 1–2)

Problems arise, then, not simply in specifying the components and character of the ethos which pervades local policy-making circles, but also in articulating how these are transferred into policy enactments. For both, the analytical problems which are raised are more daunting than those involved with identifying national political cultures. This is inevitable given the greater variety of themes that mark the historical evolution of localities. Forces which are too tepid to impress national affairs provide the centrepiece of local dispositions. What is more, on account of their smaller spatial extent, the pace of change in localities can be rapid (as when new towns are planted on formerly agrarian communities). Variety and change are important, but research on local political cultures has only scraped the surface of understanding either. The temporal dimension in particular has received scant attention; so we know little about the durability or volatility of prevailing political orientations.

Of course, one reason why a temporal appreciation is difficult to develop is lack of agreement on what local political cultures are. Seeing them as dominant value dispositions in policy-making circles does not get us far, given that this specification allows much latitude for interpretation. For example, if we adopt a person-centred approach, such cultures could be specified by the attributes of policy-makers. This view is integral to calls for a more equitable representation of women and minorities amongst elected officials. In such arguments, the implication is that increased group representation changes the governing ethos and leads to different polices (e.g. Hills 1982). This understanding has led to negative reactions from established officials and the propertied classes to the 'threat' of racial minority control of cities (Greer 1979; Kleppner 1985).[1] Such electoral victories add weight to this conviction. At least for mayors from racial minorities, US evidence suggests that their election does lead to more attention to the problems of poor people (e.g. Karnig and Welch 1980; Browning *et al.* 1984; Button and Scher 1984), with both public services and municipal employment prospects for non-whites improving (e.g. Dye and Renick 1981; Garza and Weaver 1986). However, these effects produce deviations about a central theme, not fundamental reorientations in policy. As Karnig and Welch (1980) noted, most black mayors control poor municipalities and need to appease white investors in order to preserve their tax base (i.e. to stop or at least stem white flight). A change in who runs a local institution does not mean that a new operational *modus vivendi* follows. There are structural dimensions to behaviour patterns that do not alter with the assumption of new political leadership.

This point is merely an extension of the general pattern of behaviour which is being conditioned by, and in turn reinforces, social structure. Local political cultures are components of that structural matrix, in that they specify the ground rules for the acceptability of political action. The assumption of a new leadership offers the potential for a change in ground rules. In the longer term this could lead to a reorientation in core values. However, until such values are widely accepted, the operational tone of local policy-making can be at variance with more stable cultural traces. In other words, operational styles are embedded in cultural traits but not in a fixed way. The relationship between the two is subtle rather than

**direct**, flexible rather than rigid, dynamic rather than stable. This raises interpretive problems because it can mean that operational styles do not openly express core values. Admittedly, if these styles are wildly out of phase with underlying values, then either they are unlikely to survive long or else value stances will themselves change. Since ongoing behaviour reinforces and yet changes structural relationships, only investigation can reveal whether seemingly dissonant operational styles are temporary aberrations or steps on the way to new cultural forms. Hence, in seeking understanding of local political cultures, an unresolved question concerns their temporal specificity. Put simply, at what point, or over how long a period, does it take the values in new operational styles to become central to more enduring cultural traits?

One thing that is certain is that there is no single pace of change for the evolution of political cultures. The normal course of events can be disrupted and the pace of change heightened in a number of ways. Revolution aside, economic recession provides one notable prompt, although any major threat to system stability can have the same effect. At the national level, examples of such reorientations include the abandonment of *laissez-faire* by the US government in response to the economic depression in the 1930s, the emergence of fascism under Adolf Hitler at a time of high inflation and economic uncertainty in Germany, the acceptance of new public housing and welfare state programmes in Britain during the two world wars, and 1960s programmes for the poor as a US response to the civil rights movement and nationwide city rioting. Examples at the local level are less well known, but two instances are the assertion of business dominance in New York City after its fiscal collapse in 1975 (e.g. David and Kantor 1979), and the reorganisation of municipal government in Jacksonville after the near collapse of public services and revelations of official corruption (Harrigan 1976). More commonly, however, change occurs over a longer period. Even during eras of severe fiscal disorder, the norm is to resist major realignments in policies, favouring short-run expedients to maintain the sanctity of core values.[2] Outside such time-spans, change emphases are even more likely to be evolutionary rather than revolutionary, if only because the basic structural foundations of (national and) local societies are not subject to violent fluctuation. Yet the literature has not gone far in exploring relationships between political culture and social structure. Only in more recent neo-marxist formulations have these considerations been prevalent, and these fall short of a comprehensive account.

## CLASSIFICATORY THEMES

Amongst the various formulations that have been presented on local political cultures, perhaps the most well known in the USA is Banfield and Wilson's (1963) distinction between a public-regarding and a private-regarding ethos. The former of these is where policy-makers (and area residents in general) hold value dispositions that are conscious of the general community welfare. The latter is where the promotion of sectional interests have more pull. In terms of what distinguishes localities on these dimensions, Banfield and Wilson almost repeat the arguments of nineteenth century élites who fled the cities to avoid new immigrants. Then, private-regarding values were linked more to lower income, 'ethnic' populations, while public-regarding orientations were held to see most light in centres dominated by the middle classes and by white, Anglo-Saxon Protestants. The simplicity of this formulation has proved both alluring and troubling to political scientists. At one level, the emphasis on ethnicity is troubling because of its normative overtones. This formulation, at least by implication, suggests that public-regarding behaviour is superior, and so certain ethnic groups are more fit to govern. Based on nineteenth century US experiences, it could be argued that political machines were a manifestation of a private-regarding ethos. However, to transpose this into a typology of local political cultures is to mistake the appearance of local politics for its substance. As the last chapter identified, the impetus that stirred the propertied classes to set up new suburban authorities was intrinsically private-regarding; the emphasis on self led to a preference for flight rather than seeking reform. Moreover, empirical evidence shows that the imputed public-regarding values of the middle and upper classes are more myth than reality. Self-interest retains a strong place in the value dispositions of those of higher income (e.g. Hahn 1970; Hennessy 1970). The weakness of this formulation is its supreme simplicity. It is naïve to expect that cultural distinctions coalesce around two polar concepts. The implication is that the same population composition produces equivalent political cultures. This fails to grasp the complexity of the causal relationships involved. Local political cultures are descriptively and causally more varied than Banfield and Wilson (1963) suggest.

A more detailed formulation has been presented by Williams (1961), who identified four dispositions in local policy-making circles: the promotion of economic growth; an emphasis on providing life's amenities; favouring the maintenance of traditional services only; and the arbitration between competing interests. In deriving these four categories, all that Williams really offered was a summary of empirical studies; these were observed dissimilarities rather than a tabulation of underlying causes. This approach differs from that of Elazar, which starts from the identification of cultural traits within national political traditions and examines how these conflict, coalesce or exist side-by-side in localities (e.g. Elazar 1966). Unlike Williams, Elazar does not concentrate on actual behaviour but on the trace elements that combine to produce it. Hence, there is allowance for the differential opposition or reinforcement of cultural elements or even for their benign cohabitation. Yet, while providing a framework for more complexity, Elazar is akin to Williams in not theorising the causal nexus. What we are left with is the argument that dominant political values are made up of a combination of three main elements: the *individualistic*, wherein the governmental role is one of limited intervention, allowing private concerns primacy; the *moralistic*, in which there is a positive emphasis on benefits from political activity – this being an activity centred on promoting the public good; and the *traditional*, in which conceptions of the public good are based on the mores of the socio-economic élite, with government having a major role in preserving the existing social order. As with Banfield and Wilson (1963), Elazar saw values linked to immigration into localities. However, rather than assuming a static model, change and interaction are elements of his formulation. New immigrant groups brought a new 'layer' of values that were set on top of existing dispositions, interacting with and being moulded by them, so a unique outcome resulted.

These points are not very different from those made in recent neo-marxist writings on differentiation in local social structures. Massey (1984), for one, has used the same geological analogy as Elazar (1966) in accounting for local orientations. In contrasting the individualistic antagonism of Merseyside workers, with a long history of casual labour, with the organised discipline of workers in the coalmines of South Wales, Massey puts her hand on a key feature of neo-marxist accounts, which is the emphasis placed on social relations in the workplace. For instance, it is readily apparent that the constraints of little job choice, employer ownership of workers' homes, and the 'family' atmosphere of the workplace which is more easily engendered in small production units, has helped to sustain a 'deferential dialect' in social and political affairs within British regions which are dominated by farms with farm labourers (Newby 1977). In effect, the underlying argument is that capitalism, by its very nature, produces uneven development, which means that labour processes vary across space (and over time). Hence, conflict between capitalists and workers does not take a spatially even form. However, as Cooke (1985) emphasised, it is important not to conceptualise local cultural traits in unduly economic terms, since cultural forms can outlast the economic base which was critical to their formation. For instance, while support for separatist movements in Scotland and Wales appears to deny the importance of social class in electoral behaviour (pointing instead to the importance of community), in fact social class is influential but its effects coalesce with those of community values. Thus, in Scotland, at a constituency level, support for the Labour Party has a similar relationship to occupational structure as in England, but the Conservatives lose out by drawing the heat of long-standing anti-English sentiments (Ragin 1977).

The relationship between local cultures and actual political practices is a dynamic, changing one. Built on the base of particular social structures, political leaders can either intensify or dampen down trace elements in cultural forms. More than this, in so far as cultures are a 'web of significance', a field within which shared meaning is attached to action, an essential component of culture is a sense of belonging. Local political cultures are defined not simply by the actions of internal agents but also by reactions to external agents. Local cultures are not given but must be valued and nurtured (Cohen 1982). An example of this nurturing process is seen in the large-scale provision of subsidised public housing in some Labour controlled local authorities (the idea being to promote a culture of labourism; with the resistance of certain Conservative authorities to public housing being aligned with promoting a more private-regarding ethos; Young and Kramer 1978; Duncan and Goodwin 1988). The necessity of maintaining orientations is very evident from the dissipation of local radical upsurges. Thus, while the literature of the left is replete with references to Red Clydeside during the First World War, little Moscows and Poplarism in the 1920s, Clay Cross in 1972 and Sheffield in the 1980s, all of which are praised in glowing terms as bastions of working class radicalism and opposition to right-wing governments, the truth is that the radicalism of each has been short-lived. Indeed, as a long-term feature, there is little evidence of distinctive local political cultures in Britain (or the United States). Through their overly sentimental accounts, the left runs the risk of belittling the theoretical merits of local social processes. That the radicalism of such areas has been transitory, that many so-called radical areas have earlier or later been decidedly conservative (e.g. Baxter 1972), should emphasise the need for caution. The underlying social structure of a locality provides a framework which greases the path to particular value dispositions and specific political practices, but it is not a sufficient cause for giving them either a radical or a conservative tinge. As Macintyre (1980) found for the little Moscows, committed militants only ever made up a fraction of the population. 'Their influence stemmed from their ability to draw on the spirit of solidarity, the sense of concern that residents felt for each other, and the willingness to defend each other against external threat' (Macintyre 1980: 179). Each of these characteristics has a much wider geographical presence than the literature on radical local political movements suggests. As Urry (1986) detailed, for workers there are significant costs and restraints attached to organising for political action. Our understanding will not be furthered if we devote attention merely to the spectacular, to the detriment of the everyday. The crux of the everyday lies less in conditions provoking unique local responses, than in general processes at the heart of capitalism. It is because researchers like Elazar (1966) do not tie their conceptualisations to the character of the capitalist State that their formulations are inevitably arbitrary. Likewise, in so far as researchers on the left focus on radical localities they are in danger of producing accounts which are more significant for their ideological acceptance than for advancing theoretical debate. At the core of local political culture is a fundamental power relationship. Put simply: 'The power of capital exists without organisation, the power of labour *only* exists with organisation, but it is an organisation which is precariously established' (Urry 1986: 22).

## CAUSAL THEMES

In effect, the primary theme of this chapter is the transposing of social structure into local political practices. The detail of such practices must await the next chapter, so readers are cautioned to interpret what follows in terms of broad policy directions rather than specific policy outputs. That stipulation made, between social structure and political practice is room for slippage; knowing one tells us not about what the other is but about its potential for taking a particular form. This dissonance between culture and behaviour is well recognised in anthropology, as Cohen (1982) explained:

The view that any event or process or structure somehow replicates the essence of the society's culture is now, I think, properly discredited. We look instead at these phenomena as comments about the culture rather than being reduced to its basic 'logic'.

(Cohen 1982: 9)

Social structures demarcate prevailing power relationships in society but these must be reproduced constantly otherwise alternative forms will emerge. In terms of understanding the local political scene, the fact that local social structures are not the same as their national equivalents must be grasped, since this establishes a framework within which variability is more easily provoked. However, the scale of deviations around a central core is not so great; were it so, we would readily be able to identify distinctly local cultures. The character of long-term distinctiveness is not oriented around fundamental values but provides different interpretations on common themes. (When such divisions are critical, attempts at national dissolution are common; cf. the US Civil War, Biafra, the Austro-Hungarian Empire.) It follows that the first concern in identifying local political cultures is to evaluate how far they revolve around nationwide processes and in what ways they deviate from them.

**Unitary interests?**

A formulation that explicitly focuses on the systematic advantages that capital has over labour in guiding principles of local government action is Peterson's (1981) unitary model of local taxation and expenditure. In his style of presentation, Peterson does not emphasise the capital–labour connection, but its centrality is obvious. This is particularly so in his designation of the primary goal of city government which he sees as the promotion of economic growth. Although Peterson's account includes a heavy dose of prescription, with an accompanying parade of normative messages, these should not detract from the theoretical thrust of his ideas. In a research field criticised for weak explanations of differences in local government policies (e.g. Sharpe and Newton 1984; Hoggart 1986a), Peterson's account offers a coherent explanation for tax and policy differences. When trying to understand local political culture, this emphasis on taxation and expenditure might seem inappropriate. However, what the unitary model fashions is an explanation of why the philosophy of growth is so central to US municipalities (Molotch

1976). The key message is that while surface impressions suggest that policy is often driven by non-material concerns, structural restraints determine that councils cannot stray far from material concerns. Only if substantial resources can be derived from non-local sources are value dispositions likely to be different. Hence, with greater reliance on higher tier aid than in the USA, Peterson's model should be less applicable to Britain.

The central concept of the unitary model is that there is a single 'city interest', which is to preserve and enhance local revenue bases. In an account not dissimilar to marxist theorising on the State (e.g. Offe 1984), the unitary model emphasises that officials must maintain the confidence of capitalists and wealthy residents in order to retain a strong fiscal base. If policies threaten profits or offend higher paid residents, there is a risk of provoking outmigration by those with the greatest resources. This migratory potential is presumed to discipline councils. This occurs not simply in avoiding policies which are viewed negatively by these groups, but also requires that positive encouragement be given to investors. In effect, failure to be positive can cast the locality in the part of a bad business environment. Central to maintaining a favourable image are low tax rates. 'To protect a community's economic resources from net outward flow, tax rates must not be significantly greater in any one community than they are in competing areas' (Peterson 1981: 46). From this a crucial point follows:

> Because cities have limits, one explains urban public policy by looking at the place of the city in the larger socio-economic and political context. The place of the city within the larger political economy of the nation fundamentally affects the policy choices that a city makes.
>
> (Peterson 1981: 4)

In the unitary model account, the regional and the national arenas are so important that considerations specific to each locality play a slight part:

> A great deal can be said about local public policy without considering any variations in the recruitment of elected officials, the strength of political parties, the degree of organized group activity, or the level of turnout in local elections. Powerful forces external to the city carry weight in local policy-making.
>
> (Peterson 1981: 64)

As with Duncan and Goodwin's (1988) theoretical account, local political practices are taken to be unintelligible outside their place in a nation's evolving capitalist economy. This is a far cry from old-style community power investigations, which explained municipal policies in terms of intra-local power distributions (e.g. Dahl 1961).

The unitary model has implications similar to business-élite views on city government, but differs from them in placing more emphasis on structural limits. Within the unitary model account, the impetus for growth is not personal advancement but municipal survival: 'growth is less a desire of all local governments than a need created for them by constraints from increasingly complex structures of State and economy' (Gottdiener 1987: 94–5). Where municipalities draw mostly on local revenues, it matters not whether local power structures are élitist, pluralist or egalitarian, since structural dependence on propertied classes results in local policies favouring private profit. The decisive point, as Elkin (1987) identified, is that US municipal leaders feel obliged to consult property interests.

For councils themselves this has two major consequences. The first is that the tax rate becomes the centrepiece of municipal concern. Eyestone (1971) caught the flavour of this in his study of the San Francisco Bay Area:

> Councilmen [*sic*] seem to think of city finances largely in terms of the property tax. The tax rate they talk about is the property tax and the tax base they worry about is the amount of wealth subject to the local property tax. They constantly look for some way to broaden the tax base and to spread the tax burden around – preferably to property owners not likely to complain about 'confiscatory taxes'. The availability of other revenue sources does not lessen the councilmen's concern over their city's tax base, even though utilization of these sources may lower the extent of a city's actual dependence on the property tax.
>
> (Eyestone 1971: 69)

US municipalities are not alone in this regard. Even where higher tier grants lessen the weight of own-source funding, local taxation decisions occupy a prime place in policy deliberations. Villadsen's (1986: 43) observations on Denmark are typical, because many have reported that 'councillors are very sensitive to the level of local taxation; a fact that cannot be explained by a similar awareness amongst the public over the matter'. This particularly applies to Britain, where researchers have found no effective association between property tax rates and election results (e.g. Newton 1976b), yet where local policy-makers view rises in local taxation with some dread (e.g. Butterworth 1966; Committee of Inquiry into Local Government Finance 1976). This quest for low property taxes benefits the wealthy both directly and indirectly: directly, because they make the largest absolute payments, indirectly, because they gain most from having low taxes capitalised into the value of their homes (Yinger *et al*. 1988).

A further implication which directs the balance of benefits away from the less wealthy comes through municipal expenditure.[3] This emerges from the requirement that tax rates be kept low. As Peterson (1981) explained it, municipal expenditure falls into one of three main camps. *Distributive* policies are those which maintain the economic base of the locality. These include the provision of water and sewerage systems, the provision of adequate transport facilities and inducements to attract new investment.[4] For such expenditure, Peterson expected equal municipal commitments, since failure to perform in these fields can damage a locality's business climate. Thus, while evidence shows that tax rates and inducements to manufacturers have a negligible impact on industrial location decisions, municipalities continue to act as if they are influential for fear that they will be seen as bad business environments (Judd and Ready 1986). Precisely this created conflict between Mayor Kucinich and local capitalists in Cleveland, the ultimate consequence being a successful, concerted effort within business circles to remove the mayor from office (Swanstrom 1985; see also Saunders [1982a] on Melbourne, Australia). Compared with distributive policies, *allocational* policies have indirect effects. These are housekeeping functions, such as street maintenance, garbage collection and library services, which generally receive a neutral evaluation from capitalists since they are necessary but do not enhance profits. What makes for negative assessments are undue costs. Consequently, councils are pressured to be cost effective; hence, for allocational policies, inter-local expenditure differences are expected to be minor. This is far from the case for *redistributive* services (e.g. health facilities, public housing and welfare). These are oriented primarily at the poor, but to fund them taxes have to be raised on those in middle or upper income brackets. Hence, greater commitments to such provisions make a locality less attractive for higher income residents and businesses. Paradoxically, the more poor people in a locality, the less the council can afford to respond to their needs. Only the availability of outside funds provides an escape from this version of Catch-22. Where incomes are higher, and demand for redistributive services is less, such expenditure is supportable because the tax rate

is little affected. Unlike pluralist accounts which portray governments as responsive to the needs of citizens, the unitary model
posits that they cannot be responsive given pressures from
capitalists.[5]

The unitary model suggests that the pursuit of what Peterson
(1981) terms the 'city's interest' inevitably leads to uneven benefits
accruing to its population. How far officials can deviate from the
thrust of this central interest is a subject for empirical evaluation.
Most certainly, the neat uniformity in expenditure patterns that the
unitary model hypothesises does not hold up on empirical
evaluation (Hoggart 1989). As Mollenkopf (1981: 321) warns,
'nothing guarantees that either the laws of the market place or the
power of economic élites will successfully dominate society . . .
Politics . . . counts heavily and can be ignored only with peril by
those who are presently winning the game.' In essence, built around
a concern for the integrity of local revenue bases are other values.
These can be local or non-local in origin. For example, Great
Society programmes which channelled federal funds to cities in the
1960s and 1970s in the main were not an attempt to counteract
inequities of local fiscal circumstances, but 'to integrate black voters
into the Democratic party coalition by the development of place-
specific entitlements which could shore up as many Democratic
urban regimes as possible' (M.P. Smith 1988: 92–3; also Mollenkopf
1983). As seen when Ronald Reagan assumed the presidency, the
Republican response has been to dismantle federal urban programmes, so as to force cities to compete for market shares (as in
the unitary model). The applicability of the unitary model is thus
place and time specific. What is more, the structurally imposed
constraints which limit activities are not deterministically aligned
with single outcomes. Even assuming that profit alone were the
critical value, this could be promoted either by placing primary
emphasis on low taxes or else by underwriting private investment
intensively (Stone 1987). To understand local political cultures
requires appreciation of how essential capital–State relations
produce dissimilar local specifications. One reason for this is the
over-writing of basic capital–State relationships. This weakening of
unitary model impulses is readily evident in localities with strong
dependencies on other governmental agencies.

**Dependent localities**

Theoreticians examining determinants of local fiscal conditions in Britain require a different perspective from their US counterparts. Fundamentally, this is because battles fought over local practices have produced different outcomes in the two nations. Not that the underlying forces were particularly dissimilar. Where a difference existed was in their power structures. In the United States, values of individualism and the early utilisation of local government as a vehicle for personal economic advancement produced local units with weak fiscal ties to higher tier authorities. Here, a unitary model view was not only accepted but encouraged. In Britain quite different forces have been in operation.

*Westminster and its local dependencies*

With the landed aristocracy having a tight hold over much of the nation, the dynamism and flexibility that was apparent in land-use in North America was absent in Britain. Thus, in the nineteenth century, growth impulses in Britain were not built upon land-use issues, but came from manufacturing and commercial links with foreign markets. Pressure for public services to underwrite private sector expansion were not evenly felt. In cities, capitalists wanted local government to provide the services that they depended on (e.g. Hennock 1973; Fraser 1979). In the countryside, however, the aristocracy had no call for such endeavours; improved public facilities meant more taxes and this meant substantial costs for the landed classes (even given grotesque anomalies in tax systems; Ashford 1980). It is no surprise, therefore, that while property tax rates in cities doubled between 1873 and 1887, in rural areas they remained roughly the same. This snippet is a key to Ashford's (1980) instructive account of the early evolution of central government grants. The main causal impetus here was that industrial capital was not sufficiently powerful to out-gun landed interests. Yet with Britain's competitors catching up on the nation's manufacturing lead, parliamentary leaders were persuaded of the necessity for new services to help the competitive position of industry (as in the promotion of applied education through the opening of technical colleges). In the face of antipathy or even antagonism from the landed classes, grants encouraged local institutions to take on new responsibilities. Landed classes accepted this arrangement, since it enhanced local control but not local fiscal burdens. A similar outcome might have resulted had funding bases been more flexible, but Treasury disapproval scotched this prospect.

Over time, as councils were asked to take on more responsibility or as extra concessions were granted (such as the de-rating of industry in 1921 or domestic rate relief in 1966; Foster *et al.* 1980), the grant component of local revenue increased. In 1913, just 15 per cent of local expenses in England and Wales were covered by central government aid, by 1945 this had risen to 34 per cent, with a peak in 1975 at 51 per cent (Committee of Inquiry into Local Government Finance 1976; Figure 3.5).[6] Despite their importance as service providers, local authorities were not able to mount effective pressure to change their funding base. The élitism of the national political culture was visible in the centre's paternalistic relationship with its local charges. Localities were looked after because they were the work horses for national policies.

It might be expected that the compromise which manufacturing and landed élites carved out, and which the Conservative and Liberal parties implemented, would have been challenged by the emergence of the Labour Party. After all, the subjugation of the local to the national gave least authority to the arena in which Labour was strongest. What worked against this threat was a belief that the redistribution of societal benefits is best achieved through national control (hence from an early date Labour leaders subverted local interests in the national cause; e.g. Branson 1979). In reality, centralisation has served the partisan interests of all major parties (provided that they looked capable of forming a government). It follows that the main tones of local political cultures in Britain are not really local, but are stage managed from above. Local political traits are significant, but, compared with other nations, national influences have a strong guiding effect. This neutralising of territorial politics makes Britain unusual amongst the advanced economies (Ashford 1982):

> No modern government can exist without making spatial and locational decisions. What differentiates Britain from France, which also has a unitary system, is how easily national policy-makers can act without careful consultation with local government and how easily national objectives are imposed on this vast subnational structure.
>
> (Ashford 1981: 168)

Thus, accounts of English local government which tie local dissimilarities to processes of uneven development end up offering little insight on either, given the weight of national impositions (e.g. Duncan and Goodwin 1988). The centrality of the national core provides a small arena for genuinely local traits.

*Intergovernmental cities USA*

This is much less true in the United States. Certainly, there are localities with a heavy dependence on higher tier authorities but only a few have reached the level that is evident in Britain, and the time span over which dependency has been central is much shorter. Nevertheless, the emergence of 'intergovernmental cities', viz. those that are highly dependent on higher tier grants, has been an important feature of US political history in recent decades (Burchell *et al.* 1984). Two distinctive forces have brought these dependencies into being. The first arose from a crisis of confidence in the responsiveness of local agencies to social problems; the main manifestation of this came in the 1960s. The second was more limited in spatial extent, emerging as a response to the fiscal problems of some local institutions. These were seen in 1930s state aid programmes, which were something of a break from previous *laissez-faire* attitudes, and in the enhanced contributions that some states have made in reacting to local taxation restraints in the late 1970s. Neither of these periods produced a level of funding increase which was comparable with the 1960s (e.g. Figure 4.1). It was in this era that the phrase 'the intergovernmental city' was coined, because it was then that new municipal philosophies had their foundations laid.

Even so, the level of dependency justifying this label has been restricted in geographical extent. Prior to the 1972 introduction of revenue sharing, which allocated federal aid to all localities, around one-fifth of US cities received neither federal nor state assistance (Clark and Ferguson 1983). Revenue sharing did not lead to an increase in federal commitments, but pinpointed the peculiar character of higher tier dependence in the USA. For instance, prior to revenue sharing, few local grants were not tied to programmes requiring explicit higher tier approval (before 1972 over 90 per cent of grant aid was categorical; MacManus 1978).[7] Even today, categorical grants occupy a much more influential place in grant giving than in Britain. This means that most grants require matching funds from local councils, have restrictions on their use and, frequently, have detailed reporting requirements (Levine and Posner 1981).[8] Certainly, some councils shunt funds for one purpose

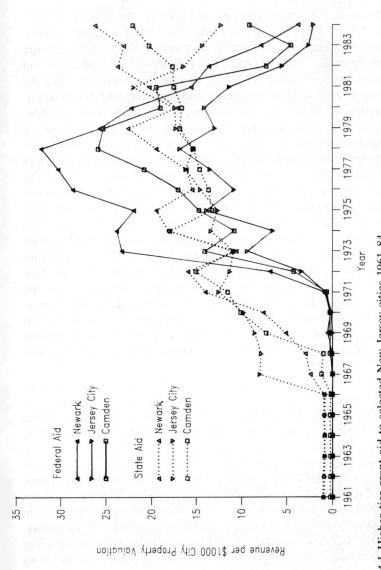

*Figure 4.1* Higher tier grant aid to selected New Jersey cities 1961–84
*Source:* calculated for Hoggart (1989)

into other expenditure categories, with state overseers turning a blind eye (e.g. Elazar 1970), but how common this practice may be is difficult to assess. Overall, categorical aid schemes enhance higher tier control.

The second theme in grant programmes is that they further the aims of higher tier authorities rather than being decided on local criteria. The infusion of state aid into local coffers after the passage of tax limitation measures such as Proposition 13 (California) and Proposition 2½ (Massachusetts), might seem to contradict this, but in both cases the state government did not support the restraint measures. Even for revenue sharing, where funds came without strings, there was a clear federal intention; namely, that of weakening Democratic control over localities by reducing the scope for grant manipulation by the Democratic controlled Congress (Mollenkopf 1983). An outcome of the tussle between leaders in the Democratic and Republican parties is the unreliability of higher tier awards. New grants often come with limited lifespans and are dependent upon the goodwill of Congress for their renewal. If the balance of party forces changes in Congress, programmes run a high risk of being terminated when up for renewal. Not surprisingly, many municipalities respond by limiting their reliance on higher tier offerings. For some, this has meant spending such gifts on frills alone. Thus, revenue sharing payments went into movable stands for Mile Hi Stadium in Denver, a coliseum (twice defeated in local referenda) for Baton Rouge, and new uniforms for the municipal band, along with an ice rink and bathhouse, in Burlington, Vermont (Stone *et al.* 1986). In more hard pressed fiscal environments such luxuries have been less evident. Poorer places rely on aid for their bread and butter (Fossett 1983); which has been problematical in the 1980s as federal funds have been cut and new grant programmes have had a weak redistributive thrust (Schneider and Logan 1985; Schneider 1986).

As for the consequences of grant provisions, two trends stand out. The first is that grant funding has a weak correlation with dissimilarities in local socio-economic conditions. In some instances this is explicit. For example, when grants to school districts have been paid on a per pupil basis; with revenue sharing likewise having a strong per capita element. In other instances it has come from the manipulation of programme rules and fund allocation criteria so as to benefit particular elected officials. This feature was readily apparent in the Model Cities Program, a 1960s scheme intended to coordinate federal aid and redistribute resources to the urban poor.

In their review of this programme, Frieden and Kaplan (1975) make a point with general relevance to much federal and state aid, which is that too many hands steer fund allocation. In this instance, trying to coordinate across numerous federal departments made matters worse, but the difficulties of assembling various congressional interests – all with different constituencies which wanted a cut – led to the dispersion of aid. The result was a weak link between money receipts and (initial) programme targets. However, while the federal system is open to severe criticism on this account, most researchers have found that federal aid is more redistributive than state assistance (MacManus 1978; Schneider 1986; Hoggart 1989). This does not get around a second major consequence of higher tier grants, which is the extra uncertainty that they introduce into local policy-making. This occurs from grant cuts and delays in receiving assistance. One example makes the point: in 'Southside' Rubin (1982) found that the Housing and Urban Development block grant for which the city applied in 1973 only arrived in 1976. Such delays not only disrupt policy implementation (especially if coordination across functions is necessary) but also have a psychological impact on local leaders.

This is the crux of the dependency phenomenon in local political cultures within the United States. In those localities which have long experienced high service demands on top of weak (or declining) tax bases, the infusion of substantial federal and state funds into local arenas has forged a new mentality in policy-making. Standing in a relatively weak position with regard to attracting private investment, such locations have built coalitions with higher tier officials in order to develop programmes and projects which help to stimulate their economies and fund their social programmes. With categorical aid holding a major place, one consequence has been the emergence of a professionalised bureaucracy intent upon extracting high levels of intergovernmental funding. One dimension to this has been the setting up of lobbying operations in Washington to appeal for resources for single cities or for groups of cities. Another has been the more prominent role of officials who are skilled at developing grant applications, responding to cues about likely future programmes and ferreting out new funding sources (Fossett 1983). To be successful at this game, prime-pumping resources are needed to get them started, as well as skilled personnel to see them through. On both counts, large cities have advantages over small ones. In many instances, of course, such cities also have severe needs which require attention. But the same is true of many small municipalities which lack the resources to collate substantial, ongoing responses to higher tier initiatives.

Adding a further dimension to local differentiation is race. The civil rights movement and the nationwide bout of city riots in the 1960s led to greater federal and state sensitivity to racial minorities. Many aid programmes were written specifically for minority populations, and black and hispanic mayors have been successful in increasing grant receipts from federal agencies (e.g. Karnig and Welch 1980). Consequently, higher tier dependencies have been more intense in localities with large non-white populations. The same places commonly have poor revenue bases (e.g. Burchell *et al.* 1984; Schneider and Logan 1985), so local leaders have had to become more outward looking than their contemporaries. Leads for action have not been dominated by local pressure groups, nor capitalists, although both can be important, but by higher tier authorities. The primary direction of change in local policies has been dictated by higher tier decisions. When budget cuts have had to be made, it has been programmes receiving most federal and state aid which have been protected (Levine and Posner 1981). Local priorities have thereby changed, much as it would be feasible to wean a vegetarian on to meat if no other food were available. In times of fiscal austerity, councils look to stretch resources as far as possible. This is more easily achieved if local reserves have to fund only part of the cost. What happens, therefore, if higher tier grants are cut?

### Dependency decline?

There is no doubt that over the last decade fiscal relationships between tiers of government have changed significantly on both sides of the Atlantic. Yet, as outlined in Chapter Two, the central features of these alterations have been different in each nation. In the United States, there has been an emphasis on withdrawal from local affairs, by the federal level at least, whereas Britain has seen more vigorous central intervention. In both cases the turn around came before the ascendancy of a new right leadership. In the United States, for example, 1978 was the peak year for federal grants to local and state authorities, since when there has been a downward trend (e.g. Figure 4.1). In Britain, it was the 1974–9 Labour government that first included local public expenditure in calculations for national economic management. The same government started the process of reducing central grants to local councils (e.g. Figure

3.5) and, as in the refusal to pay South Yorkshire's transport grant when it used local funds to subsidise services beyond Whitehall's wish, this government also initiated grant penalties for authorities not complying with its aims. The 1980s has seen an intensification of these processes. In effect, this has meant the entrenchment, or reinforcement is perhaps better, of dominant national power relations at the local level.

What Ronald Reagan offered intergovernmental cities was, as he would put it, a chance to stand on their own feet. Grants and regulatory practices would be cut, the recession would be left to run its course without a federal anti-recessionary response and tax reductions would encourage the private sector to raise investment. Cities in fact did better than many expected under this regime (Peterson 1986). Certainly, this was partly because states replaced federal programmes (e.g. Table 4.1). In addition, the economies of cities are less susceptible to economic fluctuations than non-metropolitan areas, so they did not suffer so badly from recession. Despite this, there were severe consequences for some places. Municipal grant receipts became more regressive (e.g. Schneider 1986), with the most substantial grant losses being suffered by those most dependent on federal largesse (Burchell *et al.* 1984). As Gormley and Eisenger (1988: 296) noted, despite all the rhetoric about returning authority to localities: 'What the White House thought best for private sector interests often took precedence over New Federalism principles of devolution.' And what the White

*Table 4.1* Replacement of human services block grants after federal cuts 1981–3

| Grant | Replacement in current dollars | | |
| --- | --- | --- | --- |
| | Full | Partial | None |
| Social services | 11 | 4 | 3 |
| Community services | 0 | 0 | 18 |
| Maternal and child care | 8 | 2 | 3 |
| Preventive health and health services | 9 | 1 | 3 |
| Alcohol, drug abuse and mental health | 12 | 2 | 0 |

*Notes*
(a) These figures are based on a sample of 18 states.
(b) Community services grants were for agencies outside the local government structure.

*Source*: adapted from Peterson (1986: 34)

House thought was best for the private sector was increased dependence by local institutions on private investment. However, compared with earlier decades, cities were better able to handle their new found 'freedom'. Primarily this was because the tone of private investment had changed. This shift in fashion had taken place on two fronts. On the one hand, inner cities had become profitable investment sites for new office developments and for middle to upper income housing; prestige was now attached to rejuvenating old dwellings and neighbourhoods for both offices and homes (Palen and London 1984; Smith and Williams 1986). Admittedly, this change in attitudes did not benefit all cities or all neighbourhoods, but the tone at least was set. On the other hand, through relationships built up over a number of decades – starting with urban renewal schemes and evolving through Model Cities and other economic development programmes – stronger frameworks for action had developed which linked the private sector to public institutions. In effect, local State institutions had become more central to the mediation of conflicts amongst capital and to the coordination of local capitalist interests (e.g. Bowman 1987; Doig 1987). What is more, even for intergovernmental cities, locations favourable for private sector investment, as with historical central cities, have been able to graft a broader niche for themselves by playing off the preservationist concerns of commercial gentrification interests (and in-migrant middle classes) against boosterist land development sentiments. Not too much should be made of this, however, since compromises are not that easy to maintain and the character of both the city and its particular neighbourhoods affects its government's options. Even so, the Reagan legacy has not brought a return to 1960s inner city gloom. All is not bright, and greater attention to private interests is pressing, but the scope for local action is less constrained than (say) 15 years ago.

In Britain exactly the opposite trend is evident. What the last decade and a half has seen is an intensification of national direction over local affairs. In scope these interventions have been wide ranging. Section 28 of the 1988 Local Government Act restrains local authorities from funding theatres, art galleries or libraries which, by government designation, are deemed to promote homosexuality. Since 1980, councils cannot hold on to the houses that they own, but must sell them at discount to sitting tenants (if the latter want or can afford to buy). Schools must now follow a curriculum set down in Whitehall. For many functions, private firms must be allowed to compete with local authority workforces for service contracts. As for finance, the list of central impositions is enormous. So too is the literature dealing with them. Readers can find ideological interpretations which praise them (Henney 1984) or damn them (Duncan and Goodwin 1988), legalistic accounts of their meaning (Loughlin 1986) and technical treatments of their fiscal significance (Travers 1986). The main points are well known.

Since 1979, in what so far appears to be an escalator of increasing central restrictions on local finance, councils have seen: the introduction of a new (block) grant allocation mechanism; reductions in grant levels; a move to tie more grant payments to programmes which the government prefers (Figure 4.2); a linking of grant aid to expenditure performance, so councils which spend more than an arbitrarily set figure lose grant; restrictions on councils calling on their own tax base, as in rate capping and stopping councils drawing funds from ratepayers during a financial year (i.e. levying a supplementary rate); and, in no sense making the list complete, more central direction in the fixing of fees for local services (as for council house rents). As the presenter of a vaudeville act would put it, all this and much, much more.[9] Aspects of this new legislation have had clear party political aims (as with hampering more left-wing councils; e.g. Grant 1986), yet the measures introduced have had nationwide, and often contradictory, impacts. Thus, in the calculation of grants, there are biases which in one guise give disproportionate funds to poor inner city (Labour) areas but in another take aid from these areas (Bramley 1984). The overall effect, as in the past, has seen an absence of overt political party direction to grant allocations (e.g. Bennett 1980; Hoggart 1986b). Far from making local fiscal environments simpler, and subject to less central overview, it has become more complex; 'the grant system is now a Heath-Robinson affair, so far removed from the simplicity and purity of the original block grant system' (Smith and Stewart 1985: 22). Local budgeting has become a more contorted and time consuming process, with far greater uncertainties and, as the government's own watchdog on local finances, the Audit Commission (1984), makes clear, much greater inefficiency owing to central interventions. It is hardly surprising therefore, that condemnation of the government's actions have a near universal appeal in local authority circles. The 1980 criticism of the new block grant by the chairperson of the Conservative controlled Association of County Councils was a portent to the future:

We are bitterly disappointed by the government's decision to reject our alternative to the block grant . . . The explanation for

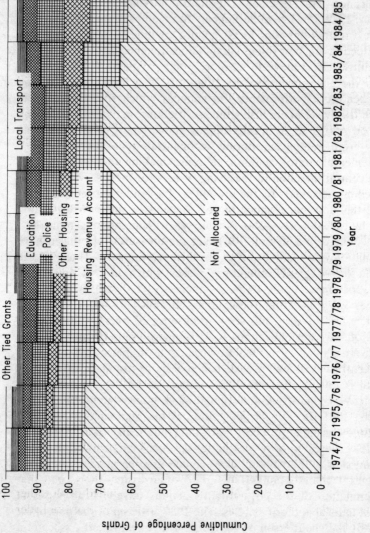

*Figure 4.2* Composition of local government grants: England and Wales 1974/5–84/5

*Source:* Central Statistical Office (1988) *Annual Abstract of Statistics 1988*, HMSO, London

the rejection of the Association's scheme is totally inadequate . . . the Secretary of State . . . gives a clear indication that the government is bent on achieving greater control over the actions of each and every individual local authority.

(from Travers 1986: 90)

Thus as early as 1980, there was disdain for local interests, even those of Conservatives. Later, this became the hallmark of the government's public image (as over the 1986 abolition of the metropolitan authorities). Local councils were to be subordinated to the central will. Change was not to loosen the reins of national direction but to tighten them. Uniformity of response, phrased differently, compliance with the government's dictate, was the new rule. Actuality has fallen well short of government intention.

In the main this is because local councils have been resilient in the face of central interventions. Most obviously this is seen in local authority expenditure not falling to government targets. Even with a contraction in councils' freedom of action, authorities have circumvented directives. Most notorious amongst the tactics employed has been creative accounting to make expenditure appear lower than it actually is. Illustrative of the principles involved is the scheme introduced by Leicester City Council to pay for the upgrading of houses suffering from cement cancer (Table 4.2). The central idea is that by paying for projects later and more slowly than normal, councils avoid expenditure limits in the immediate future and so do not lose grant income. P. Smith's (1988) analysis of such practices makes it clear that, under the convoluted system of financial targets, rate caps and grant reductions, it is economically rational for councils to act in this way; the marginal savings that accrue from efficiency savings are a pittance compared with grant gains (or losses) resulting from creative accounting. How extensive such practices are is difficult to assess, but one indication of their importance has been given by the government appointed Audit Commission, which placed a figure of over £1,000 million on 1987 creative accounting commitments in London alone (Travers 1988). Not surprisingly, the government moved to abolish this practice (in March 1988), but local authorities have responded with other ingenious devices such as swapping interest rates on loans in order to keep formal spending down.

Avoidance of central direction, in the face of strenuous efforts to impose uniformity, has occurred on a wide spectrum. Financial issues alone are not at the heart of this friction. Deeper political

*Table 4.2* Annual cost of a deferred purchase scheme in Leicester (£ Million)

| Year | Deferred payment scheme | Normal scheme |
|------|------|------|
| 1986/87 |  | 4.5 |
| 1987/88 | 0.6 | 5.3 |
| 1988/89 | 1.7 | 5.4 |
| 1989/90 | 2.8 | 5.3 |
| 1990/91 | 3.8 | 5.1 |
| 1991/92 | 4.9 | 2.7 |
| 1992/93 | 5.7 | 0.2 |
| 1993/94 | 6.0 |  |
| 1994/95 | 6.0 |  |
| 1995/96 | 6.0 |  |
| 1996/97 | 4.8 |  |
| 1997/98 | 3.7 |  |
| 1998/99 | 2.6 |  |
| 1999/00 | 1.6 |  |
| 2000/01 | 0.5 |  |
| Total | 50.7 | 28.5 |

*Source*: Stoker (1988: 167)

values are at stake. Over the government's encouragement of the privatisation of local public services, for example, councils have shown ingenuity in resisting central wishes: as in writing tight conditions for service contracts, with private firms taking fright over specifications on work conditions, rigorous insurance precautions and service quality guarantees (Ascher 1987).[10] In a war of political values, both sides can play 'dirty', and, on the government's part, caution has been required in responding to such reactions (note the time it took for creative accounting to be banned). Central authorities depend upon local councils, since local authority workforces provide services which national authorities consider desirable. This gives local councils significant power. 'Above all, central government cannot force local councils to do something *well*' (Dunleavy and Rhodes 1983: 115). Consequently councils must be encouraged to follow central wishes. When rigid adherence to central dictate is called for, this must be dressed up in a guise that sits on a higher plane than government wishes alone. Obviously, shared political ideology helps some councillors accept government messages more than others and recourse to noting that the government has an electoral mandate for its legislation helps to win over others who question a new proposal. However, as in the 1980s, when local leaders are not convinced of the legitimacy of the government's actions, have doubts about its practicability, and are certain of its political party objectives, willingness to comply lessens sharply. This does not mean that overt conflict erupts, since quiet resistance, when multiplied over numerous localities, can be as disruptive to central aims as outright refusal. Further, such covert actions are more difficult to detect and provide fewer justifications for harsh central interventions (they do not comprise absolute refusals, merely differences in 'interpretation', so strong central actions are more easily castigated as infringements on local autonomy). If the centre wishes to see its directives operationalised in an efficient way, it must seek the willing compliance of local leaders, not their enforced adherence. The restraining effect that this has on central actions possibly has not been given sufficient attention.[11] In the 1980s, for example, despite all the vitriol and charges of oppression and non-compliance, and in spite of assertions about convictionism, central–local conflicts are aptly summarised by one senior local authority officer in terms of a 'dishonourable draw' (Travers 1986: 145).

Where dominant themes in British local political cultures have changed in the last decade is in a growing sense of disenchantment with and distrust of central authorities. As Loughlin (1986) pointed out, the British central–local relationship is not grounded in legal document but in administrative practice. The law is ill-suited for keeping a check on local authority compliance with central wishes, in the same way that it offers little legal assistance to local councils who wish to avoid punitive national legislation. The system has evolved around the cooperation of 'chaps' (Bulpitt 1983); a fact long recognised in texts which characterise the British central–local relationship in terms of consultation, compromise and partnership. What the 1980s has seen is a breakdown in that relationship. It is not simply that central–local conflicts have erupted, as these have always occurred in one form or another. Rather, what has emerged is the sense that local institutions are less worthy; no longer partners of national government but its servants. Catching the headlines in the media, and dominant in some academic commentaries on central–local affairs, has been the antagonism of new left councils and the new right leadership in Westminster. This has been important, because these councils challenge the government by not complying with its wishes quietly and quickly.[12] Indeed, such councils have come to occupy a place in central–local affairs out of proportion to their real significance. Often legislation has been drafted to control the actions of these few institutions (e.g. rate capping and the 1986 metropolitan county abolitions). In some measure this has been intentional on the government's part. Through recourse to populist appeals about 'militant marxists' and 'the loony left,' attention has been diverted from broad inroads made into local autonomy.[13] Yet the policies of new left councils have hardly been radical. They would not appear out of place in a listing of US city policies. Special aid for women and homosexuals is part and parcel of numerous aid programmes (albeit not in every city, but then neither is it in Britain). Stipulations about employment practices in private firms obtaining municipal contracts is also common (as in regulations governing minority employment and work conditions). Paying special attention to the housing needs of low income people, and regulating assertive, profit-centred capitalist behaviour, also make a mark in the USA without highly emotive outbursts from national politicians (for examples see Clavel 1986).[14]

In justifying its inroads into local autonomy, the government has appealed to the conservative instincts of local activists in its own party. But when the rhetoric is put aside and the harsh reality of the policies has become evident, discomfort has resulted. After all, Conservative councils pride themselves on their 'economy', on the efficiency of their guardianship of ratepayers' money. Yet their own leaders were informing them that they were not efficient enough and had to make more cuts, that they should privatise services because this would increase efficiency, and that their running of schools and public housing was suspect, and so ratepayers should have the right to control them (with direct lines to Whitehall). It matters little that the justification for all this was dressed up as red-bashing: Conservative councils suffered along with those of the left. They lost public housing which they did not want to see go.[15] They had to cut expenditure so that they did not lose grant, although they believed that they already operated at the bone. The centralisation of authority in Britain since the mid-1970s has been achieved at the expense of fracturing the partnership between central and local authorities. Resisting central impositions, no matter whether done quietly or publicly, has become acceptable. Councils might toe the line on legislative requirements but they do so with less willingness than in the past. As in the United States, the reassertion of 'traditional values' has opened doors through which local leaders have been motivated to emphasise core values in local political cultures in defiance of the nationwide pull of materialist themes.

## DEVIATIONS ON THEMES

Additional to central materialist themes in local political cultures are a number of sub-plots. About these, researchers know much less than they would like, in spite of the long tradition of community studies. We know too little about how local political differentiations emerge and how they are sustained. It is not that empirical material is missing, but that theoretical conceptualisation is weak. Many community studies have investigated sites as if they were isolated from mainstream processes. Others have concentrated on those processes to the detriment of specifying the local political character. What we are left with is an array of empirical observations, but of uncertain comparability. One is not sure if similarity of observations emerges from the same causal processes or coincidence of empirical manifestation. At this stage, then, it is necessary to proceed with caution. That being stated, it is possible to identify with certainty some deviations around national themes (albeit we cannot be sure what produces these local themes).

In good part, local political cultures are materialistic in that their critical features relate to the distribution of society's costs and benefits. However, we cannot read political cultures from economic conditions. Even less can we assume that economic circumstances decide a council's prevailing operational style. This point has already been made, some might say with a vengeance, but its importance is such that it is worth restating, even at the risk of boring the reader. Put simply, faced with the same fiscal and service demands, in situations where there is communality in political culture, councils can have quite different operational styles. Political cultures – the frames of reference that give meaning to and place value on modes of behaviour – are linked to different operational styles, since these styles are subject to short-term variation when compared with cultural traits. They are grounded in a prevailing ethos which specifies acceptable behaviour patterns, but does not dot each 'i' nor cross each 't', so there is variability in translation processes. Hence, political cultures need not be immediately apparent in behaviour patterns. Operational styles are anchored to political cultures but they slide over them in manner that, at least potentially, varies between localities and changes over time.

Although the manner in which operational styles play out in

practice is a matter for the next chapter, it is pertinent to emphasise the point here that behaviour is not a mere reflection of structure (Cohen 1982). In terms of the economic structure–political culture relationship, this is partly because core values in political cultures are not simply economic. Maslow's (1970) suggestion that people have a hierarchy of needs to be satisfied provides a useful framework in which to analyse this. At the most basic level Maslow sees material needs. Without food, clothing and shelter, the satisfaction of other needs would be futile. Feelings of belonging, love, security and self-respect are all important personal needs, but they are subsidiary to the body's basic requirements for survival. Once these material conditions are satisfied, however, there is scope for other needs to attain importance. Of course, people differ with regard to when they believe such needs are satisfied; hence the drive for more material possessions is not uniform. What is more, when food and shelter needs are satisfied (in the sense that the search to enhance standing on them ceases), they are not supplanted as prime concerns; only in rare circumstances do threats to material standing not strike at the heart of core values. Yet people can act as if material interests were insignificant; for example, when there is confidence in the continuing existence of material support, and so possible loss is not considered, the driving force of behaviour might have little connection with materialism. In such circumstances other values come to the fore. In the context of local political cultures, the focal point around which these other interests are centred is that of community. Built into ideas of community are positive and negative implications. The cause of community is advanced on the positive grounds that it strengthens friendship, a sense of belonging, mutual support and socialisation. However, it can be a screen behind which forces of status discrimination, racism and sexism are given full throttle. As with individuals, the personality of localities reflects a balance between materialism and other (community) values. Like individuals, situations can be observed where materialism seems muted in personality traits. At both levels, surface impressions should not detract from the fundamental role of material concerns. To understand political cultures, however, both material and community interests must be central to explanatory modes.

The central emphasis on materialism given above might appear to orient explanations towards neo-marxism. However, as Mollenkopf (1981) explained, such accounts tend to be stilted and myopic because they fail to breathe the life of community into their explanations:

because Marxian theories stress the system of accumulation to the exclusion of community formation, they lack an adequate vocabulary for analyzing politics. Class analysis reveals much about the underlying distribution of interests within society but politics has a frustrating way of not responding with underlying interests . . . [local government] is suspended between community and accumulation.

(Mollenkopf 1981: 321)

This is apparent in the character of small suburban municipalities in the USA. Suburbanisation has been played out in a chamber marked capital accumulation, in which the bulk of suburban residents have had to choose between options decided for them (Walker 1981). Yet, through controlling municipal units, residents have promoted differentiation by adopting dissimilar land-use zoning stipulations. In laying down regulations about the height of buildings, the number of bedrooms in apartments,[16] and minimum lot sizes, councils influence the future character of their locality. This is not the central determinant of house price variation, because the operations of the land market and of residential developers set the framework for this (Windsor 1979), but nevertheless it is an important aspect of municipal life. Once settled with (say) high income professionals, localities might choose not to compete for outside investors in the manner that Peterson (1981) described. Provision of amenities could become the *raison d'être* of such a locality (Williams 1961). Hence, 'community' would be at the core of municipal behaviour, even though community effects would ride on the back of accumulation processes.

Acknowledging the role of community moves us in the right direction but does not take us far enough. Additional to accumulation and community, though operating not alongside but inside and across these two, are differences in local orientation. Put simply, there are differences in what householders perceive to be their community, just as there is no uniformity in how central a locality is to the profits of capitalist enterprises. Within any locality some look inward more than others. This has been recognised for a long time in the political science literature, although it has been slow to permeate into theory. Dye (1963) is one who long ago examined the extent of localist and cosmopolitan orientations with regard to municipal leaders and their constituents (concluding that leaders were more localist than their constituents once social status was taken into account). For economic enterprises, the political importance of spatial frames of reference was also recognised early. As in studies by Schulze (1958) and Mott (1970), evidence has long shown that when dominant employers are absentee-owned there is a loosening of local power structures, leading to more variety in access to positions of authority and in channels of municipal influence.[17] What should be understood therefore are the different styles of local dependence of householders and capitalists (Cox and Mair 1988), as well as how these evolve from structures of accumulation. What is evident today might not have been what established the central concerns of municipal institutions.

What follows in the rest of this section is an attempt to pinpoint some of the dissimilar outcomes which emerge when forces of accumulation and community combine. In no sense is it suggested that the treatment offered here is comprehensive. This comment applies not only to the categories of local political culture that are specified but also to the treatment of causal forces. We know too little about the forms and implications of cosmopolitan and local orientations in order to make this central to the discussion that follows. Some suggestions can and will be made, but only skin and bones are offered. This also applies to the temporal dimension of cultural traits, to how long it takes for a change in basic political values to occur. What can be stated is that recent theorising on the State does give guidance on the primary forces at work in deciding primary political values (Offe 1984; Block 1987). The importance of capital–labour relationships has already been noted by way of reference to accumulation processes. Stated in a more general vocabulary, the role of civil society has also been specified in the context of the values of community formation and maintenance. What has to be added to these is the impact of the State itself, since the political character of capitalist societies is decided by the relationships and compromises associated with all three sets of processes. Political cultures offer different visions on the acceptability of behaviour. These visions place dissimilar emphases on the centrality of accumulation, civil society and the State. Even granted the same emphasis, differences emerge in the weight that is placed on aspects of each. The sections below specify how these various forces intersect and unfold to produce dissimilar logics for local action.

## Boosterism

Boosterism is the closest political culture to a pure, unitary model (Peterson 1981). Cities with boosterist mentalities are most active in subjugating the interests of community – as expressed, for example, in householder attachment to neighbourhood – in order to promote the advancement of economic expansion. Perhaps the most visible expressions of boosterist sentiments in US city government occurred during the nineteenth century (literally across the nation), with many southern and western localities offering modern-day equivalents. Most important to the development of this sentiment is the entrenchment of business leaders, with strong local roots, at the local power apex. Their preference for growth related policies is easy to appreciate:

> Boosterism is primarily an ideology of businessmen [*sic*] oriented toward the local market and its basic urge is toward rapid population growth – more illness for the doctor, more litigation for the lawyer, more policies for the insurance agent, more customers for the retailer, more sodas from the soft drink bottler, and more subscribers and advertisers for the daily paper.
>
> (Abbott 1987: 144)

Conceptualising the impact of such sentiments on the political ethos, analysts have emphasised the centrality of land-use issues (e.g. Molotch 1976; Domhoff 1986; Dye 1986b). It is the intensification of land-use that brings more customers, higher rents and greater land sale prices. Where boosterist urges differ from Peterson's (1981) unitary model is in the manipulation of governmental channels for personal gain rather than simply to maintain the sanctity of the municipal revenue base:

> Because so many specific government decisions can affect land values and growth potentialities, leaders of the growth machine are prime participants in local government. Their involvement is even greater than that of corporate capitalists at the national level, where the power élite can rely to some extent on such 'signals' as stock prices, interest rates, and the level of new investments to tell government officials what they think of current policies.
>
> (Domhoff 1986: 62)

A hands-on approach in boosterist regimes finds expression in a variety of private–public cooperations (such as economic development councils) which make the division line between government and business hard to detect (e.g. Bowman 1987). Central to the emergence and continued operations of such growth machines is the dependence of capitalists on a locality (Molotch

1976; Cox and Mair 1988). Since this dependence need not come simply from income reliance, changes to more absentee-ownership need not weaken the impetus of boosterist sentiments. Even multinational corporations with global strategies for profit-making can possess strong local ties, perhaps owing to the special skills of the local labour force. Extra-locally oriented companies can gain substantially from pro-growth sentiments because a pro-capital orientation justifies weakening labour organisations, lowering welfare commitments and improving infrastructure for business.

Contradicting the accumulation values that capitalists attach to land-use are use values which families place on it (i.e. community dimensions). As is now well established, urban renewal and highway construction take a heavy toll on vibrant urban neighbourhoods (e.g. Gans 1962; Dunleavy 1981). Partly in response to such devastations (aided by their spread into more middle class areas), strong sentiments favouring neighbourhood survival have gained momentum in the United States (and, less spectacularly, in Britain). This assertion of use values has challenged the primacy of boosterism in some places. However, one crux of local political cultures is the sense of belonging to a locality; people must identify with the sentiments that its core values embody. Part and parcel of such feelings is the belief that these values are worthy. Such assessments emerge from internal circumstances (e.g. a belief amongst the populace that growth brings jobs for them, a view which is promoted by the media granted the benefits from growth that accrue to newspaper, radio and television companies; Logan and Molotch 1987). Additionally, it can come from area residents' impressions of where their locality stands in the national political economy. This helps to explain the perseverance of boosterist sentiments in southern states, given a long history of North–South division, a long-standing desire amongst southerners to assert their merits over the North and, in more recent years, the boost to self-image which comes from economically out-performing northern states. Even within the South, however, changes in sentiment are in evidence. In Atlanta, for example, Stone (1976) found an assertion of neighbourhood use values that directly conflicted with the merits of accumulation. The force of these sentiments led political leaders to draw in their boosterist horns somewhat. The promotion of land-use intensification and growth became less overt and the tactics employed to further these aims were more inclined to wear down the opposition than face it head on:

Politics usually result . . . not from a few key decisions but rather from a series of decisions, many of which appear to be unimportant when viewed singly. Policies are complex phenomena, and the ways in which they come to take shape are intricate. Decisions at one stage may be negated by the absence of follow-through actions at a subsequent stage. Conversely, proposals rejected at one point may be revived, altered, or even replaced by substitute proposals that still enable objectives to be realized. Policy success, then, is rarely a matter of winning spectacular battles. Rather, it is more akin to prevailing in a war of attrition. Cumulative results give shape to policies.

(Stone 1976: 14)

Given the earlier dominance of pro-growth sentiments in this city (Hunter 1953), one can speculate whether their more muted expression in recent years has been influenced by changed self-images. No doubt the civil rights movement and environmentalism have been effective here, if only through changing national legislation and so expectations. However, it is possible that the greater importance of Atlanta in national affairs has altered residents expectations about what is desirable for their city (viz. the feeling that the city has now 'made it' could provide a context in which more sophisticated urban policies are given higher priority, with 'humane' living environments consequently being given greater value). Most certainly, while accumulation is still central to Atlanta's policy dispositions, it no longer carries the force of earlier years. Its enactment must now be achieved more covertly; one symbol of the changing character of broadly accepted values within the city.

## Paternalism

Two factors distinguish localities with boosterist and paternalist political cultures. First, embodied within paternalism is a less consistent attitude towards economic growth; this even extends to an anti-growth philosophy. Second, under paternalistic political cultures the local élite is more overt. Different élite forms do exist under paternalist structures, but, like boosterism, the central focus for political values is the economy.

Two main types of paternalist regime can be recognised – those that are status based and those based on employment. The former is most commonly associated with rural areas, more particularly in

Europe. Here, through labourers' accumulated dependencies for work and housing, a deferential dialect emerges which gives large landowners a favoured, unquestioned place of superiority in social and political standings (Newby 1977). In earlier decades, such attitudes were stronger and more national in scope. Robert Roberts (1971) paints the scene aptly when describing life in Salford at the turn of the century:

> The overwhelming majority of unskilled workers remained politically illiterate still. The less they had to conserve the more conservative in spirit they showed themselves. Wages paid and hours worked might spark off discussion at the pub and street corner, but such things were often talked of like the seasons – as if no one could expect to have any influence on their vagaries. Many were genuinely grateful to an employer for being kind enough to use their services at all. Voting Conservative, they felt at one with him [*sic*]. It was their belief, widely expressed at election times, that the middle and upper classes with their better intelligence and education had a natural right to think and act on behalf of the rest, a right that one should not even question.
>
> (Roberts 1971: 167)

In British cities such sentiments broke down with the emergence of the Labour Party and the adoption of policies by the Conservative and Liberal parties which did not find working class support (e.g. Savage 1987). In rural areas their trajectory followed a more gentle downward path, as landed élites had a tighter grip on employment and housing opportunities. Up to the reorganisation of local government in 1974, when smaller towns were integrated with country areas, it was not uncommon to find reports, such as that by Dyer (1978) on Kincardineshire, which equated rural council deliberations with a gentleman's club discussing county affairs. In various county councils, the aristocracy held authority until late into the twentieth century (Table 4.3). In such regimes, preservation of the status quo is at the forefront of political tradition. These places are not the same as the caretaker governments that North American analysts have identified (e.g. Williams 1961; Stone 1987). The latter do not result from tight control by a small élite, but from the combination of little prospect of economic growth, dominance by small scale producers in competitive market sectors who want low taxes, and, consequent upon these, an espousal of the merits of community and self-reliance (Vidich and Bensman 1968). In policy terms, similar packages might result from these regimes, but their

*Table 4.3* 'Establishment' representation on English county councils

| | | Percentage of councillors with listed attributes | | | |
| | | *Dorset* | *Durham* | *Hampshire* | *Suffolk* |
|---|---|---|---|---|---|
| 'Lords' | 1973 | 3.1 | 0.0 | 8.5 | 3.1 |
| | 1988 | 1.3 | 0.0 | 0.0 | 1.3 |
| Knights | 1973 | 3.1 | 0.0 | 4.3 | 1.2 |
| | 1988 | 1.3 | 0.0 | 0.0 | 1.3 |
| DL | 1973 | 4.2 | 1.0 | 1.1 | 5.5 |
| | 1988 | 1.3 | 0.0 | 0.0 | 2.5 |
| Military | 1973 | 16.5 | 0.0 | 23.4 | 12.9 |
| | 1988 | 7.8 | 0.0 | 3.9 | 2.5 |
| JP | 1973 | 7.2 | 12.5 | 0.0 | 4.3 |
| | 1988 | 0.0 | 0.0 | 1.0 | 3.8 |
| OBE | 1973 | 4.2 | 1.0 | 5.3 | 4.3 |
| | 1988 | 1.3 | 0.0 | 1.0 | 0.0 |
| MBE | 1973 | 2.1 | 3.8 | 5.3 | 0.6 |
| | 1988 | 3.9 | 1.4 | 0.0 | 1.3 |
| CBE | 1973 | 7.2 | 1.0 | 4.3 | 3.1 |
| | 1988 | 1.3 | 0.0 | 2.9 | 0.0 |
| KBE | 1973 | 0.0 | 0.0 | 1.1 | 0.6 |
| | 1988 | 0.0 | 0.0 | 0.0 | 0.0 |

*Notes*
(a) 'Lords' includes Lords, Ladies, Baronets, Dukes and Earls.
(b) DL refers to Deputy Lieutenants.
(c) Military refers to a rank equivalent to army captain or above.
(d) JP refers to Justices of the Peace.
(e) OBE refers to Officers of the Order of the British Empire.
(f) MBE refers to Members of the Order of the British Empire.
(g) CBE refers to Commanders of the British Empire.
(h) KBE refers to Knight Commanders of the British Empire.
(i) For 1973, aldermen were assumed to be equivalent to councillors.
(j) For 1973, Suffolk means East Suffolk and West Suffolk combined.
(k) These percentages cannot be added to give a county total since people could have more than one of the attributes listed.

*Source*: Municipal Journal Ltd, *The Municipal Journal*, London (annual)

rationale is not the same, even if both are grounded in the realities of their respective economic positions.

This last point also applies to corporate paternalism. The most obvious instances of this are found in single industry towns. Most especially in isolated places, where opportunities for alternative employment are slight, corporations have dominated workers' lives through the provision of employment, company housing, company shops, company health care and company based social and recreational facilities (e.g. Lucas 1971; Gaventa 1980). Even when labour unrest has been significant, over time these relationships are capable of producing a political culture in which the hearts and minds of the populace are the company's (e.g. Gaventa 1980). In such instances corporate paternalism is little different from status based systems. However, other kinds of corporate domination are different, being more accurately conceptualised as keynotes in operational styles rather than local political cultures. Obvious examples include US Steel (now USX) in Gary, Indiana (e.g. Crenson 1971; Greer 1979) and DuPont in Delaware (Phelan and Pozen 1973). Here acceptance of company domination is not accepted as a right. On the contrary, there can be strong opposition to the company. Yet the realities of the situation, the major effect that the company has on area fortunes (e.g. by shedding jobs), and the favourable legislative provisions that it builds up over time,[18] mean that the prime value in local policy-making is what the corporation allows. Under such circumstances growth need not be a critical feature of the operational *modus vivendi*. On the contrary, growth might threaten existing power relations by introducing new economic interests. This fear also applies to places with cohesive, paternalistically inclined élites. Immediately after World War Two, for example:

> The central goal of Denver's dominant élite was the preservation of wealth earned in previous decades and of the comfortable life that it supported. They found nothing wrong with increases in white-collar government jobs, expanding tourism, or the export of raw materials to eastern producers. They balked at the growth of manufacturing because they feared environmental pollution, the possibility of strong labour unions, and the growth of economic interests independent of their own control.
>
> (Abbott 1987: 127)

Under a paternalistic power structure, growth might not be a central value. Maintenance of power and social standings, with a concomitant emphasis on people knowing their place, can be more highly prized (albeit economic rewards usually follow from these two conditions).

## Radicalism

As earlier comments in this chapter indicated, identifying truly radical political cultures is not easy. Spurts of radical sentiment have often been transitory, leaving the impression that favourable conditions for radical sentiments can exist without their being touched off. Some writers on the left are keen to pinpoint radical political actions, but whether or not these emerge from 'radical' social backgrounds is far from clear. The recent extolling of the radical heritage of Sheffield is a case in point, since over a longer time period this city's council has rarely been touched by radical tinges (Hampton 1970). Moreover, many instances of municipal radicalism cannot be traced to social structures. The 1981–6 Greater London Council is an obvious example, as its leaders worked for their party's dominance rather than drawing on a strong community base (Livingstone 1987). This is not a new pattern; the red islands of communist support in Britain in the inter-war years were also fortuitous combinations of popular leaders emerging at times of resistance to higher authorities (Macintyre 1980). Often what has been radical about such localities is little more that the political stance of their leaders. Numerous examples can be found in the existence of socialist controlled cities in the USA (Stave 1975). As with the more recent expansion of communist control in Italian cities, what distinguished such political groups was not their political philosophy but a commitment to efficient government and antagonism to corruption. Perhaps compared with US city practices of the time and with Italy's Christian Democrat Party such promises are indeed radical, but this does not merit labelling this a radical political culture.

In capitalist polities, radical governments are not likely to survive in the long term. The abolition of the GLC is not the first case of a higher tier government using the death sentence to quieten a local operation which challenged national political traditions (for example, the termination of poor law guardianship in 1929 was aimed at closing radical units like Poplar). If a locality were truly radical then the local economy would likely nose-dive or, if success were attained through municipalisation, national authorities would stamp it out lest its example was catching. The radical Labour councils that we see in Britain today cause a short-term threat to the Thatcher government, but this is more through rhetoric than action (in challenging governmental assumptions and explanations). Their policy impact has been far from radical, since constraints on local government action preclude a major deviation from national norms. That this is appreciated by politicians from the new left is signified in the title of Ken Livingstone's (1987) book about his local government experiences: *If Voting Changed Anything, They'd Abolish It.*

Radical cultural traits are more inclined to be potential than actual at any time. What distinguishes such places politically is that they do have outbursts, perhaps sustained for quite a few years, of a political activism which draws on deep-seated oppositional values (e.g. Macintyre 1980). The picture is complex, because radical sentiments can emerge around recent entrants onto the political stage (e.g. racism, feminism and gay rights). The position these hold in radical thought and action is still poorly developed theoretically. Where theoretical attention has been directed is towards links between social structure and radical politics. In Urry's (1986) formulation, five conditions ease the emergence of such activism: (1) the existence of spatially specific collectivities in which shared experiences of work and home are facilitated by residential propinquity; (2) the ability to portray group experiences as representative of a whole social group; (3) the organisation of collectivities outside work and government which reinforce social divisions; (4) a belief that gains are only – or largely – available through collective action; and (5) a substantial proportion of the population holding that collective action is worth pursuing and can be successful.[19] In combination these are difficult stipulations to meet. What is more, their existence does not lead to radicalism *per se* (as for urban political machines in the USA). Hence, for a social movement to be radical, in addition to these stipulations there should be a conscious antagonism to prevailing values in society (i.e. not simply a desire for greater shares from the existing order, but a search for a new social order). All in all, it is no surprise that radical working class collective actions which are community based have been most prevalent in locations dominated by a single occupational groups in which intense capital–labour conflict has a long history (e.g. mining towns). The mere existence of such locally dominant groups is not enough, since relationships with employers can promote class action or (as under paternalistic structures) retard it (e.g. Gaventa 1980). The veracity of this point should be obvious to those who noted the different responses of people in Nottinghamshire and South Yorkshire to the 1984–5 British miners' strike (Rees 1986).

## Consumerism

More than the other political cultures examined here, the underlying philosophy of consumerism is community centred. This ethos is most likely to be present when the dictates of profit-making and wage determination are rarely felt within the political realm. Hence, it is in residential zones with slight or non-existent local work dependencies that consumerism finds strong expression. The term consumerism should not be taken to mean rampant acquisitiveness. Instead, it refers to an emphasis on use values rather than materialism. Of course the two are not mutually exclusive. Building up a good stock of community services and helping to maintain the attractiveness of a local environment can do wonders for property values (Yinger *et al.* 1988), as most home owners are well aware. However, the ethos directing policy selections need not be property gain *per se*. Consider, for example, retirement communities where residents are primarily seeking a pleasant living environment. The aim is the provision of life's amenities not economics. Yet it is because the inhabitants in such places are economically secure that other values more easily come to the fore.

What should be noted is that larger municipal units are less likely to be dominated by consumerism alone. This is because size increases the chances of the existence of competing interests. For example, in the opposition of the London Borough of Bromley to the construction of public housing, the council's justification is given largely in terms of community (Young and Kramer 1978; Glassberg 1981). Despite the borough having approximately a quarter of a million inhabitants, councillors project an image of it as being country-like (symbolised in the 'clean and green' signs that span the borough and in the opposition to the Conservative government's proposals to weaken planning restraints in London's greenbelt). Analysts have pointed out that the borough's opposition is comparable with the use of land-use and environmental regulations to exclude low income residents from suburban USA. Yet there is a difference owing to the size of this borough which makes the provision of services and jobs important council functions. Hence, alongside opposition to growth which alters the localities' social character there has been attention to the selective promotion of retail and office expansion. Similar patterns exist in US municipalities where a large proportion of residents are middle class professionals (e.g. Dowall 1984). Amongst such groups an attachment to community is associated with a rejection of the primacy of economic values. These people are prepared to resist growth measures and have the technical skills required to make such proposals expensive to put through (i.e. amongst their ranks there are likely to be lawyers, accountants, those with political connections and media representatives). Faced with such a phalanx of potential strife, the operational style of the council is inclined to shift into a consumerist mould. If long-time councillors do not feel the incentive to favour this disposition, incomers will assume their positions. The process is very evident in rural locations 'taken over' by urban in-migrants looking for a rural idyll (e.g. Hennigh 1978; Forsythe 1980). However, what once again needs to be stressed is that the primacy of community values in such circumstances arises from the realities of materialist concerns; in the main, consumerist sentiments are dominant because income insecurity is slight.

## RESUME

The essential point of this chapter has been to emphasise the primacy of materialist concerns in the political cultures of localities on both sides of the Atlantic. The precise form taken by these cultures varies, both within nations and between them, because there are differences in the extent to which material fortunes are decided locally or extra-locally. Adding further variability are deviations around national themes which are grounded in locality-specific processes. These in some measure represent particular intensifications of materialist concerns, but they also emerge as entities in which materialism is less evident. Such surface impressions disguise the underlying materialist base which provides a foundation from which other concerns can take a lead role. Understanding the direction of municipal values in such places is inappropriately interpreted in materialist terms. But understanding what causes such directions to emerge necessitates starting from materialism. Of course, all that has been offered here has been a smattering of insights on local political culture; much has been excluded (e.g. the pariah cities that operate in permanent circumstances of fiscal stress). The specific traditions described have tended to occupy minority positions within the spectrum of variability. These are distinctive character types, when a great many localities do not possess attributes which sharply separate them from other places. This does not mean that they are not distinguishable from one another. What binds them together is the dominant impression of nationwide forces, leaving their distinctiveness to emerge more from short-term operational styles than from enduring cultural traits. It is to these operational styles that we turn in the next chapter.

# 5 Fixing operational styles

Because social structures are comprised of ongoing, evolving activities, the distinction between structure and behaviour is somewhat arbitrary. Once particular behaviour patterns are the norm, the 'right' way of doing things, it is more difficult to act in a contrary manner. Yet universal agreement on societal norms is rare. Norms are fought over and, if efforts are not consistently made to maintain them, other views will likely gain currency, if not dominance. What is more, the norms of society have a built-in flexibility; they do not delineate precise behaviour forms but favour action styles of a general kind. Hence, within national political cultures there is a variety of local cultural traits, just as local political cultures can accept a variety of operational styles. The political environments of places range from calm manifestations of a dominant ethos to turbulent disputes over what that ethos should be. Set between these two are different degrees of overt, covert and potential conflict, with variability in the dimensions along which these occur. What this chapter seeks to elucidate is the character of these conflicts and of the harmony that exists in local policy-making. The 'fixing' that is the focus of this chapter is not the setting down of societal norms, but the operational styles of local agents within those norms (although at times those styles go some way toward challenging norms). Here we are dealing not with framework but with what occurs within framework. This chapter examines the actions of individuals and groups in directing local policies; it adopts a hands-on view of local policy-making.

In moving from structure to direct action, points of terminology need clarification. In the first chapter of this book Offe's (1984) vision of the State was commented upon favourably, not for its completeness or superiority, but for the links that it gave to processes of agency and structure. Offe's conceptualisation of strategic groups is particularly pertinent in linking these two, as well as tying them to the role of societal élites. To clarify this, we need to examine what is meant by an élite. Primarily this should not be defined by position holding or success in attaining societal benefits, since the former does not focus on effects and the latter includes lottery winners. Elites are those whose acceptance is critical to the continuance of styles of political action.[1] This does not mean that the effects of élites are immediately visible in operational styles. US urban political machines are illustrative, since behind the surface appearance of working class control was direction and cooperation with factions of capital (Shefter 1976; Elkin 1987). In effect, a coalition existed between machine leaders and entrepreneurs which led to distinctive gains and losses for social groups; the middle classes and weaker factions of business lost out (Elkin 1987). What justifies viewing machine leaders and dominant business factions as élites is their control of resources which are critical for the stability of behaviour forms: machine leaders through organising electoral balances, business leaders through their resource impacts. Two critical points need to be made about such coalition biases (Stone 1986). First of all, they make clear that structural power is not equivalent to decision power. Those in an advantaged structural position might not engage in actions that overtly impinge on institutions. Hence, while capitalists in general benefit from the State's attention to profitability, only some factions of capital are actively involved in coalition biases. Following from this, the dynamic nature of links between structural and decision power is obvious. Leadership is required to transform structural power into decision power (hence, it was those from old Yankee families, not those from ethnic minorities, who first led urban political machines). Elites are those who make that transformation, either through their own actions or because government leaders recognise their value to themselves (i.e. élite standing can be bestowed as well as won). Inevitably, given the dynamism of the relationships involved, changed circumstances can lead to the loss or the acquisition of élite status. Elite support must be secure if existing political arrangements are to be maintained. What ensures that dynamism is present is the unpredictability of human agency. For one thing, State agents can make mistakes in promoting coalition biases. They might fail to appreciate the importance of a social group and, resisting their inclusion in a governing coalition, provoke conflict. Those with structural power advantages who were previously at slumber might find new reason to flex their muscles in an active way, producing new demands and conflicts within the municipal arena. Moreover, government officials themselves have goals which can be pursued by playing off one set of élite pressures against another. A confusion of forces is at play.

Perhaps contrary to expectations, the value of élitist ideas is not weakened by this confusion but strengthened by it. Set in a context of dependence on private profitability, State processes are inevitably inequitable in their effects (Offe 1984). To make this inequality acceptable, State functionaries must selectively favour those whose support is critical for the social order. This applies for elements in all of the bourgeoisie, civil society and the State apparatus (the latter being illustrated in appeasing the military in order to lessen the chance of a *coup d'état* in Latin America; e.g. Wynia 1984). In terms of understanding State processes, one reason for preferring the idea of élites to the neo-marxist vision of classes is that State actions are not directed towards classes as a whole but to specific sections of those classes. In particular it is large, monopoly sector firms which benefit most from State largess, and which have the most influence on State policy (e.g. Useem 1984; Dye 1986a). Small, competitive sector enterprises gain from general demonstrations of the State's commitment to profit-making, from their economic importance (if only in specific sectors), and from the electoral clout of their operatives (most visibly seen in farming). Yet they come a long way behind large corporations in priorities for State appeasement. This pattern should apply no matter what the ideological disposition of government leaders. Unless the monopoly, and increasingly transnational, sector is bought off, an economy is more likely to destabilise (with obvious electoral consequences). Within the bourgeoisie there is an élite; that group of capitalists whose leadership or example is critical to existing political arrangements (and these will vary across localities).

The same point is true for other segments of society. Thus, one weakness in neo-marxian accounts of local politics lies in their translation of workplace conditions into the governmental sphere. Savage (1987) offers an antidote to this simplistic formulation by emphasising how political practices are strongly related to questions of strategy and tactics rather than simply working class consciousness. Compared with the bourgeoisie, the working classes are resource poor, membership is large, and demands for action require more immediate attention. Hence, working class organisation is unstable and difficult to make effective (Urry 1986). To sustain a working class movement requires a collective identity which grants support without constant evaluations of self-interest;[2] the group must come before the individual. Critically, what this requires is leadership. Such movements do not arise in a vacuum. Their members need symbols to guide them, success to gladden them, and a sense of vibrancy to inspire them. Without leadership, even widespread discontent generally lacks political voice (spontaneous combustions such as riots are rare exceptions). Conversely, for their arguments to be persuasive, leaders require a base with broad support. The likelihood of this being found in one place is affected by local political culture:

> Working-class *interests* must be seen as the basis of political practices, but the type of politics they lead to are mediated by the role of *capacities* anchored in the local social structure, which facilitate some types of political mobilisation rather than others. Working-class politics themselves can be divided into two elements: *practical politics*, based around those activities generated by the need to reduce insecurity; and *formal politics*, which are strongly affected by purely political factors, but which operate by campaigning on the issues current in practical politics.
>
> (Savage 1987: 61–2).

In this quest for greater security, Savage (1987: 20) identified three forms of working class struggle: (1) *mutualist*, in which workers seek an independent position in society; (2) *economistic*, in which workers search for employer guarantees of job security; and (3) *statist*, in which workers look to the State to enhance security. Class conflict produces all of these outcomes. Which takes precedence is not a matter for working class leaders alone. Thus, in Savage's Preston study, it was the failure of local capitalists to sustain an economistic role that helped to turn workers to more statist strategies; something they could do because the Labour Party provided a leadership capability. Even within the same political culture, the chance of transforming potential into action is not equal. The political agendas of local institutions are influenced but not decided by structural conditions; they also depend upon the skill of people to use and stimulate resources, to grasp opportunities and to adapt to constraints.

Within the framework of constraints and opportunities afforded by political cultures, élites are those whose actions can have sufficient clout to disrupt the political system. What distinguishes élites is the roots from which their political ambitions are driven. Those grounded in the productive economy stand in a different position from those in civil society, both of whom stand apart from those whose goal satisfaction comes from the State machinery. Each of these interacts with the constraints and opportunities afforded by the State's structural dependence on capital. For some élites, such constraints are liberating (as for capitalists under boosterist political cultures), for others they are restrictive (as for black mayors in US cities). Likewise, electoral accountability has liberating and constraining dimensions, as does dependence on State officials for policy enactment.

Materialist dependence sets the broad outline of first tier considerations in policy determination. Emerging from these material interests, the political cultures of localities (and nations) constitute a second tier of policy deliberation. Cultural forms cannot be distinguished from material considerations in causal terms, since they emerge from the historical evolution of forms of accumulation, backed by the liberating and constraining effects that these have on inputs from civil society and the State. At a third tier, materialist logic can be disguised by the filtering effects of cultural form and operational style. The former is a more enduring component of the governmental scene, one that slowly adjusts to changing circumstances. The latter is the vehicle through which change occurs. Fluctuation in operational styles is common. It can lead either to minor deviations around a central theme in a political culture or it can incrementally push core values into new realms (i.e. minor changes that direct visions ever more leftward or rightward). It is these operational styles – what happens within political cultures – that constitute the primary focus of this chapter. They have undoubtedly received the most attention in research on local politics, as expressed in the community power theories of instrumentalism, pluralism and managerialism. Yet these theoretical models have not proved convincing. Too often they have been seen as contradictory theories of society as a whole, as universal explanations. This view is misguided. Placed in the context of the materialist concerns of the State and the cultural form of policy-making environments, these operational styles should be locationally variable. The liberating and constraining impetus of the first two disposes policy environments in certain directions; albeit they do not determine that a particular path is followed. The tendency of those favouring élitist, neo-marxist or pluralist theories to talk past one another leaves us in a position where conceptualisation and theorisation of the links in this chain are poorly specified. What follows, therefore, is more an articulation of the character of

operational styles than a coherent specification of the interpenetrations of structure, culture and action.

## CAPITALISTS AND PLACE ENTREPRENEURS

To this point, comments on capital–State relationships have largely
focused on capital as a class. As attention shifts on to specific policy
enactments, this framework becomes less satisfactory. The smaller
the geographical scale, the easier it is for a single faction of capital
to impose its will on policy. In Britain, for example, Sharpe and
Newton (1984) found that city expenditure is aligned with the
importance of local employment sectors; resort towns, for example,
commit sums to parks and recreation which are much greater than
in other places. Likewise, in the USA, urban renewal schemes
appear to be less associated with urban decline than with the growth
of the downtown commercial and retail economy (Friedland 1980).
In both cases, local public institutions subsidise the profits of specific
segments of capital. In pursuing this strategy, they did not act
contrary to Peterson's (1981) unitary model; they merely oriented
their pro-capital responses in particular ways. Given public sector
dependence on private profitability, it is not surprising that
municipal policies favour existing trends within the local economy.
After all, while it might be advantageous to broaden the base of
local economic activities, investing heavily in new sectors could
alienate existing businesses, and would take local officials into
economic realms about which they know little. Supporting existing
economic sectors allows for efficiency in resource allocation (in that
more advice, knowledge and expertise is on hand) and helps to
maintain favourable relations with local capitalists. All of this could
take place with little direct business involvement. Where business
representatives take a more direct, hands-on role in local public
institutions, an extra dimension is added to policy-making

### Councillors in Business

A notable feature of business links with local councils has been a
withdrawal of their representatives from the formal arena of
electoral politics. One measure of this is provided by Birmingham
City Council, where business representatives made up more than 50
per cent of elected officials in the inter-war years but less than one-
third more recently (Morris and Newton 1970). Similar trends have

been reported by Bradley and Zald (1965) for Chicago. Yet it would be incorrect to place too much emphasis on this decline, because change in business representation is not simply a matter of counting numbers. In addition, the background of capitalists who sit on councils has altered.

Behind these changes is an adjustment in the social standing and functions of local government. In Britain, for example, holding council office in the nineteenth century brought both social status and business advantage. In cities such as Bradford and Leeds, the council was a forum in which the frustrated social ambitions of new wealth (manufacturers), those thwarted by a national status system dominated by the landed gentry, found an outlet (Fraser 1979). In addition, control of city government enhanced the supply of critical business services (such as electricity, gas, sewer and water systems, and good roads). In the United States the economic centrality of municipal government was also highly visible, as in the coordination and funding of growth promoting facilities (such as railroads).

Why, therefore, has business representation declined? Four main reasons can be suggested. The first is the emergence of working class political organisations. In Britain this was through the Labour Party. In the larger cities of the United States it was in the emergence of ethnic political machines. Secondly, restrictions began to be imposed on business councillors, as over the ability of their firms to bid for council contracts. Without restrictions, lucrative returns from occupying council positions were difficult to resist. Thus, in nineteenth century England, market traders tended to seek office where councils controlled the local produce market, merchants and shippers followed suit when the docks were council operated, and tradesmen filling council contracts similarly found elected positions attractive (Hennock 1973). Most notably in London, what unfolded from this was as outcry amongst the upper classes over corruption in municipal activities. This helped to create the local government system of 1888, part of its aim being to increase responsiveness to the public.[3] Before the new system was introduced, some change had already occurred: the 1882 Municipal Corporations Act disqualified contractors from holding office (although this did not exclude directors of limited liability companies). However, over time local councils were becoming less important to larger companies. By the late nineteenth century, the most pertinent issues for larger British firms were being raised at the national level (e.g. tariff policy). In addition, average firm size was increasing rapidly

(Scott 1985), leaving business executives less time free for local government. This third cause of reduced business involvement is relevant today. Thus, when Clements (1969) questioned local notables in Bristol, he found that the most important reason for not standing for elected office was the time demands that such work made (mentioned by 77 per cent). Heclo (1969) similarly found that half of newly elected members in Manchester could not give sufficient time to their job, with 80 per cent believing that lack of time was the biggest drawback to elected office. Not only time is involved. The cliché 'time means money' is also pertinent, as estimates suggest that around one-third of councillors suffer financial loss because of their positions (Hampton 1987). Adding to time pressures is the decline in social standing associated with councils (e.g. three-quarters of Manchester councillors felt that the public did not respect their position; Heclo 1969). This is a fourth reason why there has been a decline in business representation.

In the United States time pressures nowadays are even greater, because, with so few elected officials in large cities, positions have effectively become full-time (e.g. with a population of 1.6 million Philadelphia has only 20 elected officials, whereas Birmingham, England's largest district council with just under one million residents, has 117). Amongst smaller units, part-time status is more common, leading to a pattern similar to Britain. Here again we can trace an element of national political culture. The more individualistic orientation of the USA, aligned with the earlier awarding of political rights to the working classes, provided a greater willingness to accept that municipal appointments were an occupation. In Britain, by contrast, the hierarchical tone of dominant values scorned such professionalism in favour of rule by 'gentlemen', of the virtue of amateurism. Hence, the abolition of the property qualification in 1882 did not open the floodgates for those of low income to become members of English councils; amateurism determined that compensation was not given for lost wages and meetings were held during work hours. Even today, when changes in the law have restrained employers from firing those who devote time to council affairs, there are redundancies and lost career prospects for active council involvement (e.g. in 1968 the future Labour leader of Birmingham City Council, Stanley Yapp, was made redundant by GEC partly because of his council work; Sutcliffe 1976). Since 1974, attendance allowances and expense payments have eased the financial situation somewhat, but the money paid is sufficiently low that only the particularly committed or those with other income supports are inclined to view full-time council activity with equanimity.

Hardly surprisingly, British investigators report a lack of interest in candidacy for local office and, once elected, difficulty in retaining members (thus, the Audit Commission [1984] reported that elections and resignations result in only one-fifth of London's councillors staying in office for longer than a single electoral cycle). The figure that Birrell (1981) reported for Northern Ireland, where standing for election was the personal idea of only 14 per cent of councillors, is not out of line when placed beside other British studies. Certainly, party differences exist, since Labour councillors devote a great deal of time to party activities before standing for office, and frequently hold an appointed position within the party, whereas Conservative councillors often engage in little formal political activity until asked to stand for office (e.g. Blondel and Hall 1967; Heclo 1969; Chandler 1984). All of this might seem to justify recent Conservative calls for a reduction in the number of councillors (Gyford *et al.* 1989). It does not. Other options are available. For instance, Britain could follow the Swedish example and enable a selection of councillors to occupy full-time, salaried posts (Malmsten 1983). Which option is selected reveals much about underlying values. Where representation of the electorate is favoured, more emphasis is likely on easing the burdens of office. Where, as in Britain, such values carry less weight, arrangements favourable to 'strong government' are likely to be preferred

A review of candidate selection procedures and the occupations of councillors indicates that those from business generally do not seek office for personal advancement. With restrictions on the contracts that a firm can obtain if it has a council representative, office-holding could actually damage business prospects. Understandably, then, Saunders (1979) found that a hallmark of the London Borough of Croydon, a business dominated, Conservative Party stronghold, was that councillors did not come from economic sectors gaining most from municipal decisions. This could be conclusive were contracts the only means of deriving personal benefit. But they are not. Rose *et al.* (1976) illustrate this by showing how farmer councillors' support for a lack of spending on housing, and the discouragement of new employment, helps to maintain a low wage economy with a compliant labour force. Seen from this perspective, a question mark should be placed against the growth of building and property interests on councils (e.g. Morris and Newton [1970] found that they comprised 40 per cent of business-based councillors in Birmingham in 1966, up from 6 per cent in 1920; for the USA see Banfield and Wilson 1963). Position holding on council might not bring specific personal benefits, but it can adjust local economies in ways that bring wider business gains (from which individual enterprises gather indirect spin-offs).

## Business in the community

Care is needed when the goals of business intervention in local policy-making are interpreted. By operating within a capitalist polity, a bias which favours capital is inevitable in the long run (over the system as a whole at least). Constraints imposed by capital transpire with or without direct intervention. But place entrepreneurs, those who favour growth machine strategies, are more disposed toward direct involvement to achieve their goals. This involvement is of a different calibre to that of structural restraints. In particular, place entrepreneurs tend to have ties to companies with locality-specific profit-making capacities (Domhoff 1986; Dye 1986b). Hence, their concern is to promote economic expansion *in situ*, whereas corporate capital has a more aspatial point of reference (though locational considerations are integral to their profit strategies; Massey 1984). However, the structure of capitalist polities does not preordain the emergence of growth machines. As for East Anglian farmers, State aid in profit-making need not be best achieved through growth. Moreover, in many localities private sector employers do not see the council as central to their profit-making. Hence, although there is now a statutory requirement that British councils consult non-domestic ratepayers over their budgets, local Chambers of Commerce and branches of the Confederation of British Industry have generally been satisfied with being informed rather than being active participants. 'In most cases, non-domestic ratepayers got information, sometimes tea, but little else' (Elcock 1987: 249; also Martlew 1986).

This does not mean that councils are indifferent to their economic base. It does not mean that companies are indifferent to their tax payments or to local public policies. What it does mean is that care is needed in recognising when business intervention in day-to-day council operations is provoked. In Britain a distinction is needed in this regard between nationally and locally oriented companies. As the history of urban renewal and public service privatisation reveals, national corporations court local authorities to accept policies favourable to themselves (e.g. Dunleavy 1981; Ascher 1987). Such interventions are primarily oriented around securing markets for corporate products, rather than ongoing control of local policies. They are an aspect of business intervention in local affairs; one in which the tactics employed, most especially against smaller authorities, are at times best described as bullying (e.g. Dunleavy 1981). Yet, other than viewing these as straightforward business transactions, such interactions are often more validly seen as inspired by national government, since it is usual for them to be sanctioned by central government. Corporations might well be instrumental in bringing about acceptance of such policies, but this occurs more at a national level than locally.

In Britain the potential for local authority policy either to harm or to stimulate profits is comparatively slight. The contribution of local property taxes to total business costs is small, even though it can be an irritant (Birdseye and Webb 1984; Bennett and Fearnehough 1987). What is more, evidence indicates that limits imposed on private companies by land-use planning restraints are not in the unacceptable range (e.g. North and Gough 1983). Given that the 1974 local government reorganisation placed most areas firmly in the hands of either the Conservative or the Labour parties, business intervention has little prospect of changing local party control (Dunleavy 1980b). In those few instances where such endeavours have been noted, there is no evidence that they were effective (as with Aims of Industry offering £200,000 to fund any court action against the Greater London Council, with a further £200,000 for efforts to unseat GLC Labour leader, Ken Livingstone; O'Leary 1987a). More generally, far from relations between councils and business being antagonistic, they are conciliatory. Moreover, even in their direct interventions in economic affairs, the independent actions of councils have often reinforced central government policy, not contradicted it (Armstrong and Fildes 1988). In general, local economic initiatives have affected few firms and have operated at the margins of local economies (e.g. in providing premises or grants; Chandler and Lawless 1985). Sweeping aside the ideological smokescreen in which those on left and right have shrouded economic initiatives by new left councils, even the most pro-labour stances have been played out on the edges of local economies (Gough 1986). Small firms have been primary targets for such initiatives; large employers have been unscathed (Coulson and Baker 1984; Mackintosh and Wainwright 1987). Ultimately, local councils have too little authority over issues central to profitability to be of serious concern to British capitalists.

This not the case in all nations. Democratically elected councils in both Cleveland and New York have been overthrown for pursuing policies which business élites did not accept. Describing a similar occurrence in Melbourne, Australia, Saunders (1982a) explained the rationale:

> like a spoilt child who finds himself [*sic*] losing a game of monopoly which he had expected to win, the big retailers, insurance companies and property owners of the CBD simply kicked the board over and decided to begin the game again under different rules.
>
> (Saunders 1982a: 15)

The expectation that local councils should overtly favour private accumulation is characteristic of earlier centuries in newer lands of European settlement. After all, in many centres, entrepreneurs did not own large businesses and depended on the financial clout of the council to promote services essential for their well-being. In the United States this applied particularly to inducements to attract railroads. In a context in which the lack of a railway commonly meant economic collapse (Hudson 1985), business and government had a communality of interest in obtaining this facility. Growth-favouring sentiments were further intensified by a nationwide belief in future economic prosperity (Kolko 1976). Within this value system, entrepreneurs were seen as the obvious leaders for city councils. Of course, these entrepreneurs had much to gain from growth promotion and in many cases pushed councils so far into debt that loans could not be repaid (between 1850 and the Great Depression, 35 per cent of all municipal defaults resulted from funds used as inducements for railroads; Monkkonen 1984). The raw materialism of such business-led drives was toned down in many cities once its leaders made their fortunes. In effect, the rough and tumble tactics of the growth machine were scorned by old 'aristocratic' families in northern cities whose family wealth was based on their ancestors' relying on such tactics (Bell 1962: 148). But within the United States, these 'aristocratic' families have not taken on the mantle of leadership within the public domain. They have devoted themselves to family and caste, commonly pursuing favoured lifestyles in the suburbs (Burt 1963; Baltzell 1964). They have aided the process of denuding central cities of their economic resources, leaving them open to a new kind of entrepreneur; one that is attracted less by the merits of place advancement than by the special concessions that can be wrung from desperate city councils.

Such businesses do not have the attachment to specific localities of place entrepreneurs and are more inclined to set one place off against another in searching for the highest inducement to investment (Herr 1982; and Blowers 1983 for an English example).

Place entrepreneurs have most to gain from place-specific land-use intensification and from economic growth in their home town. In the last century the centrality of these goals was aided by companies being smaller and by the locational ties of skilled labour, transport and raw materials being stronger. Moving into the twentieth century, divisions have sharpened between those seeking profits from a single location and those with more dispersed profit strategies, because technological progress has broadened the geographical availability of labour, material and efficient transport, and large corporations have become more dominant. This separation lies behind Domhoff's (1986) criticism of the weak distinction in neo-marxist accounts between mobile capital and place entrepreneurs. Yet while this division should be noted, its importance must not be exaggerated. This is because many large corporations are keen promoters of specific places. This has been seen in each of suburbanisation, urban renewal and neighbourhood gentrification (Checkoway 1980; Walker 1981; Smith and Williams 1986). Indeed, as in Australia, the real estate and property interests of place entrepreneurs are less a compilation of small, locally owned enterprises than associations of national and international interests which link into finance capital (e.g. Daly 1982). It is therefore hardly surprising that 300 of the largest 1,000 US manufacturing firms have real estate departments (Friedland and Palmer 1984). Likewise, the mass media, a sector dominated by corporate ownership (Bagdikian 1983; Parenti 1986), combines an attachment to specific places, through owning single outlets, with more global concerns for profitability. Just as corporations divest less profitable manufacturing plants, so real estate businesses, television stations, retail outlets and city newspapers face closure for poor performances. Place entrepreneurs are locked into the national corporate economy, even if their *modus operandi* has a different spatial reference.

Visualising growth machine sentiments in the United States in universal terms has one obvious drawback, which is the number of places whose inner drive owes little to such goals (e.g. in consumerist, paternalist or radical localities). Perhaps the absence of a growth impetus is a realistic response to a history of failure in place promotion (as is often the case in rural areas; e.g. Vidich and Bensman 1968). Alternatively, a monopoly employer might block growth in case it challenges the company's local supremacy (e.g. Gaventa 1980). Similarly, local élites might block it for fear that it challenges their preferred lifestyle (Wild [1974] offers a good Australian example, also Hugill 1989). Whatever the precise reasons, in numerous municipalities growth has not been a central value and business leaders have not been critical to policy-making processes. Instructively, Clark (1977) found that US cities in which mayors had significant policy influence tended to have weak business lobbies, and vice versa. This suggests that the relative power of local capital and of local State functionaries has mutually exclusive components. This is a feature of community power structures that has been little studied, but its likelihood is not surprising given the dissimilar characteristics of local political cultures.

That the influence of capitalists appears to be subdued in some locations does not necessarily damage business interests. Single municipalities are rarely fundamental to private profit. In metropolitan areas, for example, place entrepreneurs are not rigidly bound by specific municipal locations. On account of the fragmented nature of the municipal system, enterprises can move from locations with a less favourable business climate to those more amenable to profit-making (e.g. Herr 1982; Blowers 1983). Further, for many companies (newspapers, radio, television and department stores being good examples), growth in a single municipality is much less critical than growth in the metropolitan area as a whole. Certainly, if the largest municipalities are not favourably disposed to growth, this can cause frustration. But metropolitan-wide special districts can be called on to circumvent local opposition (Heiman 1988). Besides which, larger municipalities are usually central cities, places that need economic growth to help to redress an imbalance in resources and service demands (Nathan and Adams 1976). Such places have been far from reluctant in encouraging private sector investment. Often, in both Britain and the United States, it is councils themselves which coordinate attempts to promote economic growth (e.g. Bassett 1986), with poorer cities putting most effort into such programmes (Rubin and Rubin 1987). Growth machine inspiration should not be expected in the actions of all councils, but these sentiments are evident in US municipal systems as a whole. That capitalists are rarely provoked to mount coups against municipal leaders owes more to satisfaction with existing arrangements than to a lack of inclination. As earlier chapters indicated, the roles that citizens play in local polities are set within a context which is primarily decided by propertied interests, not vice versa.

## THE LOCAL STATE AND CIVIL SOCIETY

How interactions between State institutions and the public at large play out in practice is conditioned by core features of national political cultures. Not surprisingly, the dissimilar traditions of Britain and the United States are associated with distinct linkage patterns. Summarising the basic divide, Almond and Verba (1963) point to a more active involvement of US citizens in governmental affairs, compared with a more deferential acceptance of governmental actions by Britons. 'Though the British citizen became an active participant, he [sic] did not lose his respect for the independent authority of the government to the extent that this occurred in the United States' (Almond and Verba 1963: 493). This difference reflects the stronger impression of self-interest in US political values, since this is aligned with less willingness to accept unfavourable decisions and an inclination to expect policy-makers to act more for personal gain than for the public good. The importance of this underlying distrust, set though it is in a framework of overall citizen support for the governmental system (Almond and Verba 1963), is that sentiments against government actions are more easily translated into popular protest than in Britain. As Bell (1962: 114) noted, the USA has a moralising, populist temper which is fuelled by specific issues, but which is difficult to sustain as a long-term drive. Hence, over specific policy issues, US officials must be prepared for intrusive public oversight and the likelihood of public opposition to their decisions.

As we have already seen, one response to such oversight is to hide decision-making, through devices such as special districts. In addition, in the drawing up of boundaries for suburban municipalities, and in the implementation of land-use and environmental policies within them, processes aid the preservation of social homogeneity (Newton 1978). The relevance of this for council–citizen relationships is obvious. 'Since most [or at least many] suburbs are individually homogeneous, the councils are selected as "like-minded" men [sic] who can be trusted to carry on city business in the tradition of the suburb' (Murphy and Rehfuss 1976: 59). In such situations, disagreement over fundamental values is comparatively rare. Conflict centres on frills rather than core values, on tactics rather than primary goals, on issues of slight distributional importance (Newton 1978). But set alongside this pattern is a crucial countervailing condition; namely, that large proportions of US citizens live in central cities or large suburbs which have varied social compositions. Here the potential for conflict is significant. Diluting this potential has been achieved in a number of ways. Special districts apart, the most obvious vehicle has been political machines. This seeming victory for the working class cause was more apparent than real, since early leaders did not come from the lower classes (Kolko 1976), and, when working class movements began to threaten the WASP élite, a common response was to adjust electoral and managerial practices in order to strengthen the hand of the upper classes and their middle class supporters. One mechanism for achieving this was reform government.

## Reform government

According to *The Municipal Yearbook 1988*, there are 7,068 cities in the United States, of which 3,815 are run on a mayor–council system and 501 have either town meetings or representative town meetings. This leaves 2,576 cities with council–manager governments and 176 with commission governments. It is these last two types that come under the rubric of reform government. In fact, governmental form alone does not encapsulate the reform package, only one arm of it. Additional reform measures include nonpartisan elections and city-wide (viz. at-large) polls. These three components of reformism – more professional administrations, at-large elections and non-partisanship – are not a united package. Many cities have one but no other. Some have two, but in different combinations. Reformism is a hotch-potch of measures (Table 5.1); it is not unidimensional.

The character and rationale of reformism is easily explained for at-large elections and nonpartisanship. The first simply determines that, in order to attain elected office, candidates must obtain votes over a whole municipality. Representatives thereby require broad support for their candidature; sectional interests are assumed to be restrained, as electoral success rests on appealing to a spectrum of interests. Nonpartisanship is similarly geared toward restricting sectional interests. By denying political parties access to the electoral arena it is held that candidate selection will be based on personal ability, not mindless adherence to party leaders' wishes. Put together, the expectation is that those best equipped to serve the city as a whole will be elected. To aid their governance, commission and council–manager schemes heighten the authority of administrative officers. In the commission case, this is by means of each elected official being both a member of the council and heading one or more administrative departments; commissioners

*Table 5.1* City attributes by administrative type

| Percentage | City governmental form | | |
|---|---|---|---|
| | Mayor–council | Council–manager | Commission |
| Partisan | 39.0 | 18.1 | 25.4 |
| With mayor as councillor | 33.2 | 85.6 | 96.6 |
| With mayor voting on all issues | 16.8 | 72.1 | 92.3 |
| With mayoral veto as councillor | 39.5 | 7.5 | 8.6 |
| With mayoral veto as non-councillor | 80.9 | 92.5 | 91.4 |
| With direct election of mayor | 98.0 | 61.8 | 69.2 |
| With mayor selected by council | 1.9 | 35.5 | 29.1 |
| With at-large elections | 49.1 | 68.1 | 87.7 |
| With ward elections | 21.3 | 6.3 | 5.3 |
| With at-large–ward mixture | 29.7 | 25.6 | 7.0 |

*Note*
These figures refer to cities only and came from a 1986 International City Management Association survey.

*Source*: Adrian (1988) and Renner (1988)

not only make policy but also implement it. In council–manager schemes, the head of council is the manager, with elected officials acting as a legislature which approves administration policies.

The consequences of these arrangements are well recognised. Most notably, reform government has a decided upper class accent. City-wide elections are expensive to mount and, with no party labels allowed, city-wide exposure requires good relations with the mass media.[4] With media outlets being tightly bound into the growth machine (Molotch 1976), there is an impetus favouring capital within reform government institutions. Minorities, on the other hand, find their representation much lessened by reform electoral procedures (Table 5.2). Not surprisingly, as the civil rights movement gained strength, and assumptions about justice and equality in the United States were revised, these electoral practices were increasingly challenged. The 1982 Voters' Rights Act was critical here, because it changed the legal definition of discriminatory electoral practices from that of intent to that of effect (Garza and Weaver 1986). Yet racial discrimination was not a major factor behind the introduction of reform government measures, most of which were implemented in the early decades of this century in places without a large (franchised) minority population. Nevertheless,

*Table 5.2* Reform electoral procedures and black representation 1986

|  | Percentage of black councillors | | |
|---|---|---|---|
|  | Under 20% | 20–39% | Over 40% |
| At-large elections | 29.4 | 35.3 | 35.3 |
| District elections | 9.7 | 16.1 | 74.2 |
| Mixed elections | 17.3 | 44.2 | 38.5 |
| Party on ballot | 5.4 | 27.0 | 67.6 |
| Party not on ballot | 24.6 | 38.6 | 36.8 |

*Note*
These figures refer only to cities in which at least 40 per cent of the population is black.

*Source*: Renner (1988)

when the electoral (and administrative) procedures of reform government have been removed, minority influence has increased (e.g. Browning *et al*. 1984; Garza and Weaver 1986).

The creation of reformed institutions had the discriminatory intent of weakening the impress of the working classes on city government. In some cases, this was because of genuine concern over corruption. However, it seems that criticism was often levelled less at corruption *per se*, than at its benefits by-passing reform advocates. Most certainly, many cities that changed their organisation to the commission model found that costs and waste did not decline. On the contrary, they were magnified (Griffith 1974b). Too often, commissioners simply approved one another's schemes with few questions about their value for the municipality or their efficiency of provision. In response, the wealthy again pushed for organisational reform. Many places grasped the seeming professionalism of the council–manager model and ceased to experiment with commissioners. From its initial introduction in 1900, as an organisation to reconstruct Galveston, Texas, after a tidal wave destroyed half of its property, the heyday of commission government lasted only until around 1920. Afterwards council–manager forms were in the ascendancy.

In line with the hopes for commission government, council–manager schemes improved municipal efficiency. Often this was not difficult:

Introducing managers into American cities in the current century was like hiring a baseball star to be player-manager for a sandlot club. Opportunities for improvement were everywhere. And the improvements yielded obvious and immediate increases in performance and reductions in costs.

(Bollens and Ries 1969: 8)

Even so, not all cities adopted this governmental form. Significantly, larger cities, where newer immigrants comprised a large population percentage, were less likely to accept reform. Even today, of cities with more than half a million inhabitants, 25 have mayor–council systems, just five have council–manager forms and none has a commission government. For comparison, amidst places with between 100,000 and 500,000 residents, the comparable figures are 110, 116 and 10. Put simply, political machines in larger cities were powerful enough, locally and in state assemblies, to maintain their ward-based, partisan, mayor–council schemes. The rising tide of working class, immigrant influence over politics in such cities seemed irresistible, leading higher income, predominantly WASP populations to favour flight ('exit'). Where machines were less entrenched, the inclination was to stand and fight ('voice'). In essence, class conflict was critical to the implementation of reform government. This is captured in the time that it took these proposals to gain widespread support (Griffith 1974a). The real change in attitudes came during the last two decades of the nineteenth century, a time when levels of immigration from eastern and southern Europe were increasing and when labour unrest was gathering pace. In cities such as Dayton, Ohio and Oakland, California, reforms were introduced overtly to stop socialist advance (Weinstein 1968; Hayes 1972). The ethnic base of urban political machines might have intensified upper class fears, but at heart their concerns were class ones. In pursuing class interests, reform pressures occurred on a broad front. Chambers of Commerce pushed for reform measures in many cities (Weinstein 1968), but at the national and state levels numerous organisations were active (e.g. the National Municipal League, the National Civil Service Reform League, the National Voters' League and the Short Ballot Organization). The moralising zeal within US political values sanctified the cause of property by bestowing on it the aura of a 'good government' crusade. In numerous instances this proved highly successful. Utah made commission government compulsory for all municipalities in 1911, with Missouri (for second class cities) and Pennsylvania (for third class cities) both following in 1913.

The impact of reform government on working class representation is clear. What is less certain is how reform affected municipal operations. In this regard, the evidence is far from obvious. For citizen–council linkages, some studies conclude that reformism reduces responsiveness to public opinion and group demands (e.g. Getter and Schumaker 1978), but others find no difference or even an enhanced role for citizen groups (e.g. Hoffman 1976). Similarly, at least in the post-1945 era, there is little to suggest that reformed cities have distinctive policies.[5] For Peterson (1981: 7) reform is insufficiently influential to divert cities from the influence of the broader political economy. As Bollens and Ries (1969: 19) expressed it: 'Only by coming to terms with the existing political environment can the manager put himself [*sic*] into a position where he can use his administrative skills'. Above all, reformism had to adapt to the local business climate and to voter blocs in the population. Its introduction was conditioned by the comparative strength of class forces and its life has reflected their ongoing impetus. Reformism arose in environments conducive to its success in that it sat snugly inside prevailing local power relationships. Although local social structures changed, municipal organisation perpetuated old power relationships. The recent decline of reformism owes less to responsiveness to a changing local political arena than it does to external pressure (e.g. national civil rights legislation).

**Citizens and electors**

The divergence of public sentiment and government form in reformed institutions in recent decades is one example of the loose correspondence that can exist between citizen preferences and council policy. Most obviously, this slack sees expression in citizens responding more to symbols of action than to actual council practices. Evidence on the public's incomplete knowledge, and incorrect assumptions, on council affairs is extensive. Illustrating the magnitude of the problem, in a 1981 poll, only 2 per cent of Londoners correctly named the councillor for their ward and only 22 per cent knew in which two local authorities they lived (Henney 1984). Compared with many nations, electors in Britain and the United States are poor participants in local elections. Turnout rates are around 40 per cent, slightly lower in the USA, in contrast with 70–90 per cent in the Netherlands, Sweden and West Germany. Commonly, electors' views on local government are more significant for their factual inaccuracy than for their assessment of performance.

For example, in an Audit Commission (1984) nationwide survey, 37 per cent of voters thought that the police were a national responsibility and around two-fifths thought that the two main district council functions of public housing and refuse collection were in county hands. In the United States even more confusion should be expected, given the variable service packages of municipalities, the importance of private sector contracting and the role of special districts (Liebert 1976). But the ordered, uniform English system favours recognition of functional responsibility. Hardly surprisingly, councillors regard citizen interest in council affairs as low (e.g. 70 per cent of Manchester councillors rated constituents' interest as low or non-existent; Heclo 1969), with many holding that the public had insufficient knowledge to vote effectively (as reported by 60 per cent of Hampton's [1970] Sheffield councillors). Put simply, 'few [British] people vote in local elections even when they have the opportunity to do so, and that many people are ignorant of the most elementary facts about their local governments, are points which can hardly be disputed' (Dearlove 1979: 39). Similarly, in the United States, citizens are 'strongly influenced by inertia, habit, unexamined loyalties, personal attach-ment, emotions, [and] transient impulses' (Dahl 1961: 90–1).

Set in this context, it might be expected that electors, or more accurately elections, make a slight impression on council policy. In this regard a distinction should be drawn between England and the USA. In England, nonpartisanship is a rare commodity. Of the 2,992 English county councillors listed in *The Municipal Journal 1989*, only 130 were not members of one of the main parties, and no council was controlled by 'independents'. Likewise, out of 364 metropolitan and non-metropolitan districts, only 13 had a majority of councillors lacking a party label. By contrast, in the United States only 27.4 per cent of all cities are reported to be partisan (Adrian 1988). Furthermore, in England the links between local and national parties are strong, in the public's eye if not so strongly in day-to-day operations. Hence, across the nation, studies report that local elections are decided more by national than by local factors (e.g. Waller 1980; Bristow 1984); rural areas and wards where the Liberals have successfully promoted their brand of community politics provide rare breaks with the national pattern (Waller 1980; Laver 1984). Hardly surprisingly, one survey of metropolitan councillors found that 52 per cent of Conservatives and 72 per cent of their Labour counterparts believed that elections were primarily decided by national events (McGrew and Bristow 1984).[6] Related to this belief, English councillors largely view themselves as 'trustees'; once elected, they believe that they are free to decide issues irrespective of the wishes of the electorate (e.g. Saunders [1979] classified 70 per cent of Croydon's councillors in this manner; see also Newton 1976a).

Nonpartisanship and weaker local–state (or local–national) links in the United States should favour closer councillor–constituent ties. Yet, in his survey of suburban St Louis, Downes (1968) found that this was not the case; here, fully 73 per cent of the councillors defined themselves as 'trustees' and only 7 per cent saw themselves as delegates acting on behalf of constituents. Partly responsible for this is the homogeneity of many municipalities, since this reduces the likelihood of fundamental policy conflict (Newton 1978). In small municipalities with narrow functional responsibilities, political ambition appears to be weakly developed amongst elected officials. Many are encouraged to take office as a public service (Greer and Greer 1976; Murphy and Rehfuss 1976). With an 80 per cent success rate for incumbent re-election, electors seemingly have few conflicts with their representatives. In larger cities the picture is more complex. In northern states at least, these places are more likely to be partisan and socially heterogeneous. Yet, while conflict is more inclined to erupt in such places, they are also the most likely to be fiscally strapped. Far from being able to mediate between competing interests in an equitable manner, such authorities must keep a sharp eye on their image as an investment site. Shortage of funds makes them inclined to listen to and cultivate the tones of propertied élites and of aid givers in higher tier governments, while at the same time delaying and distracting other demands. As Barbara Ferman (1985) found for Boston and San Francisco, when an institution has a liberal image it can pursue conservative policies without raising public ire (the same applying for liberal policies set within a conservative image). A problem with such tactics is achieving a balance between officials' impressions of their public image and the public's views. Over time, failure to be seen to respond to citizen discontent can lead to a groundswell of opposition producing a 'critical election' which sweeps out the old guard and sets up a new era of municipal politics (Iannaccone and Lutz 1970). But when the build-up of resentment is concentrated amongst the least powerful, the prospect of alleviation can seem remote. With a sense of abandonment or neglect strong in people's minds, the chance of civil unrest is heightened.

## Civil disorder

Civil disturbances might be provoked by single official decisions, but they rarely find their causes in this guise. For rioting to occur, a seedbed of deep dissatisfaction with the status quo is usual. Rioting is a response to an accumulation of disaffections. It is grounded in an environment with an ongoing potential for minor incidents to erupt into full-blown disorder. So far, theory has not advanced far in explaining how this potential becomes reality. Disorders are temporally and spatially specific, but we have poor understanding of when and where they occur.

That civil disturbances rest on a seedbed of antagonism is evident from the incidents which cause riots. What characterises them is their everyday nature (Keith 1987). In the Brixton riot of 1981, for example, the instigating incident was the apparent arrest of a person by the police; 'apparent' because the person was actually being helped to a hospital, having been injured. On account of their presence at so many eruptions, the police have been much criticised for riot instigation (over a third of 1960s riots in the USA were started by police arrests; Morgan and Clark 1973). However, if community–police relations were the prime cause of rioting, civil disorders would occur weekly. As Roberts (1971) reflected on the turn of the century slum, antagonism to the police is a long-time feature of low income neighbourhoods:

> nobody in our Northern slum, to my recollection, ever spoke in fond regard, then or afterwards, of the policeman as a 'social worker' and 'handyman of the streets'. Like their children, delinquent or not, the poor in general looked upon him with fear and dislike . . . The 'public' (meaning the middle and upper classes), we know well enough, held their 'bobby' in patronizing 'affection and esteem', which he repaid with due respectfulness; but these sentiments were never shared by the undermass, nor in fact by the working class generally.
>
> (Roberts 1971: 100)

Disgruntlement was there but rarely made itself apparent in disorder. Commonly, when breakdowns in civil order have occurred these have come in phases (e.g. 1960s USA and 1980s England). Theorists have so far offered little to explain these phases.

Additionally, within phases, there are no convincing accounts of the incidence of civil disorder. For both Britain and the United States, objective socio-economic circumstances tell little about rioting. This applies not simply to geographical incidence but also to personal involvement. Many places with poor housing, high unemployment and poor community–police relations, where antagonism is expected to be highest, do not experience rioting, whereas areas with less adverse conditions do (Morgan and Clark 1973; Keith and Peach 1983). Similarly, contradicting the attempts of conservatives to blame rioting on deviants, evidence shows that riot participants are little different from non-participants in the same neighbourhood (see Horowitz 1983 for a review). What is more, if the conservative 'riff-raff' theory were correct, one would expect a haphazard pattern of incidents. In fact, the targets which are vandalised in riots are deliberately selected, usually owing to the actual or symbolic role that the institution has in generating dissatisfaction amongst rioters. Thus, in the South African townships, targets tend to be government buildings (whether schools or police stations; Western 1982), while the Brixton disturbances saw attacks on places with a reputation for exploiting blacks (Greaves 1984). Riots are not random events, but political messages about societal arrangements. Not surprisingly, post-riot surveys of black citizens in the United States recorded sympathy with rioters and a feeling that riots called attention to ghetto grievances and aroused white sympathy. But rioting is just one tactic in attaining these ends. For instance, in the southern states, the centrality of the church in people's lives, and the willingness of church leaders to lead civil rights actions, provided the social cohesion and organisational basis for more peaceful social protest (Horowitz 1983).

Violence is one means of seeking societal change. It is often interpreted as a tactic of the under-class. Yet, in truth, it is a tactic of all social groups. For the powerful, violence is justified in the name of authority, of the preservation of law and order. To meet this elusive entity, violence has been common against those who threaten élite privileges. Most evidently this occurs in unstable regimes, since it is infinitely less expensive to have the masses willingly cooperate than to coerce them (Pareto 1901). Nevertheless, in both Britain and the USA, the police (including immigration authorities and the judiciary) have been active agents in restricting challenges to élite standing (note the tactics of North American élites towards socialist advances; Brown and Brown 1973; Karabel 1979). Protection of social standing has also been a cause of violence amongst those of more moderate status. Good examples are the riots in US cities in the second decade of this century in which working class whites sought to exclude blacks from their neighbourhoods and workplaces (e.g. Hirsch 1983). Very similar in some regards is Protestant violence against Catholics in Northern Ireland. Of course, disorders instigated by the more powerful are dissimilar from those originating amongst the less powerful. Those in the ascendancy have resources and authority which allows for varied tactics. For those with fewer resources, action plans are rare. Their disorders are spontaneous; symbols of distress and of a sense of hopelessness over alleviating their discontent. Elites commonly claim legitimacy for their acts of violence. Usually, non-élites are denied such justification, given that the designation of legitimacy is in élite hands.

As to the effectiveness of rioting, generally riots are effective instruments of protest. Were this not the case, disturbances would likely continue (cf. Northern Ireland and South Africa). This does not mean that rioters 'get their way'. *Protest is Not Enough* is an apt title for the study on minority politics by Browing *et al.* (1984), because this is certainly the case. For one thing, two levels of government can react to disorders. In the 1960s, the US federal government enhanced social programmes for inner cities, but city governments often strengthened the arm of law and order (Welch 1975). Then again, the federal government offered palliatives rather than cures: poorly coordinated and insufficiently funded programmes with a stress on short-term measures such as summer jobs (Frieden and Kaplan 1975). The fragility of these appeasements was later revealed when the Carter and Reagan administrations cut urban aid (Cloward and Piven 1982). The British experience has also been more akin to posturing than action. The Task Force established to assist Liverpool in its plight (Parkinson and Duffy 1984), and the government's offer of enterprise zones as a cure to inner city problems, are illustrative. Both appeared at the same time as the government restricted local policy options for functions critical to the poor (e.g. housing and social services). However, what urban rioting did achieve was a change in attitudes. In the USA, corporations recognised the dangers of social unrest and made commitments to new jobs and housing in inner cities (Orren 1976). Within the black population, riots and civil rights activism helped to promote black consciousness and strengthened commitments to equality. Amidst sections, though only sections, of the white population, it enhanced support for civil rights. One result has been increased minority representation on councils (Table 5.3). Another has been more municipal jobs for minorities (e.g. Dye and Renick 1981); although minorities seem to have taken the brunt of recent

***Table** 5.3* Black elected officials in US city and county government 1970–86

| Year | Number |
|------|--------|
| 1970 | 719 |
| 1971 | 909 |
| 1972 | 1112 |
| 1973 | 1268 |
| 1974 | 1607 |
| 1975 | 1885 |
| 1976 | 2284 |
| 1977 | 2509 |
| 1978 | 2616 |
| 1979 | 2675 |
| 1980 | 2871 |
| 1981 | 2914 |
| 1982 | 3017 |
| 1983 | 3282 |
| 1984 | 3367 |
| 1985 | 3689 |
| 1986 | 3800 |

*Source*: US Department of Commerce Bureau of Census *Statistical Abstract of the United States*, annual, US Government Printing Office, Washington D.C.

municipal job losses (e.g. Thomas 1978). Thus, while civil disorder can be effective if it meets with public sympathy, to sustain the gains made requires that this sympathy is built on through effective organisation.

## Organising and presenting civic interests

A central idea in organisation theory is that institutions seek to control their external environment so as to create stability in their operations. In a local government context, this involves restricting citizen access to policy-making. Allowing free access could introduce contradictory pressures which would make difficult effective planning and, above all, the smooth operation of the organisation. Of course, the degree to which councils are in a cocoon which protects them from outside pressures is variable. To maintain such arrangements, a council would have to act in line with the prevailing political ethos. This is not necessarily an easy task. For instance, changing population compositions introduce new policy preferences. Additionally, within organisations, leaders tend to become more distant from grassroots sentiments the longer they stay in office (Michels 1959).

Empathy between community and administration does not occur naturally; it must be worked at.

Value correspondence is more likely in a conflict-free social environment. No local government meets this stipulation completely, but in small, socially homogeneous areas, it is more likely. The strategies which appease electorates in such settings can be expected to be distinctive. Since control is assured for one social group, the council can present itself as the defender of core values. This stance has relevance not only in an intra-local setting, but also in inter-municipal interactions. Even in the larger authorities of England, aspects of this practice can be identified. The London boroughs of Bromley, Kensington and Chelsea, and Westminster illustrate this in their active conflicts with Labour controlled councils. In some cases, such as Bromley's resistance to building more public housing, these conflicts have a specific locality relevance. In others, such as Bromley's taking the GLC to court over its Fares Fair policy, or Kensington and Chelsea's challenging the GLC budget, the issue is broader. Such tendencies are even stronger in homogeneous suburbs in the United States. Experiencing no fundamental challenges to central ideals, pressure group activity in such places is likely to be trivial. Indeed, community–council interactions are likely to be marked by apathy (Greer and Greer 1976). Where conflict is probable is in external relations, wherein the council acts as the champion of local values.

In larger authorities a different pattern is to be expected, since units embrace a wider variety of views. Here a distinction should be drawn between places in which one political bloc has an effective monopoly (as contrived for many authorities in the 1974 reorganisation of English local government; Dunleavy 1980b), areas which are resource deficient and localities which are socially heterogeneous but not poverty stricken. For the first of these, research in England by Dearlove (1973), Saunders (1979) and Glassberg (1981) has shown that single party rule is linked to the by-passing of demands which contradict the governing party's views. Hewitson (1969) captures the flavour of this environment:

> The first rule of the game is that if you are a member of the loyal opposition you will find yourself playing up the slope into the teeth of a howling gale, with everything against you. You may persuade yourself that you are having influence and getting somewhere, but the harsh reality is that in important matters you are well-nigh powerless. If you are a member of the majority

party you are easily persuaded of your own importance, and can achieve a good deal more, but you rapidly become aware of the second important rule. There is a small, imprecisely defined, group of more able and more senior or influential councillors, who set the pace and make the real decisions. This is the caucus.

(Hewitson 1969: 62–3)

In single party councils, the weakness of local electoral accountability provides this leadership caucus with considerable flexibility over policy. Localities under the same party's control thereby often have dissimilar ideological stances (Bulpitt 1967; Mark-Lawson *et al*. 1985). Dominant Labour groups are as capable of adopting a low spending, ratepayer mentality as Conservative authorities (e.g. Butterworth 1966; Baxter 1972). The United States offers a similar pattern in that single group domination reduces the impetus to respond to unwelcome citizen pressures, while at the same time enabling élite compromises to evolve into distinctive policies. Here, though, the narrow ideological divide between major power groups offers more prospect of cooperation: 'In reality, what occurs is often a kind of tacit collusion in which one coalition dominates at the polls for long periods and makes side payments to the losers' (Elkin 1987: 47). As far as electors are concerned, however, the result is the same as in Britain – slight citizen effects on mainstream council decisions.

For resource deficient cities, the main thrust of policy determination has been outlined earlier. These places are driven by the need either to attract private investors or to capture intergovernmental grants (or both) and must thwart citizen initiatives that threaten these goals. It is not pertinent to repeat the relevant arguments here, but it is worthwhile outlining how such initiatives respond to citizen opposition. Neighbourhood and other mass membership groups are not necessarily ineffective but their impact is highly constrained:

pressures exerted by means of protests or elections tend to be direct and simple. While such external pressures are fully capable of determining the outcome of any specific issue, they appear to be ill suited to controlling a policy direction.

(Stone 1976: 201)

Policy-making environments are more easily dominated by those with a consistent, ongoing relationship with policy-makers. This was very evident in the favoured position of business which Stone (1976) found in Atlanta:

The political resources of the business community were not

converted directly into policy benefits. Instead, resources were used to maneuver into and maintain a favorable political position from which the CAIA [Central Atlanta Improvement Association] had exceptionally good, almost unlimited, access to decision makers (and through them reasonably good access to federal officials as well). From this favorable political position, business influence extended over the process by which conflict was managed. In this way, some opposition was forestalled and some aborted, but not all opposition could be prevented.

(Stone 1976: 88)

In effect, business was granted a central role in policy-making processes. To guard this position, demands made on public officials were presented with care, so that justification for municipal acts could not be portrayed as unreasonable; hence projects were favoured which could be publicised as bringing city-wide benefits rather than favouring business over neighbourhood interests. Senior officials were given flexibility to coordinate developments, because this was mutually beneficial in that profits were enhanced at the same time that the realities of electoral politics were acknowledged; 'the stronger the light of public scrutiny, the closer officials came to being neutral arbiters' (Stone 1976: 197).

The peculiar circumstances of localities which are poverty stricken or single party dominated means that citizen groups find their greatest scope for action in socially heterogeneous areas which are moderately resource rich. Even here there is little prospect of municipal officials acting neutrally. For one thing, there are notable differences in group resources; that is, not only in funds, but more broadly in skills, ability to sustain long campaigns and personal contacts. For another, within localities there are strategic electoral blocs whose support politicians seek, but whose influence varies across places. Take, for example, black populations in English cities. In Birmingham, Newton (1976a) found a pattern of slight influence, whereas in Bradford the main parties have sought alliances with minority populations (Bentley 1972). The difference between these two cities derives largely from dissimilarities in the correspondence between marginal electoral wards and concentrations of black residents. Behind the cultivation of electoral blocs, the desire is not simply to win votes – important as that is – but also to stabilise the policy-making environment; if group leaders believe that they are favoured by the ruling coalition, they will be less likely to arouse discontent. This is important for policy-makers since an active citizenry makes policy processes more unpredictable and can lead to government which is cautious, ineffective and unwilling to take controversial decisions (Crain and Rosenthal 1967; Vidich and Bensman 1968). In the USA, one means of circumventing such inaction has been for functions critical of powerful interests to be tucked away from public view in special districts. Where this option is infeasible, negative policy consequences are commonly directed on to those who are least likely to mount opposition. Glassberg (1981) provides a good illustration in noting how the London Borough of Bromley adopted a focused 'development' strategy to place facilities with negative externalities in locations of slight electoral importance which primarily consisted of lower income residents.

All of this makes the local policy-making environment appear highly contrived. In some instances, this is so. In others, it is not. There are few certainties in politics. Unexpected issues arise. Pressures come from unusual corners. Support is given when none was expected. Outcomes are less clinical than policy-makers hope for, and can be a surprise to all concerned. Uncertainty is to be expected, even if it is worked against.

Uncertainty is most prevalent over specific demands. The response to such issues depends upon the overlap of demands and council preferences. The relationship between these two is complex. The literature abounds with examples of pressure groups being encouraged by factions within a council who wish to show that there is public support for their proposals (e.g. Bondi 1988). Bureaucrats have professional goals that can conflict with more partisan councillor aims, just as the professional priorities of engineers, housing officers, health officials and finance executives can induce inter-departmental conflicts over appropriate policy goals (e.g. Hartley 1980). Lack of clarity over dominant political values leaves more room to manoeuvre for all participants. Yet, even here, open access is denied to the bulk of citizen groups. For ease of policy-making, State functionaries seek to impose their own will and direction on public participation. Hence, citizen involvement is often to inform, rather than be informed by. Reflective of this view is an official's comments on the introduction of comprehensive schools in an English local authority:

> We held parents' meetings and all that, and some officers from the Education Office spoke to them. But this wasn't to *consult*; this was to *tell* the parents what their authority had decided to do

about comprehensive schools . . . Here we *tell* the parents what the authority has decided is best for their children.

(Peterson and Kantor 1977: 202)

As over comprehensive schools, councils can feel compelled to make unpopular decisions that place them in the public limelight. When examining such occasions a distinction should be drawn between issues which are imposed on councils (say by higher tier authorities) and those which arise from their own volition. The former create problems of evaluation, since, as Dearlove (1973) shows, councils can transpose higher tier requests into policy options which they already support. Faced with the prospect of public disquiet, such 'impositions' can be welcome mechanisms for deflecting opposition from the council.

Where unpopular decisions are firmly rooted in the local institution, it is to be expected that councils will try to isolate any opposition. Policies will be justified by a claim to their broad benefits, and opponents will be discredited through the charge of vested interest. In reality, of course, vested interest is integral to all council activities. Bureaucrats and politicians themselves have a vested interest in particular policy practices and outcomes, as do those who gain privileged policy-making access. But these components of policy-making either are legitimised by the electoral process or derive little publicity. The claims of specific neighbourhoods or small social groups are more likely to be vocal and oppositional, in that they challenge council decisions. Consequently, they are easier to tar with the brush of vested interest. In this regard, officials (and powerful interests) are aided by public exclusion from early stages of policy-making. This means that threatening decisions are hidden from public view until late in the policy-making process; perhaps until after a decision is a *fait accompli*. This adds an intensity to group opposition that can make the charge of vested interest stick more easily. The combination of poor resources, weak organisation and the immediacy of a threat provokes so-called undemocratic behaviour. As Dearlove (1974) explained:

In most cases, groups which are not sympathetically regarded by the authorities, and which urge change and innovation in the pattern of established public policies, do make a first attempt to gain access for their demands by quiet, more acceptable, methods, but their invariable failure to gain effective access by a strategy which is completely controlled by the authorities forces them into a more aggressive style of demanding representation. Protest is further encouraged by the fact that the authorities always fail to consult the interests affected before they make a decision.

(Dearlove 1974: 29–30)

This particularly applies to lower income groups. Unlike the middle and upper classes, they do not 'talk the language' of council officials (Sjoberg *et al.* 1966). Furthermore, they lack the resources that higher income groups often embody. In this context, Bondi's (1988) investigation of opposition to school closures in Manchester is instructive, because she found that the social background of most group members was a less significant contributor to success than whether or not leadership was in middle class hands. As Lipsky found in investigations of working class protest in the United States, when middle class support is won, the likelihood of success magnifies (e.g. Lipsky and Levy 1972). This is understandable given the benefits of a broad base of support. But such breadth is not easily achieved, particularly at a neighbourhood level where social classes are often segregated. More commonly, as seen in the location of noxious facilities (such as freeways) or the closure of prized possessions (such as schools), the inclination of neighbourhood groups is to heave a sigh of relief that the target was not in their patch. Councils are adept at exploiting such divisions within citizen interests in order to further their policy choices (e.g. Cockburn 1977).

## THE INNER CIRCLES

Amongst those on the left and the right there is distrust over the role that public sector bureaucrats have in policy-making. On the left, middle and upper class favouritism is highlighted; the inner drive in bureaucratic organisations is seen as the preservation of the status quo. On the right, bureaucratic goals are feared to contradict those of elected officials; the inner drive is seen to favour the growth of government rather than its efficient operation. Underlying both conceptualisations is the notion that bureaucrats are primarily self-interested:

Our bureaucrat is, like all of us, concerned with his [*sic*] own welfare. He views his agency's policies as affecting that welfare. He is interested in the agency's clients primarily as they affect the agency and, through the agency, his own welfare. He cares about his profession, another aspect of the outside environment, as a source of guidance for internal conduct and as a means of furthering his mobility, thus increasing his welfare. While others may be concerned with the distribution of an agency's resources in the city, our bureaucrat is not. To him, the shape of the resource distribution is a by-product of pursuing his own objectives.

(Levy *et al.* 1974: 227)

In so far as such forces are potent in policy-making, an understanding of State institutions must grasp the nettle of evaluating the balance of forces between bureaucratic and elected representatives. In theoretical terms, let alone ideological ones, this issue is important. Yet the reality of the situation is that the relationship between elected officials and bureaucratic officers is complex. On this score, it is not difficult to agree with Stoker's (1988) summary:

We would suggest that in most authorities there is likely to be no *single* centre of power among senior councillors and officers. Rather, we would argue, there are likely to be agreed spheres of influence and when disputes arise they are overcome through strategies of negotiation, persuasion and even manipulation.

(Stoker 1988: 88)

Theory has not advanced far in teasing out the subtlety and dominant causal themes in these relationships. We have not progressed far in identifying the character of agreed spheres of influence. We know little about their permanency or the degree to which they are disputed territory. We know very little about the extent to which such relationships vary across institutions or are tied to political party influence. All in all, this is an area in need of theoretical advancement.

## Bureaucratic officers

Perhaps the most appropriate way of starting an analysis of bureaucratic power is to note the now widely appreciated point that public servants are not the masters that they were once thought to be. Writings such as Ray Pahl's (1975) on urban managerialism are not belittled by this. Prior to managerialism there was too ready a willingness to assume that politicians ruled and bureaucrats administered. Managerialism challenged this assumption. Yet the role that bureaucrats play is still uncertain. Their actions are constrained by the realities of existing within a capitalist polity. Reliance on private sector investment, and the backcloth of elections and local political cultures, are part and parcel of a bureaucrat's work. But the balance of power between them and elected officials appears to be variable (spatially and temporally). Evidence shows that bureaucrats can take leading roles in forging alliances amongst local capitalists in order to further economic growth (Doig 1987), just as their dynamism and leadership has done much to set the political tone of localities (e.g. Caro 1974). In addition, over time the relative power of bureaucrats can change; in the 1960s and 1970s English local officers were described as a dominant force (e.g. Davies 1972; McAuslan and Bevan 1977), but in the 1980s they were cast more as highly constrained by the partisan actions of elected officials (e.g. Laffin and Young 1985; Gyford *et al.* 1989). This change brings home the cautions expressed by a number of researchers in the 1970s, that the influence of councillors was probably being over-estimated (e.g. Haywood 1977; Ribbins and Brown 1979). In particular, councillors – both personally and as reflecting local political cultures – make a significant impression on the philosophical context in which bureaucrats act.

The subtlety of this interchange appears to be lost on right-wing theoreticians of bureaucracy. Here bureaucrats are seen to be driven primarily by a desire to increase the size of their bureau or department in order to gain the salary, status and responsibility associated with a larger institution (Niskanen 1971). Backing this argument, analysts point to bureaucrats being more active partici-pants in elections and generally favouring spending options (e.g. Staaf 1977; Gramlich and Rubinfeld 1982). This public choice account is naïve (Dunleavy 1985). Its appeal owes more to the support that it gives to those who want less government expenditure than to convincing explanation. For one thing, if bureaucrats did control public agencies, they would be unlikely to seek bureau growth for its own sake. The larger a unit is, the more likely it comes under public scrutiny, is subject to the critical eye of elected officials, and is questioned about its effectiveness. Further, job satisfaction is only partially linked to finance. Trust, work autonomy, respect for professionalism and a predictable operational environment are also valued, and each can contradict financial incentives (Breton and Wintrobe 1982; Dunleavy 1985). Moreover, if bureaucrats did dominate politicians, they would hardly preside over large-scale cut-backs in their own bureaux (as has happened in the 1980s). To characterise bureaucratic objectives as predominantly growth inspired is a gross simplification.

Nevertheless, in so far as bureaucrats place their own goals before those of elected representatives, questions should be asked about their democratic tendencies. As is evident in the antagonism which police forces show towards public overview and complaint, there is a tendency within professional circles to promote a technocratic image of their rightful place in government. How far this value disposition is carried into action is not known. As Randall (1981) emphasised, evidence on the power of public bureaucracies is surprisingly shallow. Illustrative of this is our knowledge about street-level bureaucrats (i.e. those who engage in face-to-face interaction with clients). We do know that these officials often have considerable autonomy. Nivola (1978) shows this in the failure of Boston housing inspectors to act on the poor maintenance of rented properties. Faced with the prospect of landlords closing down homes if forced to make improvements (viz. of renters either having no home or having substandard housing), inspectors chose to turn a blind eye. This does not mean that such field officers are not controlled from the centre. Senior officials actively discourage appointments to street-level positions of those who might become advocates for clients (Lipsky 1980). Moreover, the centre controls the resources of street-level operatives. It also provides the backing required to see their decisions through. Thus, when mayor Hatcher took the reins of Gary, Indiana, in 1967, he pressed for improved housing conditions for private renters. Housing inspections increased but few landlords were prosecuted, because the city's legal department was controlled by the old guard Democratic machinery which opposed the policy; hence, prosecution proposals had a tendency to be rejected on technical grounds (Greer 1979). Here, the street-level bureaucrats followed the mayor's wishes, the bureaucratic centre did not. Put simply, bureaucracies are not unitary entities. There are conflicts of interest within them, just as their members can resist (or support) the initiatives of politicians.

In terms of the relationship of these two, a catalogue of examples could be given showing that senior bureaucrats are powerful. This is understandable, since they have a major say in the promotion and work roles of their subordinates. Those who acquire seniority in large authorities are also best placed to take leadership roles within professional associations. Through such roles they can help to reinforce or change the prevailing ethos of their profession; that is, the definition and articulation of what are desirable professional aims and standards. Despite the fact that these goals incorporate discriminatory outcomes, because they are couched in betterment terms, their distributional consequences are frequently ignored by politicians and bureaucrats alike. Levy *et al.* (1974) provide examples of such discriminations in their analysis of Oakland, California; and the themes they identified have been reinforced by studies elsewhere (e.g. Lineberry 1977; Mladenka 1980). For each of libraries, roads and schools, Levy *et al.* (1974) reported that bureaucratic rules governing service provision produced unequal facilities across neighbourhoods. For libraries this was partly because of a professional emphasis on 'the classics' (Dickens, Tolstoy, Twain, etc.), which encouraged middle class readership, rather than more popular titles (*Amateur Photographer*, *Car Mechanic*, etc.), which working class readers prefer. Inter-neighbourhood service inequality then arose when resources were allocated by use levels. Funds for roads were similarly usage based, with routes and areas favoured by high income residents receiving most investment because of their higher ridership levels. As for schools, here bias came from regulations which allowed senior, higher paid teachers to have first call on transfers into schools in 'better' neighbourhoods. All in all, these results add meat to the assertion by Sjoberg *et al.* (1966: 325) that 'bureaucratic systems are the key medium through which the middle class maintains its advantaged position *vis-à-vis* the lower class'. Unless other values intrude into the service provision agenda, it is likely that bureaucratic rules will favour those of higher status (albeit the precise beneficiaries might differ across service types).

Politician–bureaucrat power relationships are expressed both in the outcomes of specific decisions and in the *modus operandi* of an institution. Whichever is focused on, the relationship is interactive; in important ways it is contingent upon the persons involved. Heclo and Wildavsky (1974) point this out for the British government:

> The problem is not that the civil service is too strong and creative in devising public policy, but that politicians are too weak and not creative enough . . . Bureaucracy would only be frustrating party government if there were something there to frustrate.
>
> (Heclo and Wildavsky 1974: 378–9)

Such a view coincides with Margaret Thatcher's new right image of government, which assumes that the bureaucracy can be controlled, but that politicians have lacked conviction, and been too easily swayed by pressure groups, so bureaucrats have dominated large tracts of policy-making (Barry 1987). Lying behind this idea is the notion that personal commitment limits the scope of non-elected officers. That there is truth in this assertion is seen in the manner in which strong personalities, whether amongst politicians or bureaucrats, have made their presence felt in policy-making (e.g. Caro 1974; Doig 1987).

Phrasing explanation purely in personality terms would nevertheless be a mistake, as the framework in which politicians and bureaucrats interact is influential. Thus, when party competition is rife, bureaucrats are inclined to take a back seat (e.g. Newton 1976a; Jennings 1977). By contrast, where competition leads to an impasse, bureaucratic power can be enhanced (Bulpitt [1967] on Rochdale). Such tendencies are nevertheless conditioned by a variety of circumstances. In the nineteenth century, for example, British councillors felt that they had insufficient expertise about services such as gas provision to impose their will on officers (e.g. Garrard 1983). Today, numerous studies reveal the same phenomenon. Hence, it is no accident that investigations identifying the dominance of bureaucratic power have often analysed land-use planning. As Blowers (1980) explained for Bedfordshire:

> In general, the planning officer's appeal to 'planning merits' or 'principles' is sufficient to discourage politicians from challenging his recommendations unless there are obvious party considerations or outside pressures which urge them to do so. Over a whole range of items which are, on the face of it, not contentious, the chief officer will have his way.
>
> (Blowers 1980: 27)

Officer autonomy is not equal across policy arenas. Local authority departments overlap with influential professional communities such as those for accountants, architects, engineers, lawyers and teachers. The professional status of others is less widely accepted (Laffin 1986); housing management is one example. In Britain, once these differences are combined with political party interest in services, varying intensities of overview can be understood (e.g. weaker officer influence combines with more intense party interest over housing management). To secure a significant policy-making effect in these circumstances, officers are aided by self-selection; those favouring substantial public housing commitments find more room to manoeuvre in Labour controlled councils than in Conservative ones. Where bureaucrats are on the same policy wavelength as politicians, the need for tight overview is lessened.

But this does not lead to the influence of elected representatives being subdued. As Ribbins and Brown (1979) pointed out, what it does mean is that it is extremely difficult to disentangle the relative power of bureaucrats and elected officials.

## Elected officials

In their analysis of newly elected English councillors, Fudge *et al.* (1981) reported that after six months in office, 15 out of 19 agreed that officers tend to dominate council affairs, but felt that this was probably the fault of elected members for letting it happen. This point should not be played down. It confirms the picture that Heclo (1969) found in Manchester, but differs from it in the significant regard that it refers to the post-1974 local government system. This reform was supposed to upgrade the 'quality' of councillors (Dearlove 1979) and so favour younger, management-oriented leaders (Jennings 1982). Becoming aware of their standing *vis-à-vis* officers is commonly just one of a number of shocks for new councillors. Also to be contended with are the limits imposed by central government regulations and directions, plus the hierarchical structure of local parties that places newcomers on the backbenches (e.g. Birrell 1981). Hardly surprisingly, many newcomers become disillusioned with their inability to grasp issues and by the slowness of policy advance (Fudge *et al.* 1981). Moreover, newcomers are more likely to be representing marginal wards (by definition, councillors of longer duration are inclined to be from safer wards; Newton 1976a). Hence, efforts must be given to constituency work, leaving less time for promoting oneself within the party or pursuing policy objectives.

To be exact, a ward orientation is not something that is restricted to new councillors. One of the prevailing features of the pre-1974 England was the lack of drive and policy commitment that councillors exhibited. Blondel and Hall (1967) summarised the tone well:

> Councillors are not in political life locally in order to put their personal mark on the present and future development of the town. They are modest – both about their ambitions and their capabilities. Though they are not at all unwilling to spare their time and efforts, it is more in order to achieve political status than to modify policies crucially important to the community.
>
> (Blondel and Hall 1967: 331)

Emerging from this, council chambers were often more like a club, with officers in some authorities complaining that members were reluctant to go home (Harrison and Norton 1967; Dyer 1978). The social gratifications of office were prized, as was service to the ward. Policy orientations were reactive rather than positive, focusing on issues rather than broad trends:

> Birmingham council contains its fair share of those who are passionate about administrative detail and trivia, and who seem to take no interest in general policy issues; indeed they were surprised by the suggestion that they might have some concern with policy.
>
> (Newton 1976a: 153)

Associated with this, analysts report that party politics barely made a mark on the operations of many pre-1974 councils. Often a bi-partisan attitude was dominant (Bulpitt 1967; Corina 1974). Bureaucrats had autonomy because elected officials allowed it; their minds were on other things, not governing.[7]

The similarity of conclusions in Fudge *et al.* (1981) and Heclo (1969) warns that since 1974 all has not changed. As Ken Livingstone (1987) described, even some years after reorganisation, the London Borough of Lambeth continued to plod on in the time-honoured fashion:

> Lambeth had for years been a quiet backwater of local government where the leadership was never challenged. Like other inner-city Labour councils, a strong authoritarian, quite conservative Labour administration had been in power since the war, led by a handful of competent working-class men[8] with strong roots in the area. These men ruled over a group of mediocre councillors who were treated as lobby fodder. Many were barely literate but if they did as they were told and did not cause any trouble, they might, after ten or fifteen years' loyal service, be rewarded with a year as mayor and enjoy all the job's little perks.
>
> (Livingstone 1987: 15)

Accounting for changing council orientations requires more than a naïve assumption that the 1974 reorganisation promoted a more committed council membership. That reorganisation *per se* was not critical is evident in London's restructuring having no such effect. All that reorganisation can be credited with is introducing two governmental tiers into cities, so making it easier for local authority officers to hold office (although the Thatcher government recently placed restrictions on local government officer's holding elected positions).[9] Most especially for Labour, the growth in representation by public sector employees has raised the educational attainment and policy commitment of councillors (Walker 1983). This states what has happened but not why. For this we must look at changes in the ideological standing of political parties.

On the Labour side, the 1964–70 national government provoked a strong reaction amongst many party supporters, who accused the leadership of failing to pursue socialist aims. Starting at the local level, a groundswell of new left sentiment sought to infuse the party with a stronger ideological commitment (Gyford 1985). As Chapter Two indicated, a reaction also occurred within the Conservative Party to what some saw as a dismal performance by the 1970–4 national government. This led to a strengthening of new right forces. Here, change came first to the national level and has penetrated slowly into the local sphere. What is more, as with the new left, the local strength of this ideological stance is variable. Moreover, it is unstable, since there is much disagreement within local parties over policy direction, to the extent that intra-party conflict can be more notable than that between parties. For Labour, Keating (1988: 59) summarised the situation well: 'There is the ever-present conflict between right and left within the Labour Party, a conflict ostensibly based on ideology but with ideology often used as a pretext for personal and factional rivalry.' While some writers keenly portray the emergence of the new left in terms of the radical character of local populations (e.g. Duncan and Goodwin 1988), more realistically they should be seen in the context of disgruntlement with old leaders (with personality disputes probably receiving too slight a coverage in accounts of this; see Corina [1974] on the importance of councillors' personality traits). The emphasis given to the regular re-selection of elected officials by the new left is one symbol of the desire to weaken the old guard (re-selection providing an opportunity to de-select those out of tune with the new radicals). Another is encouraging decentralised administration within local authorities. In both cases genuine beliefs in increasing democratic tendencies in government dovetail neatly with the goal of attaining leadership positions and generating public support for new leadership styles. Extending Byrne's (1986) argument, just as increased unemployment requires the State to promote new forms of dependency, given the weaker disciplining effect of work, so the Labour Party needs a stronger non-work support base. New left councils have gone some way toward providing this by supporting coalitions of disaffected social groups long neglected by trade union elements in the party (e.g. racial minorities, gays, women, the physically disabled; Gyford 1985; Livingstone 1987). The character of links between local political leaders and their constituents are ever changing. Many of these changes are unexpected. Others are hoped for – as with the growth in middle class representation on councils – but their consequences are not (as in more radical councils). Political processes, like the agents who carry them through, do not occupy empty shells described by social structures. They maintain and change processes. Trying to control their political prospects, public sector officials adapt to the restraints of social structure, are liberated by the opportunities these provide, and endlessly engage in a dynamic interaction with a complex of forces whose lifespans, styles and potency are highly variable. It is this dynamism, and particularly its linkages to broader, more enduring social forms, that is still poorly understood.

## RESUME

The massive literature on local policy-making and community power structures provides few satisfying cues for abstract theorising. Too much of what has been written has been oriented around universalist explanations of local events. Like spoilt brats squabbling over who has told the best story, much of the history of community power research has been taken up by researchers talking past one another, pouting in disgust at the narrow-mindedness of others, while cuddling the advocate's favoured toy so as to shield it from critical evaluation (Walton 1976; Elkin 1987). The intervention of structuralist approaches in the field offered some glimmering that this impasse would be broken, but little progress has been made in linking structural conditions to the dynamism of policy processes. Too much of what has been offered fails to grasp the complexity of society. Fundamental to furthering our understanding is to appreciate Mann's (1986: 4) simple dictum that: 'Societies are much *messier* than our theories of them'. This seems obvious, something everyone agrees with, but too often it seems to be ignored. 'To conceive of societies as confederated, overlapping, intersecting networks rather than as single totalities complicates theory. But we must introduce further complexity' (Mann 1986: 17). Without structuralist ideas, pluralism and élitism offer shallow accounts of local politics. Yet structuralist accounts, as is now well recognised, are too unidimensional for comfort. 'What is needed is a theory of *political* economy, not an economic theory of politics' (Swanstrom 1988: 88). Identifying this need, analysts have sought to breathe more reality into their accounts through the mechanism of locality studies. Already, commentators are warning that such steps run the risk of a return to empiricism; to the diminution of theoretically informed analysis (e.g. Newby 1986; Jonas 1988). In addition, originating as it does from a structuralist perspective, such locality studies run the risk of simplifying the dynamism of policy processes. This chapter has provided no answers in this regard, but hopefully it has given some insight on the flexibilities and uncertainties that pervade policy-making environments. Here too much has been simplified. Empirically there is much flux. Theoretically, the links between policy processes and social structure occupy a body with the flimsiest bones which lacks sufficient muscle to give a realistic semblance of life.

# 6   Policy outcomes

Policy outcomes are the consequences of governmental action. They are the 'so-what' of State processes (Levy *et al.* 1974: 1). As such, policy outcomes are conceptually distinguishable from policy outputs, since the latter refers to the attributes of governmental policies *per se*. Questions about policy outputs – such as, do standards of road maintenance vary, which locality receives most public housing investment and how do tax breaks vary between jurisdictions – are important in political research. Further, because answers to them inform theories of the State, output issues are of theoretical importance in their own right. However, by their nature, the focus of output studies is institutional rather than societal; the prime consideration is how a governmental unit performs, not what the consequences of that performance arc. It is in the evaluation of consequences that researchers concentrate on issues of policy *outcome*:

> Consider government as a mechanism that makes decisions about what it should do. The decisions result in the production of outputs. Officials dispense these outputs to citizens in such a way that we talk about a distribution of outputs or discern a pattern of resource allocation. When anyone evaluates this distribution or pattern, we refer to outcomes. To inquire about the impact of an outcome is to ask how the lives of individual citizens are altered by governmental action.
>
> (Levy *et al.* 1974: 2)

Even if left implicit, of necessity assessments of policy outcomes are deeply penetrated by theoretical perspectives on the State. This is because the primary issues at stake concern the distribution of societal benefits. When it comes to analysing such distributional issues, the ideological disposition of both researcher and reader of necessity play an important part in an evaluation.

Subjectivity is further enhanced by the immaturity of social science theory, since this exposes substantial uncertainties over the impact and causes of social forces. Even with theoretical advancement, different interpretations will inevitably persist, because the dynamism of society itself is sufficient to raise new uncertainties and periodic vagaries. Yet theoretical advancement has been made. This can be seen in the manner in which dissimilar interpretations of the same event have been able to inform advocates of different perspectives in a manner which has deepened causal insight. The declining tendency toward economic reductionism in neo-marxist analyses (Jessop 1982), and the recognition of unequal power blocs in pluralist theory (Lindblom 1977; Dahl 1982), are two examples of advancement along these lines. Most certainly, this does not mean that theoreticians combine ideas from different theoretical traditions indiscriminately. Radical theories are difficult to inter-mesh with formulations favouring the status quo because their base line assumptions are so divergent (Taylor 1983). Yet critics of alternative postures rarely downgrade opposing ideas on the grounds of inaccuracy or distortion. More commonly critiques focus on the incompleteness or the inappropriate emphasis of competing formulations.[1] Thus, criticisms of early ideas on urban managerialism did not claim that urban managers were not powerful but that their scope for action was constrained by more powerful structural forces. To accept the latter does not lead automatically to a rejection of insights from managerialism but merely to the emphasis placed on them. As with a number of theoretical stances, the propositions of managerialism could be reformulated to be consistent either with radical ideas or (as seen in an elementary form in public choice theory) with status quo orientations.

To date, such theoretical reformulations have not taken us very far. In many regards this appears to owe much to the timidity (or perhaps narrow-mindedness is more accurate) of attempted reformulations. (To me, Saunders's dual state model is an exception here, since it does seek to integrate quite disparate theoretical ideas in a consistent, provocative way; e.g. Cawson and Saunders 1983.) Too often, while recognising the incompleteness of their accounts, analysts have continued to stress the sanctity of their preferred theory, allocating other explanatory causes to 'contingent factors'. What we need are theories of those contingent factors which help to explain why they arise (in particular forms, at particular times, in particular places) and so explain why more dominant forces are not apparent in the overt actions of human agents. This is a tall order, which will not be easy to fill. Yet it is a goal which is worth striving for. In this book, for example, a base assumption has been that the dependence of the State on private profitability is a fundamental value. Yet, in one activity sphere after another, theoretical ideas which revolve around this assumption do not get us far in explaining specific State processes. This applies at all geographical scales; even up to the international sphere, where there is increasing recognition that State policies cannot be read off from economic structures (e.g. Blake and Walters 1987; Gilpin 1987). It is not simply that States have strategic interests which are unrelated to economic consider-ations (Mann 1986, 1988), but that internal political conditions mediate between the world economy and national economic circumstances. Hence, neither marxism nor liberal economic theory provides much help in understanding how Argentina shifted from a position in 1914 when per capita income was higher than in France and Sweden, and when it had competed for 40 years with Japan as the fastest growing economy in the world, to the status of a Third World nation some 40 years later. As Waisman (1987) illustrates, ideas of dependency or 'take-off' offer little explanatory assistance, but understanding the peculiarities of Argentine politics helps to clarify why government policies worked against economic advance-ment. It is essential to recognise that the State cannot simply be read off from class structure, since it is an integral component of creating that structure. Katznelson (1986) highlights this in his comparison of France, Germany and the United States in the nineteenth century. As he noted, the French Revolution fun-damentally altered the way in which workers conceived and even talked about social class, because it created new categories of citizen rights and spawned new vocabularies of political justification. By contrast, the authoritarian character of the German State led to its becoming a fulcrum of social class formation as it became a focus for collective working class agitation over political participation. At the same time, the fragmented nature of the governmental system in the USA, aligned with the early granting of voting rights, helped to weaken class consciousness amongst workers. Current theories do not take us far in accounting for such variety in the causal forces that intersect to decide State processes and their interrelationships with social structures. At present, theories appear either to retain a firm grounding in structuralist explanation or else to show reluctance in leaving their human agency base. Few efforts have offered an integration of agency and structure that is convincing.

Going beyond this point, it has to be emphasised that cause and effect are intertwined. Take the United States as an illustration. Through the desire to maintain privileges, elements of the propertied classes had to rely on working class support in the struggle for independence from England. In payment, workers were granted the franchise, with the governmental system being fractured in order to restrict the scope of action lest too much authority fell into the hands of the lower classes. The granting of the franchise helped to limit the development of working class consciousness, as worker organisations were denied the rallying cause of striving for political rights. Further weakening of the communal working class identity arose from the lack of shared experience in the workplace. Thus, with relatively buoyant economies in northern Europe, labour shortages in the USA prompted efforts to attract immigrants from the more economically backward regions of central and southern Europe. The unskilled work which these immigrants could immediately undertake (and which many were brought to the USA specifically to do) placed them at loggerheads with more skilled indigenous workers who were opposing employers' efforts to mechanise production (Shefter 1986). Social status bigotry over the inferiority of new immigrants helped to fuel antagonism, but divisions between new immigrants and indigenous workers were fundamentally driven by class conflict. The use of immigrants as strike-breakers and their assistance in advancing mechanisation led many indigenous workers to place them on the side of capital (mechanisation being resisted because it de-skilled the workforce, so threatening wages, and was used as a device for overcoming strong labour organisations). Divisions between newer and more long-time residents weakened the effectiveness of trade unions as vehicles for advancing workers' fortunes. Indeed, with immigrant flows producing spatial concentrations of ethnic groups in cities, the openness of US governmental arrangements offered an alternative to the workplace as a channel for immigrant advance. Moreover, with ethnic political machines fuelling suburbanisation trends, there was added fragmentation of the government system. Divided by workplace, by neighbourhood, and increasingly by political jurisdiction, the opportunities for developing a collective class consciousness were severely retarded. Yet, at the same time, owing to the weakness of class consciousness, divisions by workplace, home and jurisdiction were easier to create and sustain. Throughout these events, social processes were informing governmental actions at the same time as they were being informed by them. The fragmented yet open governmental system was grounded in class conflict, yet these governmental features in turn helped to determine the future character of lower class–upper class relationships. The spatial separation of social groups and the ability to use governmental channels to further new immigrant fortunes were both cause and consequence of the social structure of the USA (though in neither case solely so).

The implications of this are central to understanding interrelations between policy outcomes and theories of the State. In a nutshell, if society informs State action which in turn informs societal organisation (and so on), then policy outcomes are written into each of the character of capital, the nature of civil society, the structure of State institutions and the relationships of capital, civil society and the State. Hence, all of the material covered in this book has dealt in one way or another with policy outcomes. The spatial structure of municipal government, its administrative organisation, its revenue bases, representation in its corridors of authority by social class, sex, race, age and ethnicity, and the differential access of pressure groups to its policy-making channels, are all the outcomes of previously decided, but ongoing decisions. But if this is the case, why include a separate chapter on policy outcomes? The answer lies in the non-government realm. To this point, attention has been directed at the manner in which forces within society at large and, importantly, prior government actions, become written into present-day operational procedures and decisions in local public institutions. What this chapter examines is the manner in which governmental policies feed into society, influencing the character of social formations and directly affecting the life chances and lifestyles of the populace.

In addressing this question, a wide variety of policies with implications for societal organisation is relevant. What is attempted here is not an overview of the specifics of numerous public policies, but an outline of themes and directions in local public actions. To be more specific, this chapter is not concerned with the organisational form of local institutions, nor with the character of its interactions with non-governmental (or even other governmental) institutions and social groups. The insights offered focus on the consequences of policy outputs. These outputs are not simply the physical or financial products of public institutions (such as new public housing, more or less school books, or changed welfare payments). In addition, they include outputs which are strictly decisions, in that they grant others the authority to act without councils making a financial or commodity contribution (examples include land-use planning decisions, the regulation of health standards in restaurants and the insistence that council contracts go to firms with equal opportunity provisions). In examining the outcomes of such outputs, three distributional patterns are concentrated upon: first, those that separate social groups; second, distinctions between local jurisdictions; and, third, differences within local jurisdictions. Surrounding each of these are temporal change and dissimilarities across policy arenas.

## SOCIAL GROUPS AND POLICY BENEFITS

Messages projected by politicians and the media concerning the distributional effects of government policy frequently portray a redistributive image of the effects of governmental actions. New right emphasis on the need to reduce public expenditure highlights this point, as do calls from the left for increased public spending. For both, the implicit message is that government intervention is generally progressive; by implication, at least, government actions are assumed to benefit those of lower income more than others. Most certainly, this pattern is not believed to hold across all sectors of government responsibility. The picture is a generalised one, taken over the totality of government, rather than being specific to every policy arena. However, amongst those who have investigated the totality, the common conclusion is that this public image is far too simplistic. For example, for the revenue and expenditure of the US federal government between 1949 and 1976, Devine (1983) found that while expenditure policies favoured labour over capital, revenue policies reversed this pattern. In combination, federal actions left inequalities, which were generated by the market economy, virtually untouched. Instructive though this conclusion is, it must be handled with some care, because the definition of labour in Devine's categorisation was extremely broad. What he really compared was employee compensation and corporate profits (plus dividend, rent and interest income). If we peel back the general cover of employee benefits we find significant differentiation within the labour camp. Such divisions have been eloquently revealed in Julian LeGrand's (1982) analysis of the British welfare state (George and Wilding [1984] offer a confirmatory account). The crux of LeGrand's findings are summarised in the simple, blunt statement that 'the middle and upper classes benefit most'. Before examining this, its counter-intuitive nature should be stressed. By itself, the idea of a welfare state projects an image of a redistributive benefit structure. What is more, working class organisations have fought hard for the statutory provisions embodied in the welfare state (with resistance principally coming from those representing propertied interests). If LeGrand is correct, why should politicians on the left argue for higher public expenditure, whilst those on the right demand less? If LeGrand is correct, then surely the distribution of gains from governmental policies might be expected to produce the opposite response?

Excluding distortions to priorities that arise for electoral reasons or to maintain the confidence of capital, one explanation for this seemingly incongruous situation is that the goals of ruling parties can be satisfied in a variety of ways. For example, if those on the left wish to aid the poor, in preference to the already wealthy (or relatively wealthy), is this best achieved by redistributing existing societal benefits or by promoting economic growth so that there is more wealth to spread around? If governmental actions discriminate too much against the wealthy and against capital, there is a risk of discouraging future investment and of encouraging the emigration of skilled workers and wealthy residents. For leftist leaders, therefore, the competing pressures of a desire to help the less fortunate and the need to appease the already wealthy must be balanced. For those on the right, there is a reluctance to favour welfare state provisions on account of a belief that social programmes reduce workers' willingness to take low paid jobs and, because higher taxes are required to pay for them, lest they weaken incentives for entrepreneurship. Additionally, by keeping down payments to the poor, the favour of small businesses is expected to be won (by helping to keep down wages), and pressures on product prices should be less, so aiding exports and weakening inflationary pressures. Hence, there is a variety of reasons why the right opposes extensive welfare state benefits for those of lower income. But, set alongside these reasons, it is generally recognised that social programmes are essential if a breakdown in social order is to be avoided (O'Connor 1973).

All of this does not explain why the benefits of State programmes favour the more wealthy. For one thing, most of the negative consequences which the right sees as resulting from social programmes are equally relevant for hand-outs to the rich (e.g. inflationary effects, increased imports, lower work incentives). Further, just as capitalists view with distrust policies which favour the poor, so too is there discomfort amongst citizens in general over policies favourable to the rich (most visibly seen in populist outbursts which call for the end of big business privileges; e.g. Burbank 1976; Karabel 1979). But such sentiments are often based on suspicion rather than known practice. A problem with evaluations of government policies is that, even amongst researchers, let alone the general public and politicians, definitions of critical concepts such as public expenditure and taxation are themselves contentious (Mullard 1987). Illustrative of this is the British government's calculations of expenditure on the National Health Service: when Conservative ministers state how much they have increased spending on health they neglect to point out that their figures include hypothetical efficiency savings and income from the sale of assets.[2] The actual performance of government is shrouded in a mist of confusing definitions, partial reporting, non-comparable figures and poor publicity; all of which the public finds difficult to penetrate (albeit part of the blame for this lies in the public's lack of attention to governmental activity). Playing on symbols rather than actual performance, popular evaluations are subject to manipulation (by State functionaries as well as others) in order to present or to perpetuate particular points of view. With a bias in State disposition toward capital, supplemented by the same leanings in primary channels of information dispersion such as the mass media, publishers and the film industry, it is no surprise that it is easier to project images which distract attention from the benefits obtained by the propertied classes and cast doubt on the validity of payments to the poor. The anecdotes of Ronald Reagan are typical of a tendency to cast suspicion on those who benefit from social programmes.

A prime example of the anecdotal approach to welfare reform was demonstrated by President Reagan when he spoke of a man in the grocery line paying for an orange with food stamp coupons and using the change to buy vodka. Another was his comment on the exorbitant federal moneys spent on mass transit, when he exclaimed that government could afford to provide every resident in one city with a limousine for a day with the money spent on the transit system. Such anecdotes quickly capture the alleged evils of a program by portraying an easily identified image. To the uninformed public, the anecdote then takes on a life of its own, conveying an entire ideology – in these cases, a negative portrayal of all 12 million households receiving food stamps and of public mass transit subsidies. But the anecdote may be factually incorrect, as in the two just mentioned. Food stamp rules allow a maximum of 99 cents in change to be given to any customer, hardly enough with which to buy vodka. And President Reagan was comparing the costs of limousines for *one* day with the total capital construction costs of a permanent transit system. The impression left by the anecdote is used as the basis for major program changes even though data consistently prove that the anecdotes are usually inaccurate or that they reflect isolated cases at most.

(Joe and Rogers 1985: 153)

Another area where suspicion is easy to generate is trade union strikes. It is obvious that harm and inconvenience can result from these actions, yet withdrawal of labour is the main, and at times the sole tool which trade unionists can employ in fighting for improved work conditions. This is rarely explained in mass media presentations; just as the similarity of such 'selfish' actions to the refusal of capitalists to invest in a nation is by-passed. (In the imagery of most mass media presentations, giving up income in trade union strikes is harmful to the nation, but giving up income by not investing in it, preferring perhaps to invest abroad, is a symbol of free choice, with the harm done to the nation ignored.) Of course, not all governmental officials, nor all media reports, adopt such tactics. However, because of the dependence of the State on capital (Offe 1984), because of the mass media being controlled by large corporations (Parenti 1986; Curran and Seaton 1988), and because of middle and upper class biases in the value dispositions of private and public sector bureaucracies (Sjoberg *et al.* 1966), there is impetus behind discriminations in the portrayal of policy costs and benefits. (For an analysis of the potency of these sentiments in television news coverage, see Glasgow University Media Group 1976, 1980.)[3] As with any social order, socialisation into capitalist society is intricately bound up with the reproduction of the established order; that is, with perpetuating the values and norms of behaviour that justify existing inequalities. Hence, dominant images of acceptable behaviour are deeply penetrated by the preferences of dominant power groups.

Criminal law provides a good example of this, because the specification of what is and what is not a crime is supremely conditioned by the ideology of the more powerful:

Rather than being a fair reflection of those behaviours objectively causing us collectively the most avoidable suffering, criminal law categories are artful, creative constructs designed to criminalize only some victimizing behaviours, usually those most frequently committed by the relatively powerless, and to exclude others, usually those frequently committed by the powerful against subordinates.

(Box 1983: 7)

It is not simply that (say) corporate crime receives scant attention in the media, so that the extent to which it occurs is lost on the general public. It is not simply that such crimes receive relatively little attention from State agencies (note how the Reagan and Thatcher administrations have stressed the need to catch illegal welfare recipients but have said little about the need to catch tax dodgers). It is not even that much white-collar crime goes unreported for fear that the employer will be embarrassed or will suffer a loss of customer confidence (computer fraud being notable for low rates of reporting). More significant is the manner in which the mass media deliberately focus upon, and indeed even manufacture, crimes that they associate with the less powerful. A good example is the British media campaign of the early and mid-1970s against 'mugging'. As Hall *et al.* (1978) have shown, press reaction was on a scale much in excess of the threat posed. However, by unnecessarily stirring fears of personal attack, and by innuendo and selective reporting, a political message was projected: 'If "mugging", by mid-1972, in Britain meant slums and cities and innocent folk and daylight robbery, it also meant liberal politicians versus decent white folks . . . the politics of "law and order" and "silent majorities"' (Hall *et al.* 1978: 28). The rise of authoritarian populism, on whose back Margaret Thatcher gained much credibility, owed much to such images, since they helped to project the myth that society was breaking down and required a strong dose of law and order (Jessop *et al.* 1988).[4] Now this all seems conspiratorial, but it should not be construed in this way. Newspapers have to be sold, just as motion pictures have to be watched, if their makers are to stay in business. Stories about mugging helped to sell papers, just as stories about governmental or corporate corruption can. The point is not that the material which is covered in the media does not criticise a wide spectrum of institutions or practices, but that reports are constrained by dominant power relationships. For one thing, the wealthy have the resources to purchase media outlets and to direct their materials in directions which they favour (Evans 1983; Curran and Seaton 1988). For another, they have the resources to penalise reports which fabricate stories (as with those over mugging and the 'loony left'), by taking court action. They also have the ability to penalise media concerns whose reports discomfort them by withdrawing advertising. And, if the outlets are like the BBC and do not depend on advertising revenue but on the government, they have their friends on the political right (or occasionally on the left) who can threaten the autonomy of the institution.

The predisposition in favour of the more powerful in dominant institutions is evident throughout the governmental system. For education, this has been revealed in Willis's (1977) excellent study of students in a Midlands school. Here, he identified how the rejection of school values by 'the lads' led to a self-perpetuating cycle in which working class youths ensured that their career options were restricted to low paid, unskilled jobs. This rejection did not come from innate or personality attributes. Rather it emerged from a realistic assessment of the life chances of working class youths in a highly stratified society. Through socialisation – in and out of school – the prospects for interesting, well-paid work were soon recognised to be slight. With the tone of school education directed toward the requirements of middle class, office oriented work, resistance to school norms became an active component of behaviour. Having little to offer those who see no prospect of (or perhaps inclination for) following a middle class career path, school teachers effectively colluded in a compromise which de-emphasised educational goals. Both Reynolds (1976) and Corrigan (1979) confirm the report of Willis in other settings, with education *per se* taking a low priority in this collusion:

> the crucial factor in determining a favourable overall response by the pupils to most of their schools lies in the degree to which both staff and pupils have reached an unofficial series of arrangements – or truces – which lay down the boundaries beyond which the participants in the schools will not carry their conflict . . . A truce situation means, simply, that the teachers will go easy on the pupils and that the pupils will go easy on the teacher.
>
> (Reynolds 1976: 132-3)

The picture is quite different in schools dominated by the middle classes. Here there is more likely to be a favourable disposition toward schooling, since formal education seems to offer the prospect of personal advancement for those following its norms. This is well expressed in the manner in which the British schooling system has been oriented around class divisions. At one extreme this is seen in the divide between private schools and the government sector, at another in the practice before comprehensive schools were introduced of selecting children at 11 years of age for entry into one of grammar, technical or secondary schools. Of course, selection was not overtly class biased, but its dependence on academic performance at so young an age favoured those whose parents believed that advancement was gained through formal education, and had the time and resources to assist their children's training. Within England there is a strong relationship between social class and school performance (e.g. Gray and Jesson 1987). Yet in the United States, where the schools have traditionally been less distinguished by social class, the link between socio-economic standing and educational outcomes is less sharp (e.g. Katzman 1968; Summers and Wolfe 1977). Racial minorities are something of an exception to this pattern, because the depth of cleavage between social classes in Britain is equally evident in the United States by race. In both nations, when attempts have been made to remove these rigid separations, through desegregation in the USA and by introducing comprehensive schools in Britain, there has been strong resistance from those with more personal resources. In both nations, the 'solution' for the middle classes (in particular) has commonly been to opt-out. Thus, the emergence of desegregated schools and comprehensive schools was accompanied by sharp increases in the number and size of private schools; when it was denied to them in the public realm, those with the resources re-created an élitist schooling system in the private sector (e.g. Clark 1988). Taken as a whole, private schooling advantages those who are already most advantaged – both socially and geographically (e.g. Bradford and Burdett 1989). Yet, even in the public sector, spending on education is regressive (with the degree of regressiveness increasing the higher one progresses up the educational ladder; Table 6.1). Education, most especially higher education, is a form of negative income tax; those of lower income pay disproportionately to benefit those of higher income (e.g. Wilensky 1975; Spangler 1979).

It is not necessary for us to run through any more sectors of State activity, as the essential point has been made in what has been examined so far. Put simply, there is an orientation within State policies which favours the more powerful and the more wealthy. Individual State programmes can certainly provide benefits that offer more to the less powerful and to the poor, but these will be ebbs that run against the main tide. When such reverse pressures threaten to develop into trends, resistance from more dominant segments is the norm. In broad terms, the distribution of benefits from State policies are a reflection of the underlying power structure

*Table 6.1* Public education expenditure by occupation group: England and Wales 1973

| Occupation group | Educational institution | | | |
|---|---|---|---|---|
| | *Primary* | *Secondary under 16 years* | *Secondary over 16 years* | *University* |
| Professional–managerial | 90 | 88 | 165 | 272 |
| Intermediate | 102 | 99 | 134 | 172 |
| Skilled manual | 103 | 105 | 65 | 37 |
| Unskilled/semiskilled manual | 103 | 103 | 91 | 50 |

*Note*
The figures given are the percentages of the mean expenditure level for each educational level which are spent on those with parents from the named occupational groups.

*Source*: LeGrand (1982: 58)

of society. This means that there are built-in biases in favour of capital, but that these are conditioned by the preferences of State functionaries themselves and by vested interests amongst the population at large. What this means, most especially when we move down to the locality level where power networks are more complex, more varied and more dynamic than their national counterparts, is that there are counter-currents, cross-currents, whirlpools and occasional rip-tides within overall trends in benefit distributions. Complexity and variety are present which ensures that the reading of dominant themes requires much more than a surface viewing. However, even when benefit structures are written in the language of universal availability and even if equitably provided, in satisfying demands from within the State apparatus and from civil society, they must in the long term respond to more powerful factions of society (although at times this can result in increased benefits for others). In effect, many of the State programmes which are available for all are disproportionately called on by the middle and upper classes because they are better placed to make use of them (i.e. they have the resources to do so). The State supports the reproduction of their social standing but through mechanisms wrapped in the cloak of equality and national advancement.

## POLICY VARIATION ACROSS LOCAL AUTHORITIES

All this does not mean that policy variation across local councils is unimportant. This is obvious, because not all policies have the same distributional consequences and the weightings given to specific local programmes is not everywhere the same. Hence, programmes which directly bring most benefit to the poor (or the wealthy) are evident in differing measure across localities. Each place will have a package of service and policy commitments that provides it with a distributional pattern unique to itself. Some similarities can be expected, of course, as with the tendency for places with radical political cultures to back tighter environmental regulations and to approve progressive legislation such as rent controls (Clavel 1986; Judd and Ready 1986). Yet even if we look within categories of cities that can be said to share a common political culture, there is variety in policy packages. At present, we know little about either the character of these local policy complexes or how they are linked to the attributes of local socio-economic or governmental environments. In good part, this is because investigations: (a) have concentrated on single policy spheres rather than the interrelationships of policy commitments within single places; (b) have tended to take broad policy commitments as their focus of investigation when much variation exists within policy arenas; and (c) have shown too little regard for the impression that nationwide or state-wide forces make on local decisions (hence providing an account of policy variation that places too high a value on local discretion). The first two of these are evinced in the tendency for investigations to focus on single policy arenas (say housing) and to assess policy differences in terms of broad measures of local activity (say per capita expenditure on housing as a whole). Few investigations have considered how contributions to housing dovetail with commitments to other policy arenas (such as education, welfare, roads, or recreation). In a few studies it has been shown that, in expenditure terms at least, the relative standing of functional allocations across localities is highly variable; local authorities which place a high priority on one of education, housing, welfare or roads, to name a few, are quite likely to place a low loading on one or more of the others; although the pattern of inter-correlations between functional areas is not captured in simple trade-off terms (Danziger 1976; Hoggart 1989). What is more, within service categories, there is unevenness in policy commitments. Thus, for 1949–74, a feature of public housing expenditure in English cities was that Labour controlled cities placed a higher priority on investing in new housing construction, but these places lagged behind Conservative controlled boroughs in their commitments to services such as repairs and maintenance which benefited those already living in council owned homes (Hoggart 1987). At present we know too little about the circumstances that produce these variable commitments, either within or across service categories.

Additional to this is a lack of depth in our appreciation of the extent to which local policy manifestations are decided by nationwide or state-wide forces. If they are largely contingent local effects, then policy variation is principally decided by nationwide forces, with their specific manifestation being determined by the spatial distribution of populations which are targeted for a policy. If, on the other hand, local causal effects are present, then the geographical incidence of target populations will be less important and such factors as local political culture will have an important part to play. Most especially in more centralised polities like Britain, fundamental tenets of State action are decided at the national level, and so strong common threads should be expected in local policies. Amongst the empirical investigations which have clearly brought this out is Newton's (1976a) analysis of housing policy in Birmingham. Here:

> when the separate performance of all the leading actors on the local stage have been weighed and appraised, it appears that the leading part in the city's housing drama has often been played by the central government on the one hand, and by general economic conditions on the other. In fact, for all the heat and fury surrounding the house building issue, for all the hard words in council debates and the contumely hurled by each party at the other, for all the activity of citizen organisations, and for all the power and influence of city architects and engineers, the city's record is remarkably like that of other large provincial cities.
>
> (Newton 1976a: 200)

The strength of such broad based causal forces is inclined to be stronger in Britain than in the United States, but in both countries few attempts have been made to assess their relative importance. Investigations by Derthick (1968) and Grubb (1984) on welfare spending in the USA show that variability in local response is more extensive the greater the local discretion over policy implementation. Jesson *et al.* (1985) offer a somewhat different insight on English local education spending when reporting that only between 10 and

20 per cent is accounted for by local voluntary contributions (most being made up of the matching of dissimilar local circumstances with non-discretionary policy commitments).

When we go beyond policy outputs to address the issue of variability in policy consequences, it is necessary to take account of both absolute and relative circumstances. Put simply, it matters little if one group of councils puts twice the resources of another group into (say) road construction, if even the higher level is woefully inadequate when compared with existing traffic congestion and future demand for road travel. Yet assessments of present demand satisfaction and future demand can only be answered through the filter of political ideology. For one thing, how congestion is responded to is dependent upon ideologically informed assumptions about the relative merits of private and public transport options. Traffic volumes could be alleviated by placing more emphasis on mass transit systems or else investment in new roads and improvements in existing ones could be increased. Even when assessing future traffic demands, the assumptions that are made about the role of public transport go a long way toward estimating future traffic volumes. Moreover, attitudes towards private and public options are intimately involved in any evaluation of the costs and gains from transport improvements. Those on the right are more inclined to favour private options which reduce governmental involvement and encourage personal initiative (and so downplay the disbenefits which fall on the poor from an emphasis on private transport modes). Those on the left more commonly promote public transport solutions which reduce negative externalities[5] and offer broad social access to transport facilities (and so favour benefits which fall across a broad social spectrum, rather than gains made by those who can most afford to pay).

Rarely is there an absolute base line for policy evaluation. This even applies for health-related issues, such as water purity or food contamination. It might be assumed that there is widespread agreement which favours the elimination of pollution. But in reality cleanliness has costs: clean water could increase manufacturing costs, thereby reducing international competitiveness and leading to job losses. Likewise, removing stimulants to plant or animal growth from the food production process will increase prices. Having clean beaches means more expensive sewerage disposal facilities and hence higher costs. Restricting smoking would lower hospital bills but would also lessen government taxes and provoke job losses in the cigarette manufacturing industry. Whatever the criterion laid down for an ideal standard, decisions concerning the implementation of that goal are fundamentally value-laden. The mismatch between ideal standards and actual performance is evident even in the actions of single institutions, most especially when higher goals are placed above meeting supposed institutional goals. For example, in his defence of the Inner London Education Authority (ILEA), Wheen (1985) points out that Her Majesty's Inspectorate for school education have concluded that out of the 96 local education authorities in England, only the ILEA and five other authorities are adequately resourced. Ninety of the 96 are inadequately funded, according to the criteria of the government's own school inspectorate. Yet a primary argument which the government put forward to justify abolishing the ILEA was that it spent more than other local education authorities and yet its pupils had poor examination performances. On the expenditure front, the government appears to be devoting most of its time to looking at the tail which is still wagging, while neglecting the body that is starving; by its inspectors' standards it should have been devoting attention to the under-performance of other authorities rather than the ILEA's position. Moreover, once the impact of social class differences (and independent schools) are taken into account, it is not inner city, high spending authorities whose examination performances are most suspect but low spending, wealthier authorities such as Bromley, Norfolk and Northamptonshire (Table 6.2).

In terms of appreciating the potential for local councils to direct policy consequences in particular ways, this last point is important. It is clear that the mainstream of local policy impacts carry a national (or state-wide) ring to them. This is understandable given that the resource base of local councils, their functional responsibilities, their geographical extent, their electoral procedures, and their management processes are all subject to extensive higher tier influence. Then again, in addition to events explicitly within the governmental sphere, there are forces within society as a whole which limit the impact of local policy initiatives. One area in which this is apparent is educational attainment, with variation in the social class compositions of schools and of local authorities going a long way toward explaining variation in examination grades. However, locality-specific deviations do add to these general trends. Thus, David Byrne *et al.* (1975) showed that at the local authority level the likelihood of pupils staying on at school after the minimum leaving age is affected by the resources that councils put into schooling (also Williamson and Byrne 1977). King (1974) adds

*Table 6.2* School examination performances for English local education authorities 1985

| | By examination performance alone | Allowing for social class | Allowing for social class and independent schools |
|---|---|---|---|
| **The best ten** | | | |
| 1 | Harrow | Harrow | Harrow |
| 2 | Barnet | Wirral | Barnet |
| 3 | Sutton | Sutton | St Helens |
| 4 | Buckinghamshire | E Sussex | Liverpool |
| 5 | Surrey | Hounslow | Coventry |
| 6 | Kingston | Cleveland | Sutton |
| 7 | W Sussex | N Tyneside | Newcastle |
| 8 | Hertfordshire | Coventry | Wirral |
| 9 | Bromley | Calderdale | Cleveland |
| 10 | N Yorkshire | St Helens | Manchester |
| **The worst ten** | | | |
| 10 | Waltham Forest | Haringey | Bedfordshire |
| 9 | Manchester | Wakefield | Brent |
| 8 | Barnsley | Suffolk | Haringey |
| 7 | Haringey | Barking | Rochdale |
| 6 | ILEA | Norfolk | Isle of Wight |
| 5 | Barking | Shropshire | Essex |
| 4 | Sandwell | Avon | Norfolk |
| 3 | Oldham | Richmond | Northamptonshire |
| 2 | Knowsley | Somerset | Oldham |
| 1 | Newham | Bedfordshire | Bromley |

*Note*
The data are by local authority area, with the first column listing best and worst by examination performance, the second identifying best and worst performers once the social class composition of areas is allowed for, and the third extending this to 'take out' the effects of independent schools (given the distorting effects of boarders and more intense educational services).

*Source*: Gray and Jesson (1987)

further spice to this conclusion by suggesting that the positive impact of service commitments are greater for children from poorer homes (also Ntuk-Idem 1978). In addition to spending on schools, councils can enhance educational attainment by assisting those from poor households to stay in education and so gain higher qualifications. Yet as Reddin (1973) reported, there are wide divergences in the willingness of councils to put money into this cause. With regard to what produces such divergences, apart from some preliminary efforts, such as that by Jesson *et al.* (1985), we still have too little information.

Many would argue that political ideology has a hand to play. Backing this view, they could point to experiences with pre-school education. Thus, in line with the present Conservative government's emphasis on home-centred family lifestyles, since the late 1970s Conservative controlled councils have cut back pre-school education provisions, at the same time as Labour councils have increased them (Pinch 1987). Put simply, Labour councils have sought to enhance opportunities for equality by making it easier for women to take up employment (or more generally for all adults in single-parent and two adult families to work), whereas Conservative councils have reduced such opportunities.[6] Yet, while such specific instances of ideological inputs can be noted, general evidence on political party effects is notable for its lack of conviction. Party effects appear to apply to particular places, and at particular times, rather than to local authority systems as a whole. Britain is somewhat unusual in this regard (amongst the advanced capitalist polities at least), because here many studies have concluded that political party effects are quite virulent. However, it has to be admitted that much analysis on this score is laced with methodological and theoretical shortcomings (e.g. Sharpe and Newton 1984; Hoggart 1986a);[7] and in other nations evidence of strong political party effects is sparse. For the United States, of course, the chances of recording party influences are slight, given the small number of places that are partisan (Table 5.1). Indeed, as Rich (1979) observed, there is not even strong evidence of service biases by social class:

> Municipal services do not appear to be consistently manipulated by the affluent to the disadvantage of the poor. Nor are they clearly redistributive instruments through which government attempts to redress inequalities in private resources with public services for the less affluent.
>
> (Rich 1979: 145)

This summary of the US scene provides an accurate summary of empirical evidence, but needs to be interpreted cautiously. The primary reason for this is that the structure of local institutional arrangements mean that overtly biased policy enactments are not required in order for significant discriminations in the benefits of governmental activity to be present:

> The question of who benefits from public services is answered at

least as much by decisions about what type of services will be provided as by decisions regarding the distribution of existing services . . . [moreover] . . . Strategic use of the tools of municipal incorporation and land use planning have, to a significant extent, replaced competition for favors from city hall as a means of securing favorable service packages.

(Rich 1979: 143 and 148)

Similar points can be made about English local government, with national government directives going a long way towards deciding the scope that local policy-makers have for distributing policy benefits. Recently this has been seen in the national requirement that councils sell their housing to tenants who want to buy (and, probably more importantly, are affluent enough to pay), while also insisting that public sector rents be raised (helping to encourage tenants to buy). With grant cut-backs, restraints on expenditure and central government antagonism toward public housing, it is no surprise that there has been a marked reduction in house building by councils (Figure 6.1). As a general point, it should also be noted that because housing is a policy arena that has been subject to intense local party political conflict (e.g. Newton 1976a: 195; Young and Kramer 1978), these national impositions lessen the scope for local initiative and local policy variation. In truth, even with strong pressures favouring conformity, resistance to national supervision can be maintained in some measure (e.g. Hoggart 1985, 1986c). However, the structural framework within which institutions operate goes a long way towards setting limits to such resistance. By fixing the boundaries of English councils in order to keep 'city' and 'countryside' apart, while also allocating land-use planning and public housing functions to the smallest local government units (i.e. the lowest tier), the 1970–4 Conservatives established a framework in which areas of poverty were most likely to be Labour controlled and places of affluence were likely to fall into Conservative hands. As with the present Conservative government, when this spatial fix is backed with restraints on social programmes (as for public housing), Labour councils find their ability to meet the demands made on them (either absolutely or relatively) difficult to handle.

But within this last comment is the implication that Conservative and Labour are unitary entities. This they certainly are not, since there are substantial ideological differences and even ideological conflicts within these parties (Bulpitt 1967; Mark-Lawson *et al*. 1985). Not surprisingly, therefore, policy choices do vary not only

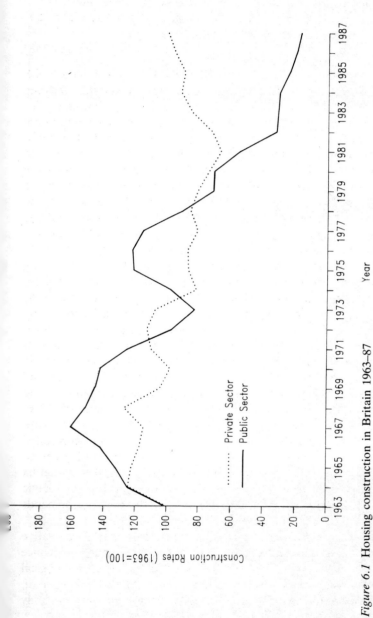

*Figure 6.1* Housing construction in Britain 1963–87

*Source*: Central Statistical Office (1989) *Annual Abstract of Statistics 1989*, HMSO, London

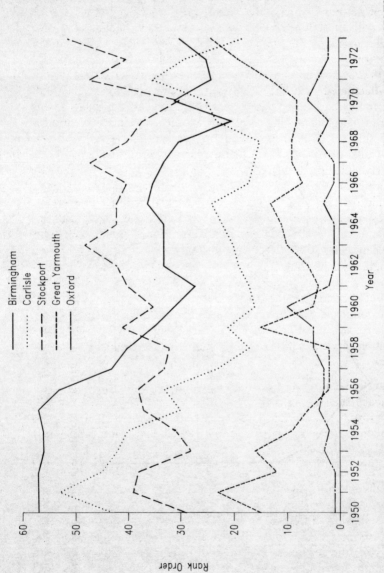

*Figure 6.2* Changes in rank order for primary education expenditure for five English cities 1949/50–1972/73

*Source:* calculated for Hoggart, K. (1984) 'Political Control and Urban Redistributive Policies', PhD thesis, University of London, London

across localities controlled by the same political party but also over time. This is apparent if we examine temporal change in the relative standing of councils with regard to their expenditure commitments. Figure 6.2 provides one instance of this for spending on primary education per school child in 57 English county boroughs over the 1949–73 period. Selecting those cities that were ranked first and last by their per pupil expenditure figures for the financial year 1949/50, along with the three cities that occupied the median and two quartile positions for that year, Figure 6.2 shows the annual expenditure ranks for these five places for each year from 1949/50 until 1972/3. This graph clearly reveals how the relative standings of cities fluctuated over the years (with annual volatilities and mid-range trends both being evident). Lest the reader presume that this pattern is particularly English, Figure 6.3 offers a similar picture for police services in Pennsylvania's urban centres between 1958 and 1982 (rank orders were calculated using expenditure per $1,000 property valuation as the index). For both countries, charts could be produced for other local functions which reveal only slightly differing patterns (e.g. Hoggart 1989). Over a number of services, most especially the more costly ones, temporal change in expenditure position is the norm. There is a dynamism to local policy that so far has received far too little research attention.

Where does all this leave us with regard to understanding inter-authority variability in policy outcomes? Firstly, we are still in the realm of uncertainty, since the links between the character of public policy outputs and their consequences are insufficiently understood. In this regard, the points that Sher and Tompkins (1977) make for education services can be extended across a spectrum of local policy arenas:

> educational research has failed to identify a single resource or practice that is consistently effective in bolstering achievement. Moreover, the presumed linkage between school success and economic success in later life has been shown to be consistently weaker than common sense would suggest.
>
> (Sher and Tompkins 1977: 61)

Secondly, even for the simpler task of specifying what causes inter-authority policy variation, the literature is weak. It is simple to draw a map showing differences in (say) commitments to nuclear free zones or rates of approval for private residential homes, but the utility of the exercise is limited. Researchers still live with uncertainty over how much variation can be ascribed to locality-

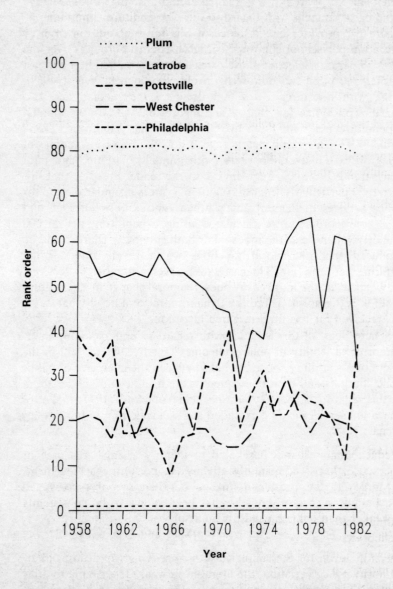

*Figure 6.3* Changes in rank order for police expenditure for five Pennsylvania cities 1958–82

*Source*: calculated for Hoggart (1989)

specific policy practices (or indeed about the relative causal weights which capture the contributions of different local factors). What is known is that the organisation of municipal government and the impositions of higher tier legislation go a long way toward explaining the core of local policy. Where you live influences the character and cost of the public services that you receive, but how important local factors are in determining these is far from being resolved.

This statement is made from the perspective of evaluating 'objective' measures of policy commitment, but a further complication arises from differential personal assessments of policy impact. Birgersson (1977) brings this out in a study of 36 Swedish communes, where he found that citizen dissatisfaction was strongest in communes which made greater commitments to service provision. Further dimensions to this relationship are revealed in Gaziel's (1982) analysis of 11 US centres. Here Birgesson's result was confirmed, but was augmented in that citizen evaluations were tied to service standards as a whole; hence, citizen views on the quality of specific services were greatly influenced by their opinions on the complete package of local authority provisions. Moreover, surveys suggest that citizen evaluations of governmental performance are linked to their personal experiences when interacting with city officials on a face-to-face basis (Gottdiener 1987). All of this means that citizen evaluations can be manipulated by elected or bureaucratic officials, perhaps irrespective of what services are being objectively provided. It also means that whatever the real impact and distributional consequences of governmental policies, these are unlikely to conform with citizen evaluations of them.

## WITHIN THE LOCALITY: POLICY AND NEIGHBOURHOOD

The absence of consistent ties between socio-economic or political attributes and the geography of public policy at the inter-authority level is matched by confusion over the spatial patterning of policy outputs at the intra-authority level. At the extremes, cases of deliberately enforced policy bias are clear (as in South Africa). However, in nations which purport to be democratic and egalitarian, evidence on the distribution of policy benefits provides few firm conclusions about who gains most. For Bolotin and Cingranelli (1983: 209), the fact that numerous studies have recorded an 'unpatterned inequality' in neighbourhood service provision is surprising, since: 'Almost everyone who has lived in a large city intuitively believes that the underclass hypothesis is correct'. This underclass hypothesis is comparable with what medical researchers refer to as 'the inverse care law'. In essence, it holds that those in most need of public services – owing to their inability to purchase facilities in the private market – actually receive the poorest quality and smallest quantities of public commitments. The literature on this issue is not particularly extensive for Britain, although US studies are more plentiful. From what evidence is available, on both sides of the Atlantic, it is clear that the distribution of public services follows a more complex patterning than the underclass hypothesis suggests. Aspects of some services are regressive, just as others are progressive. But the overall picture is confused by the intervention of private sector facilities, by contributions from higher tier governments, by differences across services within the same locality, by the importance of indirect (or externality) effects and by inertia in patterns of service provision. Furthermore, it is confused by the various interests that impose their will on the policy-making process (even if these are at times somewhat marginal). Thus, in addition to the objectives of local politicians, there are the professional goals for bureaucrats, the wishes of constituents in electorally sensitive wards, the impositions and assistances of higher tier authorities, and the demands of capital, all of which can direct patterns of provision, or perhaps just single facilities, away from the clean lines that the underclass hypothesis proposes. What some analysts argue should also be taken into account is the relationship between the benefits that householders or institutions receive and the contributions that they make toward service costs.

This point is a good starting place, since it pinpoints a key aspect of any evaluation of benefit distributions, which is the highly subjective and politically charged character of the exercise. To find that those who gain most from a service, say in terms of expenditure per household, are the highest paid is interpreted by some as evidence that a policy is regressive. However, others hold to a looser view of what is regressive. They would contend that what is critical is not expenditure *per se*. Rather it is the balance between benefit and cost. From this viewpoint, at a neighbourhood level, only when (say) public expenditure minus tax payments were positively correlated with household income would the underclass hypothesis be taken to be correct. What is certain is that expenditure minus tax distributions are quite different from those of expenditure alone. For example, in Hodge's (1988) investigation of King County (Seattle), he found that the benefits received from mass transit saw a subsidy flow from the central city to the suburbs, whereas general tax revenues which helped to pay mass transit costs produced a reverse subsidy flow. Whether expenditure should be analysed independent of revenue is a moot point. However, if it is assumed that all services should be provided in response to the ability to pay, then there seems little point in using non-market provision mechanisms. Under this scheme, the State would merely reflect the class basis of society. The ideals of democracy assume more than this in so far as they are linked to the ideal of equality of opportunity. They thereby lean towards focusing on expenditure (or provision) only, although the idea of equality of opportunity is so nebulous that it still leaves great flexibility over what is and is not a 'fair' distributional scheme.

A ready example of this flexibility is seen in evaluations of centralised facilities. For Bolotin and Cingranelli (1983), a reason why research has not strongly supported the underclass hypothesis is that investigators have equated the central business district with other city neighbourhoods. As Whitehead (1983) reported for Leeds, this is inappropriate because centralised facilities tend to be located there; so the centre has a marked over-representation of facilities (e.g. the main city library, community colleges, the largest public offices and major recreational facilities are all likely to be in the centre, giving it substantial public investment per capita). The question of how centralised facilities influence distributional questions is complex. Intuitively, it would seem that centralisation should lead to greater inequities in access to services, since many will have further to travel to reach service outlets. In rural areas, for instance, the centralisation of educational, medical and recreational facilities commonly has been discriminatory, because the poor, the young, the old, and women with families find it more difficult to gain access to outlets (e.g. Haynes *et al*. 1978). But it is pertinent to note Adrian's (1983) warning that the actual effects of centralisation will depend upon the existing distribution of facilities and the quality of transport provision. Conversely, while professionals frequently argue in favour of larger facilities in order to provide a wider range of services and more technically advanced facilities, for many users the more impersonal character of such units, the extra travel demands and the sense of loss which the closing of a local facility brings, all help to produce a negative evaluation of centralisation tendencies. Yet for others, technical improvements, alongside easier access for places on major arterial routes, means that centralisation almost inevitably brings improvement (plus, in some cases, cost reductions). In effect, any evaluation of service distributions runs into the obvious problem of users evaluating aspects of provision differently. What we can tell, by the very fact that centralisation processes are so prevalent in advanced economies, is that it is service providers who hold the whip hand in deciding provision patterns; centralisation is largely supplier driven (being preferred by service bureaucracies and suppliers of products such as hospital equipment), rather than demand (or user) driven.

That reactions to the centralisation of public sector facilities are mixed arises not simply from differences in transport availability, but also from access to other outlets. In Southampton, for example, Pinch (1984) reported that there was a correspondence between governmental nursery school provision and areas of low income housing, but because nursery schooling was so dominated by private sector and voluntary facilities, the overall spread of nursery school premises was in keeping with the underclass hypothesis. In Oakland, private sector interventions likewise altered the relationship between (governmental) provision and neighbourhood socio-economic status, giving regressive aspects to the school system as a whole (Levy *et al*. 1974). Yet the extra resources that parent–teacher associations provided for schools, which gave higher income neighbourhoods their better facilities, was in part compensated by the intervention of another 'outside' agency. This was the federal government, assistance from which was specifically targeted at schools in poorer neighbourhoods. The composite effect of these various factors was that the relationship between school expenditure per pupil and neighbourhood income was U-shaped. (Sanger [1981] found similar distributions for police and fire services in New York City, but was unable to explain this because the rules governing provision were intricate and not readily manifest.) What adds further complexity to the situation is inertia in service provision (stated differently, the difficulties of bringing rapid change to service distributions when facilities are fixed and capital investments have already been made). Two studies which suggest that inertia is important are those by Glassberg (1973), which revealed that changes in political leadership in councils in London and New York little altered provision patterns, and that by Tunley *et al*. (1979), which showed that inequities in provision across comprehensive schools in Newham were tied to the previous status of some institutions as grammar schools.

Three general points should be made about the divergent influences which determine existing service provision. The first is that what exists today is an amalgam of hangovers from the past, present trends and preparations for the future, the combined effects of which obviously add to the complexity and make difficult the identification of primary driving forces. The second is that State provision rarely compensates for inequities in the private sector; indeed, in so far as the balance of private and public sector facilities varies across services, it is to be expected that this has some influence on the character of public sector provision. The third is that the sharing of functional responsibilities between tiers of government inevitably means that services within localities are driven by more than one set of causal forces. There are those causal processes that are essentially local in origin, those that are local but set within national guidelines, those that are national but for which the local authority is the agent of implementation (with varying degrees of local support or antagonism to national initiatives), and those which are bound by direct links between facilities and higher tier government (as for schools which have recently been allowed to opt out of the English local education authority system). The variety that is present here cannot do less than produce complex relationships between socio-economic structures and public service provision. That tendencies consistent with the underclass hypothesis are in evidence is clear, but then so are other tendencies. At present, the balance of causal influences is too little appreciated to make particularly instructive statements about dominant influences on narrow policy arenas.

A further reason for this is the number of variables that intervene between policy outputs and policy consequences. A starting point for confusion here is what researchers should focus on when examining policy consequences. For example, when investigating police services should analysts concentrate upon expenditure or crime rates? In terms of policy outcomes, it seems clear that crime rates should be the object of concern; expenditure on the police is not made for its own sake but, as one important goal, to keep down crime. Yet how much influence does police activity have on crime rates? Since only a small minority of police spending is oriented towards preventing either domestic crime or corporate crime (for reasons unrelated to policing procedures), at least two major crime components should be weakly linked to police spending. Then again, the goals of service provision are themselves multiple, in terms of both their target groups and their purpose. For instance, services such as the police are directed not only at people but also at buildings (whether homes, offices, shops or factories). What is more, as with people, these buildings provide unequal enticements for crime and differential ease of achieving it. Thus, whereas residential neighbourhoods have people at hand all round the day, zones of offices and factories can be vacant for long spells of time. Then there is the problem of the police fulfilling the dual roles of protecting property and protecting lives. Whether household or institutional property is the target, protection efficiency per unit of property value is likely to be highest in higher income neighbourhoods. With regard to crimes against persons, police efforts will be utilised more efficiently in poorer areas. Perhaps this mixing of contradictory impulses alone is sufficient to justify Sanger's (1981) U-shaped distribution. But how effective commitments of police time, money and effort may be is unknown, since the potential for crime without police protection cannot be assessed.

It should not be expected that the criteria which govern distributional outcomes are the same in all localities. The balance of political forces within places will undoubtedly orient service goals towards different objectives. At a simple level, this phenomenon was seen in the policies of Cheshire County Council in the run up to the reorganisation of English local government in 1974. Fearful that restructuring would lead to the loss of land close to major conurbations, and thereby 'waste' investment which counted against the council's revenues, as early as the 1958–9 financial year a policy was inaugurated which restricted capital investment close to the conurbations and only allowed essential work to be carried out if it could be paid for from current revenues (Lee *et al.* 1974). In Boston and Chicago a more directly 'political' practice has been identified, with wards which provided electoral support for the mayor receiving the highest municipal spending (Mladenka 1980; Bolotin and Cingranelli 1983). However, such effects are far from dominant and, as a host of other studies have shown, they are either absent or tepid in many places (e.g. Levy *et al.* 1974; Lineberry 1977).

## RESUME

There is variety in the causal nexus producing dissimilar public policy commitments and the consequences of governmental decisions make complex patterns. Reflective of the divergent trends within these processes is the conclusion that service distributions are unequal, but in an unpatterned way. The essence of this unpatterned inequality is the multiple foundations from which policy outputs and their consequences can be generated. Set within any one locality the forces of national and local processes combine. These are grounded in considerations of electoral advantage, professional judgement, profit enhancement, social attachment, leadership style, political ideology and resource availability (to name a few). Where you live, both nationally and within a local government area, undoubtedly affects the range, quality and quantity of services that you receive. It will also be aligned with a particular style of decision-making. Yet what the consequences of this variability are is uncertain. Evaluations of policy outcomes are highly subjective. The issues involved concern not only the consequences of provision, but also what effect non-provision has. Poor standards of public services are essentially a hidden tax, since they necessitate purchasing facilities from the private sector (M.P. Smith 1988). Yet this does not mean that public service provision is progressive, since the wealthy and the more powerful are better able to orient the assumptions and delivery practices of public services in their own favour. It is not enough to look to the generalities of public policies, because their detail has important distributional implications. Thus, the apparent egalitarian overtones of English comprehensive schools have been diluted in many establishments by streaming (thereby retaining some features of grammar school–secondary school divisions within the framework of a single institution). Dominant power relations reveal themselves in differing form and with differing intensities in government policies. In times of plenty, and in places of wealth, it is feasible for the weak to gain substantial benefits (Peterson 1981). However, in times of stress, or where resources are scarce, dominant power relations might be expected to be more apparent (note how local fiscal stress since the 1970s has taken a toll on gains made by racial minorities and women in public service provision; Thomas 1978; Webster 1985). Yet uneven service provision is not the most important manifestation of inequity in policy outcomes. More important is the effectiveness of public sector commitments. This is inevitably conditioned by dominant power relationships. Not only do the powerful find it easier to bend public policy to their will, but they are also more likely to find its aims compatible with their wishes. Inequality in policy outcomes can involve many different mutations, but these ultimately owe much to the dynamism and character of local and national power networks.

# 7 Place in politics

That this book has not been written by a political scientist is self-evident. For one thing, the attention given to policy-making processes *per se*, as well as to elections, pressure groups and the legal framework of local public institutions, is less than would be expected in a political science text. On the other hand, within geography, reactions to the book are likely to be mixed. For some, it will have too narrow a definition of what is 'political' (most especially with regard to the slight attention to questions of gender and racism). For other geographers the book perhaps has too much politics and not enough 'geography'. (Rephrasing this, there is justification in holding that it does not go sufficiently far in drawing out the locality basis of different political practices.) That the text focuses on State processes is more a reflection of the particular concerns of this volume than of the author's views on what is or is not political. That its first line of vision is on the politics of State institutions, rather than their geography, is deliberate, since it is believed that geographers have been lax in their attentions to the analysis of political practices.

In both geography and political science, in truth often provoked by work in sociology, the last 20 years has seen a change in research emphasis which has enriched our understanding of the State. Yet this greater sense of realism has not overcome central weaknesses in the investigation of political phenomena. In political geography these shortcomings have arisen from the dual problem of not only being isolated from political science but also standing apart from the mainstream of human geographical inquiry. Although stated a decade ago, Logan's (1978) summary of the situation has not lost its veracity:

From the outset political geography developed in relative

isolation from the rest of geography, itself aloof from the main intellectual developments in the social sciences until the 1960s. Thus, while political geographers have paid much lip service to their field's position at the interface of political science and geography, in reality political geography has borrowed little from political science or the other social sciences in the past; nor does it yet reflect the paradigm unrest still being experienced in those areas. In the 1970s political geography has remained in a confused state with no clear sense of direction. The difficulty in defining a mainstream of thought may be partly attributed to the fact that the field is now thinly populated and is consequently characterised by a high degree of individualism.

(Logan 1978: 12)

Perhaps as a result of the sparsity of political geography practitioners, as well as their diverse interests, attention to the State in geography emerged largely from within social geography. (In part this was because radical perspectives which drew attention to the value of theorising the State developed within this sub-discipline.) This has had both bad and good consequences, although the evaluation of each is highly subjective. On the negative side, there has been too little attention to policy processes and too simplistic an appreciation of the subtlety and complexity of political practices. This has led to some sharp, but justified, criticisms from political scientists on the naïvety of geographical offerings. One example is Jones's (1986) debunking of geographical attempts to analyse the judicial system by pointing to the loose links between geographers' ill-formed abstract, structural theories and socio-spatial reality (also Allison 1982; Dommel 1984). On the plus side, the impetus given by social geographers (and sociologists) has helped to focus attention on distributional issues and has underlined the need to situate political practices within the context of social structure. Most especially in Britain, political scientists have been slow to integrate debates on these issues and to capture their vitality within their research (although recent years have seen improvement in these directions).

In a sense, the distinction between the vision which has commonly pervaded social geography circles and that more favoured in political science arises over a dissimilar focus in the study of 'politics'. In political science, the kind of politics which is primarily concentrated on is that concerned with everyday political acts; with the politics of policy-making processes, of elections, and of governance. Within social geography, and indeed more generally within geography, primary interest in politics is much more concerned with issues of social advantage, with who gets what, when and where. As well as being the bread and butter of political science, the first of these understandings is the Achilles heel of much geographical research. On the other hand, by engrossing themselves in the day-by-day operations of governmental institutions, political scientists have offered little insight on the distributional consequences of political processes.

If political geography is to assist in furthering understanding of the State, there are two niches within which positive contributions would be welcome. The first is to provide a stronger sense of realism in accounts of everyday political processes within human geography. Because of their stronger interest in political science, political geographers are better placed to draw attention to the intricacy of policy processes than those in other parts of the discipline. This is particularly relevant for research on the State, since there has been a tendency in recent years to favour a brand of structuralist interpretation which makes insufficient allowance for the dynamism of political practices and, despite protestations to the contrary, assumes too readily that State processes can be read off from the logic of capital accumulation processes. Akin to work in some other disciplines, one aspect of this emphasis is that the concept of social class has become elastic:

> As a concept, class has soaked up so much meaning that it has become bulky to use. Because it is often employed without a clearly specified definition, debates about class often become conversations in which people talk past each other because they are talking about different dimensions of class.
>
> (Katznelson 1986: 14)

We need a clearer specification of the dissimilar manifestations of social class, since the causal positioning of class will vary according to whether it is taken as a structural component of capitalist economies, as a nation-specific manifestation of social forces which have evolved over time, as a social group with shared social experiences or as a vehicle for collective action (Katznelson 1986). The causal impetus of both capital accumulation and class conflict is not to be denied, but interpreting social class as an expression of the structure of capitalist economies has a dissimilar theoretical meaning from seeing it as a focal point for collective action. The clean lines that structuralist accounts offer when referring to abstract social distinctions become significantly muddied and disfigured when transposed into political action. Although this is recognised in some writings on the State, too regularly there is a lack of clarity over the varying forms of class relations. This is associated with a tendency to emphasise abstract structural views on class and to produce accounts of society which extend its causal importance beyond reasonable bounds. Other causal forces, those that distort the purity of abstract social class divisions, as well as defusing their immediate causal force, have a tendency to be neglected (regrettably, at times, scornfully so) or to be treated superficially (too often being discarded as 'contingent factors'). Human geographers from all realms of the discipline have a role to play in breathing more depth and subtlety into evaluations of the causal position of class relations. As regards the State, political geographers could aid their colleagues by illuminating the variety of causal links and empirical manifestations that exist between location, social structure and political practice.

In addition, political geographers could contribute to political theory by drawing on insights within geography and sociology to help to develop a stronger appreciation of the importance of place in determining political practices. Already, as in Bulpitt's (1967) observations on inter-city dissimilarities in political party philosophy, or Sharpe and Newton's (1984) identification of the causal role of urban hierarchy influences and 'the Welsh effect' on local government expenditure, political scientists have recognised significant geographical dimensions in political events. Yet they have not convincingly theorised them. Political geographers could have a positive influence here, since the inter-disciplinary nature of human geography as a whole, and the centrality of location in the evaluative frameworks of geographical research, makes them well placed to transpose general ideas on place into specific insights on their links to political practice. From existing work by human geographers and particularly sociologists, we already know that the geographical incidence of human activities is not simply a reflection of the uneven spatial occurrence of nationwide processes. Locationally contingent events do make a significant contribution to geographical variability, but local causal effects also make notable impressions on the political landscape (Mark-Lawson *et al*. 1985; Agnew 1987). Political science is a discipline with a long history of community studies, a tradition of investigating political practices within single localities. But these studies have tended to view their research sites as laboratories for investigating nationwide phenomena rather than as stages on which local and national causal effects intersect. Despite recognition of the local grounding of some causal forces, researchers have offered little by way of assessing how far political practices are local manifestations of national occurrences, how far they are local distortions of broader processes or whether they have evolved as distinctly local practices. This is an area of interest that, by its very nature, is probably more central to geographical research than to political science. Quite legitimately, political scientists could expect to find instructive commentaries on these issues within the geographical literature, and the specific concerns of political geographers should make their contributions most pertinent.

In truth, however, political geography has not gone far in aiding theoretical progress in either of the two fields identified above. With regard to infusing geographical research with a stronger appreciation of policy processes, or indeed to adding that touch of day-to-day political realism to more structural accounts of the State, what has worked against the sub-discipline is the disparate interests of its members and the differential emphasis that they have placed in their work on understanding political processes, as opposed to the geographical dimensions of political phenomena. With regard to deepening the appreciation of the character, autonomy and causal significance of place-specific political forces, the individualism of research interests are again likely to be a handicap. At this point, the effect is not so evident, since geographers and sociologists in general have not progressed far in furthering our understanding of local causal processes (indeed, there is debate over their precise form, as well as how best to identify them in research endeavours). This is understandable, given that these effects have only recently taken a significant role in the research agendas of both disciplines. Additionally, quick answers are unlikely, because locality effects are complex processes which will require extensive research before their causal character is understood (Urry 1987). Most certainly, political scientists do have good reason to chafe at the lack of interesting insights on local causal effects in the work of political geographers (e.g. Dommel 1984; Jones 1986). But a start has been made that holds out the promise of future theoretical advance (e.g. Agnew 1987). Political geographers could add to this by infusing their work on locality effects with the political realism of the inter-penetration and dynamism of structure and human agency. By seeking a balance between these, added impetus can be given to what at present are efforts weighted towards human agency in political science and toward structure in geography. Capturing this balance will not be an easy task, but it will be a worthy goal.

It is into this gap that this book has sought to make its contribution. In no sense has the reader been offered a well rounded account which ties up loose ends and presents a coherent theoretical whole. There are far too many muddy waters and disquieting exceptions for the commentary to be regarded in a convincing theoretical light. Indeed, the concepts that have been employed in this text are at times rough and in need of substantial refinement. Perhaps they merit rejection as fruitful mechanisms for furthering understanding. This book raises questions more than it provides answers. It seeks to draw together materials from a wide variety of disciplines, to try to make sense of the complexity of political reality. In effect, its central working assumption has been that the character of social structures, and hence of structural constraints and of abstract categories such as social class, are variable in time and space, so the elegant simplicity of much structuralist writing is too naïve. Leading on from this, it has been accepted that the unique, yet structured, character of place-specific political processes provides a significant clue to understanding politics (however defined). Since I am no abstract theoretician, the attempt to grapple with the complexity of this situation has inevitably been empirically grounded. It has lacked neat lines of theoretical discourse and has left gaps of both an explanatory and an empirical kind when available materials afforded no coherent cues for categorisation, interpretation or assimilation. Thus, the answer to the question of why attention to policy-making processes is barely informed with insights on locality-specific effects is simply that, having tried to bend my mind around the evidence at hand, I have come up with nothing about which I am sufficiently convinced to put even tentative suggestions on paper. With gaps of this sort, this book offers at best a stumbling attempt to integrate causal pressures from structure and agency in a manner that does not adopt a single explanatory perspective, but calls attention to gaps in knowledge and uncertainties over effect. The approach adopted is not presented as the 'right' way forward, because, to my mind, there are too many inconsistencies and irregularities in mainstream explanatory accounts to be able to latch boldly on to one perspective. In the last 20 years, researchers in each of geography, political science and sociology have come a long way in furthering our understanding of the State. But, my word, there is still a long, long way to go.

# Notes

**PREFACE**

1 Throughout the text, State as a concept is capitalised, whereas states as governmental institutions are not. Hence there are theories of the State and 50 states in the USA.

2 I refer to Britain here but, as readers from Northern Ireland, Scotland and Wales are well aware, many texts use this designation even though their commentaries are on England alone. It is not intended to provide the reader with a mountain of footnotes or a general discourse on the different local government systems in Britain. Some feel for the complexity of the situation is provided in Page's (1980) observation that 16 distinctive local authority systems fall under the home jurisdiction of the British government. Certain consistencies can be identified across these 16, but their dissimilarities are sufficient to yield a long list of exceptions over precise details. In fact, the same point applies for the United States, since each state in the Union has its separate arrangements. To cut through the clutter of minor deviations, the factual information in this book focuses on England (with national figures for the USA). Where comparative intra-national commentary furthers understanding, this is offered.

The attention to England needs to be emphasised from the outset owing to the peculiar standing of Scotland, which at times takes on the appearance of the testing ground for legislation later applied in England (e.g. local spending targets, restrictions on local property tax rates and abolishing property taxes in favour of a poll tax). For those who wish to arm themselves with an overview of the Scottish situation, Kellas (1989) provides a brief, readable introduction. Those seeking more detail could profitably start with a series of papers by Ed Page in the *Studies in Public Policy* series (Page 1978, 1980; Page and Midwinter 1979), with Midwinter's (1984) examination of local fiscal affairs in Scotland being well worth reading. It is relevant to be aware that local government affairs in Scotland are mediated through different central government departments than in England (as they are for Northern Ireland and Wales). On the operations of the Scottish (and Welsh) Office, further *Studies in Public Policy* can be recommended (Madgwick and James 1979; Keating and Midwinter 1981; Ross 1981; Thomas 1981). For

Northern Ireland, an understanding of local politics requires appreciation of that province's religious divisions. These make the province something of a 'special case'; a position not helped by the fact that: 'In general, research into local government in Northern Ireland is almost non-existent' (Birrell 1981: 5). For those seeking basic information and useful clues on similarities and dissimilarities with England, Derek Birrell's work is a good starting place (Birrell 1978, 1981; Birrell and Murie 1980). Those who wish to pursue an interest on a more esoteric governmental system could indulge in Kermode's (1979, 1980) work on the Isle of Man.

## 1 LOCAL POLITICS IN COMPARATIVE PERSPECTIVE

1 The State refers to the array of processes through which a national society is governed and which provides for the collective survival of the nation as a political unit. Institutions such as the judiciary, Parliament, public bureaucracies and the military constitute the organisational structure of the State and are often referred to as State institutions. However, the State is really a bundle of processes, rather than a series of institutions, since it is the interactions of these institutions and their personnel, along with the relationships of each with the public at large (civil society) and with capital, that determine the character of the State.

2 This point should be read in the context of the UK–US focus of this book, because this stipulation follows from formulations of the State which are most prevalent in these countries. This stance is a reflection of a strongly felt capitalist antagonism toward public sector involvement in the private sector. As Lash and Urry (1987) make clear, such negative attitudes are less common in other nations (also Wilson 1985). With Japan, Sweden and West Germany as classic examples, the State has often taken the lead in directing private sector advancement (partly owing to the lateness of nineteenth century industrialisation in these countries). These distinctions warn against extending the commentary presented in this book beyond a UK–USA axis, as well as highlighting the necessity for theories of the State rather than a single theory of the State. As Mann (1988: viii) put it: 'Theorists of *the* state abound, but they seem not to have noticed that *states* are plural. In fact most sociologists [and other social scientists] in all fields have come up with peculiarly stateless theories.'

3 For example, when Lloyd George and Winston Churchill first entered the British Cabinet in 1908 they thought that social programmes were desirable irrespective of how the public viewed them. Thus, when the Treasury's loosening of the purse strings after the Japanese defeat of Russia lessened pressure for more naval construction (the 'Russian threat' was seen to have declined), personal initiative came to play an important part in directing policy towards providing old age pensions. As Pelling (1968) observed, there is no evidence that such social reforms were popular or were called for by those who benefited most from them. Their popularity arose after their implementation, not before it.

4 In significant ways all the main classes of State theory are structural; it is merely that they portray the most powerful influences on State actions

differently. The image of democracy promoted by almost all government officials (that of pluralism) differs from neo-marxist accounts in that it stresses the primacy of electors rather than capitalists. However, it is still structural in the sense that the general population is seen to hold a dominant power position even without acting; officials must respond to electoral wishes for fear that failure to appease voters will lead electors into action. New right theorists hold yet another position, seeing State functionaries as holding the whip hand (by implication because self-interest drives them to disguise their real behaviour intentions).

5 It is worth noting Mann's (1988) point that it was not until well into the twentieth century that the advanced capitalist polities regularly spent more on domestic civil functions than on defence against outsiders.

## 2 THE NATIONAL CONTEXT OF LOCAL POLITICS

1 An issue that will arise later in this book concerns differences in political party organisation in these two nations. However, at this point it is worth noting that US parties allow 'lateral' entry for political amateurs, in that the practice of senior officials moving through party ranks is barely evident. In Britain this is the norm (with more exceptions as one moves to the right of the ideological spectrum). Consistent with the stronger sense of hierarchy within the nation, British politicians are expected to 'learn their place'.

2 These figures are taken from a report in the *Valley Morning Star* (Harlingen, Texas) on 27 December 1988: A1, A10.

3 US papers seem to find even trivial items on the Royal Family newsworthy, as in reporting that Princess Diana had her wisdom teeth removed (e.g. 'Princess' wisdom teeth', *San Francisco Chronicle*, 1 April 1989: C11).

4 This comment is made with hindsight. At various times, the prospect of public discontent has put the Establishment in a cold sweat (as seen in reactions to the Tolpuddle martyrs). Symbolising the discomfort felt when élite supremacy is questioned: 'Bonar Law [Prime Minister during the era of working class disquiet in 1919–20] so often referred to the need to arm the stock brokers that the Cabinet Secretary had visions of militant stock brokers manning the barricades' (Hinton 1983: 109).

5 The attachment to this electoral procedure extends well beyond parliamentary elections, as seen in the 1989 contests for the European Parliament, when Britain was the only nation in the 12 not to use some form of proportional representation.

6 When national leaders have felt the legitimacy of their position severely strained, repressive and anti-democratic reactions have been more common. Even if the flamboyantly presented claims of Peter Wright (1987) about MI5 agents trying to bring down Prime Minister Harold Wilson are ignored, other documented cases of 'undemocratic' attempts to oust 'outsiders' from office are available. One of the most notorious is the concoction of the fictitious Zinoviev letter by officers in MI6 and the *Daily Mail*, which was sprung on the public during the 1924 election, when the then Labour Government was fighting to stay in office. This letter suggested that Labour's future plans called for the placement of

communists in key positions throughout the armed forces (Chester *et al* 1967). In recent years, restraints on civil rights, in order to thwart those who 'upset' the Thatcher government, offer further examples of a willingness to use repression to maintain advantaged positions (cf. the seizure of documentary films from the BBC's Glasgow offices, restraint of free movement during the miners' strike of 1984–5, the banning of local authority employees from holding political office, and the greater restrictions introduced in the new Official Secrets Act).

7 As in Britain, within the United States there is a tendency for élites to assert their lack of influence and even express bemusement over their standing. Mills (1956) accurately identified this trait:

> The truth about the nature and the power of the élite is not some secret which men [*sic*] of affairs know but will not tell. Such men hold quite various theories about their roles in the sequence of event and decision. Often they are uncertain about their roles, and even more often they allow their fears and their hopes to affect their assessment of their own power. No matter how great their actual power, they tend to be less acutely aware of it than of the resistance of others to its use. Moreover, most American men of affairs have learned well the rhetoric of public relations, in some cases even to the point of using it when they are alone, and thus coming to believe it.
>
> (Mills 1956: 4–5)

To my knowledge the only time when such a sense of insecurity provoked a serious 'anti-democratic' threat to the US government was during the Great Depression. Then, led by officers of the Morgan Guaranty Trust, a plan was devised to forcibly overthrow President Roosevelt – viewed by the plotters as a dangerous radical – but the plan was discovered before it came to fruition

8 The concept of a propertied élite includes those owning means of production, such as industrialists, landowners and financiers, and as such the expression could be replaced by the word 'capitalists'. Here it has been preferred because the politically powerful are not necessarily active profit-makers (perhaps relying on managers for this or even drawing on income from existing wealth without seeking its growth). In particular, there are those whose orientation in exerting political power is driven more by aesthetic or social status considerations. Commonly, such people have been linked to 'aristocratic' values most often associated with Britain (e.g. Wiener 1981) but similar attitudinal and behavioural dispositions had power in new lands of European settlement as well (e.g. Wild 1974; Hugill 1989). Such people sit uncomfortably inside a 'capitalist' label.

9 The above account concentrates on relations between mainstream political organisations and socialist parties. This is not a complete account of the 'failure' of socialism in the United States. Other factors to acknowledge are the internal and inter-group wranglings of socialist organisations, rising farm product prices which helped to quell farmer discontent and the release valve of opportunities in the West (Moore 1966; Husbands 1976; Karabel 1979). In Canada, the same processes, except the McCarthyite excesses of the 1950s, were evident but have

been less widely publicised (Brown and Brown 1973; McCormack 1977).

10 Today's research shows that high rates of social mobility are no more intrinsic to the USA than to European nations. It is the dynamism of the US economy which provides more opportunities for advancement than in Europe (e.g. Haller *et al* 1985; Kerckhoff *et al* 1985).

11 As Agnew (1981) pinpoints, this is manifest in differing attitudes towards housing in these two nations. In Britain a house is seen more as a home, whereas in the USA it is more likely seen as a commodity, an investment waiting to be disposed of. Thus, from interview responses, Agnew found that 72.9 per cent of householders in Dayton (Ohio) thought profit was either a very important or an important reason for owning a home, whereas only 14.4 per cent of those in Leicester did (with 43.3 per cent holding that it was very unimportant compared with a Dayton figure of 2.9 per cent).

12 It is tempting to perceive this as being tied to a greater sense of 'professionalism' within Britain. However, as noted below, in many regards professionalism is more highly developed in the USA than in Britain. The paradox of corruption and professionalism coexisting comes from the pervasiveness of individualism and the unmet aspirations of US citizens.

13 In drafting the Constitution the nation's leaders were conscious of the dangers of business control over government leading to the pursuit of short-term, vested interests which could undermine the long-term viability of a commercial society (Elkin 1987). Consequently, restraints were built into the federal apparatus which restricted too narrow a push for personal gain. At the national level, concerted, cooperative pressures were required for the sustained promotion of self-interest. If special interests identified permanence in their shared goals, concerted action was easier to sustain. Hence, sectionalism is important because shared geographical and social environments lead to the expectation of convergence in long-term interests (e.g. farmers on the Great Plains, large landowners in the South, and northern and midwestern manufac-turers). Moving down the governmental tiers, such coalitions were less central for states, where it was easier to change legislation, and even constitutions (Elazar 1988). As for the local level, it should be evident, from materials in various chapters in this volume, that here public office has long been a channel through which local capitalists have greased the wheels of personal fortune with comparative ease.

14 The socialist movement in the USA largely ignored new southern and eastern European immigrants (Aronowitz 1973; Shefter 1986). This arose from ethnic chauvinism, concern over a lack of familiarity with industrial skills, and, in practice, an orientation in socialist and trade union circles which was favourable to skilled workers (Edelstein and Warner 1975). Another possibility, which is suggested by Macdonald's (1963) research on Italy, is that immigrants were unfamiliar with effective working class movements. Macdonald showed that where labour was weak outmigration was highest. In localities where labour was stronger, workers fought rather than joining the immigrant trail.

15 A point that should be made is that, in general, early leaders of political machines were not from ethnic minorities but from old Yankee families

(Kolko 1976). Only in the 1920s did ethnic leaders attain national significance. Hence, party machines offered one more channel through which the already wealthy could gain bounty.

16 This is well captured in a 1920s labour song attributed to the Needle Workers' Industrial Union:

> The Cloakmakers' Union is a no good union
> It's a company union by the bosses.
> The old cloakmakers and the socialist fakers
> by the workers are making double crosses.
> The Dubinskys, the Hillquits, the Thomases
> by the workers are making false promises.
> They preach socialism but they practice fascism
> to save capitalism by the bosses.
>
> (from Aronowitz 1973: preface)

17 This point is still pertinent today. Whereas in the USA elected officials in municipal government, in the larger cities at least, pursue their political roles as full-time occupations, in Britain there is resistance to this route. Indeed, when councillors, largely from the new left, have accepted the low salaries that attendance allowances and expenses offer as a main income source, this move to full-time political status has been regarded as highly suspect (especially by those in other political parties). The day of the amateur has not departed from Britain. If it did, most current parliamentarians would presumably be forced either to resign their political post(s) or else give up lucrative outside business interests (e.g. Mellors 1978).

18 One symptom of élite attitudes to non-élite movements is seen in restricting non-élite access to channels of communication. In the case of Chomsky and Herman's (1979) book on US involvement in Indochina, the corporation owning the publisher which issued the book contract censored it and delayed its publication by six or seven years (although 20,000 copies had been printed). This was because the critical tone of the text was deemed 'unpatriotic'. As the authors pointed out: 'on fundamental issues the mass media in the United States . . . function very much in the manner of a system of state-controlled propaganda' (Chomsky and Herman 1979: x).

19 While Mrs Thatcher holds the distinction of being the most unpopular Prime Minister since opinion polls were first taken (Rose 1984: xv).

20 This point might seem controversial given the relative insulation of British governments from popular pressures. However, a long list of policy changes can be presented to confirm this point. Note, for example, the Prime Minister's personal intervention to change the route of the proposed railway link from London to the Channel Tunnel in order to avoid key Conservative electoral areas, the retreat from monetarism within two years of taking office, and the climb down over coal policy in the face of a threatened miners' strike in 1981. Even when policies have been introduced, these have been conditioned by external pressures. Keating (1988) provides a good example in describing the government's enterprise zone policy, which was supposed to free capital from governmental regulation:

When the Conservatives returned to office in 1979, [Chancellor of the Exchequer, Geoffrey] Howe's enthusiasm was translated into Treasury initiative, considerably modified in turn by inter-departmental bargaining. The Department of Employment, under pressure from the trade unions, refused the suspension of the Employment Protection Act. The proposal to withdraw regional policy aids and other grants and subsidies was dropped after pressure from both sides of industry. The proposal to force public authorities to auction off land was dropped as unworkable and probably very costly, though the intention was declared to select zones without substantial public land holdings. On the other hand, to maximise the attractiveness of zones, the proposal for rates relief was incorporated, though, to satisfy the local authorities, rates were not abolished but paid by the central Treasury as a straight subsidy to zone occupants . . . By the time the final proposals emerged, the idea had drifted a long way from the original free market concept and was beginning to look like an instrument of traditional spatial policy, a means of subsidising industry to locate in one area rather than another.

(Keating 1988: 177)

What has been on the side of the Thatcher administrations has been time (i.e. length of time in office). Because of this, on occasions, retreat in the face of opposition has been a temporary setback only. For some policies early reversals have been countered at a later time: the 1984–5 miners' strike bears ample witness to this, with the revival of loans for higher education students as another example. In these instances what is seen is traditional politics at work: retreat in the face of opposition, regroup, prepare a strategy to isolate opponents from their previous supporters, then wait for an opportune time of political strength and apply proposals with vigour. This is not convictionism, but pragmatic politics. Yet it is a pragmatism which, since around 1984, has been set within a 'grand vision' that has sought to reorient British society towards a new consensus which asserts the primacy of private-regarding, individualistic values (Jessop *et al* 1988). In pursuit of this hegemonic project, electoral politics has a much higher priority than specific policy enactments:

The primacy of the political class struggle in Thatcherite policy is often astonishing. Whereas the last Labour government tended to subordinate political strategy to economic crisis-management, the Thatcher governments have often treated economic policy as a subfield for the politics of hegemony . . . The general rationale seems to be that if the government can modify the balance of forces in the short-term, it will gain sufficient time to restructure society and to allow a market-generated recovery.

(Jessop *et al* 1988: 129–30)

In the context of this hegemonic project, the substantial costs of selling public assets at huge knock-down prices, so as to increase share ownership levels, is a small price to pay.

21 That inertia is found also amongst the general population is clear from

national opinion polls. Throughout the 1980s British voters have preferred expenditure increases to tax cuts, with more recent surveys showing that about half want more spending with higher taxes, 30 per cent prefer the two to stay as they are and under 15 per cent want tax cuts with less expenditure (Gyford *et al* 1989: 243). The 1980s has seen no major transformations in dispositions towards public expenditure (W.L. Miller 1988).

22 With all that has been stated so far, readers might well wonder why the Conservatives have stayed in office for so long. Undoubtedly, the party has been aided by a first-past-the-post electoral system, at a time when a new third 'party' has split the opposition vote. Obviously, the spatial expression of party support has had an effect here. This is not simply because constituencies have developed local political 'cultures' which are derived from their dominant class compositions (Warde 1986). It also draws on the uneven geographical gains from Britain's economic performance in the 1980s. This has helped to keep voters loyal to the government in some places and has been enticing others into its fold (Johnston *et al* 1988). Additionally, there have been elements of 'luck' favourable to the Conservatives. Although its precise impacts are uncertain, there seems little doubt that the party gained electoral support in 1983 on account of the Falklands/Malvinas War (Norpoth 1987). Although there were no inter-party disagreements on policy here, the Conservatives were constantly in the public eye at this time (partly through tight control of the media, but also because the government received kudos as 'champion' of the nation). This 'Falklands effect' was well recognised by the government, as seen in Margaret Thatcher's promise not to call a general election immediately after the war. If Norpoth's (1987) assessment is correct, then even a year after the war the Conservatives gained a 5 per cent increment in public support on account of it. Another aspect of 'luck' came in the form of internal squabbling within opposition parties. Certainly the Conservative media played these stories to the full. Nevertheless, at times when Conservative support has been at a low ebb, one or other opposition camp has contrived to give this party a significant boost in electoral support.

## 3 STRUCTURING LOCAL POLITICS

1 Block-busting is a ploy used by realtors in the United States which plays on the centrality of property values in people's attitudes to their home (Agnew 1981) and on social and often racist fears that minority populations are associated with high crime rates. Realtors spread rumours of an impending minority population 'invasion' of a neighbourhood – perhaps even buying a home and putting a family from a racial minority in it – to stimulate demand for house sales (at low prices as the market becomes over-supplied). Neighbourhoods can very quickly 'flip' from one social composition to another as a result of block-busting. Racial enclaves result, with further benefits for those in real estate from the placement of numerous low income families in former single family homes, thereby yielding high rent income. In an attempt to restrict such

practices, some municipalities now stipulate that any general canvass of a neighbourhood by a real estate company has to be approved by the council or its officers.

2 In France around 28,000 of the nation's 36,000 communes have fewer than 2,000 inhabitants (Mény 1983). In Italy almost 80 per cent of municipalities have less than 5,000 residents (Dente 1985) and three-quarters of Spanish municipalities contain under 2,000 people (Amodia 1986).

3 As with all aspects of local government organisation it is pertinent to ask whose interests are best served by such arrangements. Walker and Heiman (1981) point to pressures from residential developers and industrialists for land-use control functions to be vested in regional authorities. While justifications for this are couched in terms of the parochialism of local self-interest and the difficulties of efficient planning, what lies behind this preference is the assumption that large corporations can more easily influence regional units, while eradicating the right of localities to block unwanted corporate projects. As Heiman (1988) showed for New York State, when state officials are persuaded by such arguments, the beneficiaries are more inclined to be corporate shareholders than rational planning.

4 Interpret this comment as a relative rather than an absolute criticism. Decentralisation did start from a relatively early time in places with strong labour movements (Kolko 1976). However, with large companies not gaining the ascendancy until the twentieth century, the establishment of early suburban municipalities owes much more to social exclusion than to capital–labour conflict (e.g. Burt 1963; Baltzell 1964; Hugill 1989).

5 Despite this, it should be emphasised that there were differences in vision involved here and not simply party political differences. For one, there was deep antagonism towards the preference of some cities for municipally owned public enterprises (such as electricity and the trams). This opposition was manifest in the Liberty and Property Defence League, which in the 1870s and 1880s mounted campaigns inside and outside Parliament to thwart new attempts to promote municipal 'socialism' (albeit such proposals usually came from business dominated councils, where such enterprises were viewed favourably on the grounds of efficiency and the ability to set profits against lower taxes). That the landed-mercantilist élite found such tendencies dangerously radical is evinced in an insistence that the 1888 legislation did not allow the police to be directly controlled by county councils, but for the overview function to be divided between councillors and magistrates (i.e. authority was placed in the hands of a group half selected by electors and half from the élite's own ranks).

6 This standing was seen in the creation of special authorities covering numerous London councils (such as the 1902 London Water Authority, the 1908 Port of London Authority, the 1930 Licensing Authority and the 1933 London Passenger Transport Board). Outside London, these functions were usually part of mainstream local authority services. In addition, London was (and is) covered by some peculiar legislative and administrative provisions (as with the Metropolitan Police being

responsible to the Home Office, not to a local jurisdiction).

7 Contrary to neo-marxist interpretations of State restructuring as a response to economic recession, the depression of the 1920s and 1930s almost certainly vetoed the reorganisation of London's government. Problems which the 1963 legislation was designed to address were evident in the 1930s, as legislation dealing with regional issues made clear (cf. the formation of the London Passenger Transport Board in 1933 and the passing of the London Greenbelt Act in 1938). In addition, as a reading of an established political journal such as *Political Quarterly* reveals, there was a consciousness in 1930s policy circles that reform was needed (cf. Stocks 1939).

8 During Wilson's 1964–70 era as prime minister, it is evident that parliamentary boundary changes were a damage limitation exercise for the Labour Party. The tactics employed included delaying implementation of disliked proposals and selective acceptance of others. In Steed's (1969) estimation, one round of such adjustments turned proposals that would likely have increased Conservative seats by 8 to 20 into a Labour gain of 2 to 3.

9 Scotland was the exception, since here the main provisions of the Scottish Commission were accepted. The significance of this is that Scotland is a poor hunting ground for the Conservative Party (e.g. Johnston *et al.* 1988). Almost irrespective of what local government boundaries are, the Conservatives gain little advantage.

10 The ideological division between the government and the metropolitan county councils (including the GLC) over employment policies came in two forms. Firstly, at a time when Margaret Thatcher had earned the nicknamed TINA, for her reiteration of the message 'There Is No Alternative', these councils showed that there was an alternative: jobs could be saved and new opportunities could be created. Secondly, in their promotion of new jobs, these authorities – or more accurately some of them, since not all were equally active – insisted on conditions which the government found repugnant. Included amongst these were stipulations about equal opportunities, the extension of worker involvement in business decisions and compliance with minimum wage requirements (Hall 1986). None of these is particularly radical (aspects of contract compliance had been in operation in London ever since 1888). Even for small, struggling firms, these policies did not cut deeply into operational procedures. What is more, the financial backing for these programmes was insufficient to make a deep impact (Mackintosh and Wainwright 1987). In the end, market forces themselves tightly constrained these efforts (Gough 1986) and they made a slight impression on employment levels. However, for some analysts, this is less important than their ideological input. As Duncan and Goodwin (1985: 244 and 251) expressed it: 'It is not so much what local state institutions do but how they do it . . . [since] Local economic policy may be fairly impotent in directly changing, through relations at work, class relations or gender relations. But it could well be influential in terms of people's expectations about these things.' If you discount the authoritarian impetus within government actions, the fear that these policies would gain broad support could be an appealing explanation for the

government's response. However, as Stoker (1988) pointed out, the public was barely conscious of this 'ideological battle'. Indeed, as we shall see in Chapter Five, the expectation that such struggles lead to a new public consciousness relies on a poor grasp of relationships between local government and the public.

11 The technical arguments about the purity of public goods and the free-rider problem can be found in any standard text on the economics of the public sector (e.g. Stiglitz 1986).

12 This is a simplified argument about a complex issue. The point to grasp is that government ownership *per se* has no necessary implications for the efficiency or profitability of enterprises. This point has been well made in numerous criticisms of the privatisation schemes of post-1979 Conservative governments. For profit-making units, neither economic theory nor empirical evidence distinguishes private and public sector performances in their own right. Where the line is drawn is between monopolies and competitive markets, with the caution that government endeavours have an inclination towards monopoly. Additionally, in economic theory (where economic criteria alone set objectives), the dangers for efficient operations come from governments imposing political criteria on economic transactions. Both criticisms apply to 1980s Conservatives. Privatisation in Britain has not encouraged competition but has shifted monopoly power from public to private hands (Aharoni 1988). At the same time, the business decisions of nationalised industries have been interfered with (as in restricting the ability to borrow money) because of the political decision to count loans by nationalised industries in the public sector borrowing requirement. To follow up on these points in a context relevant to the main issues in this book, the reader is recommended to Meadows and Jackson (1986) and Tomlinson (1986).

13 In Britain this has been seen in the lack of applications from private companies for public service contracts. Even for services which must now be put out to competitive tender, many councils only receive bids from their own workers. It is estimated that 75 per cent of competitively tendered contracts were awarded to council staff ('Staff win most council contracts', *Guardian*, 8 May 1989: 4).

14 An appropriate way to view such tactics is to see them as a means of asserting local values (viz. forcing local preferences on to nationally dictated directions to act). The stipulations laid down in awarding contracts are often the same as those imposed on direct labour forces. If councils use their ability to write service regulations to favour public provision, this is little different from the government using its position to favour capital. Moreover, it is not dissimilar from the manipulation of services to the public by private sector firms in order to enhance profits. Notable amongst the instances of this was the deliberate running down of urban transit systems in the USA in order to increase profits for car manufacturers, oil companies, tyre companies and real estate developers, while at the same time breaking the power of one of the more active trade union movements (the transit workers). The story of transit decline, of the continuing opposition of the highway lobby to railroad systems and of the importance of capitalist power in deciding comparative rates of rail decline, has been well told by Allen Whitt and

Glenn Yago (Whitt 1982; Yago 1984; Whitt and Yago 1985). Amongst the tactics employed by the highway lobby were purchasing railways and closing them down, establishing non-competitive supply contracts for bus operations, investing in competitors to rail routes, financially squeezing rail companies through the banks and offering direct or indirect loans to companies that would compete with rail lines.

15 If one wanted to follow this line it could be done easily. Why, for instance, are the personal social services primarily in national hands when, as consumption items, Saunders's explanation suggests that they should be in local care? Similarly, is it appropriate to view public housing as a consumption service when large corporations are so intimately involved in its provision (Dunleavy 1981)?

16 For both electricity and gas, some care should be taken in reading these functions as local losses. Both moved out of local control because their industries were nationalised by the government. When this occurred, municipalities accounted for 37 per cent of gas production and two-thirds of the electricity industry. Primarily, these nationalisations were to improve the efficiency and capacity of production and supply, given the belief that larger organisations were required to meet emerging demands (see Robson 1962).

17 At local and state levels, Bennett and DiLorenzo (1983) report that there are around 17,500 'toy governments' in the United States that do not employ anyone, with around 4,000 local units only employing a single person.

18 This list of exceptions excludes such entities as the National Health Service and the Manpower Services Commission, because, while such institutions have local machineries, their actions are principally directed from Whitehall. In the light of beliefs that local authorities have little autonomy from Whitehall today (Dearlove and Saunders 1984), this distinction perhaps rests on arbitrary grounds. However, even local arms of national agencies interpret central policies in different ways and pursue them with uneven vigour. Why such units (such as district health authorities) are distinguished from organisations with primary roots in local government is because they are formally part of national government.

19 This does not mean that the greatest commitment to local economic regeneration has always come from left-wing councils. With inner city bases, many Labour councils have perhaps been more conscious of the need for action. However, rural authorities have also been active. Kent County Council, for one, has a similar enterprise board to that set up in Greater London (Stoker 1988); albeit the emphasis on trade union participation is not the same.

20 As the then leader of the GLC has pointed out in a recent book, the assumption that councils have no mandate is itself legally disputed (also Johnston 1983; Loughlin 1986). Thus, when Tameside Council opposed the 1974–9 Labour government by refusing to implement a comprehensive school system, it was supported by the Lords on the basis that the policy was part of the council's manifesto (Livingstone 1987: 195). The basis for such biases in legal rulings is suggested in Griffith's (1985) comments on the Fares Fair ruling:

Why did they make this choice? For the members of the Court of Appeal, one reason seems to have been their annoyance with the way the majority group implemented their manifesto commitment . . . In the House of Lords . . . the reason for the choice seems to have been primarily the Law Lords' strong preference for the principles of the market economy with a dislike of heavy subsidization for social purposes. Their decisions were in the tradition of individual rather than social, private rather than collective, enterprise . . . Whether or not their Lordships were politically biased, their habits of thought determined their decision.

(Griffith 1985: 211–12)

The legal process has the potential to favour councils over national government, but biases within the system more likely favour particular standpoints. Generally, local mandates do not have preference over central government dictate (Loughlin 1986).

21 The Law Lords' ruling over fiduciary duty opened a can of worms which some Conservative councils seemed eager to exploit by taking the GLC to court over any aspect of its expenditure which they found unsavoury. Kensington and Chelsea took the lead, but were refused leave to bring a case challenging the GLC budget. Whether any political pressure was brought to bear is difficult to say, but it is clear that widespread support for Fares Fair led to embarrassment for both the legal profession and the government following such an overtly political ruling. Whether intentional or not, the Kensington and Chelsea ruling clawed back the breadth of application for the concept of fiduciary duty. This is evident in Justice McNeill's comments:

It is now clear that the issue is one for the political hustings and not for the court. It is a matter of real concern that the court . . . is increasingly . . . used for political purposes superficially dressed up as points of law. The proper remedy in such matters is the ballot box and not the court. . . . The impropriety of coming to this court when . . . political capital is sought to be made . . . out of judicial review cannot be over stressed.

(from Livingstone 1987: 219)

## 4 LOCAL POLITICAL CULTURES, LOCAL POLITICAL PRACTICES

1 When Harold Washington was elected mayor of Chicago in 1983 he received 98 per cent of black votes and 18 per cent of white (Judd and Ready 1986). According to a CBS exit poll taken after the 1989 mayoralty election, even after six years with a black mayor, Chicago voters still divided by race. Thus, in 1989, the white candidate is reported to have obtained 89 per cent of the white vote but only 7 per cent of the black, while the black candidate scored 92 per cent of black votes and 6 per cent of white (*San Francisco Chronicle*, 5 April 1989: A8). Such patterns might be extreme in Chicago but they are not restricted to that city. For the 1983 mayoralty election, for instance, Philadelphia's Wilson Goode obtained 97 per cent of black votes and 23 per cent of white (Judd and Ready 1986).

2 This is well illustrated in majority responses to local fiscal stress in the USA, where cut-back strategies have taken the least disruptive route: primarily relying on non-replacement of staff, cutting capital investment rather than current programmes, reducing overtime and improving management procedures (e.g. Wolman and Davis 1980; Levine *et al.* 1981; Susskind and Serio 1983; Walzer 1985).

3 One qualification on this statement is that if local taxation systems are regressive, then lower tax rates should bring relative gains for those of lower income (although this depends upon which, if any, services are lost to keep taxes low).

4 It is not only new investment that is important but also maintaining existing investment. As Barlev and May (1976) found for Manhattan, increases in tax levels not only slow the pace of new construction but also hasten the rate of building demolition.

5 Peterson's typology of expenditure types probably should be viewed heuristically rather than theoretically. The broad categories he identified are extremely difficult to tie down in causal terms, since it is likely that a developmental expenditure in one location is better viewed as an allocational one in another, and so on. A good example of this is spending on the arts, which in recent years has become an important means of building an image favourable to the attraction of high technology industries (Whitt 1987). In many towns, arts spending has no such developmental appeal.

6 In the literature, reference can be found to a two-thirds funding level for central grants in the mid-1970s. This is calculated for relevant expenditure only; that is, for items which local institutions must provide under national law. It has been common for relevant expenditure to account for around 70–80 per cent of total spending.

7 Today, this is less true, although there is much inter-state variation. New York State is a heavy user of unrestricted aid, with two-thirds of state funds coming in this form (Schneider 1986).

8 Categorical grants generally infringe on local autonomy. Thus, as a stipulation of the Education of All Handicapped Children Act of 1975, state receipt of federal aid was conditional upon local schools integrating all physically handicapped children, including those with learning disabilities, into mainstream schools (Levine and Posner 1981). This imposed one image of how things *should* be done on a policy which is subject to debate and uncertainty.

9 In a comparative analysis it is out of place to piece together the intricate details of British legislation on local finance. What does need to be grasped is that the number of legislative provisions has been enormous. Moreover, as reviews on the scene have pointed out, these provisions have changed annually, such that there has been no evidence of a clear strategy, merely an intention to ensure, by hook or by crook, that local spending is brought under tight Treasury control. Readers wishing to become immersed in the detail of relevant Acts, circulars and statements could turn to Travers (1986) or, in much briefer guise, Jordan (1987). Focusing more narrowly on how grant allocations have been decided, Bramley (1984) provides a useful commentary on both technical and political issues. Drawing on the same calculations, the government has

set expenditure targets for each council, yet, as both Gibson (1985) and Smith and Stewart (1985) make clear, these have not proved sufficient for the Conservative leadership, and so additional stipulations have been introduced (calling for real expenditure reductions on previous spending figures). One result is that some councils have been asked to spend less than even the government's conservative calculations hold to be appropriate. How these stipulations feed into rate capping is investigated by Grant (1986). Bringing all this together with a clear, knowledgeable commentary on the politics of local expenditure, the reader cannot go wrong in spending time with Midwinter (1984), Newton and Karran (1985) or Midwinter and Mair (1987).

10 Despite the flurry of interest in privatisation in the early 1980s, by the mid-decade reductions in services in private hands had occurred. Apart from resistance to privatisation *per se*, the lack of success of this system owes something to the failures of private companies. Price rises after contracts were won, poor service quality, and sharp reductions in workers' wages and conditions have all been evident (Ascher 1987). Besides, for many councils, simply considering privatisation was enough to provoke employees to accept restructured work practices. In this regard the government's aims have been met, but within a framework which councils found acceptable, and in a manner which was removed from the government's aim of reducing the public sector.

11 It could be pointed out, quite legitimately, that central authorities have engaged in sharp conflicts with dissident local authorities on a number of occasions (e.g. Poplar, Clay Cross, Tameside, Norwich). Over financial matters, when councillors have persisted in opposing central regulations, the courts have stepped in to ban them from holding future elected office (as in Lambeth and Liverpool in the last five years). Yet these cases are rare. What is more, their outcomes are uncertain (in effect both Clay Cross and Tameside were local victories). The authority of the government to act does not lead to a ready willingness to do so. Thus, seemingly provoked in the extreme by Liverpool City Council, the government shrank back from taking over the city's affairs in recognition of how problematical such a step would be (Parkinson 1985). In times of calm, such acts are unnecessary. In times of strife they can be highly explosive, since councils which go to the brink are unlikely to submit quietly to takeover (see Livingstone [1987] for a flavour of opposition to cooperating with the Conservative government in new left councils).

12 A good summary of the attitude of new left councillors towards the Thatcher governments is captured in the following passage by the former leader of the Greater London Council:

> We had every intention of proceeding with our election manifesto, which had received the endorsement of the electorate, and nothing in Mrs Thatcher's nature led her to accept that others might have a right to follow policies contrary to her own.
>
> To add insult to injury there was also a huge gulf between the cultural values of the GLC Labour Group and everything Mrs Thatcher considered right and proper. The loud, populist style of the GLC represented a challenge to a Prime Minister who had gained power by a right-wing populist appeal to working-class voters and

racist and sexist prejudices. To fight racism while Mrs Thatcher assured white voters that she 'understood their fear of being swamped by an alien tide' was a direct challenge. To intervene in the economy to save and create jobs while the Government stood back and let market forces destroy 25 per cent of manufacturing industry showed that there was an alternative. Confidently to assert the rights of women and homosexuals while she preached Victorian family values was unacceptable. In our campaigning and in our refusal to pay lip service to the so-called impartiality of judges and civil servants we failed to accept the normal style and traditional courtesies of the Establishment. In our assertion that we believed Londoners had the right to information and a role in the administration of their city, we challenged the traditional establishment methods of administration by an élite. Mrs Thatcher droned on about 'the right of managers to manage'; we asserted that people should have a say in the day-to-day decisions which affected their lives both at their places of work and in the communities in which they lived.

(Livingstone 1987: 251–2)

13 That this campaign was well coordinated and had full backing from the Conservative controlled media is obvious. That much of the media coverage was damaging also appears clear. What is perhaps less well known is the extent to which such stories were fabricated. Well known 'loony left' stories with no foundation in truth include newspaper reports that Hackney had renamed its manholes 'access chambers', that Haringey had forbidden the use of black dustbin liners and the supposed banning of the nursery rhyme 'Baa, Baa, Black Sheep'. Research by James Curran of Goldsmith's College has found that there were around 3,000 'loony left' stories in the tabloid press between 1981 and 1987, a large percentage of which were partially or entirely fabricated (from Gyford *et al*. 1989: 312).

14 Illustrative of the government's appeals to prejudice rather than argument is the response of Cabinet Minister Norman Tebbitt to those who wrote to him opposing the ending of the GLC's Fares Fair policy:

Dear Constituent

Thank you for sending me a coupon clipped from one of Mr Livingstone's propaganda advertisements (paid for by your rates) about the London Transport fares.

Don't be conned into thinking Mr Livingstone is trying to give you something for nothing. Not only did he cut the fares for Londoners, but he cut them for such people as foreign tourists and well-paid commuters from outside London. They don't pay London rates, so you had to pay their fares out of your rates. Until Livingstone and his weird friends took over the GLC, London Transport was becoming more efficient and sensible. Now he has messed it up we've got bigger increases than we need have had and a huge bill to pay for the money he has lost. You shouldn't be surprised. Livingstone is pouring your money down the drain in many ways. Did you know this year he has given your money to his friends in some very peculiar organisations? For example, your money has gone to:

- the English Collective of Prostitutes
- Lesbian Line
- London Gay Teenage Group
- a series of left-wing propaganda sheets, including £500,000 spent on the extremist publication *The Londoner*.
And these are just a few of the items he is spending your money on. I suggest you write to Livingstone at County Hall, SE1, to ask him what benefit you get from giving money to these sorts of causes.

(from Livingstone 1987: 209–10)

15 The 1980 Housing Act allowed rural councils to apply for exemption from the stipulation that tenants have a right to buy their council home. Even given tight regulations that restricted applications, 130 districts sought exemption within the first year of the law, although less than a fifth of these were granted (see Forrest and Murie [1988] on opposition to council house sales amongst Conservative controlled councils).

16 Referred to as hysterectomy zoning, this procedure has been employed to reduce opportunities for families with children to settle in a municipality (one bedroom specifications are common). One indication of how important this practice can be, which is all that we can suggest given the lack of national data on its incidence, is that 42 per cent of suburban Philadelphia municipalities restrict the number of bedrooms allowed in apartments (Muller 1975). The obvious point of relevance here is the cost of children. Where school districts and municipalities are coterminous, by keeping the number of pupils in schools at low levels property taxes are also kept down (school costs accounting for over half total local spending). Hence, these lifestyle considerations have an economic motive. However, no neat disaggregation of the two can be provided. For instance, in their survey of Philadelphia's suburbs, Williams *et al.* (1965) asked citizens what was the most important task of their municipal government. In low status suburbs this proved to be keeping tax rates down (82 per cent) and keeping undesirables out (75 per cent), which was not much different from high status suburbs, where maintaining quality residents (69 per cent) and keeping undesirables out (62 per cent) rated highest. Both sentiments have financial implications as well as including social commentary.

17 Readers might well hold that the changes which are heralded by a move toward absentee-ownership alter operational styles rather than political cultures. This is not a point I would disagree with, once allowance is made for time-span. Political cultures are structures within which agents find direction for their actions. Once action paths change, so too must structures change. Political cultures must be reproduced over time; they are not fixed, immutable entities, but processes. Operational styles of long duration are thereby likely to add direction to core political values, even if they initially have weak links to certain central values. That it takes a long time to entrench changes in a political culture is certain. Thus, as Chapter Two explained, even after more than a decade of manipulating institutional practices to favour the private sector, while neutralising those who present alternatives to government policies, the new right principles of the Thatcher administrations are far from

accepted in Britain. People still cling to a central acceptance of equality, fair play and the necessity of public sector control over profit-making enterprises (e.g. W.L. Miller 1988).

18 In the case of DuPont, for example, Delaware law allows for voting in local elections to be based on property value, which gives the company a veto over many local decisions (Phelan and Pozen 1973).

19 In Urry's formulation, these conditions are specified for social classes, but they are applicable for other social formations, such as ethnic political machines in the USA (Shefter 1986).

## 5 FIXING OPERATIONAL STYLES

1 This point really applies to political élites rather than societal élites as a whole. In other words, it is legitimate to refer to religious élites as those who most decide religious practice, social élites as those who most establish social norms, and so on. The élites that are concentrated on in this book are those who most influence the State, not élites in general.

2 If self-interest is the primary criterion in evaluating the benefits of group membership, then, as Olson (1965) stressed, the likelihood that a single person has a critical effect on outcomes is small. For those who place self-interest first, it is more logical to be a free-rider (to obtain benefits from collective action without putting effort into gaining them; precisely the position of those who refuse to join trade unions but accept the higher wages which union action brings). If collective identity is weak, minor concessions to sub-groups or individuals are more likely to buy their acquiescence, so sapping the strength of the movement as a whole. For those with few resources, solidarity is a potent source of strength, but one that is dependent upon collective identity.

3 The word 'public' did not mean the same in the 1880s as it does today. The earlier reference in this paragraph to an 'outcry amongst the upper classes' suggests this. National officials were not concerned primarily with the population at large (what is now seen as the public). Indeed, the 1888 local government system was structured to maintain the dominance of propertied classes in town and country.

4 Evidence on newspaper and radio endorsements is far from conclusive. Banfield and Wilson (1963) long ago asserted that it was influential, but there have been few analytical tests of this claim. One study which did find that endorsements were effective was that of Stein and Fleischmann (1987). While calling for circumspection in interpreting their analysis, they found that endorsements for incumbents were almost always effective in six US cities. Yet their impact was not restricted to reform institutions, but also applied to partisan ballots and to district-based elections (although this does not preclude the possibility that relations between those endorsed and the media differs in reformed and non-reformed cities on account of the dissimilar opportunities offered by these different organisational structures).

5 Some studies have concluded that reformism is linked to distinct municipal policies (such as lower taxes and less spending). However, as Liebert (1974) argued, such findings are problematical given the difficulties of comparing places with dissimilar packages of municipal

functions. Studies examining single services, or the same places over time, have concluded that reformism has no significant policy impact once other circumstances are taken into account (e.g. Morgan and Pelissero 1980; Hoggart 1989).

6 These figures are almost exactly those reported by Newton (1976a) for Birmingham under the pre-1974 local government system. Here the Conservative and Labour percentages were 51 and 80, respectively.

7 This characteristic was even more marked in rural areas than in urban ones. Amongst pre-1974 county councils, for example, meetings of the full council were only quarterly in some cases.

8 Given the ideological position of this writer, I have assumed that this reference to 'men' is factual rather than gender-biased.

9 Since 1974 England has had two tiers of local government. Prior to this, county borough (i.e. city) employees could not hold elected office if they lived within a city's boundaries, since it was illegal to be a councillor in the authority which employed you (county boroughs being single-tier authorities). After that time, local authority employees could hold local elected office, as they could be employed by one local tier but hold office in the other.

# 6 POLICY OUTCOMES

1 To clarify this point, this does not mean that critics have not accused others of inaccurate or distorted description. Domhoff's (1978) evaluation of New Haven is a well known re-study that makes this charge against Dahl's (1961) earlier investigation. Yet the thrust of Domhoff's critique concerns that incompleteness of Dahl's study and the inappropriateness of the issues he examined. No charge of deliberate distortion is levelled. Indeed, Domhoff demonstrates a respect for Dahl's integrity even in disagreeing with him (e.g. Domhoff 1986). Where researchers charge others with distortion, most commonly their criticisms relate more to research practice than to theory.

2 To explain this point, when central funds are allocated to the health budget it is assumed that, say, a half per cent efficiency saving has been made on the previous year's performance. Thus if an increase in funds of six per cent is awarded, the government actually gives five and one-half per cent (with all its publicity stressing the six per cent figure). Then, if vacant health service land is sold, the income from this is counted as a 'negative' expenditure (even if the money is not spent) and the sum obtained is added to the total figure that the government claims has been spent on health care provision.

3 It should be emphasised that this statement might not apply to nations other than Britain and the USA (or at least it might require qualification). As Wilson (1985) argued, it is too easy for English language researchers to assume the universality of what is a particularly Anglo-American perspective on the roles of business and government in society. Elsewhere overtly hostile reactions to government intervention in the economy are often muted.

4 It is not pertinent to extend this discussion, but readers will be able to identify similar patterns both in the fabricated mass media stories about

new left councils (Gyford *et al.* 1989) and in the posturing of the British government over football hooligans.

5 An externality is a 'cost' or 'benefit' that is not incurred by those undertaking an activity. Thus, those travelling on congested roads pass on the negative externalities of increased noise, greater air pollution and lower property values to those living beside the route.

6 Another dimension of educational policy that has a party political overtone in its discriminations is subsidies for private schools. In Conservative controlled Oxfordshire in 1976, for example, the council sought to reduce its teaching staff by 10 per cent in order to save £350,000 at the same time as it was paying £500,000 to private schools to provide scholarships for 'bright' children (almost wholly from professional homes; Dunleavy 1980a).

7 For instance, contrary to the common impression that Labour dominated authorities are responsive to poorer people, there is evidence from a large number of Labour controlled councils which cautions against too ready an acceptance of this view (most especially prior to the 1980s). Thus, Butterworth (1966: 31) found that: 'Islington's mission was to keep the rate low and their [Labour's] majority constant . . . their paramount interest came to be that of stifling all public controversy' (see also Baxter 1972). As Corina (1974) recorded for Halifax:

> far from the parties giving a political aspect to the decision-making they frequently helped to eliminate political dialogue by inhibiting discussion in order to expedite decision-making and by organising the context to produce working consensus.
>
> (Corina 1974: 83)

# Bibliography

Abbott, C. (1987) *The New Urban America: Growth and Politics in Sunbelt Cities*, University of North Carolina Press, Chapel Hill, NC.

Adams, C.T. (1989) 'Spending cuts and central/local relations under Reagan and Thatcher', in H. Wolman (ed.) *Constitutional Regimes and the City*, Wayne State University Center for Urban Studies, Detroit, MI.

Adrian, C. (1983) 'Centralised service provision: an examination of the facts', *Australian Geographical Studies*, 21, 251–8.

Adrian, C.R. (1972) *State and Local Governments*, McGraw-Hill, New York.

Adrian, C.R. (1988) 'Forms of city government in American history', in *The Municipal Yearbook 1988*, International City Management Association, Washington D.C., 3–11.

Agnew, J. (1981) 'Homeownership and the capitalist social order', in M.J. Dear and A.J. Scott (eds) *Urbanization and Urban Planning in Capitalist Society*, Methuen, London, 457–80.

Agnew, J.A. (1987) *Place and Politics: The Geographical Mediation of State and Society*, Allen & Unwin, London.

Aharoni, Y. (1988) 'The United Kingdom: transforming attitudes', in R. Vernon (ed.) *The Promise of Privatization*, Council on Foreign Relations, New York, 23–56.

Aiken, C.S. (1987) 'Race as a factor in municipal underbounding', *Annals of the Association of American Geographers*, 77, 564–79.

Alford, R.R. and Friedland, R. (1985) *Powers of Theory: Capitalism, the State and Democracy*, Cambridge University Press, Cambridge.

Allison, L. (1982) 'Review: R. Muir and R. Paddison "Politics, Geography and Behaviour"', *Political Geography Quarterly*, 1, 109–12.

Almond, G.A. and Verba, S. (1963) *The Civic Culture: Political Attitudes and Democracy in Five Nations*, Princeton University Press, Princeton, NJ.

Amick, G. (1976) *The American Way of Graft: A Study of Corruption in State and Local Government, How It Happens and What Can Be Done About It*, Center for Analysis of Public Issues, Princeton, NJ.

Amodia, J. (1986) 'The Spanish Communist Party and local government', in B. Szajkowski (ed.) *Marxist Local Governments in Western Europe and Japan*, Frances Pinter, London, 20–44.

Anderson, J. (1983) 'Geography as ideology and the politics of crisis: the enterprise zone experiment', in J. Anderson, S.S. Duncan and R. Hudson (eds) *Redundant Spaces in Cities and Regions?*, Institute of British Geographers Special Publication No. 15, London, 313–50.

Arblaster, A. (1987) *Democracy*, Open University Press, Milton Keynes.

Armstrong, H.W. and Fildes, J. (1988) 'Industrial development incentives in England and Wales: the role of the district councils', *Progress in Planning*, 30, 85–156.

Aronowitz, S. (1973) *False Promises: The Shaping of American Working Class Consciousness*, McGraw-Hill, New York.

Ascher, K. (1987) *The Politics of Privatisation*, Macmillan, Basingstoke.

Ashford, D.E. (1980) 'A Victorian drama: the fiscal subordination of British local government', in D.E. Ashford (ed.) *Financing Urban Government in the Welfare State*, St Martin's Press, New York, 71–96.

Ashford, D.E. (1981) *Policy and Politics in Britain: The Limits of Consensus*, Blackwell, Oxford.

Ashford, D.E. (1982) *British Dogmatism and French Pragmatism: Central–Local Policy-Making in the Welfare State*, Allen & Unwin, London.

Ashford, D.E. (1986) *The Emergence of the Welfare States*, Blackwell, Oxford.

Audit Commission (1984) *The Impact on Local Authorities' Economy, Efficiency and Effectiveness of the Block Grant Distribution System*, HMSO, London.

Audit Commission (1987) *The Management of London's Authorities*, HMSO, London.

Bachrach, P. and Baratz, M.S. (1970) *Power and Poverty*, Oxford University Press, New York.

Bagdikian, B.H. (1983) *The Media Monopoly*, Beacon Press, Boston, MA.

Bailey, S. (1986) 'Rates reform – lessons from the Scottish experience', *Local Government Studies*, 12(3), 21–36.

Baltzell, E.D. (1964) *The Protestant Establishment: Aristocracy and Class in America*, Random House, New York.

Banfield, E.C. and Wilson, J.Q. (1963) *City Politics*, Harvard University Press, Cambridge, MA.

Barlev, B. and May, J. (1976) 'The effects of property taxes on the construction and demolition of urban areas', *Economic Geography*, 52, 304–10.

Barry, N.P. (1987) *The New Right*, Croom Helm, London.

Bassett, K. (1986) 'Economic restructuring, spatial coalitions, and local economic development strategies: the case of Bristol', *Political Geography Quarterly*, 5 (supplement), 163–78.

Baxter, R. (1972) 'The working class and Labour politics', *Political Studies*, 20, 97–107.

Becquart-Leclerq, J. (1977) 'French mayors and communal policy outputs', in R.J. Liebert and A.W. Imershein (eds) *Power, Paradigms and Community Research*, Sage, Beverly Hills, 79–119.

Bell, D. (1962) *The End of Ideology*, revised edition, Free Press, New York.

Bennett, J.T. and DiLorenzo, T.J. (1983) *Underground Government: The Off-Budget Public Sector*, Cato Institute, Washington D.C.

Bennett, R.J. (1980) *The Geography of Public Finance*, Methuen, London.

Bennett, R.J. and Fearnehough, M. (1987) 'The burdens of the non-domestic rates on business', *Local Government Studies*, 13(6), 23–36.

Bennett, S. and Earle, C. (1983) 'Socialism in America: a geographical interpretation of its failure', *Political Geography Quarterly*, 2, 31–53.

Bentley, S. (1972) 'Intergroup relations in local politics: Pakistanis and Bangladeshis', *New Community*, 2(1), 44–8.

Berg, L.L., Hahn, H. and Schmidhauser, J.R. (1976) *Corruption in the American Political System*, General Learning Press, Morristown, NJ.

Berry, B.J.L. and Bednarz, R.S. (1975) 'A hedonic model of prices and assessments for single-family homes: does the assessor follow the market or the market follow the assessor?', *Land Economics*, 51, 21–40.

Bird, R.M. and Slack, E. (1983) *Urban Public Finance in Canada*, Butterworths, Toronto.

Birdseye, P. and Webb, T. (1984) 'Why the rate burden on business is a cause for concern', *National Westminster Bank Quarterly Review*, February, 2–15.

Birgesson, B.O. (1977) 'The service paradox: citizen assessment of urban services in 36 Swedish communes', in V. Ostrom and F.P. Bish (eds) *Comparing Urban Service Delivery Systems*, Sage Urban Affairs Annual Review No. 12, Beverly Hills, CA, 243–67.

Birrell, D. (1978) 'The centralisation of local government functions in Northern Ireland', *Local Government Studies*, 4 (4), 23–38.

Birrell, D. (1981) 'Local Government Councillors in Northern Ireland', University of Strathclyde Studies in Public Policy No. 83, Glasgow.

Birrell, D. and Murie, A. (1980) *Policy and Government in Northern Ireland*, Gill & Macmillan, Dublin.

Bish, R.L. (1971) *The Public Economy of Metropolitan Areas*, Rand McNally, Chicago, IL.

Blake, D.H. and Walters, R.S. (1987) *The Politics of Global Economic Relations*, third edition, Prentice-Hall, Englewood Cliffs, NJ.

Block, F. (1987) *Revising State Theory: Essays in Politics and Post-industrialism*, Temple University Press, Philadelphia, PA.

Blondel, J. and Hall, R. (1967) 'Conflict, decision-making and the perceptions of local councillors', *Political Studies*, 15, 322–50.

Blowers, A. (1980) *The Limits of Power: The Politics of Local Planning Policy*, Pergamon, Oxford.

Blowers, A. (1983) 'Master of fate or victim of circumstance – the exercise of corporate power in environmental decision-making', *Policy and Politics*, 11, 393–415.

Blydenburgh, J. (1975) 'Party organizations', in A. Rosenthal and J. Blydenburgh (eds) *Politics in New Jersey*, Rutgers University Eagleton Institute of Politics, New Brunswick, NJ, 100–37.

Bollens, J.C. and Ries, J.C. (1969) *The City Manager Profession: Myths and Realities*, Public Administration Service, Chicago, IL.

Bollens, S.A. (1986) 'A political ecological analysis of income inequality in the metropolitan area', *Urban Affairs Quarterly*, 22, 221–41.

Bolotin, F.N. and Cingranelli, D.L. (1983) 'Equity and urban policy: the underclass hypothesis revisited', *Journal of Politics*, 45, 209–19.

Bondi, L. (1988) 'Political participation and school closures', *Policy and Politics*, 16, 41–54.

Bottomore, T.B. (1964) *Elites and Society*, Penguin, Harmondsworth.

Bowman, A. O'M. (1987) 'Elite organization and the growth machine: the nonprofit development corporation', in G.W. Domhoff and T.R. Dye (eds) *Power Elites and Organizations*, Sage, Beverly Hills, CA, 116–25.

Box, S. (1983) *Power, Crime and Mystification*, Tavistock, London.

Bradford, M. and Burdett, F. (1989) 'Spatial polarisation of private education in England', *Area*, 21, 47–57.

Bradley, D.S. and Zald, M.N. (1965) 'From commercial élite to political administrator: the recruitment of the mayors of Chicago', *American Journal of Sociology*, 71, 153–67.

Bramley, G. (1984) 'Grant-related expenditure and the inner city', *Local Government Studies*, 10(3), 15–37.

Branson, N. (1979) *Poplarism 1919-25: George Lansbury and the Councillors' Revolt*, Lawrence & Wishart, London.

Breton, A. and Wintrobe, R. (1982) *The Logic of Bureaucratic Conduct*, Cambridge University Press, Cambridge.

Bristow, S.L. (1972) 'The criteria for local government reorganisation and local authority autonomy', *Policy and Politics*, 1, 143–62.

Bristow, S.L. (1984) 'The results', in S. Bristow, D. Kermode and M. Mannin (eds) *The Redundant Counties?*, Hesketh, Ormskirk, 185–205.

Brosio, G. (1985) 'Fiscal autonomy of non-central government and the problem of public spending growth', in F. Forte and A. Peacock (eds) *Public Expenditure and Government Growth*, Blackwell, Oxford, 52–64.

Brown, L. and Brown, C. (1973) *An Unauthorized History of the RCMP*, James Lewis & Samuel, Toronto.

Brown, M.B. (1988) 'Away with all great arches: Anderson's history of British capitalism', *New Left Review*, 167, 22–51.

Browning, R.P., Marshall, D.R. and Tabb, D.H. (1984) *Protest is Not Enough: The Struggle of Blacks and Hispanics for Equality in Urban Politics*, University of California Press, Berkeley, CA.

Brunn, S.D., Hoffman, W.L. and Romsa, G.H. (1969) 'The defeat of a Youngstown school levy', *Southeastern Geographer*, 39, 67–79.

Bulpitt, J. (1967) *Party Politics in English Local Government*, Longman, Harlow.

Bulpitt, J. (1983) *Territory and Power in the United Kingdom*, Manchester University Press, Manchester.

Burbank, G. (1976) *When Farmers Voted Red: The Gospel of Socialism in the Oklahoma Countryside 1910–27*, Greenwood Press, Westport, CT.

Burch, M. (1983) 'Mrs Thatcher's approach to leadership in government: 1979 – June 1983', *Parliamentary Affairs*, 36, 399–416.

Burchell, R.W., Carr, J.H., Floridin, R.L. and Németh, J. (1984) *The New Reality of Municipal Finance: The Rise and Fall of the Intergovernmental City*, Rutgers University Center for Urban Policy Research, New Brunswick, NJ.

Burchell, R.W. *et al.* (1983) *Mount Laurel II: Challenge and Delivery of Low-Cost Housing*, Rutgers University Center for Urban Policy Research, New Brunswick, NJ.

Burt, N. (1963) *The Perennial Philadelphians: The Anatomy of an American Aristocracy*, Dent, London.

Butterworth, R. (1966) 'Islington Borough Council: some characteristics of single-party rule', *Politics*, 1(1), 21–31.

Button, J.W. and Scher, J.K. (1984) 'The election and impact of black officials in the South', in H.R. Rodgers (ed.) *Public Policy and Social Institutions*, JAI Press, Greenwich, CT, 183–218.

Byrne, D.S. (1986) 'State sponsored control-managers, poverty professionals and the inner city working class', in K. Hoggart and E. Kofman (eds) *Politics, Geography and Social Stratification*, Croom Helm, London, 144–67.

Byrne, D.S., Williamson, W.W. and Fletcher, B. (1975) *The Poverty of Education*, Martin Robertson, London.

Carnoy, M. (1984) *The State and Political Theory*, Princeton University Press, Princeton, NJ.

Caro, R.A. (1974) *The Power Broker: Robert Moses and the Fall of New York*, Vintage Books, New York.

Castells, M. (1977) *The Urban Question: A Marxist Approach* (translation of *La Question Urbaine*, 1972), MIT Press, Cambridge, MA.

Cawson, A. and Saunders, P. (1983) 'Corporatism, competitive politics and class struggle', in R. King (ed.) *Capital and Politics*, Routledge & Kegan Paul, London, 8–27.

Chandler, J. (1984) 'The selection of local candidates', in S. Bristow, D. Kermode and M. Mannin (eds) *The Redundant Counties?*, Hesketh, Ormskirk, 49–68.

Chandler, J.A. and Lawless, P. (1985) *Local Authorities and the Creation of Employment*, Gower, Aldershot.

Checkoway, B. (1980) 'Large builders, federal housing programmes, and postwar suburbanisation', *International Journal of Urban and Regional Research*, 4, 21–45.

Chester, L., Fay, S. and Young, H. (1967) *The Zinoviev Letter*, Heinemann, London.

Chicoine, D.L. and Walzer, N. (1985) *Governmental Structure and Local Public Finance*, Oelgeschlager Gunn & Hain, Boston, MA.

Chomsky, N. and Herman, E.S. (1979) *The Political Economy of Human Rights Volume One: The Washington Connection and Third World Fascism*, South End Press, Boston, MA.

Citrin, J. (1984) 'Introduction: the legacy of Proposition 13', in T. Schwadron and P. Richter (eds) *California and the American Tax Revolt*, University of California Press, Berkeley, CA, 1–69.

Citrin, J. and Levy, F. (1981) 'From 13 to 4 and beyond: the political meaning of the ongoing tax revolt in California', in G.E. Kaufman and K.T. Rosen (eds) *The Property Tax Revolt: The Case of Proposition 13*, Ballinger, Cambridge, MA, 1–26.

Clark, G. (1985) *Judges and Cities: Interpreting Local Autonomy*, University of Chicago Press, Chicago, IL.

Clark, T.N. (1975) 'Community power', *Annual Review of Sociology*, 1, 271–95.

Clark, T.N. (1977) 'Fiscal management of American cities: flow funds indicators', *Journal of Accounting Research*, 15, 54–106.

Clark, T.N. and Ferguson, L.C. (1983) *City Money: Political Processes, Fiscal Strain and Retrenchment*, Columbia University Press, New York.

Clark, W.A.V. (1988) 'School integration impacts on residential change',

*Environment and Planning C: Government and Policy*, 6, 475–88.

Clavel, P. (1986) *The Progressive City: Planning and Participation 1969-84*, Rutgers University Press, New Brunswick, NJ.

Clements, R.V. (1969) *Local Notables and the City Council*, Macmillan, Basingstoke.

Coates, D. (1975) *The Labour Party and the Struggle for Socialism*, Cambridge University Press, Cambridge.

Coates, D. (1980) *Labour in Power? A Study of the Labour Government 1974-9*, Longman, Harlow.

Cockburn, C. (1977) *The Local State: Management of Cities and People*, Pluto Press, London.

Cohen, A.P. (1982) 'Belonging: the experience of culture', in A.P. Cohen (ed.) *Belonging: Identity and Social Organisation in British Rural Cultures*, Manchester University Press, Manchester, 1–17.

Committee of Inquiry into Local Government Finance (1976) *Report* (Layfield Committee), HMSO, London.

Connors, R.J. and Dunham, W.J. (1984) *The Government of New Jersey*, University Press of America, Lanham, MD.

Cooke, P. (1985) 'Radical regions? Space, time and gender relations in Emilia, Provence and South Wales', in G. Rees, J. Bujra, P. Littlewood, H. Newby and T.L. Rees (eds) *Political Action and Social Identity*, Macmillan, Basingstoke, 17–41.

Coopers and Lybrand (1984) *Streamlining the Cities: An Analysis of the Costs Involved in the Government's Proposals for Reorganising Local Government in the Six Metropolitan Counties*, London.

Corina, L. (1974) 'Elected representatives in a party system: a typology', *Policy and Politics*, 3, 69–87.

Corrigan, P. (1979) *Schooling the Smash Street Kids*, Macmillan, Basingstoke.

Coulson, A. and Baker, W. (1984) 'Local Economic Initiatives Study: Sheffield City Council Employment Department', University of Birmingham Centre for Urban and Regional Studies Research Memorandum No. 106, Birmingham.

Cousins, P. (1988) 'PGOs on London', in C. Hood and G.F. Schuppert (eds) *Delivering Public Services in Western Europe: Sharing Western European Experience of Para-Government Organization*, Sage, London.

Cox, A., Furlong, P. and Page, E. (1985) *Power in Capitalist Societies*, Harvester, Brighton.

Cox, K.R. and Mair, A. (1988) 'Locality and community in the politics of local economic development', *Annals of the Association of American Geographers*, 78, 307–25.

Cox, K.R. and Nartowicz, F.Z. (1980) 'Jurisdictional fragmentation in the American metropolis', *International Journal of Urban and Regional Research*, 4, 196–209.

Crain, R.L. and Rosenthal, D.B. (1967) 'Community status as a dimension in local decision-making', *American Sociological Review*, 32, 970–85.

Crenson, M. (1971) *The Un-Politics of Air Pollution*, Johns Hopkins University Press, Baltimore, MD.

Crossman, R. (1975) *The Diaries of a Cabinet Minister Volume One: Minister of Housing 1964–66*, Hamish Hamilton and Jonathan Cape, London.

Cullingworth, J.B. (1966) *Housing and Local Government in England and Wales*, Allen & Unwin, London.

Curran, J. and Seaton, J. (1988) *Power Without Responsibility: The Press and Broadcasting in Britain*, third edition, Routledge, London.

Dahl, R.A. (1961) *Who Governs?*, Yale University Press, New Haven, CT.

Dahl, R.A. (1982) *Dilemmas of Pluralist Democracy*, Yale University Press, New Haven, CT.

Dahrendorf, R. (1959) *Class and Class Conflict in Industrial Society*, Routledge & Kegan Paul, London.

Dailey, G.H. and Campbell, R.R. (1980) 'The Ozark–Ouachita Uplands: growth and consequences', in D.L. Brown and J.M. Ward (eds) *New Directions in Urban–Rural Migration*, Academic Press, New York, 213–27.

Daly, M.T. (1982) *Sydney Boom, Sydney Bust*, Allen & Unwin, Sydney.

Danielson, M.N. (1976) *The Politics of Exclusion*, Columbia University Press, New York.

Danziger, J.N. (1976) 'Twenty-six outputs in search of a taxonomy', *British Journal of Political Science*, 5, 201–12.

Danziger, J.N. (1978) *Making Budgets*, Sage, Beverly Hills, CA and London.

David, S.M. and Kantor, P. (1979) 'Political theory and transformations in urban budgetary arenas: the case of New York City', in D.R. Marshall (ed.) *Urban Policy Making*, Sage, Beverly Hills, CA, 183–220.

Davies, H.J. (1988) 'Local government under siege', *Public Administration*, 66, 91–101.

Davies, J.G. (1972) *The Evangelistic Bureaucrat*, Tavistock, London.

Davis, D.H. (1974) *Energy Politics*, St Martin's Press, New York.

DeHoog, R.H. (1984) 'Theoretical perspectives on contracting out for services: implementation problems and possibilities of privatizing public services', in G.L. Edwards (ed.) *Public Policy Implementation*, JAI Press, Greenwich, CT, 227–59.

De Tray, D., Fernandez, J., Pascal, A. and Caggiano, M. (1981) 'Fiscal Restraints and the Burden of Local and State Taxes', Rand Corporation Report No. R-2646-FF/RC, Santa Monica, CA.

Dearlove, J. (1973) *The Politics of Policy in Local Government*, Cambridge University Press, Cambridge.

Dearlove, J. (1974) 'The control of change and regulation of community action', in D. Jones and M. Mayo (eds) *Community Work One*, Routledge & Kegan Paul, London, 22–43.

Dearlove, J. (1979) *The Reorganisation of British Local Government*, Cambridge University Press, Cambridge.

Dearlove, J. and Saunders, P. (1984) *Introduction to British Politics*, Polity, Cambridge.

Debnam, G. (1984) *The Analysis of Power: A Realist Approach*, Macmillan, Basingstoke.

Dente, B. (1985) 'Intergovernmental relations as central control policies: the case of Italian local finance', *Environment and Planning C: Government and Policy*, 3, 383–402.

Derthick, M. (1968) 'Inter-city differences in the administration of the

Public Assistance Program', in J.Q. Wilson (ed.) *City Politics and Public Policy*, Wiley, New York, 243–66.

Devine, J.A. (1983) 'Fiscal policy and class income inequality: the distributional consequences of governmental revenues and expenditure in the United States 1949–76', *American Sociological Review*, 48, 606–22.

Dickens, P., Duncan, S.S., Goodwin, M. and Gray, F. (1985) *Housing, States and Localities*, Methuen, London.

Dilnot, A. and Stark, G.K. (1986) 'The distributional consequences of Mrs Thatcher', *Fiscal Studies*, 7(2), 48–53.

Dilnot, A., Kell, M. and Webb, S. (1988) 'The 1988 budget and the structure of personal taxation', *Fiscal Studies*, 9(2), 38–47.

Dilnot, A., Stark, G.K., Walker, I. and Webb, S. (1987) 'The 1987 budget in perspective', *Fiscal Studies*, 8(2), 48–57.

DiLorenzo, T.J. (1981) 'Special districts and local public services', *Public Finance Quarterly*, 9, 353–67.

Doig, A. (1984) *Corruption and Misconduct in Contemporary British Politics*, Penguin, Harmondsworth.

Doig, J.W. (1987) 'Coalition building by a regional agency: Austin Tobin and the Port of New York Authority', in C.N. Stone and H.T. Sanders (eds) *The Politics of Urban Development*, University of Kansas Press, Lawrence, KS, 73–104.

Domhoff, G.W. (1969) 'Who made American foreign policy 1945–63', in D. Horowitz (ed.) *Corporations and the Cold War*, Monthly Review Press, New York, 25–69.

Domhoff, G.W. (1975) 'Social clubs, policy-planning groups and corporations: a network study of ruling class cohesiveness' *Insurgent Sociologist*, 5(3), 173–84.

Domhoff, G.W. (1978) *Who Really Rules? New Haven and Community Power Reexamined*, Transaction Press, New Brunswick, NJ.

Domhoff, G.W. (1983) *Who Rules America Now? A View for the '80s*, Prentice-Hall, Englewood Cliffs, NJ.

Domhoff, G.W. (1986) 'The growth machine and the power élite: a challenge to pluralists and marxists alike', in R.J. Waste (ed.) *Community Power: Directions for Future Research*, Sage, Beverly Hills, CA, 53–75.

Dommel, P.R. (1984) 'Review: K.R. Cox and R.J. Johnston "Conflict, Politics and the Urban Scene"', *Environment and Planning C: Government and Policy*, 2, 111–12.

Douglas, M. and Wildavsky, A. (1982) *Risk and Culture*, University of California Press, Berkeley, CA.

Dowall, D.E. (1984) *The Suburban Squeeze: Land Conversion and Regulation in the San Francisco Bay Area*, University of California Press, Berkeley, CA.

Downes, B.T. (1968) 'Municipal social rank and the characteristics of local political leaders', *Midwest Journal of Political Science*, 12, 514–37.

Downs, A. (1957) 'An economic theory of political action in a democracy', *Journal of Political Economy*, 45, 135–50.

Dresser, M. (1984) 'Housing policy in Bristol 1919-30', in M.J. Daunton (ed.) *Councillors and Tenants: Local Authority Housing in English Cities 1919–39*, Leicester University Press, Leicester, 156–216.

Drury, J.W. (1965) *Home Rule in Kansas*, University of Kansas Governmental Research Center, Lawrence, KS.

Duncan, J.S. (1973) 'Landscape taste as a symbol of group identity', *Geographical Review*, 63, 334–55.

Duncan, S.S. and Goodwin, M. (1982) 'The local state: functionalism, autonomy and class relations in Cockburn and Saunders', *Political Geography Quarterly*, 1, 77–96.

Duncan, S.S. and Goodwin, M. (1985) 'The local state and local economic policy: why the fuss?', *Policy and Politics*, 13, 227–53.

Duncan, S.S. and Goodwin, M. (1988) *The Local State and Uneven Development: Behind the Local Government Crisis*, Polity, Cambridge.

Dunleavy, P.J. (1980a) *Urban Political Analysis*, Macmillan, Basingstoke.

Dunleavy, P.J. (1980b) 'Social and political theory and the issues in central–local relations', in G.W. Jones (ed.) *New Approaches to the Study of Central–Local Government Relationships*, Gower, Aldershot, 116–36.

Dunleavy, P.J. (1981) *The Politics of Mass Housing in Britain 1945–75*, Clarendon, Oxford.

Dunleavy, P.J. (1985) 'Bureaucrats, budgets and the growth of the state', *British Journal of Political Science*, 15, 299–328.

Dunleavy, P.J. (1986) 'The growth of sectoral cleavages and the stabilization of state expenditures', *Environment and Planning D: Society and Space*, 4, 129–44.

Dunleavy, P.J. and O'Leary, B. (1987) *Theories of the State*, Macmillan, London.

Dunleavy, P. and Rhodes, R.A.W. (1983) 'Beyond Whitehall', in H. Drucker, P. Dunleavy, A. Gamble and G. Peele (eds) *Developments in British Politics*, Macmillan, Basingstoke, 106–33.

Dunleavy, P. and Ward, H. (1981) 'Exogenous voter preferences and parties with state power: some internal problems with economic theories of party competition', *British Journal of Political Science*, 11, 351–80.

Dye, T.R. (1963) 'The local–cosmopolitan dimension and the study of urban politics', *Social Forces*, 41, 239–46.

Dye, T.R. (1964) 'Urban political integration: conditions associated with annexation in American cities', *Midwest Journal of Political Science*, 8, 430–46.

Dye, T.R. (1966) *Politics, Economics and the Public*, Rand McNally, Chicago, IL.

Dye, T.R. (1986a) *Who's Running America? The Conservative Years*, fourth edition, Prentice-Hall, Englewood Cliffs, NJ.

Dye, T.R. (1986b) 'Community power and public policy', in R.J. Waste (ed.) *Community Power: Directions for Future Research*, Sage, Beverly Hills, CA, 29–51.

Dye, T.R. and Renick, J. (1981) 'Political power and city jobs: determinants of minority employment', *Social Science Quarterly*, 62, 475–86.

Dye, T.R. and Zeigler, L.H. (1978) *The Irony of Democracy: An Uncommon Introduction to American Politics*, fourth edition, Duxbury, North Scituate, MA.

Dye, T.R., Liebman, C.S., Williams, O.P. and Herman, H. (1963) 'Differentiation and cooperation in a metropolitan area', *Midwest Journal of Political Science*, 7, 145–55.

Dyer, M.C. (1978) 'Leadership in a rural Scottish county', in G.W. Jones and A. Norton (eds) *Political Leadership in Local Government*, University of Birmingham Institute of Local Government Studies, Birmingham, 30–50.

Edelstein, J.D. and Warner, M. (1975) *Comparative Union Democracy: Organisation and Opposition in British and American Unions*, Allen & Unwin, London.

Edelstein, M. (1982) *Overseas Investment in the Age of High Imperialism: The United Kingdom 1850–1914*, Methuen, London.

Edwards, F.R. and Stevens, B.J. (1978) 'The provision of municipal sanitation services by private firms', *Journal of Industrial Economics*, 27, 133–47.

Elazar, D.J. (1966) *American Federalism: A View from the States*, Crowell, New York.

Elazar, D.J. (1970) *Cities of the Prairie*, Basic Books, New York.

Elazar, D.J. (1988) *The American Constitutional Tradition*, University of Nebraska Press, Lincoln, NE.

Elcock, H. (1987) 'Dimensions of the budgetary process', in H. Elcock and G. Jordan (eds) *Learning from Local Authority Budgeting*, Gower, Aldershot, 243–55.

Elkin, S.L. (1987) *City and Regime in the American Republic*, University of Chicago Press, Chicago, IL.

Etzioni, A. (1984) *Capital Corruption: The New Attack on American Democracy*, Harcourt Brace Jovanovich, New York.

Evans, C. (1985) 'Privatisation of local services', *Local Government Studies*, 11(6), 97–110.

Evans, H. (1983) *Good Times, Bad Times*, Weidenfeld & Nicolson, London.

Eyestone, R. (1971) *The Threads of Public Policy*, Bobbs-Merrill, Indianapolis, IN.

Farnham, P.G. (1986) 'The impact of governmental functional responsibility on local expenditure', *Urban Affairs Quarterly*, 22, 151–65.

Fenwick, I.G.K. (1976) *The Comprehensive School 1944–70: The Politics of Secondary School Reorganization*, Methuen, London.

Ferman, B. (1985) *Governing the Ungovernable City: Political Skill, Leadership and the Modern Mayor*, Temple University Press, Philadelphia.

Fielding, G.J. (1964) 'The Los Angeles milkshed: a study of the political factor in agriculture', *Geographical Review*, 54, 1–12.

Fincher, R. (1987) 'Space, class and political processes: the social relations of the local state', *Progress in Human Geography*, 11, 496–515.

Florestano, P.S. and Gordon, S.B. (1984) 'A survey of city and county use of private contracting', in J.H. Carr (ed.) *Crisis and Constraint in Municipal Finance*, Rutgers University Center for Urban Policy Research, New Brunswick, NJ, 252–63.

Flynn, N., Leach, S. and Vielba, C. (1985) *Abolition or Reform? The GLC and the Metropolitan County Councils*, Allen & Unwin, London.

Flynn, R. (1986) 'Urban politics, the local state and consumption', in M. Goldsmith and S. Villadsen (eds) *Urban Political Theory and the Management of Fiscal Stress*, Gower, Aldershot, 77–99.

Ford, R.G. and Brown, C.J. (1978) 'Rating reform and urban structure', *Area*, 10, 8–14.

Forrest, R. and Murie, A. (1988) *Selling the Welfare State: The Privatisation of Public Housing*, Routledge, London.

Forsythe, D. (1980) 'Urban incomers and rural change', *Sociologia Ruralis*, 20, 287–305.

Fossett, J.W. (1983) *Federal Aid to Big Cities: The Politics of Dependence*, Brookings Institution, Washington D.C.

Foster, C.D., Jackman, R.A. and Perlman, M. (1980) *Local Government Finance in a Unitary State*, Allen & Unwin, London.

Fraser, D. (1979) *Power and Authority in the Victorian City*, Blackwell, Oxford.

Freeman, R. (1979) 'The Marshall Plan for London's government', *London Journal*, 5, 160–75.

Freeman, T.W. (1968) *Geography and Regional Administration: England and Wales 1830–1968*, Hutchinson, London.

Freitag, P.J. (1975) 'The Cabinet and big business: a study of interlocks', *Social Problems*, 23, 137–52.

Frieden, B.J. and Kaplan, M. (1975) *The Politics of Neglect: Urban Aid from Model Cities to Revenue Sharing*, MIT Press, Cambridge, MA.

Friedland, R. (1980) 'Corporate power and urban growth: the case of urban renewal', *Politics and Society*, 10, 203–24.

Friedland, R. and Palmer, D. (1984) 'Park Place and Main Street: business and the urban power structure', *Annual Review of Sociology*, 10, 393–416.

Friedman, J.J. (1977) 'Community action on water pollution', *Human Ecology*, 5, 329–53.

Fudge, C., Murie, A. and Ring, E. (1981) 'First steps to a career? The problems of being a newly elected member in an English local authority', University of Bristol School for Advanced Urban Studies Occasional Paper No. 4, Bristol.

Gamble, A. (1974) *The Conservative Nation*, Routledge & Kegan Paul, London.

Gamble, A. (1988) *The Free Economy and the Strong State: The Politics of Thatcherism*, Macmillan, Basingstoke.

Gans, H.J. (1962) *The Urban Villagers: Group and Class in the Life of Italian Americans*, Free Press, New York.

Garrard, J.A. (1983) *Leadership and Power in Victorian Industrial Towns 1830–1880*, Manchester University Press, Manchester.

Garza, R. de la and Weaver, J. (1986) 'New participants, old issues: Mexican–American urban policy priorities', in J.K. Boles (ed.) *The Egalitarian City*, Praeger, New York, 75–92.

Gaventa, J. (1980) *Power and Powerlessness: Quiescence and Rebellion in an Appalachian Valley*, Clarendon, Oxford.

Gaziel, H.H. (1982) 'Urban policy outputs: a proposed framework for assessment and some empirical evidence', *Urban Education*, 17, 139–55.

George, V. and Wilding, P. (1984) *The Impact of Social Policy*, Routledge & Kegan Paul, London.

Getter, R.W. and Schumaker, P.D. (1978) 'Contextual basis of responsiveness to citizen preferences and group demands', *Policy and Politics*, 6, 249–78.

Gibson, J.G. (1985) 'Have expenditure targets converged towards GREs?', *Local Government Studies*, 11(5), 69–81.

Giddens, A. (1984) *The Constitution of Society: Outline of the Theory of Structuration*, University of California Press, Berkeley, CA.

Gilpin, R. (1987) *The Political Economy of International Relations*, Princeton University Press, Princeton, NJ.

Girvin, B. (1988) 'The United States: conservative politics in a liberal society' in B. Girvin (ed.) *The Transformation of Contemporary Conservatism*, Sage, London, 164–92.

Glasgow University Media Group (1976) *Bad News*, Routledge & Kegan Paul, London.

Glasgow University Media Group (1980) *More Bad News*, Routledge & Kegan Paul, London.

Glassberg, A. (1973) 'The linkage between urban policy outputs and voting behaviour: New York and London', *British Journal of Political Science*, 3, 341–61.

Glassberg, A. (1981) *Representation and Urban Community*, Macmillan, Basingstoke.

Gold, S.D. (1984) 'Contingency measures and fiscal limitations: The real world significance of some recent state budget innovations', National Conference of State Legislatures Legislative Finance Paper No. 43, Denver, CO.

Gormley, W. and Eisenger, P.K. (1988) 'Fear and loathing in the Midwest', in P.K. Eisenger and W. Gormley (eds) *The Midwest Response to the New Federalism*, University of Wisconsin Press, Madison, WI, 295–306.

Gottdiener, M. (1977) *Planned Sprawl: Private and Public Interests in Suburbia*, Sage, Beverly Hills, CA.

Gottdiener, M. (1987) *The Decline of Urban Politics: Political Theory and the Crisis of the Local State*, Sage, Beverly Hills, CA.

Gough, J. (1986) 'Class relations and local economic planning', in K. Hoggart and E. Kofman (eds) *Politics, Geography and Social Stratification*, Croom Helm, London, 168–98.

Gramlich, E.M. and Rubinfeld, D.L. (1982) 'Voting on public spending: differences between public employees, transfer recipients and private workers', *Journal of Policy Analysis and Management*, 1, 516–33.

Grant, M. (1986) 'Controlling local government expenditure in Britain: the experience of rate capping', *Environment and Planning C: Government and Policy*, 4, 165–76.

Grant, W. (1987) *Business and Politics in Britain*, Macmillan, Basingstoke.

Gray, J. and Jesson, D. (1987) 'Exam results and local authority league tables', in A. Harrison and J. Gretton (eds) *Education and Training UK 1987*, Policy Journals, Hermitage, Berks, 33–41.

Greaves, G. (1984) 'The Brixton disorders' in J. Benyon (ed.) *Scarman and After*, Pergamon, Oxford, 63–72.

Greenberg, E.S. (1974) *Serving the Few: Corporate Capitalism and the Bias of Government Policy*, Wiley, New York.

Greenberg, S.B. (1981) 'Race and business enterprise in Alabama' in M. Zeitlin (ed.) *Political Power and Social Theory Volume Two*, JAI Press, Greenwich, CT, 203–38.

Greene, K.V., Neenan, W.B. and Scott, C.D. (1974) *Fiscal Interactions in a Metropolitan Area*, Heath, Lexington, MA.

Greer, A.L. and Greer, S. (1976) 'Suburban political behavior: a matter of trust', in B. Schwartz (ed.) *The Changing Face of the Suburbs*, University of Chicago Press, Chicago, IL, 203–19.

Greer, E. (1979) *Big Steel: Black Politics and Corporate Power in Gary, Indiana*, Monthly Review Press, New York.

Griffith, E. (1974a) *A History of American City Government: The Conspicuous Failure 1870–1900*, Praeger, New York.

Griffith, E. (1974b) *A History of American City Government: The Progressive Years and their Aftermath 1900–20*, Praeger, New York.

Griffith, J.A.G. (1985) *The Politics of the Judiciary*, third edition, Fontana, London.

Grubb, W.N. (1984) 'The price of local discretion: inequalities in welfare spending within Texas', *Journal of Policy Analysis and Management*, 3, 359–72.

Guttsman, W.L. (1968) *The British Political Elite*, MacGibbon & Kee, London.

Gyford, J. (1985) *The Politics of Local Socialism*, Allen & Unwin, London.

Gyford, J., Leach, S. and Game, C. (1989) *The Changing Politics of Local Government*, Unwin Hyman, London.

Haar, C.M. (1974) *The President's Task Force on Suburban Problems*, Ballinger, Cambridge, MA.

Hahn, H. (1970) 'Ethos and social class: referenda in Canadian cities', *Polity*, 2, 295–315.

Hall, D. (1983) *The Cuts Machine: The Politics of Public Expenditure*, Pluto Press, London.

Hall, P.A. (1987) 'The evolution of economic policy under Mitterrand', in G. Ross, S. Hoffman and S. Malzacher (eds) *The Mitterrand Experiment: Continuity and Change in Modern France*, Polity, Cambridge, 54–72.

Hall, P.G. (1974) 'A new political geography', *Transactions of the Institute of British Geographers*, 63, 48–52.

Hall, S., Critcher, C., Jefferson, T., Clarke, J. and Roberts, B. (1978) *Policing the Crisis: Mugging, the State and Law and Order*, Macmillan, Basingstoke.

Hall, W. (1986) 'Contracts compliance at the GLC', *Local Government Studies*, 12(4), 17–24.

Haller, M., König, W., Krause, P. and Kurz, K. (1985) 'Patterns of career mobility and structural positions in advanced capitalist societies: a comparison of men in Austria, France and the United States', *American Sociological Review*, 50, 579–603.

Hampton, W. (1970) *Democracy and Community: A Study of Politics in Sheffield*, Oxford University Press, Oxford.

Hampton, W. (1987) *Local Government and Urban Politics*, Longman, Harlow.

Hannah, L. (1983) *The Rise of the Corporate Economy: The British Experience*, second edition, Methuen, London.

Harrigan, J.J. (1976) *Political Change in the Metropolis*, Little Brown, Boston, MA.

Harrison, M. and Norton, A. (1967) *Local Government Administration in England and Wales*, (Maud Committee Report on the Management of Local Government Volume Five), HMSO London.

Hartley, O.A. (1980) 'The second world war and after', in D. Fraser (ed.) *A History of Modern Leeds*, Manchester University Press, Manchester, 437–61.

Hawkins, B.W. (1966) *Nashville Metro: The Politics of City–County Consolidation*, Vanderbilt University Press, Nashville, TN.

Hawkins, B.W. (1967) 'Lifestyle, demographic distance and voter support of city–county consolidation', *Southwestern Social Science Quarterly*, 48, 325–37.

Hawkins, R.B. (1976) *Self Government by District: Myth and Reality*, Hoover Institution Publication No. 162, Palo Alto, CA.

Hayes, E.C. (1972) *Power Structure and Urban Policy: Who Rules Oakland?*, McGraw-Hill, New York.

Haynes, R.M., Bentham, C.G., Spencer, M.B. and Spratley, J.M. (1978) 'Community attitudes towards the accessibility of hospitals in West Norfolk', in M.J. Moseley (ed.) *Social Issues in Rural Norfolk*, University of East Anglia Centre for East Anglian Studies, Norwich, 45–58.

Haywood, S. (1977) 'Decision-making in local government – the case of an "independent" council', *Local Government Studies*, 3(4), 41–55.

Heclo, H.H. (1969) 'The councillor's job', *Public Administration*, 47, 185–202.

Heclo, H.H. and Wildavsky, A. (1974) *The Private Government of Public Money*, Macmillan, Basingstoke.

Heidenheimer, A.J., Heclo, H.H. and Adams, C.T. (1983) *Comparative Public Policy: The Politics of Social Choice in Europe and America*, second edition, St Martin's Press, New York.

Heiman, M.K. (1988) *The Quiet Revolution: Power, Planning and Profits in New York State*, Praeger, New York.

Helstrom, C.O. (1977) 'The city in Pennsylvania government', Pennsylvania Department of Community Affairs Bureau of Local Government Services, Harrisburg, PA.

Hennessy, T.M. (1970) 'Problems of concept formation: the ethos "theory" and the comparative study of urban politics', *Midwest Journal of Political Science*, 14, 537–64.

Henney, A. (1984) *Inside Local Government: A Case for Radical Reform*, Sinclair Browne, London.

Hennigh, L. (1978) 'The good life and the taxpayers' revolt', *Rural Sociology*, 43, 178–90.

Hennock, E.P. (1973) *Fit and Proper Persons: Ideal and Reality in Nineteenth Century Urban Government*, Edward Arnold, London.

Herr, J.P. (1982) 'Metropolitan political fragmentation and conflict in the location of commercial facilities: South Bend versus Mishawaka', in K.R. Cox and R.J. Johnston (eds) *Conflict, Politics and the Urban Scene*, Longman, Harlow, 28–44.

Hetzner, C. (1985) 'Social democracy and bureaucracy: the Labour Party and higher civil service recruitment', *Administration and Society*, 17, 97–128.

Hewitson, J.N. (1969) *The Grammar School Tradition in a Comprehensive World*, Routledge & Kegan Paul, London.

Hildebrand, G.H. (1979) *American Unionism: An Historical and Analytical Survey*, Addison-Wesley, Reading, MA.

Hill, B.E. (1984) *The Common Agricultural Policy*, Methuen, London.

Hill, R.C. (1974) 'Separate and unequal: governmental inequality in the metropolis', *American Political Science Review*, 58, 1557–68.

Hills, J. (1982) 'Women local councillors – a reply to Bristow', *Local Government Studies*, 8(1), 61–71.

Hinton, J. (1983) *Labour and Socialism: A History of the British Labour Movement 1867–1974*, Wheatsheaf, Brighton.

Hirsch, A.R. (1983) *Making the Second Ghetto: Race and Housing in Chicago 1940–60*, Cambridge University Press, Cambridge.

Hirschman, A.O. (1970) *Exit, Voice and Loyalty: Responses to Decline in Firms, Organizations and States*, Harvard University Press, Cambridge, MA.

Hoare, A.G. (1985) 'Dividing the pork-barrel: Britain's enterprise zone experiment', *Political Geography Quarterly*, 4, 29–46.

Hoch, C. (1984) 'City limits: municipal boundary formation', in W.K. Tabb and L. Sawers (eds) *Marxism and the Metropolis*, second edition, Oxford University Press, New York, 101-19.

Hodge, D.C. (1988) 'Fiscal equity in urban mass transit systems: a geographic analysis', *Annals of the Association of American Geographers*, 78, 288–306.

Hoffman, W. (1976) 'The democratic response of urban governments', *Policy and Politics*, 4, 51–74.

Hoggart, K. (1985) ' Variation in public housing rents in England 1974–83', *Tijdschrift voor Economische en Sociale Geografie*, 76, 356–62.

Hoggart, K. (1986a) 'Geography, political control and local government policy outputs', *Progress in Human Geography*, 10, 1–23.

Hoggart, K. (1986b) 'Property tax resources and political party control in England 1974–84', *Urban Studies*, 23, 33–46.

Hoggart, K. (1986c) 'Political party control and the sale of local authority dwellings 1974–83', *Environment and Planning C: Government and Policy*, 3, 463–74.

Hoggart, K. (1987) 'Does politics matter? Redistributive policies in English cities 1949–74', *British Journal of Political Science*,17, 359–71.

Hoggart, K. (1989) *Economy, Polity and Urban Public Expenditure*, Gower, Aldershot.

Horowitz, D.L. (1983) 'Racial violence in the United States' in N. Glazer and K. Young (eds) *Ethnic Pluralism and Public Policy*, Gower, Aldershot, 187–211.

Howard, K. (1987) 'Composition of municipal revenues 1979–84', in *The Municipal Yearbook 1987*, International City Management Association, Washington D.C., 8–14.

Hudson, J.C. (1985) *Plains Country Towns*, University of Minnesota Press, Minneapolis.

Hugill, P.J. (1989) 'Home and class among an American landed élite', in J.A. Agnew and J.S. Duncan (eds) *The Power of Place*, Unwin Hyman, Boston, 66-80.

Hunter, F. (1953) *Community Power Structure*, University of North Carolina Press, Chapel Hill, NC.

Hunter, F. (1959) *Top Leadership USA*, University of North Carolina Press, Chapel Hill, NC.

Husbands, C.T. (1976) 'Introductory essay', in W. Sombart *Why is There no Socialism in the United States?* (translation of *Warum Gibt es in den Vereinigten Staaten Keinen Socialismus?*, 1906), Macmillan, Basingstoke, xv–xxxvii.

Husbands, C.T. (1985) 'Attitudes to local government in London: evidence from opinion surveys and the GLC by-election of 20 September 1984', *London Journal*, 11, 59–74.

Iannaccone, L. and Lutz, F.W. (1970) *Politics, Power and Policy: The Governance of Local School Districts*, Merrill, Columbus, OH.

Ingham, G. (1984) *Capitalism Divided? The City and Industry in British Social Development*, Macmillan, Basingstoke.

Institute for Local Self Government (1970) *Special Districts or Special Dynasties? Democracy Denied*, Berkeley, CA.

Isaac, J.C. (1987) *Power and Marxist Theory*, Cornell University Press, Ithaca, NY.

Jennings, R.E. (1977) *Education and Politics: Policy-Making in Local Education Authorities*, Batsford, London.

Jennings, R.E. (1982) 'The changing representational roles of local councillors in England', *Local Government Studies*, 8(5), 67–86.

Jesson, D., Gray, J., Ranson, S. and Jones, B. (1985) 'Some determinants of variation in expenditure on secondary education', *Policy and Politics*, 13, 359–91.

Jessop, B. (1982) *The Capitalist State: Marxist Theories and Methods*, Martin Robertson, Oxford.

Jessop, B., Bonnett, K., Bromley, S. and Ling, T. (1988) *Thatcherism: A Tale of Two Nations*, Polity, Cambridge.

Joe, T. and Rogers, C. (1985) *By the Few, For the Few: The Reagan Welfare Legacy*, Heath, Lexington, MA.

Johnson, R.W. (1985) *The Politics of Recession*, Macmillan, Basingstoke.

Johnston, R.J. (1979) *Political, Electoral and Spatial Systems*, Oxford University Press, Oxford.

Johnston, R.J. (1980) 'Political geography without politics', *Progress in Human Geography*, 4, 439–46.

Johnston, R.J. (1983) 'Texts, actors and higher managers: judges, bureaucrats and the political organisation of space', *Political Geography Quarterly*, 2, 3–19.

Johnston, R.J., Pattie, C.J. and Allsopp, J.G. (1988) *A Nation Dividing? The Electoral Map of Great Britain 1979–87*, Longman, Harlow..

Jonas, A. (1988) 'A new regional geography of localities?', *Area*, 20, 101–10.

Jones, B.D. (1986) 'Political geography and the law – banishing space from geography', *Political Geography Quarterly*, 5, 283–7.

Jordan, G. (1987) 'Budgeting: changing expectations', in H. Elcock and G. Jordan (eds) *Learning from Local Authority Budgeting*, Gower, Aldershot, 1–22.

Judd, D.R. and Ready, R.L. (1986) 'Entrepreneurial cities and the new politics of economic development', in G.E. Peterson and C.W. Lewis (eds) *Reagan and the Cities*, Urban Institute, Washington D.C., 209–47.

Karabel, J. (1979) 'The failure of American socialism reconsidered', in R. Miliband and J. Saville (eds) *The Socialist Register 1979*, Merlin Press, London, 204-27.

Karnig, A.K. and Welch, S. (1980) *Black Representation and Urban Policy*, University of Chicago Press, Chicago, IL.

Karp, W. (1973) *Indispensable Enemies: The Politics of Misrule in America*, Penguin, Baltimore, MD.

Karran, T. (1988) 'Local taxing and local spending: international comparisons', in R. Paddison and S. Bailey (eds) *Local Government Finance: International Perspectives*, Routledge, London, 53–84.

Katzman, M.T. (1968) 'Distribution and production in a big city elementary school system', *Yale Economic Essays*, 8(1), 201–256.

Katznelson, I. (1981) *City Trenches: Urban Politics and the Patterning of Class in the United States*, Pantheon, New York.

Katznelson, I. (1985) 'Working class formation and the state: nineteenth-century England in American perspective', in P.B. Evans, D. Rueschemeyer and T. Skocpol (eds) *Bringing the State Back In*, Cambridge University Press, Cambridge, 257–84.

Katznelson, I. (1986) 'Working class formation: constructing cases and comparisons', in I. Katznelson and A.R. Zolberg (eds) *Working-Class Formation: Nineteenth Century Patterns in Western Europe and the United States*, Princeton University Press, Princeton, NJ, 3–41.

Kavanagh, D. (1985) *British Politics: Continuities and Change*, Oxford University Press, Oxford.

Keating, M. (1988) *The City that Refused to Die: Glasgow, the Politics of Urban Regeneration*, Aberdeen University Press, Aberdeen.

Keating, M. and Midwinter, A. (1981) 'The Scottish Office in the United Kingdom Policy Network', University of Strathclyde Studies in Public Policy No. 96, Glasgow.

Keith, M. (1987) '"Something happened": the problems of explaining the 1980 and 1981 riots in British cities', in P. Jackson (ed.) *Race and Racism*, Allen & Unwin, London, 275–303.

Keith, M. and Peach, C. (1983) 'The conditions in England's inner cities on the eve of the 1981 riots', *Area*, 15, 316–9.

Keith-Lucas, B. and Richards, P.G. (1978) *A History of Local Government in the Twentieth Century*, Allen & Unwin, London.

Kellas, J.G. (1989) *The Scottish Political System*, fifth edition, Cambridge University Press, Cambridge.

Kerckhoff, A.C., Campbell, R.T. and Winfield-Laird, I. (1985) 'Social mobility in Great Britain and the United States', *American Journal of Sociology*, 91, 281–308.

Kermode, D. (1979) *Devolution at Work: A Case Study of the Isle of Man*, Saxon House, Farnborough.

Kermode, D. (1980) 'The changing pattern of Manx devolution', University of Strathclyde Studies in Public Policy No. 52, Glasgow.

King, R. (1974) 'Social class, educational attainment and provision', *Policy and Politics*, 3(1), 17–35.

Kirby, A., Knox, P.L. and Pinch, S.P. (eds) (1984) *Public Service Provision and Urban Development*, Croom Helm, London.

Kleppner, P. (1985) *Chicago Divided: The Making of a Black Mayor*, Northern Illinois University Press, De Kalb, IL.

Kolko, G. (1976) *Main Currents in Modern American History*, Pantheon, New York.

Kornhauser, W. (1960) *The Politics of Mass Society*, Free Press, New York.
Laffin, M. (1986) *Professionalism and Policy: The Role of the Professions in the Central–Local Government Relationship*, Gower, Aldershot.
Laffin, M. and Young, K. (1985) 'The changing roles and responsibilities of local authority chief officers', *Public Administration*, 63, 41–59.
Langrod, G. (1953) 'Local administration and democracy', *Public Administration*, 31, 25–34.
Lash, S. and Urry, J. (1987) *The End of Organized Capitalism*, Polity, Cambridge.
Laski, H.J. (1935) *The State in Theory and Practice*, Allen & Unwin, London.
Lasswell, H.D. (1958) *Politics: Who Gets What, When, How*, Meridian, New York.
Laver, M. (1984) 'Are Liverpool Liberals really different?', *British Journal of Political Science*, 14, 243–9.
Leach, S. and Stewart, J. (1988) 'The politics and management of hung authorities', *Public Administration*, 66, 35–55.
Lee, J.M., Wood, B., Solomon, B.W. and Walters, P. (1974) *The Scope of Local Initiative: A Study of Cheshire County Council 1961–74*, Martin Robertson, London.
LeGates, R. (1972) 'Can the federal welfare bureaucracies control their programs? The case of HUD and urban renewal', University of California Institute of Urban and Regional Development Working Paper No. 172, Berkeley, CA.
LeGrand, J. (1982) *The Strategy of Equality: Redistribution and the Social Services*, Allen & Unwin, London.
Lenski, G.E. (1966) *Power and Privilege: A Theory of Social Stratification*, McGraw-Hill, New York.
Levine, C.H. and Posner, P.L. (1981) 'The centralizing effects of austerity on the intergovernmental system', *Political Science Quarterly*, 96, 67–85.
Levine, C.H., Rubin, I.S. and Wolohojian, G.G. (1981) *The Politics of Retrenchment*, Sage, Beverly Hills, CA.
Levy, F., Meltsner, A.J. and Wildavsky, A. (1974) *Urban Outcomes*, University of California Press, Berkeley, CA.
Leys, C. (1984) 'The rise of the authoritarian state', in J. Curran (ed.) *The Future of the Left*, Polity, Cambridge, 58–73.
Liebert, R.J. (1974) 'Municipal functions, structure, and expenditures: a reanalysis of some recent research', *Social Science Quarterly*, 54, 765–83.
Liebert, R.J. (1976) *Disintegration and Political Action: The Changing Functions of City Governments in America*, Academic Press, New York.
Lindblom, C.E. (1977) *Politics and Markets*, Basic Books, New York.
Lineberry, R.L. (1970) 'Reforming metropolitan governance: requiem or reality', *Georgetown Law Journal*, 58, 675–717.
Lineberry, R.L. (1977) *Equality and Urban Policy*, Sage, Beverly Hills, CA.
Lineberry, R.L. and Masotti, L.H. (1976) 'The new urban politics', in L.H. Masotti and R.L. Lineberry (eds) *The New Urban Politics*, Ballinger, Cambridge, MA, 1–15.
Lipset, S.M. (1960) *Political Man*, Heinemann, London.
Lipsky, M. (1980) *Street-Level Bureaucracy*, Russell Sage Foundation, New York.

Lipsky, M. and Levy, M. (1972) 'Community organization as a political resource', in H. Hahn (ed.) *People and Politics in Urban Society*, Sage Urban Affairs Annual Review No. 6, Beverly Hills, CA, 175–99.

Livingstone, K. (1987) *If Voting Changed Anything, They'd Abolish It*, Collins, London.

Logan, J.R. and Molotch, H.L. (1987) *Urban Fortunes: The Political Economy of Place*, University of California Press, Berkeley, CA.

Logan, J.R. and Schneider, M. (1981) 'The stratification of metropolitan suburbs 1960–70', *American Sociological Review*, 46, 175–86.

Logan, W.S. (1978) 'Post-convergence political geography – death of transfiguration?', Monash University Publication in Geography No. 18, Melbourne.

Lojkine, J. (1981) 'Urban policy and local power', in M. Harloe and E. Lebas (eds) *City, Class and Capital*, Edward Arnold, London, 89–104.

Loughlin, M. (1986) *Local Government in the Modern State*, Sweet & Maxwell, London.

Lovell, C.H. and Tobin, C. (1980) 'Mandating – a key issue for cities' in *The Municipal Yearbook 1980*, International City Management Association, Washington D.C., 73–9.

Lucas, R.C. (1971) *Minetown, Milltown, Railtown: Life in Canadian Communities of Single Industry*, University of Toronto Press, Toronto.

Lukes, S. (1974) *Power: A Radical View*, Macmillan, Basingstoke.

Lyons, W.E. (1977) *The Politics of City–County Merger: The Lexington – Fayette County Experience*, University of Kentucky Press, Lexington, KY.

Lyons, W.E. and Engstrom, R.L. (1973) 'Life-style and fringe attitudes toward the political integration of urban governments', *American Journal of Political Science*, 17, 182–8.

McAuslan, J.P.W.B. and Bevan, R.G. (1977) 'The influence of officers and councillors on procedures in planning', *Local Government Studies*, 3(3), 7–21.

McCandless, C.A. (1970) *Urban Government and Politics*, McGraw-Hill, New York.

McCormack, A.R. (1977) *Reformers, Rebels and Revolutionaries: The Western Canadian Radical Movement 1899–1919*, University of Toronto Press, Toronto.

Macdonald, J.S. (1963) 'Agricultural organisation, migration and labour militancy in rural Italy', *Economic History Review*, 16, 61–75.

McGrew, T. and Bristow, S. (1984) 'Candidate to councillor: a study of political recruitment', in S. Bristow, D. Kermode and M. Mannin (eds) *The Redundant Counties?*, Hesketh, Ormskirk, 69–100.

MacInnes, J. (1987) *Thatcherism at Work: Industrial Relations and Economic Change*, Open University Press, Milton Keynes.

Macintyre, S. (1980) *Little Moscows: Communism and Working Class Militancy in Inter-War Britain*, Croom Helm, London.

Mackintosh, M. and Wainwright, H. (eds) (1987) *A Taste of Power: The Politics of Local Economics*, Verso, London.

MacLeod, R.M. (1968) *Treasury Control and Social Administration: A Study of Establishment Growth at the Local Government Board 1871–1905*, Bell, Occasional Papers in Social Administration No. 23, London.

MacManus, S.A. (1978) *Revenue Patterns in US Cities and Suburbs*, Praeger, New York.

MacManus, S.A. (1983) 'State government: the overseer of municipal finance', in A.M. Sbragia (ed.) *The Municipal Money Chase*, Westview, Boulder, CO, 145–83.

Madgwick, P.J. and James, M. (1979) 'Government by Consultation: The Case of Wales', University of Strathclyde Studies in Public Policy No. 47, Glasgow.

Malmsten, B. (1983) 'Sweden's salaried local politicians', *Local Government Studies*, 9(3), 6–10.

Mann, M. (1986) *The Sources of Social Power Volume One: A History of Power from the Beginning to AD 1760*, Cambridge University Press, Cambridge.

Mann, M. (1988) *States, War and Capitalism: Studies in Political Sociology*, Blackwell, Oxford.

Manwaring, T. and Sigler, N. (1985) *Breaking the Nation: A Guide to Thatcher's Britain*, Pluto Press, London.

Mark-Lawson, J., Savage, M. and Warde, A. (1985) 'Gender and local politics: struggles over welfare politics 1918–39', in Lancaster Regionalism Group *Localities, Class and Gender*, Pion, London, 195–215.

Martin, R. (1977) *The Sociology of Power*, Routledge & Kegan Paul, London.

Martin, R.L. (1986) 'Thatcherism and Britain's industrial landscape', in R.L. Martin and B. Rowthorn (eds) *The Geography of De-Industrialisation*, Macmillan, Basingstoke, 238–90.

Martlew, C. (1986) 'Consulting non-domestic ratepayers in Scotland: the first year', *Local Government Studies*, 12(1), 57–66.

Maslow, A. (1970) *Motivation and Personality*, second edition, Harper & Row, New York.

Massey, D.B. (1984) *Spatial Divisions of Labour*, Macmillan, Basingstoke.

Massey, D.B. (1986) 'The legacy lingers on: the impacts of Britain's international role on its internal geography', in R.L. Martin and B. Rowthorn (eds) *The Geography of De-Industrialisation*, Macmillan, Basingstoke, 31–52.

Meadows, W.A. and Jackson, P.M. (1986) 'U.K. local government: alternative economic strategies', in M. Goldsmith (ed.) *New Research in Central–Local Relations*, Gower, Aldershot, 60–89.

Mehay, S.L. (1979) 'Intergovernmental contracting for municipal police services', *Land Economics*, 55, 59–72.

Mellors, C. (1978) *The British MP: A Socio-Economic Study of the House of Commons*, Saxon House, Farnborough.

Mény, Y. (1983) 'Permanence and change: the relations between central government and local authorities in France', *Environment and Planning C: Government and Policy*, 1, 17–28.

Michels, R. (1959) *Political Parties: A Sociological Study of the Oligarchical Tendencies of Modern Democracy*, (translation of *Zür Soziologie des Parteiwesens in der Modernen Demokratie*, second edition, 1925), Dover, New York.

Midwinter, A. (1984) *The Politics of Local Spending*, Mainstream, Edinburgh.

Midwinter, A. and Mair, C. (1987) *Rates Reform: Issues, Arguments and Evidence*, Mainstream, Edinburgh.

Milch, J.E. (1974) 'Influence as power: French local government reconsidered', *British Journal of Political Science*, 4, 139–61.

Miliband, R. (1969) *The State in Capitalist Society*, Weidenfeld & Nicolson, London.

Miliband, R. (1982) *Capitalist Democracy in Britain*, Oxford University Press, Oxford.

Miller, G.J. (1981) *Cities by Contract: The Politics of Municipal Incorporation*, MIT Press, Cambridge, MA.

Miller, J.C. (1988) 'Municipal annexation and boundary change', in *The Municipal Yearbook 1988*, International City Management Association, Washington D.C., 59–67.

Miller, W.L. (1988) *Irrelevant Elections? The Quality of Local Democracy in Britain*, Clarendon, Oxford.

Mills, C.W. (1956) *The Power Elite*, Oxford University Press, New York.

Minogue, M. (ed.) (1977) *Documents on Contemporary British Government Volume Two: Local Government in Britain*, Cambridge University Press, Cambridge.

Mizruchi, M.S. (1982) *The American Corporate Network 1904–74*, Sage, Beverly Hills, CA.

Mladenka, K.R. (1980) 'The urban bureaucracy and the Chicago political machine', *American Political Science Review*, 74, 991–8.

Mollenkopf, J. (1981) 'Community and accumulation', in M.J. Dear and A.J. Scott (eds) *Urbanization and Urban Planning in Capitalist Society*, Methuen, London, 319–37.

Mollenkopf, J.H. (1983) *The Contested City*, Princeton University Press, Princeton, NJ.

Molotch, H. (1976) 'The city as a growth machine', *American Journal of Sociology*, 82, 309–32.

Monkkonen, E.H. (1984) 'The politics of municipal indebtedness and default 1850–1936', in T.J. McDonald and S.K. Ward (eds) *The Politics of Urban Fiscal Policy*, Sage, Beverly Hills, CA, 125–59.

Moore, B. (1966) *Social Origins of Dictatorship and Democracy*, Beacon Press, Boston, MA.

Morgan, D.R. and Pelissero, J.P. (1980) 'Urban policy: does political structure matter?', *American Political Science Review*, 74, 999–1006.

Morgan, W.R. and Clark, T.N. (1973) 'The causes of racial disorders', *American Sociological Review*, 38, 611–24.

Morris, D.S. and Newton, K. (1970) 'Profile of a local political élite: businessmen as community decision-makers in Birmingham 1838–1966', *New Atlantis*, 1(2), 111–23.

Mott, P.E. (1970) 'The role of the absentee-owned corporation in the changing community', in M. Aiken and P.E. Mott (eds) *The Structure of Community Power*, Random House, New York, 170–9.

Mullard, M. (1987) *The Politics of Public Expenditure*, Croom Helm, London.

Muller, P.O. (1975) *The Outer City: Geographical Consequences of the Urbanization of the Suburbs*, Association of American Geographers Resource Paper 75-2, Washington D.C.

Muller, P.O. (1981) *Contemporary Suburban America*, Prentice-Hall, Englewood Cliffs, NJ.

Murphy, T.P. and Rehfuss, J. (1976) *Urban Politics in the Suburban Era*, Dorsey Press, Homewood, IL.

Nathan, R.P. and Adams, C. (1976) 'Understanding central city hardship', *Political Science Quarterly*, 91, 47–62.

Nelson, F.H. (1982) 'School finance in Chicago: a study of failure in a city that works', *Urban Education*, 17, 123–37.

Newby, H. (1977) *The Deferential Worker: A Study of Farm Workers in East Anglia*, Allen Lane, London.

Newby, H. (1986) 'Locality and rurality', *Regional Studies*, 20, 209–15.

Newton, K. (1976a) *Second City Politics: Democratic Processes and Decision-Making in Birmingham*, Oxford University Press, Oxford.

Newton, K. (1976b) 'The impact of rates on local elections', in Committee of Inquiry into Local Government Finance (Layfield Committee) *Appendix Six*, HMSO, London, 98–101.

Newton, K. (1978) 'Conflict avoidance and conflict suppression: the case of urban politics in the United States', in K.R. Cox (ed.) *Urbanization and Conflict in Market Societies*, Methuen, London, 76–93.

Newton, K. (1980) *Balancing the Books*, Sage, London.

Newton, K. and Karran, T.J. (1985) *The Politics of Local Expenditure*, Macmillan, Basingstoke.

Niskanen, W.A. (1971) *Bureaucracy and Representative Government*, Aldine, Chicago.

Niskanen, W.A. (1988) 'Reflections on Reagonomics', in D. Boaz (ed.) *Assessing the Reagan Years*, Cato Institute, Washington D.C., 9–15.

Nivola, P.S. (1978) 'Distributing a municipal service: a case study of housing inspection', *Journal of Politics*, 40, 59–81.

Norpoth, H. (1987) 'Guns and butter and government popularity in Britain', *American Political Science Review*, 81, 949–59.

North, D.J. and Gough, J. (1983) 'The impact of local authorities on manufacturing firms: recent experience in London', in K. Young and C. Mason (eds) *Urban Economic Development*, Macmillan, Basingstoke, 155–83.

Ntuk-Idem, M.J. (1978) *Compensatory Education*, Saxon House, Farnborough.

O'Connor, J. (1973) *The Fiscal Crisis of the State*, St Martin's Press, New York.

O'Connor, J. (1981) 'The fiscal crisis of the state revisited', *Kapitalistate*, 9, 41–61.

Odell, P.R. (1986) *Oil and World Power*, eighth edition, Penguin, Harmondsworth.

Offe, C. (1976) 'Political authority and class structures', in P. Connerton (ed.) *Critical Sociology*, Penguin, Harmondsworth, 388–421.

Offe, C. (1984) *Contradictions of the Welfare State*, Hutchinson, London.

Oldman, O. and Aaron, H. (1969) 'Assessment – sales ratios under the Boston property tax', *Assessors' Journal*, 4(1), 13–29.

O'Leary, B. (1987a) 'Why was the GLC abolished?', *International Journal of Urban and Regional Research*, 11, 193–217.

O'Leary, B. (1987b) 'British farce, French drama and tales of two cities:

explaining the reorganization of Paris and London governments 1957–86', *Political Studies*, 65, 369–89.

Olson, M. (1965) *The Logic of Collective Action*, Harvard University Press, Cambridge, MA.

Orren, K. (1976) 'Corporate power and the slums', in W.D. Hawley (ed.) *Theoretical Perspectives on Urban Politics*, Prentice-Hall, Englewood Cliffs, NJ, 45–66.

Ostendorf, W. (1986) 'Municipal housing-market policy and the socio-spatial differentiation of the Amsterdam urban region', *Espace Populations Sociétés*, 1986-1, 45–58.

Ostrom, E. and Parks, R.B. (1973) 'Suburban police departments: too many or too small?', in L.H. Masotti and J.K. Hadden (eds) *The Urbanization of the Suburbs*, Sage Urban Affairs Annual Review No. 7, Beverly Hills, CA, 367–402.

Page, E. (1978) 'Why should central–local relations in Scotland be any different from those in England?', University of Strathclyde Studies in Public Policy No. 21, Glasgow.

Page, E. (1980) 'Comparing local expenditure: lessons from a multi-national state', University of Strathclyde Studies in Public Policy No. 60, Glasgow.

Page, E. (1985) *Political Authority and Bureaucratic Power*, Harvester, Brighton.

Page, E. and Goldsmith, M. (1985) 'Centralisation and decentralisation: a framework for comparative analysis', *Environment and Planning C: Government and Policy*, 3, 175–86.

Page, E. and Goldsmith, M. (1987) 'Centre and locality: explaining crossnational variation', in E.C. Page and M. Goldsmith (eds) *Central and Local Government Relations*, Sage, London, 156–68.

Page, E. and Midwinter, A. (1979) 'Remote bureaucracy or administrative efficiency? Scotland's new local government system', University of Strathclyde Studies in Public Policy No. 38, Glasgow.

Pahl, R.E. (1975) *Whose City?*, Penguin, Harmondsworth.

Palen, J.J. and London, B. (eds) (1984) *Gentrification, Displacement and Neighborhood Revitalization*, State University of New York Press, Albany, NY.

Parenti, M. (1986) *Inventing Reality: The Politics of the Mass Media*, St Martin's Press, New York.

Pareto, V. (1901) *The Rise and Fall of Elites*, Bedminster Press, Totowa, NJ.

Pareto, V. (1935) *Mind and Society: A Treatise on General Sociology* (translation of *Trattato di Sociologia Generale*, 1915–19), Jonathan Cape, London.

Paris, C. (1983) 'The myth of urban politics', *Environment and Planning D: Society and Space*, 1, 89–108.

Parkinson, M. (1985) *Liverpool on the Brink: One City's Struggle Against Government Cuts*, Policy Journals, Hermitage, Berks.

Parkinson, M. and Duffy, J. (1984) 'Government response to inner-city riots: the Minister for Merseyside and the Task Force', *Parliamentary Affairs*, 37, 76–96.

Parmet, R.D. (1981) *Labor and Immigration in Industrial America*, Twayne, Boston, MA.

Pascal, A. *et al.* (1985) 'Financing local government in tough times', in T.N. Clark (ed.) *Research in Urban Policy Volume One: Coping with Urban Austerity*, JAI Press, Greenwich, CT, 135–60.

Pateman, C. (1970) *Participation and Democratic Theory*, Cambridge University Press, Cambridge.

Peele, G. (1988) 'British Conservatism: ideological change and electoral uncertainty', in B. Girvin (ed.) *The Transformation of Contemporary Conservatism*, Sage, London, 13–34.

Pelling, H. (1968) *Popular Politics and Society in Late Victorian Britain*, Macmillan, Basingstoke.

Peretz, P. (1982) 'There was no tax revolt!', *Politics and Society*, 11, 231–49.

Peterson, G.E. (1984) 'Federalism and the states: an experiment in decentralization', in J.L. Palmer and I.V. Sawhill (eds) *The Reagan Record*, Ballinger, Cambridge, MA, 217–59.

Peterson, G.E. (1986) 'Urban policy and the cyclical behavior of cities', in G.E. Peterson and C.W. Lewis (eds) *Reagan and the Cities*, Urban Institute, Washington D.C., 11–35.

Peterson, P.E. (1981) *City Limits*, University of Chicago Press, Chicago, IL.

Peterson, P.E. and Kantor, P. (1977) 'Political parties and citizen participation in English city politics', *Comparative Politics*, 9, 197–217.

Phelan, J. and Pozen, R. (1973) *The Company State*, Grossman, New York.

Pickvance, C.G. (1980) 'Theories of the state and theories of urban crisis', *Current Perspectives in Social Theory*, 1, 31–54.

Pinch, S.P. (1984) 'Inequality in pre-school provision', in A. Kirby, P.L. Knox and S.P. Pinch (eds) *Public Service Provision and Urban Development*, Croom Helm, London, 231–82.

Pinch, S.P. (1985) *Cities and Services: The Geography of Collective Consumption*, Routledge & Kegan Paul, London.

Pinch, S.P. (1987) 'The changing geography of pre-school services in England between 1977 and 1983', *Environment and Planning C: Government and Policy*, 5, 469–80.

Piven, F.F. and Cloward, R.A. (1982) *The New Class War: Reagan's Attack on the Welfare State and its Consequences*, Pantheon, New York.

Poulantzas, N. (1973) *Political Power and Social Class*, New Left Books, London.

Pred, A. (1984) 'Place as historically contingent process: structuration and the time–geography of becoming places', *Annals of the Association of American Geographers*, 74, 279–97.

Ragin, C. (1977) 'Class, status and "reactive ethnic cleavage"; the social bases of political regionalism', *American Sociological Review*, 42, 438–50.

Randall, M.V. (1981) 'Housing policy-making in London boroughs: the role of paid officers', *London Journal*, 7, 161–76.

Reddin, M. (1973) 'Which LEAs help children stay on at school?', in J. Raynor and J. Hardin (eds) *Equality and City Schools*, Routledge & Kegan Paul, London, 118–25.

Rees, G. (1986) '"Coalfield culture" and the 1984–5 miners' strike', *Environment and Planning D: Society and Space*, 4, 469–76.

Renner, T. (1988) 'Municipal election processes' in *The Municipal*

*Yearbook 1988*, International City Management Association, Washington D.C., 13–21.

Reynolds, D. (1976) 'When pupils and teachers refuse to truce: the secondary school and the creation of delinquency', in G. Mungham and G. Pearson (eds) *Working Class Youth Culture*, Routledge & Kegan Paul, London, 124–37.

Rhodes, R.A.W. (1984) 'Continuity and change in British central–local relations: the "Conservative threat" 1979–83', *British Journal of Political Science*, 14, 261–83.

Rhodes, R.A.W. (1986) 'Corporate bias in central–local relations: a case study of the Consultative Council on Local Government Finance', *Policy and Politics*, 14, 221–45.

Ribbins, P.M. and Brown, R.J. (1979) 'Policy-making in English local government: the case of secondary school reorganisation', *Public Administration*, 57, 187–202.

Rich, R.C. (1979) 'Neglected issues in the study of urban service distributions', *Urban Studies*, 16, 143–56.

Roberts, R. (1971) *The Classic Slum: Salford Life in the First Quarter of the Century*, Penguin, Harmondsworth.

Robson, W.A. (1962) *Nationalized Industry and Public Ownership*, second edition, Allen & Unwin, London.

Rose, D., Saunders, P., Newby, H. and Bell, C. (1976) 'Ideologies of property', *Sociological Review*, 24, 699–730.

Rose, G. (1988) 'Locality, politics and culture: Poplar in the 1920s', *Environment and Planning D: Society and Space*, 6, 151–68.

Rose, H.M. (1978) 'The geography of despair', *Annals of the Association of American Geographers*, 68, 453–64.

Rose, R. (1984) *Do Parties Make a Difference?*, second edition, Macmillan, Basingstoke.

Ross, J.M. (1981) 'The Secretary of State for Scotland and the Scottish Office', University of Strathclyde Studies in Public Policy No. 87, Glasgow.

Royal Commission on Local Government in England (1969) *Report*, HMSO, London.

Royal Commission on Local Government in Scotland (1969) *Report*, HMSO, London.

Rubin, I.S. (1982) *Running in the Red: The Political Dynamics of Urban Fiscal Stress*, State University of New York Press, Albany, NY.

Rubin, I.S. and Rubin, H.J. (1987) 'Economic development incentives: the poor (cities) pay more', *Urban Affairs Quarterly*, 23, 37–62.

Ruck, S.K. and Rhodes, G. (1970) *The Government of Greater London*, Allen & Unwin, London.

Ryder, R. (1984) 'Council house building in County Durham 1900–39', in M.J. Daunton (ed.) *Councillors and Tenants: Local Authority Housing in English Cities 1919–39*, Leicester University Press, Leicester, 40–100.

Sahlins, M. (1981) *Historical Metaphors and Mythical Realities: Structure in the Early History of the Sandwich Islands Kingdom*, University of Michigan Press, Ann Arbor, MI.

Samuelson, P.A. (1954) 'The pure theory of public expenditure', *Review of Economics and Statistics*, 36, 387–9.

Sanger, M.B. (1981) 'Are academic models of urban service distribution relevant to public policy?', *Policy Studies Journal*, 9, 1011–20.

Saunders, P. (1979) *Urban Politics: A Sociological Interpretation*, Hutchinson, London.

Saunders, P. (1981) 'Community power, urban managerialism and the local state', in M. Harloe (ed.) *New Perspectives in Urban Change and Conflict*, Heinemann, London, 27–49.

Saunders, P. (1982a) 'The day they sacked the City Council', University of Sussex Urban and Regional Studies Working Paper No. 27, Brighton.

Saunders, P. (1982b) 'The relevance of Weberian sociology for urban political analysis', in A. Kirby and S. Pinch (eds) 'Public provision and urban politics', University of Reading Geographical Paper No. 80, Reading, 1–24.

Saunders, P. (1985) 'The forgotten dimension of central–local relations: theorising the "regional state"', *Environment and Planning C: Government and Policy*, 3, 149–62.

Savage, M. (1987) *The Dynamics of Working-Class Politics: The Labour Movement in Preston 1880–1940*, Cambridge University Press, Cambridge.

Savage, M., Barlow, M.J., Duncan, S.S. and Saunders, P. (1987) 'Locality research', *Quarterly Journal of Social Affairs*, 3, 27–51.

Schain, M.A. (1985) *French Communism and Local Power*, Frances Pinter, London.

Schattschneider, E.E. (1960) *The Semi-Sovereign People*, Holt Rinehart & Winston, New York.

Schneider, M. (1986) 'Changing intergovernmental aid and local government expenditure patterns', *Polity*, 19, 254–69.

Schneider, M. and Logan, J.R. (1985) 'Suburban municipalities: the changing system of intergovernmental relations in the mid-1970s', *Urban Affairs Quarterly*, 21, 87–105.

Schulze, R.O. (1958) 'The role of economic dominants in community power structure', *American Sociological Review*, 23, 3–9.

Schumpeter, J.A. (1943) *Capitalism, Socialism and Democracy*, Allen & Unwin, London.

Scott, J. (1985) *Corporations, Classes and Capitalism*, second edition, Hutchinson, London.

Scott, J. and Griff, C. (1985) 'Bank spheres of influence in the British corporate network', in F.N. Stokman, R. Ziegler and J. Scott (eds) *Networks of Corporate Power*, Polity, Cambridge, 215–33.

Searle, G.R. (1987) *Corruption in British Politics 1895–1930*, Clarendon, Oxford.

Sen, A, (1982) *The State, Industrialization and Class Formations in India*, Routledge & Kegan Paul, London.

Sharpe, L.J. (1970) 'Theories and values of local government', *Political Studies*, 18, 153–74.

Sharpe, L.J. (1973) 'American democracy reconsidered: part one', *British Journal of Political Science*, 3, 1–28.

Sharpe, L.J. (1978) 'Reforming the grass roots: an alternative analysis', in A.H. Halsey and D.E. Butler (eds) *Policy and Politics*, Macmillan, Basingstoke, 82–110.

Sharpe, L.J. (1982) 'The Labour Party and the geography of inequality: a puzzle', in D. Kavanagh (ed.) *The Politics of the Labour Party*, Allen & Unwin, London, 135–70.

Sharpe, L.J. and Newton, K. (1984) *Does Politics Matter?*, Clarendon, Oxford.

Shefter, M. (1976) 'The emergence of the political machine', in W.D. Hawley (ed.) *Theoretical Perspectives on Urban Politics*, Prentice-Hall, Englewood Cliffs, NJ, 14–44.

Shefter, M. (1986) 'Trade unions and political machines: the organization and disorganization of the American working class in the late nineteenth century', in I. Katznelson and A.R. Zolberg (eds) *Working Class Formation*, Princeton University Press, Princeton, NJ, 197–275.

Sher, J.P. and Tompkins, R.B. (1977) 'Economy, efficiency and equality: the myths of rural school and district consolidation', in J.P. Sher (ed.) *Education in Rural America*, Westview, Boulder, CO, 43–77.

Short, J.R. (1982) *An Introduction to Political Geography*, Routledge & Kegan Paul, London.

Simmie, J.M. (1981) *Power, Property and Corporations: The Political Sociology of Planning*, Macmillan, Basingstoke.

Sjoberg, G., Brymer, R.A. and Farris, B. (1966) 'Bureaucracy and the lower class', *Sociology and Social Research*, 50, 325–37.

Smith, M.P. (1988) *City, State and Market: The Political Economy of Urban Society*, Blackwell, Oxford.

Smith, N. and Williams, P.R. (eds) (1986) *Gentrification of the City*, Allen & Unwin, London.

Smith, P. (1988) 'The potential gains from creative accounting in English local government', *Environment and Planning C: Government and Policy*, 6, 173–85.

Smith, P. and Stewart, J. (1985) 'Local authority expenditure targets', *Local Government Studies*, 11(4), 21–41.

Spangler, E. (1979) 'Small winnings: blue collar students in college and at work', in M. Lewis (ed.) *Research in Social Problems and Public Policy Volume One*, JAI Press, Greenwich, CT, 15–41.

Staaf, R.J. (1977) 'The growth of the educational bureaucracy: do teachers make a difference?', in T.E. Borcherding (ed.) *Budgets and Bureaucrats*, Duke University Press, Durham, NC, 148–68.

Stave, B.M. (1975) 'Socialism and the cities: an introduction', in B.M. Stave (ed.) *Socialism and the Cities*, Kennikat Press, Port Washington, NY, 3–12.

Steed, M. (1969) 'Callaghan's gerrymandering', *New Society*, 26 June, 996–7.

Stein, L. and Fleischmann, A. (1987) 'Newspaper and business endorsements in municipal elections', *Journal of Urban Affairs*, 9, 325–36.

Stetzer, D.F. (1975) *Special Districts in Cook County: Toward a Geography of Local Government*, University of Chicago Department of Geography Research Paper No. 169, Chicago, IL.

Stiglitz, J.E. (1986) *Economics of the Public Sector*, Norton, New York.

Stocks, M. (1939) 'London government', *Political Quarterly*, 10, 365–74.

Stoker, G. (1988) *The Politics of Local Government*, Macmillan, Basingstoke.

Stone, C.N. (1976) *Economic Growth and Neighborhood Discontent: System Bias in the Urban Renewal Program of Atlanta*, University of

North Carolina Press, Chapel Hill, NC.

Stone, C.N. (1986) 'Race, power and political change', in J.K. Boles (ed.) *The Egalitarian City*, Praeger, New York, 200–23.

Stone, C.N. (1987) 'Urban regimes, development policy and political arrangements', in C.N. Stone and H.T. Sanders (eds) *The Politics of Urban Development*, University of Kansas Press, Lawrence, KS, 269–90.

Stone, C.N., Whelan, R.K. and Murin, W.J. (1986) *Urban Policy and Politics in a Bureaucratic Age*, second edition, Prentice-Hall, Englewood Cliffs, NJ.

Stone, D. (1985) 'Municipal Socialism 1880–1982', University of Sussex Urban and Regional Studies Working Paper No. 44, Brighton.

Summers, A.A. and Wolfe, B.L. (1977) 'Do schools make a difference?', *American Economic Review*, 67, 639–52.

Susskind, L.E. and Serio, J.F. (1983) *Proposition 2½. Its Impact on Massachusetts*, Oelgeschlager Gunn & Hain, Cambridge, MA.

Sutcliffe, A.S. (1976) 'Political leadership in Labour-controlled Birmingham: the contrasting styles of Harry Watton (1959–66) and Stanley Yapp (1972–4)', *Local Government Studies*, 2(1), 15–32.

Svara, J.H. (1988) 'The complementary roles of officials in council–manager government', in *The Municipal Yearbook 1988*, International City Management Association, Washington D.C., 23–33.

Swann, B. (1972) 'Local initiative and central control: the insulin decision', *Policy and Politics*, 1, 55–63.

Swanstrom, T. (1985) *The Crisis of Growth Politics: Cleveland, Kucinich and the Challenge of Urban Populism*, Temple University Press, Philadelphia, PA.

Swanstrom, T. (1988) 'Semi-sovereign cities: the politics of urban development', *Polity*, 21, 83–110.

Syed, A.H. (1966) *The Political Theory of American Local Government*, Random House, New York.

Taylor, P.J. (1977) 'Political geography', *Progress in Human Geography*, 1, 130–5.

Taylor, P.J. (1983) 'The question of theory in political geography', in N. Kliot and S. Waterman (eds) *Pluralism and Political Geography*, Croom Helm, London, 9–18.

Taylor, P.J. (1985) *Political Geography*, Longman, Harlow.

Thomas, I.C. (1981) 'The Creation of the Welsh Office: Conflicting Purposes in Institutional Change', University of Strathclyde Studies in Public Policy No. 91, Glasgow.

Thomas, J.C. (1978) 'Budget-cutting and minority employment in city governments: lessons from Cincinnati', *Public Personnel Management*, 7, 155–61.

Thompson, E.P. (1965) 'The peculiarities of the English', in R. Miliband and J. Saville (eds) *The Socialist Register 1965*, Merlin Press, London, 311–62.

Thrall, G.I. (1979) 'A geographic criterion for identifying property tax assessment inequity', *Professional Geographer*, 31, 278–83.

Tiebout, C.M. (1956) 'A pure theory of local expenditures', *Journal of Political Economy*, 64, 416–24.

Tocqueville, A. de (1835) *Democracy in America Volume One*, 1961 edition, Schocken Books, New York.

Tomlinson, J. (1986) *Monetarism: Is There an Alternative?*, Blackwell, Oxford.

Tonbee, J.C. (1986) 'The labour movement, local politics and spatial sociology: some recent Danish experience', in M. Goldsmith and S. Villadsen (eds) *Urban Political Theory and the Management of Fiscal Stress*, Gower, Aldershot, 179–205.

Travers, T. (1986) *The Politics of Local Government Finance*, Allen & Unwin, London.

Travers, T. (1988) 'The finance of local government in London', in M. Hebbert and T. Travers (eds) *The London Government Handbook*, Cassell, London, 153–61.

Trelease, A.W. (1981) 'Southern violence: the Ku Klux Klan', in M. Black and J.S. Reed (eds) *Perspective on the American South Volume One*, Gordon and Breach, New York, 23–33.

Tunley, P., Travers, T. and Pratt, J. (1979) *Depriving the Deprived: A Study of Finance, Educational Provision and Deprivation in a London Borough*, Kogan Page, London.

Tylecote, A.B. (1982) 'German ascent and British decline 1870–1980: the role of upper class structure and values', in E. Friedman (ed.) *Ascent and Decline in the World-System*, Sage, Beverly Hills, CA, 41–67.

Urry, J. (1986) 'Class, space and disorganised capitalism', in K. Hoggart and E. Kofman (eds) *Politics, Geography and Social Stratification*, Croom Helm, London, 16–32.

Urry, J. (1987) 'Society, space and locality', *Environment and Planning D: Society and Space*, 5, 435–44.

Useem, M. (1984) *The Inner Circle: Large Corporations and the Rise of Business Political Activity in the US and UK*, Oxford University Press, New York.

Vance, J.E. (1972) 'California and the search for the ideal', *Annals of the Association of American Geographers*, 62, 185–210.

Verba, S. (1987) *Elites and the Idea of Equality: A Comparison of Japan, Sweden and the United States*, Harvard University Press, Cambridge, MA.

Vidich, A.J. and Bensman, J. (1968) *Small Town in Mass Society: Class, Power and Religion in a Rural Community*, second edition, Princeton University Press, Princeton, NJ.

Villadsen, S. (1986) 'The dual state and corporatism: reflections in the light of recent Danish experience', in M. Goldsmith and S. Villadsen (eds) *Urban Political Theory and the Management of Fiscal Stress*, Gower, Aldershot, 41–62.

Vogel, D. (1983) 'The power of business in America', *British Journal of Political Science*, 13, 19–43.

Vogler, C.M. (1985) *The Nation State: The Neglected Dimension of Class*, Gower, Aldershot.

Waisman, C.H. (1987) *Reversal of Development in Argentina: Postwar Counterrevolutionary Policies and Their Structural Consequences*, Princeton University Press, Princeton, NJ.

Walker, D. (1983) 'Local interest and representation: the case of "class" interest among Labour representatives in inner London', *Environment and Planning C: Government and Policy*, 1, 341–60.

Walker, R.A. (1981) 'A theory of suburbanization: capitalism and the construction of urban space in the United States', in M.J. Dear and A.J. Scott (eds) *Urbanization and Urban Planning in Capitalist Society*, Methuen, London, 383–429.

Walker, R.A. and Heiman, M.K. (1981) 'Quiet revolution for whom?', *Annals of the Association of American Geographers*, 71, 67–83.

Waller, R. (1980) 'The 1979 local and general elections in England and Wales: is there a local/national differential?', *Political Studies*, 28, 443–50.

Walton, J. (1976) 'Community power and the retreat from politics: full circle after twenty years', *Social Problems*, 23, 292–303.

Walzer, N. (1978) 'Fiscal Note and Reimbursement Programs for State Mandates', Illinois Cities and Villages Municipal Problems Commission, Springfield, IL.

Walzer, N. (1985) 'Fiscal austerity in mid-size cities', in T.N. Clark (ed.) *Research in Urban Policy Volume One: Coping With Urban Austerity*, JAI Press, Greenwich, CT, 161–73.

Warde, A. (1986) 'Space, class and voting in Britain', in K. Hoggart and E. Kofman (eds) *Politics, Geography and Social Stratification*, Croom Helm, London, 33–61.

Warner, S.B. (1968) *The Private City: Philadelphia in Three Periods of its Growth*, University of Pennsylvania Press, Philadelphia, PA.

Webster, B. (1985) 'A women's issue: the impact of local authority cuts', *Local Government Studies*, 11(2), 19–46.

Weicher, J.C. (1972) 'The effect of metropolitan political fragmentation on central city budgets', in D.C. Sweet (ed.) *Models of Urban Structure*, Heath, Lexington, MA, 177–203.

Weinstein, J. (1967) *The Decline of Socialism in America 1912–25*, Monthly Review Press, New York.

Weinstein, J. (1968) *The Corporate Ideal in the Liberal State 1900–18*, Beacon Press, Boston, MA.

Welch, S. (1975) 'The impact of urban riots on urban expenditures', *American Journal of Political Science*, 19, 741–60.

Western, J. (1982) 'The geography of urban social control: Group Areas and the 1976 and 1980 civil unrest in Cape Town', in D.M. Smith (ed.) *Living Under Apartheid*, Allen & Unwin, London, 217–29.

Wheen, F. (1985) *The Battle for London*, Pluto Press, London.

Whitehead, P. (1983) 'Intra-urban spatial variations in local government service provision: application and results', *Environment and Planning C: Government and Policy*, 1, 229–47.

Whitt, J.A. (1982) *Urban Elites and Mass Transportation: The Dialectics of Power*, Princeton University Press, Princeton, NJ.

Whitt, J.A. (1984) 'Structural fetishism in the new urban theory', in M.P. Smith (ed.) *Cities in Transformation*, Sage Urban Affairs Annual Review No. 26, Beverly Hills, CA, 75–89.

Whitt, J.A. (1987) 'Mozart in the metropolis: the arts coalition and the urban growth machine', *Urban Affairs Quarterly*, 23, 15–36.

Whitt, J.A. and Yago, G. (1985) 'Corporate strategies and the decline of transit in US cities', *Urban Affairs Quarterly*, 21, 37–65.

Wickham, C. (1988) 'Historical materialism, historical sociology', *New Left Review*, 171, 63–78.

Wiener, M.J. (1981) *English Culture and the Decline of the Industrial Spirit 1850–1980*, Cambridge University Press, Cambridge.

Wild, R.A. (1974) *Bradstow: A Study of Status, Class and Power in a Small Australian Town*, Angus & Robertson, Sydney.

Wildavsky, A. (1971) *The Revolt Against the Masses*, Basic Books, New York.

Wildavsky, A. (1989) 'Political culture and risk', paper presented at the Institute of Governmental Studies, University of California, Berkeley, CA, 1 February 1989.

Wilensky, H.L. (1975) *The Welfare State and Equality*, University of California Press, Berkeley, CA.

Williams, O.P. (1961) 'A typology of comparative local government', *Social Forces*, 5, 150–64.

Williams, O.P. (1971) *Metropolitan Political Analysis: A Social Access Approach*, Free Press, New York.

Williams, O.P., Herman, H., Liebman, C.S. and Dye, T.R. (1965) *Suburban Differences and Metropolitan Policies: A Philadelphia Story*, University of Pennsylvania Press, Philadelphia, PA.

Williamson, W.W. and Byrne, D.S. (1977) 'The structure of educational provision and patterns of educational attainment', in P. Raggatt and M. Evans (eds) *Urban Education Three: The Political Context*, Ward Lock Educational, London, 216–41.

Willis, P.E. (1977) *Learning to Labour: How Working Class Kids Get Working Class Jobs*, Saxon House, Farnborough.

Wilson, G.K. (1985) *Business and Politics: A Comparative Introduction*, Macmillan, Basingstoke.

Wilson, J. (1987) 'Introduction', *Current Perspectives in Social Theory*, 8, ix–xviii.

Windsor, D. (1979) *Fiscal Zoning in Suburban Municipalities*, Heath, Lexington, MA.

Wolman, H. (1982) 'Local autonomy and intergovernmental finance in Britain and the United States', in R. Rose and E.C. Page (eds) *Fiscal Stress in Cities*, Cambridge University Press, Cambridge, 168–97.

Wolman, H. and Davis, B. (1980) *Local Government Strategies to Cope with Fiscal Pressures*, Urban Institute, Washington D.C.

Wright, P. (1987) *Spy Catcher*, Viking Penguin, New York.

Wyatt, C.M. (1983) 'The effects of rating reform in Britain: a case study of Derby', *Environment and Planning C: Government and Policy*, 1, 57–71.

Wynia, G.W. (1984) *The Politics of Latin American Development*, second edition, Cambridge University Press, Cambridge.

Yago, G. (1984) *The Decline of Transit: Urban Transportation in German and US Cities 1900–70*, Cambridge University Press, Cambridge.

Yinger, J., Börsch-Supan, A., Bloom, H.S. and Ladd, H.F. (1988) *Property Taxes and House Values: The Theory and Estimation of Interjurisdictional Property Tax Capitalization*, Academic Press, San Diego, CA.

Young, K. (1975a) 'The Conservative strategy for London, 1855–1975', *London Journal*, 1(1), 56–81.

Young, K. (1975b) '"Values" in the policy process', *Policy and Politics*, 5, 1–22.

Young, K. (1986) 'The justification for local government', in M. Goldsmith (ed.) 'Essays on the future of local government', University of Salford Department of Politics and Contemporary History (on behalf of West Yorkshire Metropolitan County Council), Salford, 8–19.

Young, K, and Garside, P.L. (1982) *Metropolitan London: Politics and Urban Change 1837–1981*, Edward Arnold, London.

Young, K. and Kramer, J. (1978) 'Local exclusionary policies in Britain: the case of suburban defence in a metropolitan system' in K.R. Cox (ed.) *Urbanisation and Conflict in Market Societies*, Methuen, London, 229–51.

Zeitlin, M. (1982) 'Corporate ownership and control: the large corporation and the capitalist class', in A. Giddens and D. Held (eds) *Classes, Power and Conflict*, Macmillan, Basingstoke, 196–223.

Zelditch, M., Harris, W., Thomas, G.M. and Walker, H.A. (1983) 'Decisions, nondecisions and metadecisions', in L. Kriesberg (ed.) *Research on Social Movements, Conflicts and Change*, JAI Press, Greenwich, CT, 1–32.

# INDEX